A Record of Service

Len Stahl

Canadian Utilities Limited

1st Printing Nov. 1987, 1,200 copies
2nd Printing July 1988, 500 copies

Stahl, Len – A Record of Service

ISBN 0-921146-00-0

Published by:
Canadian Utilities Limited
10035 – 105 Street
Edmonton, Alberta
Canada T5J 2V6
(403) 420-7310

Cover Design: Alfred Gardenits, Edmonton Alberta
Printing: Ronalds Printing, Calgary, Alberta
Binding: Atlas Book Bindery Limited, Edmonton, Alberta

Printed and bound in Canada

Table of Contents

Chapter 1 — The Early Beginnings

Chapter 2 — Edmonton and Central Alberta

Chapter 3 — Power for the Twenties

Chapter 4 — The Depression Years

Chapter 5 — The War Years

Chapter 6 — Post-War Boom

Table of Contents — Chapter 6 (Continued)

Table of Contents — Chapter 6 (Continued)

Chapter 7 — The Late Fifties

Chapter 9 — The Seventies

Chapter 10 — Recession and New Challenges

Table of Contents — Chapter 10 (Continued)

Chapter 11 — Seventy-five Years of Service

Photographic Section

The editors acknowledge with thanks the contributions of the Provincial Archives of Alberta and the Glenbow Foundation.

Appendices

Editing and Production Credits

Source material compiled by: Len Stahl
Editor and Project Co-ordinator: Mills Parker
Assistant: Gwen Gray
Editorial Assistant: Jack Fleming
Photographic Editor: Mike France
Assistants: Alice Major
Doreen Barry
Typesetting and Word Processing: Suzanne Slade
Claire Burke
Janice Ambrose
Lillian Rydicki
Indexing: Debi Froh
Suzanne Gagne
Historical Research and Editing: Vi Anderson
Ron Chapman
Bob Choate
Ray Cordell
Evelyn Dixon
Bob Duncan
John Fisher
Scotty Gilliland
Dennis Havrelock
Phil Hindmarch
Jerry Manegre
Sam McBride
Walter Prausa
Hal Robbins
Gene Zadvorny

Preface

Publication of *A Record of Service* in 1987 coincides with the seventy-fifth anniversary of Canadian Western Natural Gas Company Limited, the oldest company in the Canadian Utilities group. It also marks the sixtieth anniversary of Alberta Power Limited and Northwestern Utilities' sixty-fourth year of service.

The first book about a company is often a reference work in which the author has attempted to establish a chronology and to capture the names and contributions of as many as possible of the key players, particularly those from the all too easily forgotten early days. *A Record of Service* is no exception. Sources for this book were employee publications, reports to shareholders, news clippings and long dormant files. It helped that author Len Stahl is a former employee of Alberta Power Limited and knew generally what was available and where to find it.

No single volume could tell the whole story of seventy-five years of a corporation's development, least of all a book with no pretensions to being a scholarly study or investigative journalism. Inevitably, there will be names, places and events that should have been mentioned but have been inadvertently overlooked. For this we apologize. We will welcome comments, corrections and suggestions, which will be taken into consideration in any later editions of the book.

A Record of Service, we hope, will be enjoyed especially by employees, former employees and pensioners of Canadian Utilities Limited and its subsidiaries. At the very least, the book will serve as a convenient reference for anyone with an interest in the company, including the future scholar or journalist who some day will write about the company for a wider and more objective readership.

The Editors

CHAPTER 1
The Early Beginnings

Natural Gas Comes to Southern Alberta

As he walked across the lonely prairie, some seventy miles east of Lethbridge, Eugene Coste muttered to himself. "There has to be natural gas down there — billions of cubic feet of it."

Some people called him a dreamer. He was a bit cracked upstairs, they said. He had delusions of grandeur. But petty criticisms like this didn't worry the stranger with the far-away gaze in his eyes.

He was of French descent, with an interesting face which featured a romantic Parisian moustache complemented by a neatly trimmed King George V beard. His name was Eugene Coste, and he was a consulting geological engineer with the Canadian Pacific Railway, looking for gas in the Bow Island area of southern Alberta.

The spot where Coste was standing was just downstream from the point where the two major rivers of southern Alberta join. The Bow River, flowing through Calgary, and the Oldman River, flowing through Lethbridge, come together to form the South Saskatchewan.

Coste gazed at the river for a long time and then his imagination took over. It seemed he could see a shimmering, ethereal vapor flowing in the opposite direction. Again it broke up into two major streams as it flowed back across the prairie to Lethbridge and Calgary. It wasn't a river of water he was looking at now, it was natural gas; billions of cubic feet of it, flowing back the way the river had come, but through pipelines. Gas to warm and light huge cities and energize giant industries.

The Canadian Utilities energy story was just a dream when Alberta became a province in 1905. A dream which Coste shared with W.R. Martin, a driller widely known as Frosty Martin, who had acquired his trade in Pennsylvania and in the Petrolia-Sarnia oilfields of Ontario. Coste always depended on Martin, his right-hand man.

Four years after the province was founded, on a February day in 1909, Coste and Martin brought in Old Glory on the bank of the South Saskatchewan River and the dream began to evolve into reality. Old Glory yielded about nine million cubic feet of natural gas per day, making it the largest gas well in Western Canada, and putting Alberta on the energy map.

Coste has been called the father of the natural gas industry in Canada, having also brought in the first commercial discovery of natural gas in Ontario in 1889.

Eugene Marius Coste was the son of Napoleon Alexandre Coste of Marseilles, France, who emigrated to Canada in the middle of the nineteenth century. Napoleon married the daughter of a French-Canadian farmer and later became the reeve of Malden township, on the Detroit River below Windsor, Ontario. This is where Eugene was born, at Amherstburg, on July 8, 1859.

Napoleon Coste then went to Egypt with his family and became a major contractor in the construction of the Suez Canal. He returned to Canada in 1882 and in his home town of Amherstburg was again elected reeve of the county.

The Coste children meanwhile had been sent to school at Grenoble, France. Later Eugene studied at the University of Paris. On November 9, 1876, Eugene received the degree of Bachelor of Science from the Academie de Paris and went on to the Ecole Polytechnique, where he studied until 1879. He then entered the Ecole National Superieure des Mines, graduating on July 23, 1883, as a mining engineer.

That same year Eugene sailed for Canada. He joined the Geological Survey of Canada in a junior position and in 1887 was named a mining engineer with the survey. In 1887 he married Catherine Louisa Tims, daughter of Thomas Dillon Tims, inspector general of finance for the federal government.

Eugene then entered private practice as a mining engineer. With some financial assistance from his father, in 1888 he began drilling Coste No. 1 in Essex County. The well came in on January 23, 1889, with an initial open flow of 10 million cubic feet. It was the beginning of the natural gas industry in Ontario.

There followed a period of more than a decade during which many wells were drilled in Ontario, and commercial use of natural gas widened, some gas even being exported to Detroit. Then Coste left Ontario for the West on retainer by the Canadian Pacific Railway to find more oil and gas.

The success of the discovery well on the bank of the South Saskatchewan River in the Bow Island field was the beginning of Coste's fame in the West. He was soon convinced that the field might be big enough to supply Lethbridge, Calgary and most of southern Alberta for many years to come. Then began a series of drillings, and thirteen more wells were brought in with a total open flow of approximately 160 million cubic feet a day. The largest of these wells, No. 4, had a measured rate of open flow of 29 million cubic feet per day. The rock pressure of the field was seven hundred and seventy pounds per square inch. The average cost to drill a well was fifty thousand dollars.

Frosty Martin's Account

B ow Island No. 1 was drilled with a cable tool rig which had one big chisel as the bit. It was pounded into the ground. The surface hole, through sand, gravel and clay, was kept empty and kept open by drive casing which was also pounded down just behind the bit. Smaller casing was lowered, and sometimes pounded in, whenever the hole caved so badly that drilling progress ceased.

Periodically a bailer was run down the hole to bring the cuttings to the surface.

The rig was built of wood on the spot. Unlike the portable steel rigs of today, it took many days to erect. A water tank also had to be built to store the water that powered the boiler that in turn ran the rig. The water was drawn by horses from the nearest water supply. Once these tasks were completed, steam lines had to be connected and the boiler fired up.

Coste was not the first man associated with the CPR who discovered gas in Alberta. Gas was discovered twenty-six years earlier at Langevin — in the Suffield area, about twenty-five miles northeast of Bow Island — in 1883, by an engineer of the railroad who was seeking water for the steam locomotives on Canada's first transcontinental railway. But it was Coste's discovery in 1909 which led to major commercial developments. It was largely due to his efforts that Canada's two oldest natural gas companies were founded. One in Ontario, now known as Union Gas Company of Canada Limited; and the other, Canadian Western Natural Gas Company Limited, in Alberta.

There is a tendency to credit major discoveries like Bow Island's Old Glory entirely to certain individuals who happened to be in the limelight at the time. In this respect it is interesting to note that if Eugene Coste hadn't had drillers like Frosty Martin and his assistant, A.P. Phillips, known to his friends as Tiny, Old Glory might never had blown in as the Bow Island discovery well.

Some holes had been drilled in the vicinity of Dunmore and other areas in southeastern Alberta, and then Coste chose a location on the bank of the South Saskatchewan river near Bow Island.

Martin later recalled the events that led to the bringing in of that well. They were all set to go, with the wooden drilling rig in place and the pipe stacked on the ground. But Coste decided this wasn't the right place and ordered the rig torn down and the tools removed to another location. "I was able to reason with him," Martin said, "due to the fact that we had all the equipment ready to go and our camp established, that it wouldn't take long to drill the well on down to Medicine Hat sand. With this he agreed."

Coste left for Winnipeg and the crew went to work. They reported to him regularly, and everything seemed to be going quite well. It was not uncommon in those days for the man in charge at the well site to create what he called a "bank roll" in reporting progress. This was simply a hold-back on the actual depth of the well, saving a few hundred feet from time to time in case something went wrong, at which time he could keep reporting progress while he was in trouble.

The bank roll came in handy, because the crew did run into trouble. First there was water, but they finally reached the Medicine Hat sand at about eleven hundred feet. At seventeen hundred feet they ran into more trouble. They started to run out of bank roll and alibis. Martin and Coste were sending wires back and forth, with Martin urging Coste to let them keep on drilling, as they had "a nice hole," everything was in good shape, and there was lots of pipe and fuel left.

Coste wanted to quit, and then to make matters worse something jammed in the hole and the crew frantically used "fishing" tools to clear it out.

Martin waited another couple of days, and then wrote a long letter rather than wiring, hoping in this way to gain a few more days. Meanwhile, he kept getting wires from Coste ordering him to abandon the well.

They kept on working, though, and a few days later they were down to nineteen hundred feet in what was called the Dakota sandstone. There they struck a huge supply of gas.

This time Martin used the wire service again, to rush the glad news to Coste that Old Glory was producing about nine million cubic feet per day. Coste immediately ordered the necessary equipment to tube the well, and then came to see it for himself.

From that time on it was one success story after another.

Canadian Western is Born — 1911

The first step in Coste's plan to bring natural gas to Calgary was to acquire a lease of the Bow Island reserves from the CPR. He then convinced Sir Clifford Sifton, former minister of the interior, and Sir William Mackenzie, president of the Canadian Northern Railway, that building a pipeline from the Bow Island field to Lethbridge and Calgary was a sound investment. With these two men on his side, he went to England to raise money for what he called the Prairie Natural Gas Company.

That trip to London brought little success, so he came back to Canada, changed the name of the company to The Canadian Western Natural Gas, Light, Heat and Power Company Limited, and returned to England to try again. Either the new name struck a responsive chord with English investors or Coste was learning by experience how to raise money, because this time he had no difficulty putting the deal together. Four and a half million dollars' worth of debenture stock was underwritten by the British Empire Trust Company Ltd.

Ralph E. Davis, one of the foremost geologists and natural gas consultants in the United States, claimed years later this was the first public financing ever carried out for the construction of a natural gas pipeline, preceding the financing of Houston Gulf Gas Company by about fifteen years.

On July 19, 1911, Canadian Western was incorporated, with Eugene Coste as its first president and Alex McLeod as managing director. The new company took over two existing franchises — one held by the Calgary Gas Company, owner of a coal gas plant with some thirty miles of mains and about twenty-two hundred customers, and the other held by the Calgary Natural Gas Company. It was distributing gas from a shallow well in east Calgary, known as the Colonel Walker well, to about fifty customers including Calgary Brewing & Malting and for street lighting in that part of the city.

Then began the work on the pipeline from Bow Island to Calgary via Lethbridge. Construction of the main transmission line, sixteen inches in diameter and one hundred and seventy miles long, started on April 22, 1912, and was completed in eighty-six days. It was the third longest gas pipeline in North America and the most northerly gas transmission line in the world.

On July 12, at the Oldman River eight miles north of Lethbridge a flare-lighting ceremony lit up the area for several miles around. The following Monday Lethbridge ratepayers voted 275 to 112 in favor of granting a franchise to Canadian Western.

However, many of the citizens of Lethbridge resisted switching from coal to gas as coal mining was the main industry of the town. Veteran Lethbridge newspaperman Harold G. Long remarked many years later that he "shovelled coal a couple of years" after gas arrived "before taking the plunge to the new fuel," noting at the same time that "it took the coal miners a couple of decades before they followed the trend; they felt like traitors."

Although the inaugural flare-lighting north of the town took place in July, it was not until October that actual hook-up of homes took place in Lethbridge. On October 9, at 9:30 in the evening, another flare-lighting ceremony was held at the southwest corner of the North-West Mounted Police barracks, on the occasion of a visit of the Governor General the Duke of Connaught, the Duchess and Princess Pat.

Calgary Turn-on — 1912

The official Calgary turn-on took place on the night of July 17, 1912, when an estimated twelve thousand citizens gathered to witness the ceremony at Ninth Avenue East and the CPR tracks. That was an event long to be remembered. It began with a flare-lighting ceremony when a flame several hundred feet high illuminated the sky and suitably impressed everyone. This was followed by a banquet at the Empress Hotel at which Eugene Coste entertained the company staff along with the city council and various city officials.

Over the years that day stood out indelibly in the mind of Porter D. Mellon, who had begun his long career with the gas company in February that year, followed by many years of supervising plant construction in the Canadian Western system. Known to all as P.D., Mellon retired as a vice-president in 1949, remaining on as a member of the board of directors with the distinction during the company's fiftieth anniversary of having the longest record of service among Canadian Western directors.

Here is how he recollected the turn-on ceremony fifty years after it took place:

I remember clearly the events of that historic day in Calgary when gas from Bow Island was turned into the Calgary system and a flare-lighting ceremony was held.

During the day the pressure in the line was being built up to three hundred pounds. Suddenly we got word that the line had blown out in a slough at DeWinton. Things looked pretty gloomy, but we rushed several gangs of men down there and they were able to get the line coupled up again, and the pressure built up.

That evening, just after dark, some ten thousand to twelve thousand people gathered in the area in East Calgary around the standpipe. Eugene Coste and his wife were there.

Whitey Foster was in charge of the control valve.

At a signal from Coste, Whitey turned on the valve.

With a roar, there came out of the pipe first a cloud of dust, followed by stones, splinters and other debris.

The gas came out with a tremendous roar, and the people started to back up. In the meantime, Mrs. Coste was standing by with Roman candles.

Mrs. Coste started shooting the candles at the standpipe trying to light the gas. Finally away she went . . . with a terrible bang.

Coste then signalled to turn down the flow. However, Whitey thought he meant to open the valve still further.

This almost caused a panic. People were backing into each other and yelling but finally order, and the flare, were restored to normal.

That was the introduction of natural gas in the City of Calgary fifty years ago.

A week of testing and preparing the mains followed the flare-lighting, and on July 24, 1912 the *Calgary Herald* announced:

This morning marked a new epoch in the history of lighting and heating insofar as gas is concerned in Calgary. Artificial gas in the city is now a thing of the past. The ringing out of the old and the ringing in of the new has taken place, and the natural product has supplanted the artificial.

The towns of Nanton, Okotoks and Brooks became part of the Canadian Western system later that year, with Fort Macleod, Granum and Claresholm joining the following year.

Eugene Coste built a splendid residence in the Mount Royal district of Calgary in 1913. Many years later it became an art centre under the Calgary Allied Arts Council and finally was again taken over as a private residence. Coste left Calgary in 1922. He lived for some time in Toronto and also in Europe. He died in Toronto on January 22, 1940, at the age of eighty-one.

Early Employees

C anadian Western's first offices were located in Calgary in the Alberta Loan and Savings Building, next to the Beveridge Building on the corner of Seventh Avenue and First Street East.

One of the first meter setters, Oscar Doten, recalled years later that he began hauling meters and pipes with a horse called Cayuse, which he jokingly claimed was not much bigger than an oversized jackrabbit. Sometimes the roads were very muddy, and Oscar had to help Cayuse pull the wagon up some of the Calgary hills.

Later Oscar became a complaint man, working twelve hours a day. He recalled one particular complaint he took at night, when there was no transportation available other than a bicycle in the shop. He rode to east Calgary, looked after the complaint, and then came out to find the bicycle gone. It cost him nearly thirty dollars to replace it.

Another of the company's first drivers was Bill Lindsay, who joined Canadian Western in July, 1912. The horse assigned to him was called Swift. Bill delivered everything from pipe and tools for various jobs to ranges being installed for customers. The livery stable where the horses were kept was known as The Palace and was located opposite City Hall.

After years of driving teams, sometimes getting up as early as five o'clock in the morning during emergencies, Bill graduated in 1918 to driving the company's first one-ton truck.

Bill Lindsay went into stockroom work and the truck-driving was taken over by Fred Humphries, who came to the gas company from the cement plant at Exshaw.

Another old-timer who stayed with the gas company for forty-nine years and often recalled those early days was William Lloyd McPhee. Lloyd came to Canadian Western from the Trust and Guarantee Company (later Crown Trust). He started work as a ledgerkeeper, with a bottle of ink, a pen that used nibs, the old Boston ledger, and little postcards which he sent to customers as bills. Lloyd went on to become treasurer of the company.

Still another colorful old-timer was Jim Bailey, who worked for the company from 1920 to 1954. He started on May 2, 1920, and for fifteen years was on the company's payroll as Joe, until the insurance company in 1935 asked to see his birth certificate. It identified him as James rather than Joe. So the official record was changed.

7

Jim was a hard worker. Once, when working on repairs to the sixteen-inch line at Burnsland on the avenue south of the cemetery, he was told by supervisor Bill Larkham to bicycle over to the West End Shop and get five gallons of tar paint. Jim pedalled to the shop with the five-gallon bucket in a sack slung over his shoulder. On the way back he rode his bike to the foot of the cemetery hill and then had to walk up the hill. Riding down the other side of the hill the forks on his bike broke and he went head over heels, tar paint and all. Fortunately the tar didn't spill and he managed to deliver it despite the broken bike. Bill told him to get the forks on the bike braized, for which the welder charged him thirty-five cents. After due consideration the company agreed to pay the thirty-five cents.

Then there was Tommy Dodds, born near Belfast, Ireland, who started with the old Calgary Gas Company as a water boy in 1908, later transferring to Canadian Western, where he stayed until 1951.

In 1923 Tommy was given the job of testing pressures for Canadian Western. "They gave me an old Model T Ford," he recalled in later years, "and they said that would be my job from then on — to go around to the stations and boost pressures. Nowadays they have two guys going around in huge cars!"

Tommy was promoted a year later despite having been told he would be a permanent pressure booster. He was made service foreman.

Another of the interesting first employees was Phil Heather, who served with Canadian Western for fifty years. Phil, who came from England, had a brother who was a salesman in the appliance department in the Beveridge Building. Phil's brother took him to see the manager, and introduced him as "my kid brother from England who doesn't know a damn thing, but I would like to get him a job." So Phil started in the West End Shop as a fitter's helper, at twenty-five cents an hour.

Another employee who received a fifty-year service pin when he retired was Arthur J. Smith, corporate secretary of Canadian Western.

The 1915 Floods

At the end of Canadian Western's first full year of operation, in 1913, it was serving nearly sixty-four hundred customers, with gas sales totalling over six hundred thousand dollars. Sales reached the million-dollar point the following year. Twenty wells were now producing in the Bow Island field, with an open flow capacity of 170 million cubic feet per day.

Business was good for the gas company in 1915, despite some economic problems occasioned by the First World War. Then came the first major jolt — the disastrous 1915 floods which hit Alberta with unprecedented vehemence. On Saturday, June 26, the banner headlines of the *Calgary Herald* shouted: Calgary Practically Isolated by Storm; Gas Cut Off, Railway Lines Washed Out; Several Dead in Tornado East of City.

Rainstorms, accompanied by lightning, thunder and terrific winds, dumped one and a third inches of precipitation in less than forty-eight hours, in a district where fifteen inches of rainfall is considered heavy for an entire year. Rivers in the area became raging torrents. Sheep Creek, running through the oil district and the town of Okotoks, turned from a placid streamlet to a flooded river which rose to the top of the bridge, covered the main streets of Okotoks with water, and washed out the CPR tracks between Okotoks and Sandstone, the next station to the north.

It was near Sandstone that Canadian Western's main line from Bow Island crossed Sheep Creek by means of two twelve-inch pipes, sunk in the bed of the creek and protected by a crib filled with rock. The tremendous torrent rushing down Sheep Creek, carrying sand and rocks, scoured out the bed of the stream and washed out both pipes, reducing the cribwork to chips and carrying everything downstream. By 3:50 a.m. that Saturday the gas was escaping from the broken ends of the two pipes in Sheep Creek with a terrific roar. All gas in Calgary went off. No hot coffee and warm meals from gas ranges in Calgary that day!

Gas company president, Eugene Coste, and superintendent, H.B. Pearson, immediately began to muster their forces and to commandeer a train to take them out to Okotoks with the necessary supplies to begin repairs to the broken mains. The most formidable handicap, however, was the washout of the tracks near Sandstone. Water five feet deep was flowing over what were formerly tracks, and CPR officials said it would take at least forty-eight hours to repair the washout after the flood subsided. The gas company couldn't wait for that! Supplies would have to be transported overland around the washout!

The location was Mile 25, a little more than a mile from Okotoks. The superintendent unloaded the materials near the Bonny Brae farm and with almost superhuman efforts scoured the neighborhood for teams of horses to haul the pipes and supplies. By one o'clock in the afternoon they were fording the six-foot stream near the farm, the bridge having been washed away during the night. The roads were a veritable quagmire, and a long detour had to be made.

Meanwhile, back in Calgary not only were homeowners getting up to cold breakfasts, the *Herald* couldn't use its "modern" linotype machines because there was no gas to melt the metal which cast the type! What to do? The *Herald* put out a handset extra edition, distributed free of charge, while it made arrangements with a company supplying compressed gas in tanks to furnish gas for the linotype machines for the regular edition.

The *Herald* and all Calgarians were happy when the gas came back on. "Splendid work by gas company repair gang," said the *Herald*. "Record time made in fixing bad break . . . The herculean task which confronted Superintendent Pearson was carried out successfully through an incredibly short period . . . The torrential rain and a howling gale greatly interfered with the work over the CPR trestle bridge. At times the wind was so strong that the workmen were in imminent danger of being swept off into the raging torrent below."

By Sunday morning the gas was flowing again through the lines, and the company had survived another crisis.

Franchise Problems

During its first three years, the company was kept busy staying ahead of the demand for gas. The outbreak of the First World War brought about some emergency measures and cutbacks in industrial business, but residential consumers continued to increase and kept the earnings at an acceptable level.

Then in 1915 the company entered its first battle with the city of Calgary. The town fathers claimed the company's franchise covered only the original part of the city (three sections) that was in place at the time the franchise was granted. The company's interpretation of the franchise, however, was that it meant the entire city. The matter went to court. The city won its case, but this was appealed to the Supreme Court of Alberta, which ruled that the franchise did cover the whole city, present and future.

This was not satisfactory to the city. It appealed to the Supreme Court of Canada, which confirmed the decision of the Alberta court, the case being finally settled in 1917.

Lethbridge Offices

Canadian Western's first headquarters in Lethbridge were in the Hull Block on the corner of Third Avenue and Seventh Street South and the first regional superintendent was K. McLaws. Later the office was located in a wooden building on Seventh Street South in the six hundred-block. In 1939 the company built a much larger and more modern office building on Sixth Street. Today the company has a modern office and service centre complex on Stafford Drive. It was completed in 1966.

Only on one occasion did natural gas service fail for any length of time during the early years in Lethbridge. In the fall of 1917, when the weather was bitterly cold, a blowout occurred in the main line near Chin Lake. It was followed by a seventy-two-hour period of cold meals and cold water in Lethbridge homes. When the blowout occurred Canadian Western once again rushed a load of equipment and a repair crew from Calgary by train, followed by unusually fast work getting the supplies from the unloading point at Taber to the trouble point at Chin Coulee.

Calgary Headquarters

Having opened its first offices at 128 Seventh Avenue East in Calgary, the company began to branch out with a showroom in the adjoining Beveridge

Block. There was also an office at First Street West and Tenth Avenue, acquired from the Calgary Gas Company Limited.

In 1913, premises at 215 Sixth Avenue West were purchased. There an office building was erected in 1914, and occupied by Canadian Western until 1952. There were two shop areas: the East Calgary Shop, which was later sold, and the West End Shop at Eleventh Avenue and Tenth Street West, which at that time consisted of four lots and in later years was expanded to about one-and-a-half city blocks.

Exploring for New Fields

At first it seemed the Bow Island field would supply all the gas that was needed for many years. When Eugene Coste discovered the field he believed he had trapped a near inexhaustible supply. Coste was a believer in the inorganic origin of oil and gas and long before the Bow Island discovery he was addressing engineering groups on what he called the volcanic origin of natural gas and petroleum. It is recognized today that his theory was quite unscientific, as oil and gas have a biological origin and are not generated volcanically.

Towards the end of the first decade the demand for gas grew so quickly that the need for new producing fields became evident. Over the years Canadian Western obtained gas from sources other than Bow Island. Chin Coulee No. 1 was brought in on November 11, 1921, near the company's main transmission line, forty miles east of Lethbridge.

Continuing the search for further gas fields, No. 1 in Forty Mile Coulee (sixteen miles south of the Bow Island field) was drilled but proved unproductive. Three other wells were sunk in Chin Coulee, again they were unproductive. In 1922 drilling resumed at Chin Coulee and Monarch but with little success.

The Foremost field, thirty miles south of Bow Island, was more successful. By 1924 well No. 4 brought the total field capacity to 44 million cubic feet. The following year the company established a geological department and began systematic exploration for gas reserves by mapping, geophysical surveys and core drilling along its entire pipeline system commencing at Burdett and Foremost.

A ten-inch Turner Valley line was constructed in 1921, followed by a fourteen-inch line in 1928, as the developed capacity of that field continued to increase. In later years other fields were connected: Jumping Pound in 1951 (developed by Shell Canada), Nevis in 1956, Carbon in 1958, Okotoks in 1959 and Jumping Pound West in 1968. Connections were also made with the Alberta Gas Trunk Line system at various points.

In the period from 1912 to 1930 the Bow Island field produced a total of 38 billion cubic feet, and eventually became a storage field, with natural gas from Turner Valley being pumped into its depleted gas sands in summer as a reserve for winter peak-load demands.

Gas Shortage — 1920

River flood conditions in 1917 caused the company considerable expense, but these difficulties were surmounted. Everything went along fairly well until 1920 when the pressure in the Bow Island field began diminishing rapidly and the company's revenue that year dropped about ten percent. To ensure enough gas for residential consumption some large industrial accounts had to be severely cut back.

Canadian Western's annual report that year noted that "the available supply of gas is now reserved for domestic customers, over twelve thousand in number."

Old-timers still recall the shortage and the low-pressure problems it caused. Telephones were installed in all the regulator stations in Calgary, so they could be in constant communication with each other, increasing the pressure by a few ounces in one station and decreasing it correspondingly in another station where demands were less critical.

The operator at the central switchboard was instructed to suggest, when a customer would call in about having no gas in severe sub-zero weather, that he warm up his meter by draping a hot towel over it. If that didn't cause the gas to flow through the meter a serviceman would be sent out to by-pass the meter and give the customer a temporary straight connection.

The company was forced to ask the city for a rate increase. This was not a popular move, to say the least, and the city resisted. Originally, when it appeared there was an almost unlimited supply of gas in the Bow Island field, the company started out with a domestic gas rate of thirty-five cents per thousand cubic feet (MCF) net, dropping as low as thirty cents the next year, and coming back to thirty-five cents in 1914. Now, in 1920, with the serious loss of pressure in the field, the company was asking for a rate of fifty-five to sixty-five cents during the winter, and seventy-five cents during the summer months.

Nothing came of the company's request until May 1921, when the city reluctantly agreed to go before the Board of Public Utility Commissioners (which had been established on November 4, 1915). Unfortunately one of the members of the board became ill and the hearing could not be held, although the experts had already been engaged. What became known as the Technical Conference was then arranged, consisting of two representatives from the city, two from the company and an independent chairman. This conference agreed unanimously on the need for a rate increase, but the plan was rejected by the city.

It was not until September that the case was heard by the board, which approved an increase from thirty-five cents to forty-eight cents per thousand cubic feet, on the following conditions:

a) That a line be built from Turner Valley connecting with the company's main line at Okotoks, to be completed by December 31, 1921. Otherwise, the rate would revert to thirty-five cents.

b) That an energetic drilling program be conducted for the development of the Chin Coulee and Foremost fields.

"The decision of the board was received at the end of September 1921, leaving us very little time to complete the Turner Valley line," commented company comptroller H.S. Tims in recalling the events. "As usual, when a difficult task was to be undertaken, the operating force rose to the occasion and although hampered by bad weather conditions the work was finally completed and on January 1, 1922, Calgary received its first gas from Turner Valley."

Mellon, who supervised the laying of that line, recalled that construction of the line was complicated by the fact that the company decided it needed some contract help, and brought in a group of pipelayers from Winnipeg. It turned out that they knew more about laying water lines than gas lines and after about three weeks it was obvious they were getting nowhere fast. In desperation gas company crews took over, with only five weeks left in which to complete the job. They finished it — about five o'clock on the evening of the last day of grace.

The following summer the Royalite Company increased its supply by about four million cubic feet per day, and the gas company managed to squeeze through the winter of 1922-1923.

In 1923, after continued arguments between the gas company and the city of Calgary, the utility board ordered the company to augment its supply by October 1. An energetic drilling program at Chin Coulee and Foremost was immediately undertaken. Chin Coulee proved disappointing, but the finds at Foremost warranted the building of a pipeline the following year, 1924. Meanwhile, Turner Valley produced another seven million cubic feet a day and the situation was saved.

International Utilities — 1925

The mid-twenties marked a turning point for Canadian Western, as the company became associated with a United States company known as International Utilities Corporation. International Utilities began its operations in the state of Maryland, and then opened a Wall Street office in the financial centre of New York City. The corporation was engaged in the financing, engineering and management of a variety of public utilities ranging from electric and gas companies to urban street railway systems.

The beginning of Canadian Western under Eugene Coste's leadership had been financed largely by pounds sterling raised in London, but now the U.S. dollar entered the scene in a much more pronounced way. At first International Utilities simply became an agency for Canadian Western for the purposes of raising money in the United States. The minutes of a Canadian Western board meeting in Calgary on December 18, 1925, noted the resolution:

. . . That the International Utilities Corporation be agents of the Company in the United States of America, and that the proper officers of the Company be authorized to pay to them in respect of their services in this connection a sum equivalent to 3% of the gross earnings of the Company, such sum to be payable monthly, commencing November 1st, 1925.

Very quickly, however, International Utilities began acquiring the common shares of Canadian Western, and in this way over a period of years bought controlling interest in the company.

Eugene Coste, the original president, left the company in 1922, turning the presidency over to H.B. Pearson, who had been general superintendent from 1912 until the twenties when he became general manager and vice-president. With International Utilities' involvement came C.J. Yorath, a leader already associated with International Utilities' natural gas and electric operations in other parts of western Canada. Yorath became president and managing director of Canadian Western on June 15, 1925. The next year F.W. Bacon, who was associated with Yorath in other utilities, became vice-president.

The new association with International Utilities was not only a management turning point for Canadian Western; it also meant access to vast new sources of capital, as well as a link with other utilities which gave the company the benefit of valuable outside help and engineering expertise.

Rates Start to Go Down

The original sources of natural gas were becoming depleted, but Turner Valley was producing large supplies, so the company built a ten-inch line to bring more Turner Valley gas to Calgary. This assured an adequate supply to consumers, and Canadian Western reduced its rate to forty-three cents per thousand cubic feet.

Rate reductions are always popular, and the *Calgary Albertan* commented:

If utility companies elsewhere in Canada earned the same commendation that must justly be accorded the Canadian Western Natural Gas, Light, Heat and Power Company Limited in this case, there would be little or no room for discussion in respect to public versus private ownership.

The tide of Canadian Western's fortunes had turned for the better. The drop in consumption, with its corresponding drop in revenue, had started with the year 1919 and reached its low ebb in 1923 when the company was seriously in the red. Now the company organized a new business department to help promote the sale of gas, and by the late twenties sales volumes were increasing steadily. As sales went up rates came down voluntarily.

By 1929 the company's net rate was thirty-three cents per thousand cubic feet, and annual revenue had climbed well over the two million dollar mark.

Canadian Western was in a healthy condition to begin weathering the storms of the imminent great depression.

Home Service Department — 1929

In the early years the company operated with the bare essentials, but by 1923 it was well established and had time to turn to more artistic endeavors with the creation of a company crest. The basic design was developed by Fred Heuperman, general superintendent. This crest, displaying the torch of service, served to identify the company until 1962 when it was replaced by a more contemporary corporate logo, used to this day.

As Canadian Western took on a progressive look it attracted a growing number of new investors.

The first customer stock ownership campaign was conducted in 1924, with conspicuous success. Then in 1926 employees sold more than two thousand cumulative preference shares to over seven hundred subscribers. Eventually three and a half million dollars worth of these hundred dollar par value shares were taken up.

Gas service was extended to High River, Stavely and Parkland in 1927, and an inspection department was formed to inspect every gas installation in the system. Billing, too, became more sophisticated that year with the installation of the first mechanical billing machines, replacing hand billing in the Boston ledgers.

The year 1929 brought installation of gas service at Taber. In October a home service department was organized. The new department came about when Harold E. Timmins, manager of new business, persuaded Hesperia Lee Aylsworth to leave a similar position in Vancouver with B.C. Electric Company and join Canadian Western as home service director.

In October Miss Aylsworth, a graduate of the University of Alberta, began the first home service work, including home calls, visits to new customers and calling on customers who had purchased new gas ranges. During the first year over six hundred calls were made. Soon a series of cooking schools was arranged, and over the years the home service department kept pace with the growth of the company, with telephone calls, interviews and recipes for homemakers.

The *esprit-de-corps* among gas company personnel was excellent. There were sports competitions of various sorts, and a variety of social events. The annual dance in the fall of 1928 was a good example. It was a masquerade ball at the Bowness Golf Club, with music by Jimmy Holden and his orchestra. Costumes ranged from stately Quakers to delicate Japanese damsels, and from tough-looking pirates to dazzling aristocratic Elizabethan ladies. "A truly splendid evening," said the reporter who covered the event for the staff magazine. "As usual the success of the whole affair was largely due to the untiring efforts of the various committees."

A year later — Friday, October 18, 1929, the annual dinner of Canadian Western was held in the new Elks Auditorium in Calgary and by that time the company was serving well over twenty thousand customers.

President C.J. Yorath noted that the properties of the various companies in the group were "scattered over many hundreds of miles in the provinces of Saskatchewan, Alberta and British Columbia." Canadian Western, as the oldest member in the group of companies, was "progressing with leaps and bounds," and there was now "a very happy relationship between the public, our customers, and ourselves" — a relationship which he attributed to the "loyalty, integrity, hard work and above all the excellent teamwork" of the company employees.

Three employees who received awards for twenty years' continuous service since starting with the Calgary Gas Company were W.E. Larkham, city mains foreman in Calgary; George Watson, sub-foreman; and Thomas Dodds, foreman of services.

CHAPTER 2

Edmonton and Central Alberta

The Viking Field

Early explorations for natural gas in the northern half of the province date back before the turn of the century. The first natural gas well in northern Alberta was drilled by the Geological Survey of Canada in 1897, northeast of the town of Athabasca, about one hundred and sixty-five miles from Edmonton, near a fur trading post at Pelican Rapids.

The hope was expressed that wells in this area would supply Edmonton with natural gas, but it was twenty-six years before Edmonton's hope for gas became a reality — not from this field, but from the Viking field, eighty miles east of the city.

In 1913 the City of Edmonton retained a geologist to report on possible sources of supply for the city. Although a local company, the Pelican Oil and Gas Company, was drilling wells in the Pelican Rapids area, and good flows were encountered, the geologist reported in favor of drilling in the Viking field. Accordingly, a group of Edmonton citizens, incorporated as The Edmonton Industrial Association Drilling Company, Limited, started drilling in the Viking area. At the same time they began negotiating with the city for a natural gas franchise.

The association consisted of about six hundred members, including Edmonton mayor, Billy McNamara. Ex-mayor William Short, whom McNamara had defeated in a close-fought mayoralty contest, was a member of a rival group which was promoting a gas field at Vermilion Chutes on the Peace River. Short saw an opportunity to get McNamara out of the mayor's chair on the technicality that he was a member of a company trying to do business with the city and had disqualified himself as mayor. He took McNamara to court — all the way to the Alberta Supreme Court — and won. The Supreme Court ruled that an election would have to be held to choose another mayor.

While Edmonton was getting ready for the election, Short took members of the Alberta Legislature to the Peace River country to inspect his gas discovery. The MLA's were impressed, but the scheme didn't get off the ground for the simple reason that the gas field was too far away. It could not compete with the Viking field.

The Industrial Association Company struck gas at Viking on November 4, 1914. At a depth of 2,340 feet, the well blew in with a volume of more than nine million cubic feet per day.

The *Viking News* announced the discovery in a front-page banner headline story, the editor commenting: "Viking sprang into gas fame early Wednesday morning, November 4, 1914, when the drillers at the Viking gas wells struck a flow of gas that exceeded the expectations of the experts who located the well."

The citizens of Edmonton wanted gas, but apparently were not prepared to risk their money to get it. Three successive by-laws submitted to raise the money for development of this field were rejected by the ratepayers.

It took a private firm, The Northern Alberta Natural Gas Development Company, to prove, at a cost of hundreds of thousands of dollars, that this field was in fact one of the largest deposits of gas discovered in Canada to that date, capable of supplying Edmonton's requirements for many years. One of the principals of this firm was Eugene Coste, founding president of Canadian Western Natural Gas Company. Another was R.B. Bennett, who later became prime minister of Canada.

The First World War interrupted plans to lay a pipeline from Viking to Edmonton. Following the war the development company entered into protracted negotiations with the city to establish a satisfactory basis for supplying Edmontonians with natural gas. The company had already paid the city in cash for the expenses it had incurred earlier with respect to Viking, including obtaining reports on the field and the cost involved in the drilling of the first well.

The Board of Public Utility Commissioners entered the picture on November 27, 1922, with an order which fixed the rates for domestic consumption of gas at forty and a half cents per thousand cubic feet (MCF) and thirty cents per thousand cubic feet for industrial consumption. Now the development company had to find the money to launch the project, estimated by the utilities board to require more than four million dollars.

Northwestern Utilities — 1923

T he development company was unable to raise the money and subsequent negotiation resulted in the formation of a new company, Northwestern

Utilities, Limited. It was incorporated on May 26, 1923, with a federal charter, to engage in the production, transmission and distribution of natural gas. Northwestern Utilities bought the assets of The Northern Alberta Natural Gas Development Company and laid plans to bring natural gas service to Edmonton.

Northwestern Utilities, Limited, opened its first offices in the Agency Building on Edmonton's Jasper Avenue on June 1, 1923. The staff occupied the third floor of the building, located on the south side of Jasper Avenue just east of the Capitol Theatre.

A contract was let to the engineering firm of Ford, Bacon and Davis Inc. of New York to construct and operate the gas system for one year, and work began soon after that. Time was of the essence. A construction timetable was set which to many seemed impossible. The hope of bringing gas to Edmonton before fall freeze-up was highly ambitious if not presumptuous.

All pipe mills were overloaded with orders and immediate deliveries could not be arranged, so careful schedules of deliveries were drawn up, based on the output of American, Canadian and Scottish mills. Work programs were built around the scheduled delivery dates.

Close supervision by the company's inspectors kept mill production in line, but transportation was harder to predict. The Scottish pipe was shipped via the Panama Canal and Vancouver. It left Scotland on time, but that did not necessarily mean it would arrive on time as became apparent when the ship ran into traffic snarls at the canal. The situation was tense. Further delays in the field could mean running into fall freeze-up before the project was completed. When the ship arrived at Vancouver the stevedores went aboard and pipe was being unloaded the instant the ship docked. A Canadian Pacific special train was waiting with steam up, ready to leave as soon as it was loaded. As the results testified, the plans were carried through and the pipe was delivered on time.

The first carload of pipe arrived July 6 and ditching was started immediately. On the main transmission line and field gathering lines, ditching was carried out by machine with the exception of approximately fifteen miles of rough terrain, sloughs and muskeg. Ditching for city lines was done principally by hand.

While the pipeliners were busy, Northwestern's office staff was swinging into operation preparing to serve customers eagerly awaiting the new fuel. The staff quickly outgrew the space in the Agency Building, and on August 1 the company moved to a one-storey brick building on the corner of 103 Street and Jasper Avenue — a building which stood for many years kitty corner from the Hudson's Bay Company in downtown Edmonton.

Back on the transmission line project, a heavy rainfall caused almost complete suspension of work for five days during the week of August 19. Then work was entirely suspended during four days in September by a six-inch fall of snow. However, the project moved quickly to completion after that.

The main transmission line was finished October 24. It was tested over the next three days and gas began flowing into the city plant on the afternoon of October 27, just 116 days after the arrival of the engineers of Ford, Bacon and Davis.

Eighty-eight working days after the first carload of pipe arrived, a system had been built consisting of one hundred and eighty miles of pipeline, fifteen regulator stations, a warehouse, shop and various other buildings. To finance the venture, four million dollars of capital had been raised.

It was the beginning of November in 1923 when natural gas was served to the first Edmonton customer. This was at a time when bread was selling at four loaves for a quarter; a new 1924 Maxwell club sedan was being offered for $1,795; Tom Mix was playing at the Monarch Theatre and Harold Lloyd was convulsing patrons in a six-reeler at the Empress.

On November 9 Edmonton's mayor, D.M. Duggan, and city officials lit a gas flare on the 105 Street Bridge to proclaim the completion of work. The ceremonial turn-on heralded the arrival of the clean blue flame of natural gas, with a system designed to serve the metropolis of Edmonton and the smaller communities of Tofield, Ryley, Holden, Bruce and Viking.

Prior to the distribution and sale of gas by Northwestern Utilities in 1923, ten wells had been drilled in the Viking field with a total daily open flow capacity of just over 47 million cubic feet. From the data obtained from these wells the field was estimated to contain 60 billion cubic feet of gas.

Northwestern Utilities had a selling job to do and did it well. Edmontonians were soon aware of the many advantages the new fuel offered over coal. About half the floor area in the company's new offices was used for displaying natural gas appliances which were aggressively promoted and sold. Head office staff that first year totalled about fifteen, all new to the gas business but all eager to do their part to make the new venture a success. By the end of 1923 eighteen hundred customers were being served.

C.J. Yorath — 1924

The controlling interest in Northwestern Utilities as well as Ford, Bacon and Davis was held by International Utilities, which meant there was a very close working relationship between the engineering firm and Northwestern Utilities. E.G. Hill, resident manager of the engineering firm, became president of Northwestern Utilities. Then shortly after the operating contract with Ford, Bacon and Davis terminated on September 30, 1924, the presidency was turned over to C.J. Yorath, who resigned his position as chief commissioner of the City of Edmonton to take on the leadership of the utility.

Yorath experienced a dramatic career change from being dedicated to municipal operation of utilities (usually thought of as public ownership) to investor ownership. His son, Dennis K., who in later years became president and then chairman of both Northwestern Utilities and Canadian Western, recalled those early years in a speech he made at an oldtimers' get-together in January 1962.

"I was away at school in Victoria, B.C.," Dennis said. "and came back to find my father engaged in a sort of battle with an organization that wanted to bring natural gas into the city of Edmonton."

C.J. battled the group for a year and a half, but the city finally decided to give Northwestern Utilities the franchise. It was H.R. Milner, then legal counsel for the utilities, who persuaded Yorath that working for a privately-owned utility would not be a compromise of principles, and that Yorath might, in fact find more self-fulfilment in heading such a utility than staying with the city.

In short, Northwestern Utilities offered Yorath the presidency, and he accepted. "Overnight, he walked into a completely different field," Dennis recalled. "It was amazing how quickly his attitude changed."

Main Line Break — 1928

C ustomer growth in the late twenties was slow but steady. The newly installed system operated without serious difficulties until 1928, when the first setback occurred.

It was about 9 a.m. on New Year's Day when shifting ice caused a separation in a section of the Viking line which ran across a farmer's dugout. An hour later Edmonton was without gas. The temperature was twenty degrees below zero with a wind.

While repair crews rushed to the scene of the break, the rest of the staff in Edmonton had to decide on a course of action. The first thing was to inform Northwestern's customers of the break and so a handbill was produced to assure them there was no reason to panic.

John Whelihan, who later became company treasurer, rushed the handwritten message to Hamly Press for printing. The company then contacted John Michaels, owner of Mike's News, who enlisted the help of the Newsboys Band plus all his regular newsboys to distribute the notices to customers' homes throughout the city.

Meanwhile, radio stations were broadcasting the information to their listeners. Cars were dispatched to communities between Edmonton and Viking, giving the information to customers in the towns along the line. A special train was chartered to rush a crew of men, and general superintendent Charles Spencer, to the break in the line.

The citizens of Edmonton took the emergency in their stride. Some fired up their converted furnaces with coal for the emergency, removing the gas burners and replacing them when gas service was restored at four o'clock that same afternoon.

The conscientious and efficient way in which Northwestern Utilities' staff handled the crisis saved the day. The public understood, and the staff achieved a new measure of strength and unity as well as a sense of accomplishment by teamwork, which helped them through similar circumstances in the years ahead.

Duplicating Main Line

In the fall of 1928 it became obvious that steps would have to be taken to increase the capacity of the main line. The peak hourly demand for the winter of 1929-1930 was estimated at well over one million cubic feet. Various plans were considered to increase transmission capacity from year to year to meet the demand.

The company decided that the most economical plan was to start duplicating (looping) the existing line. This was accomplished by the end of 1936. During the three years that followed, the company continued to duplicate other lines at the rate of about five miles a year.

Line protection included treatment with Barrett's enamel, a substance which looked like tar and formed a hard protective coating when it solidified. At the end of the thirties an additional safeguard was instituted by wrapping the pipe with tar-impregnated asbestos. Automatic back pressure valves of the swing-check type were installed in both lines at frequent intervals to conserve the gas in the main between the valve and Edmonton, should a break occur.

Many long hours of hard work went into those early years in the twenties. But there were times of relaxation as well. Staff picnics, held annually, often took the form of day trips by train to Alberta Beach or Edmonton Beach. Annual staff parties were also instituted, the first ones being held in the Masonic Hall, north of Jasper Avenue on 116 Street.

Sale of Shares — 1928

In those days the staff was closer to the financial side of the business than in later years when the selling of shares became a specialized function involving outside brokers. A good example of activities by company salesmen was a ten-day sale of shares in the spring of 1928.

The campaign, to sell six percent Prior Preference Shares, began on May 28, after a get-together banquet the previous evening at which the president outlined the objectives. When the final reports were in on June 8, it was found that fourteen hundred and twenty-five shares had been sold, making an average of approximately twenty-two shares per salesman. First prize of fifty dollars for the lady selling the greatest number of shares was won by Ella Jonason. First prize for the man selling the greatest number of shares was won by John Holgate, who had more than tripled his quota. The team prize was won by the C.E. Wiggins team, with a total of two hundred and seventy-eight shares.

Home Service — 1930

Northwestern Utilities launched its home service department on March 1, 1930, under the supervision of Kathleen Esch, a graduate of the University of Alberta in household economics. Miss Esch came to the company from Holy Cross Hospital in Calgary where she had been in charge of the diet kitchen. She also held cooking classes and had given lectures on the composition and preparation of foods. The home service department was a popular innovation from the start, bringing enthusiastic public response and generating goodwill for the company.

New Office Building — 1930

In the summer of 1930 Northwestern moved into its consolidated quarters at 10124 – 104 Street, just north of Jasper Avenue. Two years previously the company had begun building on this location, with a garage, warehouse office, meter testing room, stock room, workshop and yard adjoining. Construction on the second and main unit was started in April 1930. All the company's buildings in Edmonton were now on one property, providing more efficiency and economy through centralization.

The property was half a block from Jasper Avenue, with trackage facilities in the rear. The building was well lit and ventilated, finished on the outside with tapestry brick and Indiana limestone. The main entrance featured a marble floor, and up above was the company crest. A twelve-foot neon sign at the front depicted a lighted bunsen burner with the words Heat with Gas on one side and Cook with Gas on the other, the words Heat and Cook being mounted on panels which were interchangeable. The main floor included a showroom, a long oak counter with two cashiers' cages and the commercial department. At the rear, beside a wainscotted stairway was the switchboard and an information desk.

The second floor included a reception desk, executive offices, general offices, a board room, and the engineering department. The basement included a model boiler room for demonstrations of furnace burners, and a large room complete with a display of kitchen appliances for gas cooking demonstrations by the home service director.

Northwestern continued to operate from this location until its move to The Milner Building in April, 1959.

CHAPTER 3

Power for the Twenties

The Start at Vegreville

Natural gas is one side of the Canadian Utilities energy picture. The other side — electric power — began to unfold in the late twenties. A company called Mid-West Utilities, Limited took over the operation of a number of small power plants in east-central Alberta, beginning in the town of Vegreville, and in Saskatchewan.

Mid-West Utilities, Limited was granted a charter by letters patent under the Companies Act of Canada on May 18, 1927, to carry on business as a light, heat and power company.

The new venture was organized as another subsidiary of International Utilities Corporation, New York, and C.J. Yorath was appointed president. The first general manager was E.W. Bowness who had been engaged by International Utilities in 1925 to negotiate electric franchises. The company's first acquisition was Vegreville Utilities Limited, which had been incorporated the previous year by Bowness to serve the town of Vegreville. On June 12, 1928, to avoid being associated with a holding company in the United States which had a similar name, Mid-West was officially changed to Canadian Utilities, Limited.

The consumption of electricity in those years was a far cry from what it is today. The first use to which most homeowners put the exciting new form of energy was to light their homes during the evening hours, replacing the old kerosene lamps. Then it was used on Monday mornings for the weekly wash, when wringer washing machines began replacing the old tub and scrub board.

When the company took over the Vegreville system it was supplied from a coal-fired, hand-stoked, non-condensing, reciprocating steam engine and two generating units producing about 25 kilowatts in total. The fixed assets were valued at almost twenty-nine thousand dollars and about three hundred and eighty customers were receiving service. The plant operator was H.R. Johnston. Vegreville Utilities increased the generating capacity of the plant to 100 kilowatts almost immediately, and later it was more than tripled again, to 375 kilowatts.

Johnston wrote a short item on Vegreville for the first issue of *The Courier*, the staff magazine of the energy group, published in April 1927. He said, in part:

Vegreville is a town with a population of about nineteen hundred, situated seventy miles east of Edmonton. It is in the centre of one of the best farming districts in northern Alberta. Farmers here are now going in more for mixed farming, although they continue to grow wheat extensively.

After the company obtained ownership of the Vegreville electrical facilities, W.P. MacDonald was appointed the first district superintendent in July 1928. Working with him were H.R. Johnston, Jim Fraser, Eric King and Ralph Provan. This small group made up the Vegreville staff in the first year of operation under the new organization.

The ambitious little company proceeded to acquire franchises in other communities. After Vegreville came Lloydminster, Drumheller, Stettler, Hanna and Grande Prairie. There were others as well, particularly in Saskatchewan, but these six are the major ones which have remained and grown with the company and are today regarded as the "six original communities."

Office Moves to Calgary — 1928

C anadian Utilities' head office was originally in Edmonton, in the CPR Building on Jasper Avenue, but less than a year later, in the spring of 1928, it was moved to Calgary, where it remained until Canadian Utilities was moved back to Edmonton in 1948. The new head office in Calgary was located at 215 Sixth Avenue West, where an additional storey had been added to the building which housed the office of the Canadian Western Natural Gas, Light, Heat and Power Company Limited.

The principal officers of the company at the beginning of 1948 were: chairman of the board, P.M. Chandler; president and managing director, C.J. Yorath; vice-president, F.W. Bacon; secretary-treasurer, Julian Garrett; assistant treasurer, H. Williams; assistant secretary, E.J. Hallberg.

Personnel in the Edmonton office at the time of the move to Calgary were: E.W. Bowness, plant manager in charge of all property acquisitions; C.S. Nance, chief accountant; W.J. Murphy, business and operating manager responsible for new business and all local managers; H.S. Tims, controller; A. Montador, power plant superintendent; E. Kelly, superintendent of construction for Alberta; D.K. Yorath, purchasing; Ivy Cialis, billing; Blanche Crozier, stenographer; and B.M. Hill, who later became president of Canadian Utilities.

On March 26, 1928, Julian Garrett resigned his position of secretary-treasurer, and D.K. Yorath was appointed the new secretary with H.S. Tims as treasurer and controller. Garrett by this time was deeply involved with Northwestern Utilities, and chose to concentrate on the natural gas operations which were head-quartered in Edmonton. In addition to having served as secretary-treasurer of the new electrical company, he also served as secretary-treasurer of Northwestern, and at the end of 1947 was promoted to become general manager of Northwestern.

Electric Grid System Begins

Having started in Vegreville with a hand-stoked steam engine and a lot of hope for the future, Canadian Utilities moved towards a grid system supplied by major power plants in key locations. The company's first transmission line was built from Vegreville northwest to Mundare. This 13,800-volt line, extending nineteen miles from the Vegreville power plant, was built under contract by Ed Kelly, who previously owned Kelly Electric Company in Edmonton. He was hired by the company to supervise its line construction and eventually became chief electrical engineer and a director of Canadian Utilities.

The line to Mundare was followed by a 13,800-volt line, seventy-two miles in length, to Lloydminster on the Saskatchewan border. Communities connected along the way were Innisfree, Islay, Kitscoty, Lavoy, Manville, Ranfurly and Minburn. At that time Lloydminster only had a small plant of its own, so the interconnection considerably enhanced the availability and reliability of power service.

At the same time Canadian Utilities brought service to Lloydminster, it acquired franchises and purchased plants and distribution facilities in Watrous and Rosetown in Saskatchewan, and Raymond and Mundare in Alberta.

As lines were extended to additional communities, the small inefficient plants serving the local loads were shut down and the generating equipment scrapped, sold or placed on standby for emergency duty. Central power plants were built and the generating capacity enlarged to take care of expanding loads.

While the Vegreville-to-Lloydminster line was being built, a seventy-mile, 13,800-volt three-phase line was constructed in the Castor, Alberta district, joining the towns of Castor and Coronation, along with the villages of Alliance, Galahad and Forestburg, to an oil engine plant at Castor.

In Saskatchewan, a further one hundred and fifteen miles of lines were built in 1928 in the Watrous district. These lines tied several small towns in the vicinity of Watrous to a small diesel plant at that point. The Watrous plant was subsequently shut down and a new diesel plant built at Kokomis, a few miles to the east. This system was sold to the Saskatchewan Power Commission in 1931.

In 1928, Canadian Utilities also acquired the diesel-fueled power plant at Yorkton, as well as small plants at Foam Lake and Wilkie and a three-phase line was extended from Yorkton to Saltcoats.

Electric Service in Drumheller

The history of Canadian Utilities in Drumheller dates back to November 1927, when Union Power Company Limited became an associate company of Canadian Utilities. Although Union Power continued to operate under its own name for a time, it gradually merged with the new company and by 1935 operated as the Canadian Utilities Drumheller District.

The Drumheller plant had an interesting history prior to its acquisition by Canadian Utilities. In the fall of 1916, the town first granted a ten-year franchise to the Northwest Engineering and Supply Company of Calgary to provide electric power mainly for lighting purposes. Service began with a twenty-five horsepower unit, providing electricity from sunset to sunrise. It wasn't until 1919 that twenty-four-hour service was initiated. That year the company was reorganized and became the Drumheller Power Company.

On February 12, 1923, Drumheller Power Company was sold to the Union Power Company Limited. Union Power was bought by the Enloe brothers of Spokane, Washington in September 1924, but continued to operate as Union Power, with Raymond Enloe as manager. Lines were extended to several small surrounding coal-mining communities.

In 1925 Union Power absorbed an operation called Mines Power, which had been formed in 1922 by a group of mine operators to provide electric service to mines in the Drumheller valley from Rosedale to Nacmine. The plant was located south of the elevators by the old Drumheller mine.

Following the purchase of Union Power by International Utilities, the company carried on an aggressive policy of expansion. In the spring of 1928 it purchased the power plant and obtained the franchise for the town of Stettler. This was followed by the purchase of private plants in Big Valley and Three Hills.

These franchises opened the door to further expansion of the transmission system emanating from the Drumheller plant. The 13,800-volt line to Munson and Craigmyle was raised to 33,000 volts and extended north to Stettler and east to Hanna, where the company had purchased the town plant and been granted the franchise in December 1927.

The following year, the line to Carbon was extended north to Three Hills and lines were built east and west from Stettler to the villages of Botha and Erskine, where Canadian Utilities had recently acquired franchises.

At the same time, major coal developments were taking place at Willow Creek and East Coulee, on the Red Deer River downstream from Drumheller. The company extended a line from Rosedale to service these new industrial loads and the communities which grew up around them.

In 1929 Union Power built a 13,200-volt line east from Botha to Castor to tie in the Canadian Utilities system in the Castor-Coronation area with the high-voltage line serving Stettler from the Drumheller plant.

The construction of a line to Castor also enabled the company to extend service to the villages of Gadsby and Halkirk, which were on the CPR line along the route of the new transmission line east of Stettler.

With all the expansion into new areas underway during 1928 and 1929, and with future plans in mind, it was obvious to management that the Drumheller plant would have to be rebuilt and its generating capacity increased. This was carried out during 1928 and 1929, under plant chief Charlie Jamieson. A 2,500-kilowatt General Electric turbo-generator and two 500-horsepower boilers with coal stokers and ancillary equipment were added to the 1,500-kilowatt unit which had been installed in 1927. The new equipment brought the Drumheller plant capacity up to 4,000 kilowatts and this remained unchanged through the depression and Second World War years.

Stettler and Hanna

The purchase of the Stettler plant by Union Power was a major step in the development of Canadian Utilities, particularly with the upgrading of the line to Munson and Craigmyle to 33,000 volts and its extension north to Stettler and east to Hanna.

Although there were probably some Hanna residents who believed at the time that the utility should have remained in the hands of the municipality, there is no doubt that this opinion was a minority one when the rates dropped from twenty cents per kilowatt hour to twelve cents per kilowatt hour after the Union Power take over. In the years that followed the rate per kilowatt hour eventually dropped to about five and a half cents.

The Hanna plant was operated by the company until the transmission line was extended from Craigmyle and then placed on emergency standby duty. Because Hanna was a CNR divisional point, it was necessary that the town be assured of a constant supply of electric energy and for this reason the plant was not dismantled.

The decision to keep the Hanna plant on standby duty turned out to be a wise one the following winter. During a severe cold period considerable trouble was experienced with breakdowns on the transmission line and it was necessary to put the standby plant in operation on several occasions.

The initial problems with the Hanna line were rectified by splicing additional slack into the line and the situation was made even more secure by the construction of eight miles of line from the Drumheller substation to provide a parallel tie-in with the Hanna line. The Hanna plant was not operated again after the building of this line.

Grande Prairie — 1928

T he plant and distribution system at Grande Prairie were acquired by the company on March 1, 1928. At that time the plant was located almost directly under the original overhead water tower back of the town hall. It had a total capacity of 45 kilowatts, obtained from three generators driven by 25 horsepower single-cylinder horizontal gasoline engines.

Prior to the company taking over the operation of the system, electric service was provided only in the evening from dusk until midnight, and on Monday and Tuesday morning so that housewives in the community could do their washing and ironing.

Meters in the town were owned by the customers, and later were all bought by the company at a flat rate of five dollars each.

The original staff at Grande Prairie consisted of Roy Nurse, who remained with the company until retirement in December 1963, and Vic Baxter, who had been operating the plant for the town. The following year Ernie Cookshaw joined the staff of the expanding power station and he too remained with the company until retirement forty years later.

The original plant contained two well pumps, providing the town's water supply. "We were subject to flooding if the water tower overflowed," Roy Nurse said. "Then our fuel oil tanks would float out and we'd be in a mess."

When the company acquired the Grande Prairie plant there were only one hundred and thirty customers and thirteen streetlights in the town. The only industrial power account consisted of a half-horsepower motor that ran a coffee-grinder in Morrison's store. There was only one rate when the town owned the electric system and that was a flat rate of twenty-five cents per kilowatt hour.

The conditions on which Canadian Utilities obtained the franchise included a substantial reduction in energy rates, along with all-night service as well as Monday and Tuesday mornings. Domestic rates under the terms of the franchise started at eighteen cents, with a sliding scale to fourteen cents after the first 100 kilowatt hours.

The company built a new power plant which was put into operation in September 1928, and marked the beginning of around-the-clock electric service in Grande Prairie. A new 120-kilowatt unit supplied electric needs at night, and a 15-kilowatt generator from the old plant was used during the day. The following year the small generator was removed and a new 175-kilowatt generator was installed to handle the growing load.

Many years later Nurse recalled with a chuckle the first night the power stayed on all night. Bridge party participants had been in the habit of breaking up at midnight when the power went off, but that night some of them went on until three and four o'clock in the morning before the players realized it was past their usual bedtime.

Nurse's enthusiasm and his skill with diesel engines became a legend in the company. His talents at improvising in times of emergency many times kept the energy on the line when it appeared there would be a blackout. At retirement he was technical assistant to the president of the company.

During Canadian Utilities' first year of electric operations its sales of electric power totalled 677,420 kilowatt hours, operating revenue was eighty-one thousand dollars and net earnings were twenty thousand dollars. The total number of customers was just over nineteen hundred in the original six communities with a combined population close to eight thousand. No farm customers were connected at that time. For the most part the rural electrification movement was still nearly two decades in the future.

Town of Raymond — 1927

In August 1927, Canadian Utilities arranged for the purchase of the Raymond Electric Company from the private owners who were supplying electricity to some three hundred and eighty customers in the southern Alberta town. On May 1 the following year a ten-year franchise was signed with the town. At that time, Raymond was supplied with power from two 100-kilowatt diesel generators. In 1929 the company entered into a five-year agreement with Calgary Power Limited for the purchase of electricity in bulk. Calgary Power had a 13,800-volt transmission line that came within half a mile of Raymond.

Following the signing of the agreement, a short tie line was built to the Calgary Power line and the Raymond plant went on standby. The Raymond franchise and distribution facilities remained the property of Canadian Utilities until 1936, when Calgary Power took over the Raymond properties in exchange for its franchise and facilities in the town of St. Paul.

One of the stalwarts who joined Canadian Utilities with the purchase of Raymond in 1927 was George D. O'Brien, plant operator and serviceman. Later he was to play a significant role in the management of the company.

Beginnings of Northland

While all this was going on in Alberta, an interesting development at Indian Head, Saskatchewan involved two men who later spearheaded the formation of Northland Utilities Limited, a company that amalgamated with Canadian Utilities in 1961.

The two men were Walter Schlosser and Warren DuBois. Schlosser was born at Grand Forks, North Dakota, on December 27, 1892. He graduated in arts and law from the University of North Dakota, and served in the U.S. infantry during the First World War. While in North Dakota he served in the state senate for four years.

In 1919, returning from military service, Schlosser became one of several pro-
prietors of a small electrical contracting firm, Electric Construction Company,
with a franchise for Delco farm lighting plants in the Red River Valley in Manitoba.
By 1926 the firm had installed alternating current distribution systems in several
communities, and was looking for a wider market. Of particular interest was
the almost complete lack of power development in Saskatchewan.

Schlosser went to Indian Head, Saskatchewan, early in 1927 with Helen, his
bride of four months. Here he established Northern Light and Power Ltd., beginning with a franchise to serve Indian Head; then Moosomin, where he installed
a diesel plant, followed by Wolseley, Grenfell and Balcarres. These communities
were all in an area east of Regina. The plan was to buy power from Regina until
it became possible to build a steam plant and a high-voltage line from Estevan
to Yorkton.

Schlosser took a few members from various town councils on trips to North
Dakota for demonstrations of power systems there, but he soon discovered that
being a planner, operator and promoter all at the same time was just too much.
So he engaged as his helper, a young graduate in mechanical engineering from
the University of Minnesota, N. Warren DuBois, who was then working in the
meter reading department of Northern States Power. That was the beginning of
a working relationship which lasted, with only a few short interruptions, until
DuBois' retirement as general manager of Northland Utilities in 1961.

Financing the "Schlosser dream" was a major challenge in those years, and
to keep expenses down DuBois found it necessary to board with the Schlossers.
The winter of 1927-1928 was a very cold one, DuBois recalled in a history he
wrote in later years, but service was maintained in reasonable shape despite the
severe weather. The only casualty was a cast iron gas unit at Wolseley that cracked
and had to be replaced. Since there were no standby facilities, Wolseley went
for a weekend without lights.

In 1928 Canadian Utilities started negotiations for the purchase of Northern
Light and Power, and a substantial down payment was made. In view of the
impending purchase, the remainder of the lines and substations which were on
the planning boards for interconnecting various towns to Indian Head were
completed by Canadian Utilities. DuBois stayed on as Canadian Utilities' superintendent of construction for the district and by the end of the year over one
hundred and eighty miles of 22,000-volt line had been built.

On March 1, 1929, the purchase of Northern Light and Power by Canadian
Utilities was completed, the price being about eight hundred thousand dollars,
and the operation became the company's Indian Head District.

Schlosser was an ambitious young man and he felt there was not enough scope
for him to stay with Canadian Utilities. He went to work for a group called
Dominion Electric Power Ltd., serving Estevan, some surrounding mines, and
a one hundred and twenty-five-mile strip connecting Assiniboia, Shaunavon and

Gravelbourg. By the summer of 1929 the need for a distribution supervisor at Dominion Electric was obvious, so DuBois was approached. He accepted the job and moved to Shaunavon with Alice, his bride of six weeks. Three months later he moved to the company's head office in Regina.

Meanwhile, at Indian Head on October 15 Canadian Utilities entered into an agreement with Montreal Engineering Company Limited for the purchase of electricity in bulk to supply the needs of the district. The electricity was to be delivered over the lines of Prairie Power Company, a subsidiary of Calgary Power Limited, which was owned by Montreal Engineering.

Prairie Power, at that time, was buying electricity from the city of Regina and distributing it in the Qu'Appelle area east of the city. To supply power for this area Canadian Utilities built a 22,000-volt tie line between Indian Head and Qu'Appelle. The Indian Head system was operated in this manner until taken over by the Saskatchewan Power Commission in 1947.

Further Expansion

On September 16, 1929, Canadian Utilities acquired the franchise in the town of Melfort, Saskatchewan, along with a small municipally owned oil engine plant and distribution system. The plant was then rebuilt and a larger unit installed.

Under the terms of the franchise the company agreed that the Melfort plant would be maintained as the central generating point for a radius of fifty miles. However, this clause in the agreement was regretted when the Prince Albert plant was purchased in 1931 and became the main generating station for Canadian Utilities operations in that part of Saskatchewan. The company negotiated with town council for removal of the clause from the agreement and the matter was settled by a payment of two thousand dollars to the town. Canadian Utilities then built a generator at Prince Albert with a capacity of 375 kilowatts at a cost of fifty thousand dollars.

As the company continued to expand its operations during 1929, franchises were obtained — Sexsmith, Wembley and Clairmont in the Grande Prairie District; Willingdon in the Vegreville District; Summerberry in the Indian Head District and Kerrobert in southwestern Saskatchewan. New lines were built in both the Grande Prairie and Vegreville Districts to serve the newly acquired communities.

Early Innovations

Among the many firsts for Canadian Utilities in those early years was Canada's first mobile rail car generating plant, which the company built in 1929 and subsequently operated for emergency power service in Alberta and Saskatchewan.

The years that followed brought many more firsts, including the first electrified oilwell in western Canada, connected in 1944. That same year the company electrified Alberta's first farm experimental area in the Swalwell district. In 1965 the company introduced the first truck-trailer mobile generating stations in Alberta, built by the company to supply power to the rapidly developing oilfields on a short-term basis.

CHAPTER 4

The Depression Years

The Corona Hotel Disaster

The second decade of the century saw the beginning of the energy story with spectacular natural gas developments. The third decade, aptly called the "roaring twenties" brought further exciting gas developments followed by the successful beginnings of the electric utility system. Then, almost without warning, in 1929, came The Great Depression. Not only did the whole continent suffer economically, the energy group itself went through some severe tests.

Northwestern Utilities in particular suffered a series of adversities which strained its resources to the limit. In 1931 a second major break in the main line, just outside of Edmonton, caused a city-wide outage of gas. As was the case in the 1928 New Year's Day break, all members of the staff were pressed into immediate service, and the crisis was handled satisfactorily. That incident was mild compared to what lay ahead.

It was ten minutes after nine on Sunday evening, February 21, 1932. James Christie, the night engineer at the Corona Hotel, 10629 Jasper Avenue in Edmonton, had just come on duty. He went to the basement to look after the coal-fired furnace, and as he opened the furnace door a blinding blast hurled him against the wall. He was stunned momentarily, and when he returned to his senses he was engulfed in flames. "My clothing was burning and my hair, eyebrows, chest and face seemed to be on fire," he told a reporter from the *Edmonton Journal* in recalling the incident later that night. "It was an awful experience. I thought I was a goner sure."

Christie groped through the flames and smoke to the stairs and then on up to the office, shouting to everyone who could hear that the hotel was on fire, warning them to evacuate. His helpers extinguished the flames on his clothing and then turned on all the fire alarms, at the same time calling the city fire department.

The Corona Hotel, built in 1909, was a landmark in Edmonton. It was booked to capacity that night, with one hundred and fifty guests. Many of them were members of the provincial legislature who made the hotel their home while the legislature was in session. The fire drove them all out into the streets, where the temperature was near zero Fahrenheit.

Within minutes the fire trucks arrived, and every available fireman in the city fought the blaze. It was one of the stiffest battles in their memory, with flames shooting two hundred feet into the air and hot embers landing on the shingled tops of buildings for many blocks around. It disrupted streetcar service on Jasper Avenue and caused sufficient radiant heat to shatter the plate glass windows of the Balmoral Block on the other side of Jasper Avenue and ignited doors and window casings.

At various times it seemed as though the fire had been brought under control, but it quickly surged up again and again. Although Northwestern turned off the gas supply to the building, the flames were being fed by what seemed like a mysterious supply. At the same time there were explosions in the utilities corridor under the street, which blew the lid off a manhole, narrowly missing bystanders. That no one was killed that night was a miracle.

For seven hours ice-sheathed firemen fought the blaze, while their black coats turned white with layers of spray-ice and their mitts froze to their hands. Two of them were hurt as walls collapsed and blasts continued. For a time the fire threatened to wipe out the whole block of buildings from 106 to 107 Street. Men were sitting astride the rooftops of their homes nearby, using garden hoses to put out fires caused by falling embers from the hotel.

Some of the hotel guests, many of whom escaped with only what they were wearing, sought refuge in a big white frame rooming house immediately west of the Corona, but it soon became apparent that this place was in imminent danger as well. Only through superhuman effort on the part of firemen was it saved.

The blaze swung through the offices of the Motor Car Supply Company (Canada) Limited, adjacent to the Corona, and in the basement found ready fuel in eighty thousand dollars worth of tires.

Thousands of people turned out to watch the fire, and the police force had to join the fire fighters to keep the crowd back and prevent people from getting hurt.

After night engineer Christie had been rushed to a doctor, and treated for burns, he returned to the fire, and then a reporter from the *Edmonton Journal* took him home. Calls to the *Journal* office came from many worried people. Even Premier Brownlee called. He was anxious about one of his cabinet ministers, Hon. Irene Parlby, who was a resident of the hotel. But no one knew if she had got out in time.

It turned out later that the minister had gone to the home of another MLA, but only after having had a frightening escape from the hotel. She had retired and was in bed reading when she heard the fire alarm, but thought the fire was in some building nearby. When smoke began to roll down the hallway and seep in under the door and the lights flickered, the minister dressed hastily and made a frantic dash out of the building.

Many of the MLA's went to the Cecil Hotel for the remainder of the night. On Monday some appeared in the legislature minus a few frills such as shirt collars. One MLA bemoaned the fact that his speech on the budget was a victim of the flames.

Mabelle Slick was one guest at the Corona that night who escaped with only what she was wearing, and unfortunately what she was wearing did not include her fur coat. She was in town to arrange the Kinsmen Club show, Oh Dear Me. Her fur coat and many of the show's un-insured costumes were destroyed.

Damage to the Corona was estimated at well over half-a-million dollars, along with considerable damage to adjacent and nearby buildings.

Shortly after the fire, employees of the gas company found a leak in a twelve-inch gas main at about the centre of 107 Street, south of Jasper Avenue. It appeared that gas escaping from the main had travelled through the conduit of the street railway return cables and found its way into the Corona Hotel basement. The leak was not easy to detect, as in those days the gas in the company's mains was not odorized. However, soon after the fire an odorization program was instituted to help prevent future tragedies.

Northwestern appears to have been the first gas company in Canada to adopt odorization as a safety procedure. The program went into effect in the fall of 1932, after exhaustive study of gas leak detection. The equipment used was the Papico Natural Gas Odorizing System, with an odorant produced by Imperial Oil Limited. It had a distinct and penetrating effect on one's nostrils, but was harmless and had no smell during combustion.

After the Corona Hotel fire Northwestern was inundated with lawsuits. Some forty insurance companies and several individuals filed claims against the company totalling about three hundred and sixty thousand dollars. Soon the courts were asking what caused the explosion and who was responsible.

The plaintiffs claimed the fire was caused and was fed by the gas which escaped at the break in the distribution line. Whether or not the break was caused by any fault or negligence of the company, however, was a debatable point.

Death of the President — 1932

The Corona Hotel fire put the gas company in jeopardy. It could ill afford the kind of financial losses with which it was now being threatened as a result of lawsuits.

There was one man upon whom this catastrophe, along with numerous other problems created by the depression, weighed heavily. That man was C.J. Yorath, who had led the company through its formative years. Several weeks after the fire he suffered a heart attack, and two weeks later, on Saturday, April 2, 1932, he died. He was only fifty-two. The loss of a president of his stature was a stunning blow to the companies. His untimely death brought deep sorrow to all who knew him.

Christopher James Yorath was not only well known in the utility industry, he was an international figure. His speeches on financial and management matters had attracted widespread interest.

He was born in Cardiff, Wales, November 4, 1879, the son of William and Mary Yorath. Upon graduating from Cardiff College he was articled to an engineering contractor. Later he joined the staff of the city engineer of Cardiff, where he gained practical experience in city development.

In 1913 he accepted an appointment as commissioner for the city of Saskatoon. He was now married, with a growing family, and settled down to devote the remainder of his life to western Canada. Saskatoon and other neighboring municipalities had overspent during boom days and had fallen into financial difficulties. In re-establishing them on a firm financial footing Yorath made valuable connections with eastern financial houses and earned a reputation as a sound administrator.

In 1921 he became commissioner for the City of Edmonton with more responsibilities than ever. Before he came to Edmonton the city's utilities — power, water, sewage and transit — were showing a net annual loss. In a short time Yorath had completely revamped their financial structure and operating basis, with the result that they were able to show a substantial profit.

In 1924 Yorath left the city to accept the presidency of Northwestern Utilities when the company was still very much in its infancy. It was not long before he was also president and managing director of Canadian Western Natural Gas, and then Canadian Utilities when the electrical operations came into being in 1927. He also supervised the Nanaimo Electric Light, Power and Heating Company and Duncan Utilities Limited on Vancouver Island.

Under Yorath's leadership the revenues of the International Utilities group increased steadily, and friendly relations were established with the public.

Yorath was succeeded by H.R. Milner, K.C., who was elected president and managing director of the energy group on May 6, 1932. Ray Milner was born in Sackville, New Brunswick in 1889. At the age of twenty he obtained a Bachelor of Arts degree at King's College, and two years later graduated from Dalhousie University as Bachelor of Laws. Almost immediately he set out for the West and settled in Edmonton in 1911.

For three years he was occupied in building a law practice, but this came to an abrupt halt when war was declared in 1914 and he became a lieutenant in the

194th Infantry Regiment. His unit went overseas in 1916 and was used as a source of replacements for other units. The 26 New Brunswick Regiment wound up with an adjutant named Captain Milner. He was wounded twice before being returned to Edmonton where he renewed his interrupted law practice.

Milner became connected with the utility industry in 1919 when he became solicitor for the Northern Alberta Natural Gas Company Limited, which held an Edmonton franchise. After this firm became Northwestern Utilities in 1922 he was retained as its solicitor and later as solicitor for the other Canadian companies acquired by International Utilities.

The depression years were well underway when Milner became president in 1932. Maintaining the financial stability of the company was a big assignment, particularly when the gas companies were facing keen competition from coal which was selling as low as two dollars a ton in Edmonton.

And there was the matter of three hundred and sixty thousand dollars in lawsuits as a result of the Corona Hotel fire. Milner personally took on the burden of defending the company in court.

The case dragged on for about two years. Experts on natural gas systems, welding, pipeline construction, earth and frost actions, from all over the continent were called by both sides. Working with Milner on behalf of the gas company were three other lawyers — A.L. Smith, K.C., R. Martland and S. Kerr.

Early in 1934, after three weeks of hearings in Edmonton, before Mr. Justice Ford, the court found in favor of Northwestern Utilities. The decision was based chiefly on the fact that the break in the company's line was caused by subsidence of the soil due to sewer construction by the city of Edmonton directly below the gas company's distribution line.

Northwestern's officers and staff had been burning the midnight oil for many months working on the case, and they heaved a sigh of relief when the judge brought down the ruling. Their relief was short-lived, however. The plaintiffs appealed the case to the Supreme Court of Canada, and continued to press it until it reached the Privy Council in England.

The last court of appeal at that time, the Privy Council in Great Britain, ruled in favor of the claimants. The decision was handed down in 1934 at the height of the depression in Alberta. It was the blackest year in the company's history. But when Milner gathered the staff to announce the result he declared: "We lost the case but we're not dead yet!"

During that same year there was actually a decline (for the first time) in the number of customers served by Northwestern. Many residents, due to economic circumstances, were forced to convert from natural gas back to coal.

But Northwestern hung on. As the country slowly moved out of the depression, the winds of change brought a gradual but steady growth in the company's operations. By the beginning of the Second World War the company was again on a sound financial footing, its plant in good order with a well-trained and dedicated staff. Management's philosophy respecting service to the public was paying off, and Northwestern was among the most highly regarded business organizations in the city.

Canadian Western Leads the Way

The thirties were not as hard on Canadian Western as they were on Northwestern. There were challenges, particularly competition from inexpensive coal in communities like Lethbridge. But on the whole the company moved steadily forward with a gradual increase in customers and improvements to the system. Canadian Western, it seems, had already weathered its major tempests, particularly its disputes with the city of Calgary in the decade between 1915 and 1925.

The company kept adding new communities to its system. There was Black Diamond, then Burdett, Cayley and Foremost. The system was growing, and so was the need for more gas. Gas pressure in the Bow Island field was so low that withdrawing more gas would only speed up the drowning of the whole field by the encroachment of water.

There was plenty of gas at Turner Valley which was flared by the operators in their search for oil. So much gas was being flared that the skyline seen from Calgary glowed red at night. P.D. Mellon, vice-president of Canadian Western, gazed at this red glow one night and the thought occurred to him that some of this wasted gas could be stored in the depleted sands of the Bow Island field. He had studied an experiment of a similar nature in the United States in 1919, which had had moderate success.

Mellon talked to S.E. Slipper, chief geologist for Canadian Western, who was so enthusiastic about the idea that he, too, began to promote it. It was not practical to store gas in the Turner Valley field itself, because the sands there were not porous enough.

The idea caught on. A compressor station was built at Bow Island, and in August 1930, underground storage of compressed natural gas got under way. The compressor had a capacity for pushing three to five million cubic feet of gas per day underground at high pressure. Bow Island became the second field in the world to be used for storage.

Over the next eight years the company pumped about twelve billion cubic feet of gas from Turner Valley into the Bow Island field. The arrangement of the piping made the operation reversible, so gas could be stored during the summer months and used for peak loads in the winter. The field has remained a vital storage reservoir to this day.

There was a great deal more gas in Turner Valley than could be stored in Bow Island, however. As the thirties began, the flow of gas in this field was completely uncontrolled. The situation was serious. It could mean this valuable resource would be entirely wasted in a few short years if something was not done to curb the reckless development.

Canadian Western was worried. It had experienced its own boom-to-bust period in the Bow Island field and learned the importance of always looking ahead with a view to ensuring an adequate supply of gas. The company used its influence and presented to the government a startling picture of the state of affairs as shown by the investigations of its geological staff. This action, along with support from the City of Calgary, brought about the organization of the Turner Valley Conservation Board in 1932. This board placed restrictions on the field and finally regulated its production by a quota system.

Geologist Slipper, in a summary of gas company developments, concluded that "it requires years of trial and error to develop a gas supply and the only satisfactory insurance against lack of supplies is constant and systematic exploration."

Private Enterprise Extolled

The greatest loss to Canadian Western in the early thirties — a loss which it shared with its sister company in Edmonton — was the death in 1932 of its president, C.J. Yorath. Ray Milner was appointed to the board of directors and became the company's fourth president and managing director.

One of Milner's unique characteristics was his strict adherence to his philosophy of private enterprise. A staunch Conservative in every way, he maintained that the primary responsibility of government was "to govern," and not to run businesses. At the height of the depression there were suggestions from many quarters that the state should assume control of all industry. "Such ideas should be resisted to the utmost," Milner stated in a 1934 New Year's editorial in the utilities staff magazine, *The Courier.* He went on:

> *Democratic political bodies have consistently shown themselves incapable of administering their own affairs. Democratic institutions are not adapted to the control and administration of great business undertakings. We have always before us the example of the history of the Canadian railroads. Hundreds of millions of the debt of the Canadian people, both federal and provincial, resulted from political participation in railway expansion programs. Bonuses and grants of land were given in respect of thousands of miles of railroad which either have been torn up or have been operated at a consistent loss. Not only has this added tremendously to our present-day burdens, but it made impossible any reasonable agrarian settlement policy, either in relation to markets or to transportation.*

For government to manage businesses, Milner contended, would destroy economic freedom, and ultimately it would destroy personal freedom. This had come about in Russia and he suggested could come about in the United States.

Milner's expertise in financial affairs stood the companies in good stead on many occasions during the depression. In 1932, for example, by taking advantage of the heavy discount on sterling Canadian Western redeemed much of its debt at a considerable saving. Canadian Western's revenue continued to hold steady, but taxes imposed on the company were becoming an increasing burden.

While operations in northern and central Alberta were having tough sledding in the early thirties, the gas operations in southern Alberta were expanding at an encouraging rate. This was true of Canadian Western as well as the gas industry as a whole. The first gas processing plant in Western Canada was built by Royalite Oil Company Limited at Turner Valley in 1933.

By the end of 1934 customers on the Canadian Western system numbered nearly twenty-three thousand, including seventy farm service connections.

Despite the depression, the gas companies in Calgary and Edmonton put on exhibits in 1934 in the Grandstand Building during the Calgary Stampede and in the Manufacturers' Building at the Edmonton Exhibition. It was the first time in Western Canada that composite displays of gas appliances and heating equipment had been brought together.

Operations of Canadian Western in 1934 were highlighted by continuation of repressuring operations in the Bow Island field with "waste" gas from Turner Valley. By now some seven billion cubic feet of gas were stored in the Bow Island field.

The new business department made a breakthrough that year by acquiring the heating load in the Western Canada High School. The school had called for tenders on coal stoker equipment for its two boilers, but the gas company put in a quotation and acquired the full load, worth around twenty-six hundred dollars a year. Up to this time the company had been unable to budge the Calgary School Board's determination not to burn gas until the company was prepared to group all of the school system's accounts.

The Noble Hotel was another load acquired — or more precisely, re-acquired — that year. Three years previously the hotel had pulled out its burners and gone back to coal.

An interesting load addition that illustrates the ingenuity of gas company personnel in developing industrial applications was a new hog-singeing appliance at the Burns packing plant. As hog carcasses moved along on a conveyor belt they were surrounded by natural gas flames that removed the hair efficiently. It was believed to be the first instance in North America of this use of natural gas. Most of the credit went to N.D. MacKinnon, shop superintendent, and Tom Cavanaugh, who were reported to have worked day and night experimenting with different types of burners before developing the successful No. 5 Gwynn Burners which used gas at eight ounces pressure and thirty-five pounds of compressed air.

In Edmonton, Northwestern acquired as customers both the Burns and Swift's packing plants in 1934, with Burns installing a large hog-singeing gas furnace.

This marked the beginning of Burns tapping major export markets for hogs. Two years later Canada Packers installed similar equipment in its new Edmonton plant, described as "the most modern and efficient plant of its kind in the Dominion."

Northwestern reported that during 1934 a small high pressure distribution system in Edmonton was extended to a "west end subdivision called Jasper Place," where fifty-one services were installed. And word came through that the gas company was to serve the Macdonald Hotel in Edmonton.

At Viking Northwestern continued its well servicing program. There were two ways of cleaning the wells at that time. Sometimes the accumulations of sand, water and mud in wells could simply be removed by opening the valve and utilizing well formation pressure to blow them out. More often, however, the pipes became so plugged that the old Star drilling machine had to be used to clean them. In contrast to modern rotary drilling rigs that use drilling bits, the Star drilling machine was a percussion type of instrument not unlike a pile driver. It punched a hole rather than drilled it. In later years when it was no longer used for digging new gas wells it was still useful for cleaning out the old ones.

Canadian Western Glee Club

The depression years were not all gloom and doom. In the mid-thirties the Canadian Western Glee Club was formed under the direction of company employee, Jesse Walker. This group won many trophies in festival competitions and performed at community functions as a goodwill gesture.

One of the first trophies the club won was the T. Eaton Company Shield at the Alberta Musical Festival. With Walker as conductor and Ted Forsey as accompanist, the club impressed the adjudicators who said they hardly thought it possible for twelve men to put up such a splendid performance with such difficult test pieces.

The Glee Club started with a small get-together in November 1932. It planned to sing Christmas carols at the office party on Christmas Eve. The idea originated with W.J. Gray, who became the first president of the club. Conductor Jesse Walker had to start from scratch, as only three of the men even knew how to read music!

The carol singing was so well received that the idea of a permanent Glee Club was promoted. So, with fourteen members who made up with enthusiasm what they lacked in technical knowledge of music, the group set its sights on the first festival. Because of the difficulty in obtaining a place to practice at times that would suit all the members, only eight rehearsals were held before entering the festival.

In 1935 the organization became officially known as the Gas Company Men's Chorus. The first festival entry in the choir class brought it the Ingraham cup for the most artistic performance. In later years, at the provincial festival in

Edmonton, it won permanent possession of the Service Club Shield by virtue of three successive wins.

In the field of sports there was the Gas Company Cricket Club, with F.A. Smith as president and C.L. Metcalfe as secretary. The club defeated the Calgary Municipal Team on June 22, at Parkdale Grounds, by a score of 112 to 86. The cricket club was not to be outdone by the company bowlers or by the baseball league, under the direction of W. Lloyd McPhee. Golf was also popular and competition was always keen at intercompany tournaments.

New Headquarters — 1935

C anadian Western's new office building in Calgary, completed in 1935, was one of the most modern buildings in the city. Located immediately east of the old office on Sixth Avenue Southwest to which it was attached by a passageway, the new building had space for five departments on the ground floor and there was an auditorium in the basement.

The auditorium stage was set up as a permanent demonstration kitchen, particularly adapted to cooking schools. A radio broadcasting panel was used for broadcasts of cooking schools.

The furnace room contained an air conditioning plant and a gas-fired steam boiler. Here the sales department could show customers a model plant in actual operation.

Meanwhile, in Edmonton, Northwestern opened an all-gas model bungalow that received a great deal of attention not only from customers but also from the building trades. The company built the bungalow on a choice lot in the west end residential district, fronting on 102 Avenue. It demonstrated everything from the value of good insulation to the comforts of controlled heating, humidity, and the use of gas for cooking, refrigeration, air conditioning, and incinerating garbage.

Northwestern acquired well over five hundred new domestic customers in 1935 and ninety-two new industrial and commercial loads, including Canada Packers, Canadian Bakeries, Misericordia Hospital, St. John's College, Metals Ltd., Taylor & Pearson Ltd., and several large blocks such as Devonshire Apartments, Westminster Apartments, Viking Hotel, Balmoral Block, Mount Royal Block, Scott Block and Cattistock Block.

In Calgary, 1936 saw more modernization with installation of Burroughs mechanical billing machines and the stub system for customer accounting as Canadian Western's revenue from gas sales passed the two million dollar mark.

That year, also, the companies acquired a four-seater aircraft for transporting key personnel around the far-flung properties and service areas.

The plane, brought from Wayne, Michigan, was a Stinson Reliant monoplane, equipped with a Lycoming motor, with a cruising speed of one hundred and thirty miles per hour. The plane was equipped with skis during the winter, had the registration letters CF-AZC, and was piloted by E. George Clark, formerly an instructor with the Calgary Aero Club.

Search for More Gas

The worst disappointment of 1937 was a well drilled southwest of High River. It was sunk to a depth of 8,990 feet, to the limestone formation, to become the deepest well in the British Empire at that time. It was known as the Arca Well. As neither gas nor oil was obtained in commercial quantities, the well was abandoned.

This failure hurt, but there was no bitterness, especially on the part of Ray Milner, who had been one of the main supporters of the project. The company would intensify its search for gas, he announced. If gas could not be found on the plains it would be found in the foothills. It had to be found.

When the well failed someone in the gas company penned the following ballad, sung at the annual Calgary banquet by the Glee Club:

ARCA!

Arca Herald Angels sing
Mr. Milner's had his fling,
For the casing has gone wild
"Dry-hole" Slipper's angel child.
Listen to the broker's yell,
Arca shares are shot to hell.
Listen while directors groan,
They have lost most all they own.
Arca Herald Angels sing.
Phooey to the new Oil King.

On the sidelines with a grin,
P.D. stands, and lifts his chin.
Fred Smith, too, is in the soup
As to sign the cheques he stoops.
H.S. Watts, that crafty gink,
Laughs as he sees Arca sink.
Down to China, so they tell,
Is the casing of this well.
Arca Herald Angels sing,
9,000 feet and not a thing.

Years have passed and still no oil,
Harry Hunter's in a boil.
Men gaze at him with a sneer —
No one wants to buy him beer;
But the gladsome tidings sound,
Oil is coming from the ground.
Arca's in at last you see,
They struck oil in the China sea.
Arca Herald Angels sing,
Milner is a real Oil King!

A copy of the ballad fell into the hands of a Calgary stockbroker who circulated it around the stock exchange one morning, thinking it a big joke on the Arca company and its president. Several broker friends telephoned the editor of *The Courier* to read it to him, and were surprised when he told them that it was a homegrown product and would be published in the company's house organ.

During the summer and fall the company intensified its exploratory work. Geologists and the ground survey party were aided for the first time by a Canadian Airways photographic survey.

The exploration program was under S.E. Slipper, director and chief geologist for Canadian Western and its associated companies, who in 1938, was elected a Fellow of the Royal Society of Canada at the society's annual meeting in Ottawa.

Slipper was a graduate of Queen's University, and worked for the federal government on the early geological surveys of Alberta. Later he carried out the first detailed mapping of Turner Valley, Wainwright and various other oil and gas areas of Alberta.

In 1913, when the federal Geological Survey Branch opened an office in Calgary, Slipper was placed in charge.

Both Gas Companies Progress — 1937

M ore work was done on transmission pipelines, including the line serving Lethbridge. Distribution lines in Calgary and various outlying towns were extended and improved. An up-to-date brick combination office, workshop and regulator station was built in Taber, and a new regulator station was built in Fort Macleod.

Harold Timmins of the new business department reported that what had looked as though it might be a discouraging year actually turned out quite well, with the acquisition of around twenty-eight thousand dollars additional revenue.

The home service department functioned more effectively than ever. More than seventy-five hundred copies of a new canning booklet were distributed, and the radio program increased in popularity. As 1937 closed with Christmas festivities Canadian Western's popular choir recorded half an hour of carols in the radio studios of CFCN, Calgary. The broadcasts featured Kathleen Tierney, violinist, accompanied by Josephine Chamberlain. This appears to have been the first time in the province that a choir "recorded on electrical transcriptions for commercial rebroadcasting purposes." The recordings were heard on Christmas Eve and again on Christmas Day on radio stations in both Calgary and Lethbridge.

In Edmonton Northwestern's general manager, Julian Garrett, reported that the company had again acquired more than five hundred new domestic heating consumers as well as many valuable commercial loads. The major extension of the distribution system in Edmonton during the year was an intermediate pressure line to serve the municipal airport and some adjoining greenhouses.

A new garage was built on a lot next to the company's premises on 104 Street and four lots were purchased on 106 Street, north of 105 Avenue. This property was fenced and made ready for pipe storage and reconditioning of distribution line pipe.

On the Viking main line, Northwestern concentrated on the western end of the system, primarily west of Tofield. Over one hundred test holes were dug, large enough to inspect each section of the pipe when uncovered. About eight thousand feet of pipe were replaced with pipe reconditioned by sandblasting, spot welding, priming and enamelling and about nine hundred feet of pipe were lowered because of roadbuilding activities.

Northwestern's Fifteenth Anniversary — 1938

The year 1938 was Northwestern's fifteenth anniversary year. The company had made giant strides since it was incorporated in the spring of 1923. It now owned nineteen producing wells in the Viking field. The company also purchased gas from two wells owned by the Hudson's Bay Oil and Gas Company, Limited. The total open flow capacity of all wells in the field was 130 million cubic feet per day.

This was ample gas supply. The possible peak hourly demand for 1939 was estimated at 1,125,000 cubic feet, or at a rate of about 26 million cubic feet per day. The wells in the field were capable of producing about twice this amount under peak load conditions.

Apart from the Viking field, the company owned or controlled about twenty-two thousand acres of petroleum and natural gas rights in the Kinsella field, twelve miles southeast of the Viking field station. In this field the company had already drilled two wells, one with a daily open flow capacity of eight million cubic feet and the other with 19 million cubic feet. Another well was drilled in this field by the Duluth Syndicate, with an original open flow of about 25 million cubic feet. Between the Viking and Kinsella fields the company felt it had ample supplies for half a century to come.

In Edmonton, Northwestern's general manager, Julian Garrett, reported that good weather during the year assisted considerably in construction and maintenance work, including the laying of more than five miles of new twelve-inch transmission line on the looping system, with practically no hitch.

As Garrett was compiling his report at mid-December, his only regret was that the mild weather was continuing too late in the year, cutting into the gas company's heating load. But by December 28, as his report was getting ready to go to press, the mercury in Edmonton had dropped to fifty-five degrees below zero, Fahrenheit.

Canadian Western was in the limelight in 1938 as well. There was the natural gas exhibit at the Calgary Stampede for example, considered by many to be the most outstanding exhibit on the grounds that year. The exhibit was built around a huge figure of the god Pan holding a lighted torch from which a gas flame burned constantly during exhibition week. Set at the base of the figure was a Hammond electric organ, which at that time was considered "the newest in modern musical instruments." The organ was played daily, afternoon and evening, and performances were broadcast over CFAC radio.

In addition to the broadcast, the Musical Gas Men — guitarists Ben Banks and George McDougal, and organist Ted Forsey — performed each evening in front of the grandstand.

Electric Utilities Slowdown

During the bleak years which followed the stock market crash of October 1929, the electric side of the utility business experienced a severe slowdown. Farm prices dropped drastically and many businesses went bankrupt. The depression was accompanied by drought, grasshopper infestations, hailstorms, and wind which swept away rich but dried-out topsoil in the "black blizzards" of the prairies.

Unemployed people were everywhere — walking the streets looking for work, or "riding the rods" across the country. Money was scarce and the future looked grim. Many customers had difficulty meeting their monthly bills, including their electric power accounts. It was not uncommon to find people tampering with their meters in an effort to beat the electric company.

Trying to catch customers suspected of "stealing juice" brought such measures as check meters, which looked like birdhouses mounted on distribution poles. The check meters were read monthly on the same day as the house meters, and sometimes they helped catch customers defrauding the company. One method of getting free electricity was discovered when a house meter was changed for a routine government retest, required every five years at that time. This customer had drilled a very small hole in the metal meter cover and had inserted a fine wire through the hole to stop the meter disc from rotating.

Meter readers, naturally, were the butt of many jokes during the depression. There was the cartoon, for example, which appeared in the company magazine showing a lady and her buxom daughter talking to a sharp-looking gentleman carrying a black briefcase. "Now that you've examined my daughter, doctor," says the lady, "what do you think is wrong with her?" "Strange that you should have asked me," replies the gentleman. "I'm not the doctor. I'm your new meter reader."

Considering the pressures under which the staff of the energy group were working, their ability to laugh was an important outlet. An in-joke was the one quoting an oculist. "Yes," says the eye doctor, "that man had a curious affliction. Everything he looked at he saw double." "Poor fellow, I suppose he found it hard to get a job?" comes the reply, to which the oculist immediately retorts: "Not at all. The utility company snapped him up, and now he's reading meters."

48

Another one which made the rounds claimed to have originated in Scotland. At the conclusion of a wedding ceremony the groom approached the minister hesitantly and said: "I'm terrible sorry, I have nae money to gie you, sir, but if ye'll take me down to your cellar, I'll show you hoo to fixe up yer gas meter so that it winna register."

During these difficult times anyone employed by the utility company was considered fortunate. Although wages were frozen and there were no raises in pay for years, there were no layoffs. This attitude of loyalty towards staff members on the part of the company was unquestionably a major factor in the company's outstanding record of long-service employees.

The onset of the thirties brought a slowdown in new acquisitions and capital projects, particularly in the electrical company. In Saskatchewan there was another development which was beginning to gain momentum — the Saskatchewan Power Commission, originally set up to regulate the utility companies, was already showing signs of entering the power business in direct competition with investor-owned companies.

Canadian Utilities acquired three small oil-fired generators in the Saskatchewan communities of Star City, Birch Hills and Kinistino in 1930.

In Alberta franchises were signed with the villages of Beaverlodge and Hythe and a start was made on a 13,800-volt line to connect these communities to the plant at Grande Prairie. When this line was completed in October six towns were receiving service from the newly rebuilt plant. By the end of 1930 over sixty miles of transmission line had been built in the district.

The first farm customer in the Grande Prairie area, situated eight miles west of Wembley, began receiving electric service from the company in September of that year.

The Vegreville-Lloydminster area experienced greatly improved service through a tie line to Calgary Power during the year. On July 31 Canadian Utilities entered into an agreement with Calgary Power for the purchase of electricity in bulk for the district, with the point of delivery being at Vegreville. A twenty-one-mile, 22,800-volt line, owned by Calgary Power, was built from Holden to Vegreville for this purpose. Following completion of the tie line the Vegreville and Lloydminster oil-fired generators were placed on standby duty and operated only on peak and emergency service thereafter.

In addition to the agreement with Calgary Power for the supply of electricity to the Vegreville area, an arrangement was entered into with the Saskatchewan Power Commission to supply electricity in bulk to Rosetown, which was served from a local isolated oil-fired generator having a capacity of 375 kilowatts.

Despite the rapid growth of Canadian Utilities since its incorporation, followed by aggressive load building efforts, an operating loss was experienced in 1930, the third consecutive year in which a loss was sustained. The best performer in the company's systems was the Union Power Company in Drumheller. With its lucrative coal-mining business providing about twenty-five percent of total revenue, Union Power continued to show a profit. It operated at a profit every year, in fact, from the time it was acquired by International Utilities until it merged with Canadian Utilities in 1935.

Dominion Gas and Electric Company — 1930

A significant event at the international level occurred in 1930 when the ownership and control of Canadian Utilities companies passed into the hands of Dominion Gas and Electric Company. This holding company was a subsidiary of the American Commonwealths Power Corporation, which owned and operated electric, natural and artificial gas companies throughout the United States. The total assets of all these properties exceeded two hundred and fifty million dollars and the annual gross earnings of the corporation were over thirty million dollars.

The president of the holding company, American Commonwealths Power Corporation, was F.T. Hulswit. President of Dominion Gas and Electric was F.W. Seymour. A.F. Traver and C.J. Yorath were appointed vice-presidents.

The former Canadian gas and electric subsidiaries of International Utilities Corporation were operated as Dominion Gas and Electric Properties until July 1, 1944, when they were again acquired by International Utilities through a merger of the two companies.

Prince Albert District — 1931

The highlight of Canadian Utilities operations in 1931 was the purchase of the city-owned steam plant and distribution system at Prince Albert, and the formation of the Prince Albert District. The acquisition of this property exemplified the struggles taking place at the time between private power interests in their efforts to maintain distribution rights in Saskatchewan on the one hand, and the Saskatchewan Power Commission, supported by proponents of government ownership, on the other.

The first offer for the purchase of the electric utility in Prince Albert had been made two years earlier, on May 10, 1928, by Canadian Utilities president C.J. Yorath. The proposed terms were the payment of three hundred thousand dollars in cash, thirty thousand dollars annually to the city in lieu of taxes and a portion of the gross receipts, along with an offer to spend two hundred thousand dollars in improving the plant.

This offer was rejected by the city as being too low. In fact there was considerable opposition to selling the plant on any terms. The Liberal government in Saskatchewan had established its power commission with the objective of setting up a publicly owned distribution system in the province, and there was considerable pressure on the city from the provincial government not to sell its utilities to private interests.

Further action on the sale of the electric utility was deferred until March 1930, when the city decided to call for tenders for the sale of the plant and distribution system. Out of seven groups invited to tender only two bids came in. One was from Canadian Utilities and the other from the Saskatchewan Power Commission.

The bid by the company was more attractive in every way. Canadian Utilities offered eight hundred and seventy-five thousand dollars and volunteered to pay five percent of gross revenue in lieu of taxes, as well as spend two hundred thousand dollars within two years on improvements. The power commission offered only four hundred and twenty-five thousand dollars, or three hundred thousand dollars for the plant without the distribution system, and refused to pay any taxes to the city. However, if the commission bought the plant alone the city could set the electric rates and retain any profits from the sale of energy. If the commission bought both plant and distribution system it would set the rates so that power was supplied at cost.

The city appointed a special committee to analyze the two bids, taking all things into consideration, including the position Prince Albert would occupy as a power generating centre in the event a provincial power grid was built. The committee recommended that the city accept the Canadian Utilities tender with certain modifications.

After numerous meetings and much discussion the issue was finally decided by plebiscite. On January 14, 1931, in the largest vote on a by-law in the history of Prince Albert, the sale of the electric utility to Canadian Utilities Limited was approved by the ratepayers by a vote of 741 to 254. Two months later, a representative of Canadian Utilities presented the city with a cheque for eight hundred and seventy-five thousand dollars. This was the largest single expenditure made by the company to that date and, indeed, for a good number of years in the future.

The power plant had been built by the city in 1907 — a substantial and attractive brick building. It contained three generators and four boilers. Much of the equipment was obsolete, and the rapid increase in the demand for electric power had forced the city to embark on an improvement program which by the end of 1929 had cost one hundred and sixty-two thousand dollars.

Canadian Utilities took over the Prince Albert system on April 1, 1931. The first district superintendent was W.J. Murphy, who joined the company in 1928. He had been superintendent of the City of Edmonton electric light department. Prior to moving to Prince Albert, Murphy was in head office in Calgary as business and operating manager. He had been instrumental in obtaining numerous franchises in Alberta and Saskatchewan. He remained in Prince Albert until March 1947, when the Saskatchewan Power Commission took over the operation.

Following the purchase of the Prince Albert system, lines were extended to Beatty, Star City, Melfort, Weldon, Brancepeth, Birch Hills and Kinistino. Old generating equipment in some of these communities was sold or placed on standby for emergency use. Eventually eleven towns were connected to Prince Albert, with about thirty-two hundred customers receiving electric service in the district.

Canadian Utilities was committed to spending two hundred thousand dollars on improvements by April 1933. However, because of the depression and tightening of capital spending, the company obtained an extension to this time commitment from the city. By the end of 1934 the company had spent almost eighty-seven thousand dollars, mainly on rebuilding the distribution system. Finally, by early 1937, the company completed its commitment with the installation of new generating equipment, bringing the installed capacity of the plant to 6,250 kilowatts, making it the largest plant in the Canadian Utilities system.

In 1933 the Saskatchewan Power Commission obtained options from the company for the purchase of the transmission line between Indian Head and Qu'Appelle, expiring December 1, 1936, and certain other lines in the Prince Albert District, expiring December 1, 1938. The power commission failed, however, to exercise its option and the lines remained the property of the company until the general take over of all Canadian Utilities operations in Saskatchewan in 1947.

Out west the B.C. Power Commission was growing too. In 1934 it bought the Nanaimo Electric Light, Power and Heating Company and Duncan Utilities Limited from Canadian Utilities' parent company, Dominion Gas and Electric. This left Canadian Utilities with its main operations centered in Saskatchewan and Alberta.

The year 1936 was a difficult one in many areas. There was Yorkton in Saskatchewan, for instance, where operating expenses increased considerably because local taxes had more than doubled. The company was denied the right to appeal to the Supreme Court of Canada against the increased assessment, and it seemed there was nothing that could be done about such unilateral municipal measures except to economize more and to work harder than ever.

With expenditures kept to the bare essentials in Alberta and Saskatchewan, the company concentrated on a maintenance and rebuilding program which lasted through most of the depression years. Where existing distribution systems had been taken over by the company the lines were usually in poor condition. This rebuilding, along with plant upkeep, was where most maintenance activities were directed. All the work was carried out by company crews.

Appliance Merchandising

During the 1930s Canadian Utilities relied heavily on merchandising of electrical appliances as a means of building customer load. Showrooms were opened in company offices in most of the larger communities to display and promote the sale of appliances. In communities where the company still operated a local plant it was not unusual to see electrical merchandise on display in the plant office.

Electric range and refrigerator sales were promoted through cooking schools where home service directors demonstrated the latest in electric kitchen appliances to large gatherings of housewives. To promote the use of proper lighting, a Better Light — Better Sight campaign was established under the direction of Ed Kelly, featuring such things as the new high wattage tri-lite lamps. Some of the women employed by the company for these promotions in the early thirties were Anne Adams, Effie Ternan, Grace MacKinnon, Marie Kirk, Mrs. L. McKinnon and Mary Hunt.

Union Power in Drumheller had been active in electrical merchandising as far back as 1929. Drumheller sales manager Fred O'Beirne had three salesmen to help him — Ernie Elkins, Ian MacIntyre and Les Stirling. In 1933 Union Power bought a two-ton truck chassis on which was installed a specially built van. All the latest in electrical appliances available were loaded into the van and Ian McIntyre with his helper, Liston Anderson, would travel the Union Power and Canadian Utilities territories putting on demonstrations.

MacIntyre had a well earned reputation of being able to sell "refrigerators to Eskimos." This was no vain boast, for sometimes his monthly earnings from sales commissions exceeded the district manager's salary.

Merger with Union Power — 1935

D espite the rapid growth of the company in the first few years of its existence and the close attention given to the efficient operation of the newly acquired properties, Canadian Utilities sustained an operating loss every year between 1928 and 1934.

By the end of 1934 accumulated losses for the seven-year period came to three hundred and eighty-one thousand dollars. Fixed assets had grown to four point three million dollars but because of the stagnant economic conditions the net increase in property assets in the previous three years amounted to only eighty-five hundred dollars.

With the company losing money each year, a great deal of belt-tightening was carried out by the staff, so that losses were gradually reduced from one hundred and ten thousand dollars in 1931 to thirteen thousand dollars in 1934. It was still obvious, however, that operating losses could not continue and that drastic action was needed to put the company on a sound financial basis if it was to survive.

During the years in which Canadian Utilities was having financial difficulties, its affiliate company, Union Power, was making a profit. This was due in some measure to the large number of coal mines that Union Power served in the Drumheller area, providing it with a substantial part of its total revenue. During six years of operation as a Dominion Gas and Electric property, Union Power had never experienced an operating loss, and by the end of 1933 had managed to earn two hundred and eighty-six thousand dollars for the parent organization.

In addition to this accomplishment, the outlook for Union Power appeared quite good. The market for Drumheller coal had been gradually extended and efforts were being made by the provincial government to build up a market for the coal as far east as Toronto.

This factor, combined with the usual optimistic Western Canada philosophy that things would be better next year, convinced company management that economic conditions would gradually improve. In 1935, the decision was made to merge the two companies as part of a major overhaul of the capital structure of Canadian Utilities.

Under the merger arrangements Canadian Utilities acquired all the assets of Union Power, effective August 1, 1935, and undertook the operations of that company from then on. The most difficult period in the company's history was now behind it. Canadian Utilities' electric operations continued to grow and managed to show a profit every year thereafter.

In the first full year of operations following the merger with Union Power the number of customers increased by nearly four hundred to fifteen thousand seven hundred and energy sales jumped by 1,678,000 kilowatts.

Floods in Peace River Area — 1935

In the Peace River country 1935 was the year of the big flood caused by the rain-swollen waters of Lesser Slave Lake. At its worst there were two feet of water on the floor of the powerhouse in Peace River. A.E. (Gus) Gudmundson reported that Grande Prairie was completely isolated except for air traffic during part of June and most of July.

The most serious condition was at the village of Slave Lake itself. The community was inundated, with boats being the only méans of travel. To enter the village's only hotel, travellers would be rowed as far into the door of the hotel as possible. Guests then stepped from the prow to the stairs leading to the upper storey. "In spite of all the disasters of the summer," Gudmundson wrote, "late spring, excessive rains, floods, interrupted train service, and early frost, the residents have not lost confidence in their Peace River Country and look forward to recuperation of losses with the next crop."

That spirit of hope was typical of the optimism which upheld people throughout the company's service areas during the depression. No matter what the calamity, they always knew there were better days ahead.

Alberta Social Credit Government — 1935

In 1935 the first Social Credit government was elected to power in Alberta. This movement was started in 1932 by a radical monetary reform group under

William Aberhart, a school teacher and lay clergyman in Calgary. The party found fertile soil in depression-ridden Alberta when Aberhart began attacking the monetary system and the "fifty big shots" who were said to be controlling the Canadian economy.

By expounding the unconventional monetary theories of Major Douglas, an English economist, and promising to pay a basic dividend of twenty-five dollars a month to every Albertan, Aberhart was successful in getting his party elected in August 1935.

The new government made numerous unsuccessful attempts to introduce Social Credit theories and financial reform in its operations, but was foiled at every turn. Nor was the government ever successful in meeting its pre-election promise to pay twenty-five dollars a month to every Albertan. In August 1937, the federal cabinet disallowed the Alberta banking legislation.

Finally it became apparent to even the most faithful of the party that Social Credit monetary theories just would not work, at least under the conditions that existed in Alberta at that time. The Social Credit government under the leadership of Premier Ernest C. Manning, Aberhart's successor following his death in 1943, evolved into a stable and ultra-conservative one, dedicated to the philosophy of free enterprise.

After controlling the destiny of the province for thirty-six years, making it the oldest democratically elected government in the world at the time, the Social Credit party was defeated at the polls in 1971 by a resurgent Conservative party under the leadership of Peter Lougheed. With the passing of Social Credit from power a memorable era in the history of Alberta had come to an end.

Particular note is made in this volume of the Social Credit era in Alberta because of its impact on the utility companies.

The free enterprise philosophy of Ernest Manning remained a powerful force in Alberta. Because of Manning's strong belief that government should stay out of business except in cases of extreme necessity, Alberta was one of the few areas in Canada where a large segment of the electric power supply was provided by investor-owned utilities rather than by government-owned corporations. It is open to debate whether the privately owned utilities operating in Alberta could have survived the clamor for public ownership of power generation and distribution which was displayed from time to time by certain political parties and pressure groups if the Social Credit party had not been in power during this period of Alberta history.

As a matter of interest, fourteen years after Social Credit defeated the United Farmers of Alberta government, its leader, Richard Reid, came to work for Canadian Utilities in Edmonton at the age of seventy. Reid became premier of Alberta when Premier J.E. Brownlee resigned in 1934. He remained premier until the party was defeated in 1935. Reid was placed in charge of the company library and was also active in public relations matters on behalf of the company. Dick

Reid established a record in the history of Canadian Utilities that will never be repeated when he was presented with a twenty-five-year long service award at the 1975 company banquet at the age at ninety-six, five years before his death.

Second Decade of Electricity

In the mid-thirties Canadian Utilities launched its second decade of electric service, serving nearly sixteen thousand customers in one hundred communities, with the number of kilowatt hours generated per year well over the twenty million mark.

Vegreville District superintendent J.G. MacGregor made an analysis of the first ten years of service in Vegreville. The town, he noted, had, since the Canadian Utilities' acquisition of the franchise in 1926, suffered some severe blows, first by losing a vast trading area to the north when railway lines were built to St. Paul and other communities formerly serviced from Vegreville. "On top of this," he noted, "we have had the world's worst depression for the last five years. In the face of all this the record of the electric utility is somewhat amazing."

Although the number of customers decreased with the decline in trading activity, the consumption of electricity per customer rose from 216 kilowatt hours in 1927 to 445 kilowatt hours in 1934.

Aside from the benefit to individual customers from a steady decrease in rates the town as a whole enjoyed many benefits. In 1926 the waterworks department was charged forty-two hundred dollars for power. This decreased to about a thousand dollars in 1934, even though water customers and power consumption had both increased. In 1926 the town paid twenty-four hundred dollars for street lighting. In 1934, by comparison, it paid the company the same amount but the number of lights had increased from fifty-three to one hundred and five. In 1926 the town electric plant paid no taxes; but since that time the company had paid an average of eighteen hundred and fifty dollars a year in taxes.

The company always maintained a larger staff at the plant than had been there formerly and took charge of all electrical inspection work in the town. The provincial inspector on one of his trips stated that generally the wiring in Vegreville was of a higher standard than in any other town in the province.

In addition there were other benefits, such as the company's Better Light — Better Sight campaign, and the numerous occasions on which company staff provided free appliance repairs, particularly during the community's annual Appliance Repair Week. The staff, MacGregor said, considered it its duty and pleasure to provide "service in the fullest meaning of the word."

Canadian Utilities' construction program was substantial in 1936 and was more varied than usual. That was the year the company took over the Calgary Power plant and franchise in St. Paul de Metis (now St. Paul), Alberta, in exchange for the Canadian Utilities property in Raymond. The acquisition of St. Paul required construction of a new forty-five-mile 13,800-volt transmission line to the nearest point on the Vegreville district system.

The new line enabled the company to serve the villages of Hairy Hill and Two Hills, as well as the hamlets of Lafond, Duverney and Brosseau. As well the agreement with Calgary Power provided for Canadian Utilities to take over the twenty-one-mile tie line between Holden and Vegreville which Calgary Power had built in 1930.

On completion of the line to St. Paul the oil-engine plant there was taken out of service and the small plants at Two Hills and Hairy Hill were dismantled and scrapped. Ralph Provan, who had been with the company from its beginning, was transferred to St. Paul from Vegreville and placed in charge.

Along with the purchase of the St. Paul property from Calgary Power, the company acquired the services of Paul Drolet, who had been hired by Calgary Power in 1930 to operate the distribution system. Although small in stature, Paul was an energetic, likeable individual. He was always active in community affairs. Paul remained at St. Paul in the service of the company until his death on May 28, 1971, just a few months before he was due to retire.

In Saskatchewan, a seven-mile extension was built from Star City to Valparaiso in the Prince Albert District. This brought the Canadian Utilities line to within five miles of the Tisdale system of the Saskatchewan Power Commission. This system served several communities between Tisdale and Nipawin from an isolated plant located at Tisdale. However, in spite of the Valparaiso extension Tisdale was never supplied with power by Canadian Utilities, although it was eventually tied in to the Valparaiso line after the Saskatchewan Power Commission acquired ownership of the company line in 1947.

At Drumheller the company moved into its new office building, next to the post office on Third Avenue. The building was constructed on the most modern lines with the latest in lighting and air conditioning. It was heated through an insulated copper pipe brought underground from the power plant three blocks away. A large showroom was provided for the display of electrical merchandise. The total cost of the building was about thirty thousand dollars.

The West was still struggling with the depression, low wheat prices and crop failures. At Prince Albert, wheat prices rose from fifty-seven cents a bushel in June 1936, to a dollar-eighteen in December, but by August 1938, they had fallen below fifty cents and remained near sixty cents until the fall of 1939. In 1937 the worst crop failure in the history of Saskatchewan occurred and drought reached into the northern districts of the province which had escaped much of the dry weather of earlier years.

At Kindersley George O'Brien was spreading the story that "the drought is so bad that the trees are beginning to chase the dogs."

In 1937 a twenty-four-mile 13,800-volt line was constructed near Prince Albert to serve the three small communities of St. Louis, Hoey and Domremy. One of the interesting features of this line was the construction of a fourteen-hundred-foot span over the South Saskatchewan river. This span was one of the longest the company had built up to this time and featured two heavily guyed three-pole structures, each supporting a cable on the river crossing.

In the Indian Head District a 22,000-volt line was extended twenty miles from Wapella to Esterhazy. The line had to cross the Qu'Appelle Valley, three miles long. Much of the valley was heavily timbered with oak trees. "The tough language used by the cutting crew in working their way through the oak groves was reported to have a melody all its own," Bill Marsh said.

Although business in general continued to stagnate throughout the West, Canadian Utilities was emerging from the dirty thirties with moderate growth in all areas. In 1937, power sales increased and the company managed a net profit of one hundred and forty-four thousand dollars for the year. By the end of the year, the electrical operations had assets of some six and a half million dollars and were serving about sixteen thousand customers in one hundred communities in Saskatchewan and Alberta.

Due to steadily increasing consumption in the Melfort district it was decided to upgrade the Prince Albert-Melfort line to 22,000 volts for a distance of some one hundred miles. Nels Hansen, line superintendent at Prince Albert, and his crew made remarkable time on the change-over. Starting at six o'clock on a Sunday morning they had the whole line cut over by five o'clock the same day, without a hitch. This meant reconnecting, phasing out and changing taps on some thirty-five transformers. In addition, they found time to change forty defective insulators.

Some customers had a little difficulty making the switch from kerosene lamps to electric lights. Fred O'Beirne, district superintendent at Indian Head, told the story of a customer in his district who, while paying the minimum charge each month, did not use any current. Fred became suspicious but could find nothing wrong, so he asked the customer why he was paying the minimum every month and not using any electricity. The customer replied, "Well, it's pretty handy to have the electric light; one of these days I might run out of coal oil."

In the Drumheller District a 25,000-volt line was extended a few miles from Rowley and Rumsey in the fall of 1937, serving a number of farms along the route. This was the only new line construction in the Drumheller District that year.

The Drumheller power plant acquired a new switchboard, of which the plant staff was justifiably proud. All the work was done by the plant staff and local line crew, with the exception of the wiring on the back of the board and the relay and meter work, which was expertly carried out by Nels Bjerre of the Prince Albert staff. With the new board all main circuit switches in the plant were operated by remote control.

Some eight hundred new customers were added to the Canadian Utilities electrical system during 1937. Approximately forty of these were in the recently acquired village of Rumsey. Another one hundred were secured by small extensions to town distribution systems and the balance were additional domestic, commercial and power customers connected to existing lines.

The year 1938 marked the end of the first ten-year period since the company acquired many of its properties and consequently it was faced with the renewal of franchises in twenty-five towns and villages. With the poor business conditions prevailing in both Alberta and Saskatchewan during the 1930s, the general public and town councils were difficult to deal with when it came to renewing franchise agreements. In spite of the pressure for lower rates, however, the company was successful in renewing twenty-three franchises by the end of the year.

CHAPTER 5
The War Years

Defence of the Empire

By the end of the thirties the associated companies in the energy group were well established. They had weathered severe setbacks and adversities, particularly during the early years of the Great Depression. But all was not well. There were ominous rumblings from Europe. There were ugly war clouds on the horizon.

President H.R. Milner, in his New Year's message at the beginning of 1939, said (in part):

> . . . *That Great Britain could be destroyed would have appeared preposterous until a few short months ago. Well over one hundred years have passed since any part of this country has been invaded by a hostile force. That has now entirely changed. At any moment we may have to go to the aid of the British people and the freedom and toleration they represent. It may be wiser to fight in foreign lands than to wait and meet the day of reckoning in Canada itself.*
>
> *The Canadian people in this difficult period should show a practical form of sympathy with their British cousins. This is an ideal country for the training of aviators. The establishment here of British flying schools would be of benefit to both countries. We accept the protection of Britain. We should be prepared to make some return. This situation may result in the movement of large amounts of British capital to Canada. It is greatly needed for the development of the country.*

It is often said that Canada is the interpreter of the two great English speaking peoples. That is true only because we are a part of the Empire.

Patriotism found a resurgence in millions of hearts across Canada during the summer as King George VI and Queen Elizabeth toured the North American portion of their Empire. The Calgary and Edmonton offices decorated the front of their buildings lavishly for the royal visit. *The Courier* said the visit "caused our blood to tingle with loyalty, love and admiration for this charming couple."

What was happening in the Old Country stirred memories of the First World War. Many recalled Private John George Pattison, an employee of the Calgary gas company, for example.

On April 10, 1917, Pattison leaped from shell hole to shell hole across No Man's Land. His objective: an enemy machine gun nest which was seriously holding up the British attack on Hill 143, Vimy Ridge. Pattison got to within thirty yards of his objective, hurled a hand grenade and followed up with a single-handed bayonet attack, completely demolishing the machine gun and its crew. For his bravery in action he was awarded the Victoria Cross by King George V. Unfortunately he did not live to receive the honor. He was killed at Vimy Ridge on June 3, 1917.

Twenty-two years later, on June 2, 1939, one day prior to the anniversary of his death, his widow, Sophia, also an employee of the gas company, met and talked with King George VI and Queen Elizabeth on their tour of Canada. Mrs. Pattison was so excited that she hadn't slept for days. She was sitting on the steps of the legislative building at Edmonton wearing her husband's Victoria Cross and was accompanied by her daughter-in-law. As the King and Queen walked down the steps of the building during part of their tour of Western Canada they walked over to Mrs. Pattison, shook her hand, and chatted with her. Mrs. Pattison's daughter-in-law was overjoyed and burst into tears. Mrs. Pattison's son, who enlisted and went overseas with his father, was at that time a member of the tank corps in Calgary.

Now on Sunday, September 3, 1939, the news broke as a numbing shock — what had happened in 1914 was happening again. Great Britain and the Empire were once more engaged in a world war.

Some staff members were already in the armed forces at the time of the announcement. Many others joined immediately. Some of them never returned.

The outbreak of war once again meant economic belt-tightening for the utility group, as the country's military needs imposed a priority on materials and supplies. A good deal of innovation and imagination was required to maintain the gas and electric systems.

The large number of employees, including some senior management, who were leaving to join the army, navy and air force placed an added burden on those remaining. The companies announced a policy that all permanent employees serving their country would retain their seniority on staff, and they were paid the difference between their regular salary and their military pay. They all knew they had a job to come home to when hostilities ended.

Apart from the outbreak of war, however, the year 1939 dealt very kindly with the companies in many ways. While there were no spectacular developments there were gratifying increases in revenue as customer numbers continued to grow and the sales of kilowatt hours of electricity and thousands of cubic feet of gas mounted.

Electric revenue for the year passed the million-dollar mark — accomplished without adding any more towns to the system and in spite of rate reductions which had been made in many towns when franchises came up for renewal.

The summer of 1939 brought an end to the drought cycle which had been plaguing the West for most of the thirties. There was a record-breaking crop all over the prairies. An increase in the price of wheat put more money into the hands of farmers and, with the whole economy heavily dependent on agriculture, everyone in business in Western Canada felt the benefits.

Despite the economic freeze imposed on most business activities not related to the war effort, there was a feeling of optimism on the part of the staff. The properties of the companies were all in good shape and their financial position was sound. Their securities, which were widely distributed across Canada, had the highest credit rating in their history.

At the beginning of the war an eight percent sales tax was imposed on utility domestic sales. The tax was accepted by the customers with very little comment or criticism. At first it had the effect of reducing electrical usage somewhat, but this did not last long and by the end of 1939 the average yearly consumption for residential customers was up to 504 kilowatt hours.

Along with the sales tax the federal government introduced a corporation excess profit tax. Taxes paid by the electric company practically doubled and resulted in a substantial decrease in net earnings from the previous year.

On December 2, 1940, the federal government prohibited the importation of electrical merchandise from the United States, and also imposed a twenty-five percent tax to apply to the manufacturer's cost on what was made in Canada.

Such wartime measures had a similar impact on the company's natural gas operations. They had the decided effect of curtailing the sale of load-building appliances for the balance of the war.

New Office at Lethbridge — 1939

On Friday, November 3, 1939, Canadian Western opened its new office and warehouse building in Lethbridge. Built at a cost of slightly over fifty thousand dollars, it was described in the staff magazine as "one of the smartest and most up-to-date buildings in Western Canada."

The main entrance featured oak doors framed in aluminum and surrounded with glass brick. Just inside the main entrance was a small tile-floored vestibule containing a desk, letterbox and cheque receptacle for the convenience of customers after office hours. Through two sets of swing doors this vestibule gave access to the large general business office and display room.

The main office was divided by an oak counter running the entire length of the room and containing two cashier windows. At one end of the office were the offices of district superintendent James J. Morrison and his assistant, F.W. Paterson. Morrison's office included a large glass brick panel and an oak-finished fireplace.

The basement contained a large auditorium with kitchen, filing and storeroom, and the heating and air conditioning equipment.

Between four and five thousand people attended the grand opening. It was fourteen years since the company had opened its office in the business block adjoining the Marquis Hotel.

Also at Lethbridge that year the company used a new metal drill and special pressure control fittings equipped with bypass connections to install three gate valves in the transmission line supplying the city, as well as a bypass at the high pressure station. The valves and bypass were successfully installed under eighty pounds line pressure without interrupting service to customers.

Especially good and fast work was done by the Calgary construction department at the outbreak of war when the company was called on to supply gas to the buildings erected for newly enlisted troops. A distribution plant was installed to serve some twenty-five buildings within a week from the time the military authorities requested the installation.

Out in the field the compressor plant at Bow Island was shut down in the spring, as the conservation board felt enough gas had been stored. The results of repressuring operations had exceeded expectations and a valuable reserve had been built up for emergency use and future supply. Some twelve billion cubic feet of surplus gas from Turner Valley had been transported and stored in the field. Repressuring operations started on August 4, 1930, when the average rock pressure of the field was 248 pounds per square inch. By February 1939, the average rock pressure had been brought up to 565 pounds.

Gas Appliance Approvals — 1939

In Edmonton, Northwestern added nearly five hundred customers during 1939, bringing the total served to more than twelve thousand. Work started, too, on extending the second floor of the office building over the warehouse to provide accommodation for the new business and inspection departments as well as the accounting department.

In the field there was the usual well cleaning, testing and tubing activity. Reconditioning and upgrading of transmission lines continued. A new system of cathodic protection was introduced to lengthen the life of the main line.

In Edmonton the distribution system was expanded to serve new customers. Six additional lots were acquired for an extension of the North Yard. The yard now had ten lots, providing ample room for expansion for many years to come.

Research by the companies' laboratories on new equipment being offered for sale brought about significant contributions to the industry throughout Canada. In several instances the companies co-operated with manufacturers in designing improvements to products. "Inefficient, poorly-made and cheap gas appliances cannot be purchased in Calgary," boasted Canadian Western's general superintendent P.D. Mellon. Before offering any gas appliance for sale dealers were obliged to submit it to the Calgary Gas Committee, a permanent board composed of representatives of the city, the gas fitting and plumbing trades and the gas company. The committee issued a certificate only after the appliance had been tested in the laboratory maintained by the gas company and met the requirements for safety and efficiency as established by the board.

New Edmonton Rate — 1940

O ne of the highlights of 1940 was the annual convention of the Canadian Gas Association and the Northwest Conference of the Pacific Gas Association, held at Jasper during July. It was the first time that a gas convention of this importance was hosted in Alberta. President of the Canadian Gas Association at the time was Northwestern's own Julian Garrett.

Delegates from Alberta's gas companies impressed visitors with what was being done in this province. Canadian Western's secretary-treasurer H.S. Watts, for instance, wrote an article on rates for the convention. Using his own home as an example, he demonstrated the exceptionally low cost of using gas for all purposes at the company's "domestic combination rate" of twenty-seven cents per thousand cubic feet after the first four thousand cubic feet. Watts' gas bill for a whole year was less than one hundred dollars for a seven-room bungalow with twelve gas appliances.

At the same time as Watts' report was written for the Jasper convention, Northwestern was negotiating with the City of Edmonton for a new rate for domestic and small commercial customers. A revised rate for these customers was finally agreed on, which replaced the old "block" schedules. The new "domestic and small commercial general rate" called for two dollars per month for the first four thousand cubic feet, and twenty-five cents per thousand cubic feet for all additional consumption.

A few of the convention delegates took in the Calgary Stampede, of which Canadian Western has always been an enthusiastic supporter. It was in 1940 that Canadian Western donated a chuckwagon trophy for competition at the Calgary Stampede. The trophy was competed for annually, becoming the property of the outfit which won the championship in any three years. Each year a plaque was given to the winner, bearing a carved replica of the trophy. The original sculpture was created by the well-known cowboy artist, Charles Beil of Banff.

Flying Training Schools — 1940

I t was in 1940 that Dennis Yorath temporarily left the companies, to become the manager of Lethbridge Flying Training School Limited. Later he moved to High River as manager of the new Elementary Flying Training School. Yorath was a director of Canadian Western and secretary of Canadian Utilities. He had always shown a keen interest in aviation, having been one of the first directors of the Calgary Aero Club. He had a private pilot's licence.

The Alberta air training schools were among a number of such establishments set up in Western Canada. New airfields were opened by the British Commonwealth Air Training Plan.

Some of these schools were in the service areas of Canadian Utilities including an Elementary Flying Training School and an Air Observer School at Prince Albert, a Flying Training School at Yorkton and a Military Training Centre at Grande Prairie. The construction of these military projects was given top priority by the government and the company. By July 1940, the Prince Albert training school was in operation, and by November two classes of pilots had graduated. Before the end of the year the Military Training Centre at Grande Prairie was in full operation with two hundred and sixty trainees and a staff of eighty-five men and women.

Much of the activity of the RAF and the RCAF took place in southern Alberta because climatic conditions permitted the greatest number of flying hours per year, enabling the British Commonwealth Air Training Scheme to reach a maximum production of trained personnel in the shortest possible time.

The gas company was called on to provide service to three service flying training schools, one in Fort Macleod and two in Calgary. In addition an airplane repair depot for Western Canada was established. Wireless training schools to turn out WAGS (wireless air gunners), and WOGS (wireless operators, ground) were established, the latter being located at the Normal School and Provincial School of Technology and Arts. The RAF and RCAF equipment depots were moved from Winnipeg to Calgary where sixty-four buildings were erected to house material and personnel.

Construction of the necessary gas transmission lines, mains and services for these military projects could not be started until August and it became a race against time to complete the program before cold weather set in. The Department of National Defence requested the gas company to prepare heating plans for all the buildings. The company had close liaison with No. 4 RCAF Training Command at Regina and the RCAF Buildings and Construction Department, Ottawa, as well as the Department of Munitions and Supply. The heating needs for more than two hundred buildings were supplied to everyone's satisfaction and the work was actually completed ahead of schedule. In every instance natural gas service was available at the time trainees moved in and even before they had sewer and water connections.

Rapid Increase in Heating Load — 1940

In Edmonton Northwestern designed, supplied and installed practically all of the equipment for heating, cooking and water heating for two air training schools, consisting of four hangars and eighteen other buildings constructed at the Edmonton airport, as well as a large airplane assembly plant that was nearing completion at year-end.

The fall of 1940 was particularly busy for Northwestern's new business department. From the time the company's new rate schedule was approved until the end of the year, there was an increase of more than seven hundred new domestic heating loads, compared to three hundred during the first eight months of the year.

No reference to Northwestern's new general rate is complete without crediting E.W. Bowness, vice-president and managing director, whose persistence against much opposition led to the new rate. He had felt for some time that the main factor impeding Northwestern's progress was the form of the old block rate schedule with its low monthly minimum charge. This encouraged customers to use gas only for convenience uses, but discouraged the large volume furnace load in the face of competition from cheap local coal. He proposed a significant increase in the minimum monthly charge and a decrease in the commodity charge. Some felt that this would lead to reduced revenues and the loss of many existing customers, but Bowness argued that the existing customers would not return to the use of coal and wood in the kitchen and the lower commodity charge would promote the large volume furnace load which would generate much-needed increased revenue for the company.

Bowness' arguments won the day. This turned out to be a major breakthrough for Northwestern, which never looked back from then on.

The first part of the year had seemed busy enough with a considerable amount of new business, despite an eight percent tax that one might have expected to dampen business. But if the staff thought they were busy during the first eight months, it was an "illusion," commented Cody McPherson, new business and service department manager. "This part of the year was like the Chamberlain era compared with the blitzkrieg which descended upon us following the first of September when city council approved the new rate schedule," he said. The new rates seemed to make customers very gas-minded because, on top of all the burner work and the commercial installation the company had to handle, there were five hundred more service calls during this period than during the same period the previous year.

The town of Vegreville, where Canadian Utilities' electrical operations began fourteen years previously, was supplied with gas by Northwestern in 1940. A four-inch all-welded high pressure line was run from a point just west of the village of Holden in almost a direct line nineteen miles to Vegreville.

At Vegreville a brick regulating station was built at the southern edge of town. From there, enamelled, wrapped and cathodically protected lines were run throughout the town. Service to the town was originally provided by the Vegreville Gas Company Limited, a subsidiary of Northwestern Utilities.

The construction of the line to Vegreville was made possible by the Viking-Kinsella connecting line, probably the most important part of the 1940 construction program for Northwestern. The Kinsella field was tied into the company's system by a pipeline running from the Viking control station across country to Kinsella Well No. 2. The line was made up of six miles of ten-inch pipe and eight miles of six-inch pipe from the edge of the field to Well No. 2.

Another five miles of twelve-inch duplicate pipeline were laid between Edmonton and the Viking field, and in Edmonton the company laid an intermediate pressure line to supply the Swift Packing Plant. All in all, Northwestern's capital budget in 1940, totalling nearly half a million dollars, was the largest since 1929, the year that three new wells were drilled in the Viking field and a stretch of twenty miles of transmission line was duplicated.

Saskatchewan Air Training Fields — 1940

During the summer of 1940 Canadian Utilities negotiated with the town of Melfort for a release from its standby obligations in connection with the Melfort generating plant so that the 550-horsepower Mirrlees unit could be moved to the Yorkton plant to help handle the additional airport load at that centre.

The main air training field at Yorkton was located about four miles north of town, with an illuminated landing field for night flying about the same distance east of Yorkton. New lines were required to serve these facilities. Pete Telfer and his crew from Indian Head were moved to Yorkton to do the line work, along with the distribution system to the base. Pete and his gang were to spend many months in Yorkton before they could return home to Indian Head.

Meanwhile the staff at Melfort rebuilt the two small generating units there and dismantled the Mirrlees for transportation to Yorkton. Bert Stringer was ready at Yorkton to take the new unit. The Yorkton air base was scheduled to go into full operation in the spring of 1941, so everyone was kept hopping to meet the deadline.

While a great deal of utility activity was taking place in connection with various military establishments, in the Drumheller District the necessary permits and materials were obtained to extend a 13,800-volt line from Trochu to serve the villages of Huxley and Elnora — a distance of some fourteen miles. This was the only line construction carried out in the Drumheller District in 1940.

Mobile Radio Systems Started — 1941

Lee Drumheller, the visionary district superintendent (the town was named after his father, Sam Drumheller), had been thinking for some time that it would be a good idea if some of the service vehicles in the district could be equipped with two-way radios to facilitate communication with the crews and servicemen in times of trouble on the power lines. He discussed the idea with Bill Marsh, merchandise and radio technician and an amateur radio operator, who agreed it had definite possibilities. Accordingly, an application was made to the Department of Transport for a license to operate a fixed radio station at Drumheller and to equip two service vehicles with mobile two-way radio sets.

The DOT looked favorably on the application and a license was granted to the company to operate a two hundred-watt transmitter at Drumheller on a frequency of 2,238 kilocycles with the call letters CG8V. The company was also licensed to operate two mobile units with a transmitting power of ten watts. A start was made immediately on building the main transmitter and installing the transmitting antenna on the roof of the company office at Drumheller. The radio receiver was located in an isolated area on a hill on the north side of the valley to improve reception. It was operated by remote control from the office.

By the end of July 1941, the main transmitter was completed and two mobile sets were in operation. The experiment was a success. Although communication with the vehicles was generally limited to a thirty-mile radius and reception was affected by terrain and static from lightning storms or power lines, the radio set-up proved invaluable during power outages and other emergencies. It was soon decided to expand the system and in a few months three more trucks were equipped with two-way sets. This small beginning, with much of the equipment locally built, was the start of the extensive radio communication system operated by the company today.

12 Air Training Centres — 1941

For Canadian Western, 1941 was one of the busiest years the company had ever had. The load taken on due to military activities and war industries totalled more than three and one half billion cubic feet. By this time thirty-five employees were in the armed forces, leaving the company short-handed in most departments.

Twelve air force training centres were being served. Serving these was always a rush job due to military secrecy. Then there was the red tape involved in clearing everything through Ottawa and sometimes through Washington. Bowness cited one example of ordering valves for a job and having to fill out in great detail thirty-four forms which went first to Ottawa and then to Washington for approval before the material could be ordered. Before final approval was obtained the forms came back for additional information not considered necessary when the forms were first completed.

Most of the training centres were built at considerable distance from existing lines, requiring construction of eighteen miles of high pressure mains.

The biggest load by far was the Alberta Nitrogen Company plant just outside Calgary. It manufactured ammonia and ammonium nitrate to be shipped to eastern Canada and the United States for the manufacture of explosives. The nitrogen plant was a hundred and fifty ton per day mill, built at a cost of twenty million dollars. Also served were a number of army training centres, barracks and war industries. One plant manufactured parts for Corvettes and destroyers and a gun factory produced small gun barrels.

With all this increased load and activity, however, Canadian Western's earnings for common stock were only two percent for 1941 — the lowest in all years but one since 1925, and only half the average earnings of the preceding fourteen years. It was necessary to give military establishments the lowest possible rates and the highest possible service. The company's own servicemen were being subsidized in the way of wages, insurance policies and pension schemes. Employees' purchases of War Savings Bonds were being supplemented by the company. And then the greatest expense of all was the increase in corporate income tax. "The company, and, we believe, each employee, has in 1941 and will until the war is over, do its full share," said Bowness.

Big Increase in Heating Loads — 1941

T he situation in Edmonton was similar. Cody McPherson, new business and service department manager, reported there was no let-up in growth in 1941. New heating loads again numbered a thousand alone, and then there was the military activity. The Edmonton Exhibition Grounds were taken over by the RCAF and converted into No. 3 Manning Depot. Gas heating was installed in over thirty buildings, including the large Manufacturers' Building and the Arena. The main building of the aircraft assembly plant was doubled in size and a number of smaller buildings added. A large drill hall was constructed on the University of Alberta grounds in connection with the No. 4 Initial Training School, making it necessary to increase the capacity of the university central heating plant by installing gas in two boilers that had been standing idle for a number of years.

Servicemen worked night after night to keep up with the demands. "However, it would appear that this pressure did not in any way affect the efficiency of their work," McPherson noted.

Julian Garrett, Northwestern's general manager, reported that to meet increasing demands the company had contracted with a subsidiary of Anglo-Canadian Oil Company Limited for drilling of five new wells in the Kinsella field. Drilling started on May 30 and the last well, Kinsella No. 7, was completed on July 18. Northwestern's engineers had anticipated a total open flow from the five wells of something less than 40 million cubic feet per day, but the wells turned out much better than expected, with a total flow of over 76 million cubic feet.

Another nine miles of twelve-inch transmission pipe were ordered for delivery May 1, but because of delays the pipe didn't arrive until October 16. Construction of seven miles of pipeline started two days later and was completed on November 14 at a cost of one hundred and twenty-six thousand dollars.

Electricity Sales also Increased — 1941

The Canadian Utilities electrical operations in 1941 experienced similar increases in sales — and similar problems, too, with a scarcity of certain materials and higher prices to pay for everything that was needed. The establishment of military training centres in Canadian Utilities territories required the building of new transmission and distribution lines and the purchase and installation of additional generating equipment at three power plants. New records for peak load and daily output were established.

The franchise agreement with the City of Prince Albert expired on January 30, 1941. Company officials met with the city council and reached an agreement extending the franchise for another ten years.

On September 18 a fire occurred at the Drumheller plant. It started about 10:30 p.m. in the intake flue of the forced draft fan and soon the whole roof of the boiler house was ablaze. All switches in the plant were pulled with the exception of the one feeding the city, thus depriving the whole district of electric power. The plant was completely shutdown at 11:15 p.m., but sufficient electric power was obtained from the ABC mine, which operated a small steam generating plant, to feed the city circuit.

Despite heavy damage to the buildings, coal elevator and conveyor system, the plant was turned back on, feeding all lines, at 3:15 a.m. The plant staff and everyone else who was available worked many long hours to get the fire under control and then to clean up the mess afterwards. Full repairs to the building and equipment were not completed until the following spring.

War Effort Through 1942

In the summer of 1942 E.W. Bowness, vice-president and managing director of the three utilities, summed up what was being done in the war effort. Virtually all employees were regularly buying War Savings Certificates and bonds.

About ten percent of the total payroll was invested in this way. Taxes at both the corporate and individual level had increased greatly.

By this time ninety employees of the companies had enlisted in the active armed forces, with most of them overseas. At home, practically every male employee was serving part-time in the reserve army or some voluntary defence corps. The women, too, were doing their full share. Some enlisted in the auxiliary services and were on active duty. All others were working through numerous organizations such as the Red Cross, IODE and the Navy League. Practically the whole administrative and training staff of several sea, air and army cadet corps were members of the companies.

H.R. Milner, president of the companies, noted in his 1942 Christmas message to the staff that this was the fourth "War Christmas," but that the tide appeared to have turned and victory was now something which could be looked forward to with "reasoned confidence." Much of this, of course, was due to the gallantry of many allies, he said, but

> . . . to my mind, however, we should remember with the deepest gratitude that everything was made possible by the heroic defence of the British Isles in the fall of 1940. If they had fallen there could have been no united resistance to Germany and Japan. Russia would have been surrounded — the isolation of the North American continent complete. No effort, no sacrifice of ours, can repay the debt now owing by the whole world to the British people. Their grim and heroic determination is equalled only by the momentous character of the events which it alone made possible.

Go North, Young Man — 1942

The year 1942 brought the beginning of an exciting new development for the energy group — the romance of the North. It was the year that Canadian Utilities reached up the Alaska Highway to Fort St. John, B.C. with electric service and began a series of projects which have been pushing into the far North to this day.

The fascination of the North, of course, had been there for a long time, but it took the war years and the building of the Alaska Highway to make the North accessible.

When Canadian Utilities acquired the franchise, Fort St. John was served by a small plant consisting of two diesel engines and two 10-kilowatt alternating current generators installed in the back of a garage operated by two local businessman named Bowes and Herron.

United States military activities on the Alaska Highway were turning Fort St. John, at Mile Forty-Six, into an active centre and there was a need for a bigger power plant and distribution system. Canadian Utilities gained the necessary permit and then gathered together enough power plant equipment from its other districts to go ahead with the project.

R.E. (Bob) Duncan was hired to assist Roy Nurse, Ed Kelly and W.M. (Bill) Whitley with the building of the plant and the system. By a prodigious effort on their part and with the help of the line crew from Grande Prairie under Pete Telfer, the plant and lines were completed in record time. The newly installed 20-kilowatt Caterpillar unit went into operation on November 10.

The bringing of electric power to Fort St. John was unique in many respects. The story written for the staff magazine by Whitley illustrates some of the problems which were encountered and overcome before the lights could be turned on.

The project began with a preliminary trip by Kelly, transmission chief, and Nurse; followed by the gathering of ten tons of power plant equipment from the districts, all of which was assembled at Edmonton, shipped to Dawson Creek by rail and taken the remaining sixty miles by truck.

On October 23, Kelly and Whitley headed up to Grande Prairie by train, and then, accompanied by Grande Prairie superintendent J.A. Whitlock, left with a truck full of material for Fort St. John, one hundred and seventy-five miles north. They travelled along a fairly good road past Hythe, where now and then the old wagon trail used by prospectors going to the Yukon could be seen; through Brainard, a stopping place in early days; and on up to Tupper Creek. The road passed through the Sudetan Colony with its four farms together on a section corner, one farm for each section, and into Pouce Coupe. Ten miles farther on they arrived at Dawson Creek, B.C., the end of the steel and the start of the Alaska Highway. "Dawson Creek reminds one of the early days of which we have all read and seen in the movies," Whitley wrote, "A boom town! Trucks carrying huge loads, small cars scurrying here and there, restaurants jammed to capacity. Where the dress is high boots, bright colored shirts and mackinaws, with some wearing moccasins and parkas. A town of the early days but in modern times; all freight yards filled with railroad cars and the first real glimpse of the work on the Alaska Highway."

When they left Dawson Creek they took the old trail to Fort St. John, as construction of the Alaska Highway was still under way. The next event was to cross the Peace River. Coming to the top of the riverbank there was a thousand-foot drop to the riverbed, the road twisting and turning back and forth to get down with numerous hairpin turns. Loaded trucks customarily went down the hill in their lowest gear. Two ferries were in use for the half-mile crossing of the river. At a location down the river the U.S. Army was completing a one-way bridge of wood piles. It took three weeks to build the bridge and it was used for a month when cold weather set in, freezing the river. Then followed a week of chinook winds, which sent the ice down on the bridge and carried away a hundred and fifty feet of it.

Leaving the river, the company crew arrived at Fort St. John and spent that week sorting material, staking out the pole lines, setting the engine and generator and numerous other jobs. Later came the line crew and other helpers from Grande Prairie. While the poles were being set up, a thirty-five hundred-gallon bolted tank had to be put together — quite a job in cold weather. The tank was aptly called the "nut house" by Bob Duncan, who became the new superintendent.

It was 5 p.m., November 10, when H.W. Kearney, the secretary of the Fort St. John Board of Trade, stepped up to the switchboard of the new power plant and pushed home the main switch which gave Fort St. John its first electric service by Canadian Utilities.

Whitley concluded his report with the remarks:

In years to come, when we slip up to Alaska on summer holidays, it will be hard to realize the huge amount of work entailed in pushing this road through the wilderness and the obstacles that had to be overcome, but it will be a great scenic trip. But this is in years to come, as the thousands of trucks are hauling army supplies over this route now.

System Total Increase — 1942

L ooking at the total electrical picture in 1942, Canadian Utilities' kilowatt-hour sales showed a healthy increase over the previous year, due in large part to the military training centres in the company's operating territories. Not only did the camps themselves provide a good load for light and power, they helped stimulate business in adjoining communities as well.

Due to the war the coal mines in the Drumheller valley were much more active than they had been in many years and the load on the plant increased accordingly. As it was impossible to secure a new steam turbine in order to have standby power for peak loads and emergencies, a used 2,000-kilowatt Westinghouse turbo-generator was purchased from the City of Edmonton. To secure space for this machine the generator room was extended about fifteen feet and a foundation and base were put in that would be suitable for a 5,000-kilowatt unit in the future. The installation of this unit in 1942 brought the Drumheller plant up to a 6,000 kilowatt capacity.

The increased load in the old Yorkton District brought about by the establishment of the Flying Training Centre there made it necessary to install further generating equipment in that plant. A Dominion-Crossley 380-horsepower unit was purchased, installed and put into operation early in the year.

The same condition arose at Grande Prairie and the 300-horsepower Polar unit from Rosetown was moved north during the summer. This gave the Grande Prairie plant five generators.

Record Gas Sales — 1942

N atural gas sales in 1942 rose dramatically. The year-end report of Canadian Western showed that while 1941 recorded an unprecedented increase of about a billion cubic feet in gas sales, 1942 shattered all records with an increase over 1941 of more than three billion cubic feet. A large portion of this was due to the steadily increasing load of the Alberta Nitrogen Company. Military projects were greatly expanded, and there was considerable building activity in both Calgary and Lethbridge.

Some five hundred new service lines were installed in Calgary and a hundred and fifty in Lethbridge and other towns served by the company. In spite of the large number of new houses built, the demand for housing accommodation continued. Many more new residences would have been erected had it not been for the wartime restrictions put on building by the federal government and the increasing difficulty of obtaining materials.

Three-quarters of a mile of eight-inch intermediate pressure line was installed during the year, principally to supply gas to the Broder canneries at Lethbridge, working mainly on war contracts. A new district regulator station was constructed in the southeastern section of Lethbridge to serve a fast-growing district and to relieve the demands made on existing regulating equipment.

After surmounting numerous difficulties in connection with the obtaining of priorities and the final delivery of material, two miles of six-inch transmission line were installed to a large prisoner-of-war camp and a complete gas distribution plant was constructed to serve over one hundred buildings. In addition, one of the air force schools was doubled in size, requiring another mile of six-inch transmission line to meet its requirements.

In anticipation of large peak loads and high line pressures, a great deal of work was done on the transmission lines, including installation of new drips at Turner Valley and Foremost, reconditioning of pipe and replacing old pipe with new.

Edmonton, along with Calgary, was growing by leaps and bounds. In fact, Edmonton was now reported to be the fastest growing city in Western Canada, its population having increased by eighteen hundred in one year to 95,725 in 1942.

System at Capacity — 1942

N orthwestern, however, was having problems. There wasn't enough steel pipe available to enable the company to keep ahead of the demand for gas. Julian Garrett, general manager, reported that the activities of the new business department had to be curtailed because of this.

There was enough gas in the field, but the problem was getting it to the city. Two new wells were drilled and two more were on the drawing boards. Orders for large size transmission pipe had been placed as early as December 1941, but by late summer 1942 it had become apparent that the company would not receive additional supplies of transmission pipe before freeze-up, so they had to do the best they could with material available.

On September 21 there appeared to be a real danger of overloading the system, and Northwestern began refusing to take on any new loads except where the need was urgent. Edmonton also was suffering from an acute shortage of coal. Plumbers and gas fitters in the city were side-stepping the gas company and installing gas furnace burners in homes themselves. Northwestern applied to the city to forbid the installation of gas-burning appliances on its system without a permit. After weeks of negotiations the city claimed it did not have the necessary authority and at year-end the situation was not yet resolved.

Despite shortages, the gas company's number of customers served at December 31, 1942, had risen to 14,600. The increase of eight hundred over the previous year included one hundred customers at Vegreville. Annual value of the new business was about two hundred thousand dollars, involving additional annual sales of nearly a billion cubic feet of gas.

Among the additions to the distribution system in Edmonton were a four-inch extension of more than four thousand feet to serve the United States Army Air Force at the airport; and the enlargement of the distribution system to No. 2 Air Observers School.

A record-breaking storm visited Edmonton and district early in December, depositing more than nineteen inches of snow overnight. Streetcar and automobile traffic were paralyzed and citizens were forced to brave sub-zero temperatures and negotiate waist-high snowdrifts to get to their place of business.

All provincial government snow removal equipment was brought to the rescue as the city dug itself out of the worst blizzard in the history of Northern and Central Alberta. In some areas deliveries of milk, bread, mail and merchandise were held up for several days, while snow-clearing crews continued to work around the clock.

Several members of Northwestern's Edmonton staff skied to work, and some were unable to get to work at all during the crisis. Cody McPherson, by slide rule calculation, estimated he shovelled eighteen tons of snow before reaching the highway.

The winter of 1942–1943 was a long, cold one. On January 20, with the temperature at fifty-two degrees below zero (Fahrenheit) in Edmonton, one of the main transmission lines broke. Fortunately the break was not far from Edmonton where the line had been duplicated, and as the repairs were completed in about six hours, customers suffered little inconvenience.

Temperatures in Calgary during that cold spell were said to be "relatively mild" — only forty-one degrees below zero! There was some difficulty due to ice formation on the inside of the transmission lines, but the only curtailment of gas service was to two large industries which were not greatly inconvenienced.

Northwestern's Twentieth Year — 1943

The year 1943 marked the twentieth anniversary of Northwestern Utilities. Nineteen employees stayed with the company all through those years. They were: D. Airth, E.W. Bell, A.J. Danes, J. Farquhar, I.C. Ferrier, Julian Garrett, G.W. Green, H. Hind, J.C. Jefferson, G.W. Lineker, E.F. McGarvey, T. Megas, E. Nelson, W.E. Philpot, Mrs. L. Robinson, B.J. Shalin, D. Watson, J.B. Whelihan and C.E. Wiggins.

During these twenty years the number of customers served by Northwestern increased from eighteen hundred in 1923 to sixteen thousand at year-end 1943. Annual sales in thousands of cubic feet increased from fifty-one thousand in 1923 to more than six million in the same period. Population in the company's service area was more than one hundred thousand by 1943.

In December, Milner, as president of the companies, announced that the pensionable age of employees was now reduced to sixty-two from sixty-five years for male employees and to sixty for female employees. Under the circumstances, however, the company was asking a number of employees who had reached retirement age to remain for another year or two, due to the wartime labor shortage.

The highlights of Northwestern's developments during 1943 were the drilling of five new wells in the Kinsella field and the laying of nearly thirteen miles of twelve-inch pipe to bring the main line capacity to two and a half million cubic feet per hour. The five new wells had a total open flow of 71 million cubic feet per day. The combined open flow of the Viking and Kinsella Fields was now 363 million cubic feet per day.

New service connections totalled nearly thirteen hundred — an all-time high since 1923. Five large extensions were made in the Edmonton distribution system to serve the naval barracks, a wartime housing project, and several U.S. military installations.

Canadian Western's gas sales were running almost neck-and-neck with Northwestern's and with an average rate of about twenty-five cents per thousand cubic feet, the companies were selling gas at one of the lowest rates on the North American continent. A coal strike caused people to become even more gas-minded than before. Some large commercial buildings and schools that previously used coal exclusively in their heating plants suddenly appealed to the gas company for help.

Aided by good weather, Canadian Western crews carried out a complete inspection and overhaul of over three hundred miles of transmission lines. In addition to transporting gas from the Turner Valley field, both the repressured Bow Island and the Foremost fields in southern Alberta were now on standby for peak load periods.

It is worthy of mention here that in 1943, Gordon M. Tranter, Canadian Western's collection manager at that time, was recognized for his outstanding work in photography by being made an Associate of the Royal Photographic Society of Great Britain. Tranter's photos had been published in the company staff magazine on many occasions and won a host of awards throughout Canada, the United States and the British Commonwealth. Tranter later became secretary of the Group Accident and Sickness Fund for the companies. He was also editor of *The Courier* for a time.

Employees at the Front

Meanwhile the war was still raging and several employees were awarded medals for distinguished service. One of them, the Distinguished Service Order (DSO), went to Colonel John Begg for his contribution at Dieppe. Begg was married to Georgina Dey who spent nine years with Canadian Western as cashier, ledgerkeeper and assistant contract clerk.

Pilot Officer J.R. Price, a member of the Canadian Utilities staff at Indian Head, Saskatchewan, who joined the RCAF, received the Distinguished Flying Cross on June 14, 1943. Price took part in numerous large-scale raids over France, Holland, Denmark and Italy. He was one of five Canadians in a Halifax bomber that blasted Stuttgart with blockbusters and incendiaries. Then, with three of its engines knocked out by a fighter plane, they managed to limp home on one engine. Over France the crew stood by to bail out. Over the English Channel they prepared to crash on the water. However, through the skill of the pilot, the flight engineer's ability to balance gasoline tanks, and the jettisoning of equipment, the bomber managed to reach a Midlands airdrome and crash landed. No one was injured, but as the craft touched the runway an engine fell out.

In Italy, in the shade of an olive grove within sight and sound of battle, General Bernard Montgomery pinned the Distinguished Service Order on Lt. Col. J.C. Jefferson, commander of the Loyal Edmonton Regiment, for the courageous leading of his unit through the Sicilian campaign. Jefferson had just completed twenty years of service with Northwestern Utilities. He later went on to become a Brigadier and the company's highest ranking soldier.

Rural Electrification

Prior to the start of the war there was little demand in the prairie provinces for farm electrification. Many theories have been advanced as to why rural electrification did not develop along with the construction of the original transmission lines that brought central station electricity within economic reach of a large number of farmers.

One theory was that the costs were too high. Undoubtedly the cost had some deterrent effect. But that was not the only reason. In 1939 Canadian Utilities had tried to interest farmers to install electricity in their homes and on their farms.

The response was discouraging, possibly due to the unfavorable economic conditions and the low returns being realized by the farmer for his grain and other produce.

Individual farmers located close to the transmission lines and town distribution systems were offered service for a construction contribution of less than one hundred dollars but they did not accept. It is now thought that, along with the initial cost, the farmers were not ready to accept electric service because they did not realize how much time and labor could be saved, nor did they realize how the use of electricity could increase farm production.

By the end of 1939 the company was serving only ninety-three farms with electricity on its entire system, and by December 31, 1941, this number had only increased to ninety-six. Less than five hundred farms out of the one hundred thousand in all of Alberta were receiving electric service from a utility.

As the war progressed a great deal of emphasis was placed on obtaining peak production of agricultural products. With the heavier demand and higher prices of all farm products the prairie farmer was better off than ever before. The shortage of farm labor made it apparent many tasks could be done by electric motors and appliances. It became obvious to both the power companies and the provincial governments that an end to the war and subsequent release of manpower and material would bring about a great demand for electrification on farms in Western Canada.

It was realized, too, that the interests of the company were closely linked with agriculture. Canadian Utilities served a territory which was largely rural in nature and where the prosperity of the towns and villages depended, in large measure, on the prosperity and well being of the farm families in surrounding areas.

With this in mind, in 1942, under the direction of construction superintendent Ed Kelly and new business supervisor Jack Bagshaw, the company undertook a survey on the feasibility of a post-war farm electrification program.

Kelly made trips to Eastern Canada and the United States to study what had been done and what was planned in farm electrification. He made a particular study of rural electrification in Montana and Idaho where conditions approximated those in Alberta and Saskatchewan. Kelly had been in the electric power business for many years. Born in Edmonton in 1886, he was the son of a director of Edmonton Electric Light Company, one of Alberta's first electric utility companies. For ten years he was actively engaged as a contractor in the construction of transmission lines, distribution systems and power plants that supplied some of the first electricity in Alberta.

With the inception of Canadian Utilities in 1928 he joined the new company, with his crew, and was given major construction responsibilities in Alberta, Saskatchewan and B.C. Now Kelly took a critical look at rural electrification in the northern states. Bagshaw and his group of company field men gathered information on what might be encountered in districts close to company lines.

In 1943, at the invitation of the Alberta Post-War Reconstruction Committee, which had been set up by the provincial government, company representatives met with the committee and officials of Calgary Power to discuss the feasibility of a general plan of farm electrification after the war.

The information already gathered by the company in a preliminary report was the nucleus for the discussions at that original meeting on farm electrification.

Following the meeting, Professor Andrew Stewart of the University of Alberta was commissioned to conduct his own survey for the Alberta legislature and to report to the Research Council of Alberta relative to a post-war rural electrification program for the province. Almost immediately a co-ordinated study of eighteen separate farming districts was undertaken by Calgary Power, Canadian Utilities and professor Stewart.

The survey was completed in 1944 and became the basis for Stewart's report, "Rural Electrification in Alberta."

Professor Stewart estimated that approximately twenty-three thousand of the one hundred thousand farms in Alberta might be connected over a ten-year period under an extensive program of farm electrification. Of this number, forty-nine hundred farms were estimated to be within the territory served by Canadian Utilities. He also estimated that thirty thousand farms might be hooked up eventually in the province.

Before the report was tabled in the legislature Canadian Utilities management concluded that a theoretical survey, no matter how carefully conducted, would not give sufficient information on such important matters as line design, construction and operating costs, the usage to which the power would be put, rates to be charged and revenues which might be expected. Knowing the answers to these questions was vital before any comprehensive program of farm electrification could be undertaken.

To obtain this information first hand, it was decided to proceed with the construction of a farm electrification test area. The necessary materials were assembled and Experimental Area No. 1, as it was termed, was built during the summer of 1944 in a prosperous dairying area near Swalwell in the Drumheller District. The building of these lines made electricity available to seventy-eight farms and a cheese factory in the small community of Linden.

President Milner closed the switch to energize the lines on October 19, 1944. It was a day of great rejoicing in the area. A highlight of the day was a lamp-burying ceremony. Claude Webb, a prominent citizen of the community and one of the most enthusiastic backers of the farm electrification project, buried his kerosene lantern in a deep hole beside a new 6,900-volt substation. He said this was the happiest day of his life.

The Swalwell test project was Alberta's first large-scale rural electrification undertaking and became the forerunner of a network of farm power lines that would eventually reach into virtually every corner of the province.

The Swalwell experiment was built at a cost of thirty-four thousand dollars. The information obtained proved valuable. Costs averaged four hundred and thirty-seven dollars per customer, but the density of farms taking service was considerably higher than could be expected over the entire farming community. It was felt further experiments should be carried out. Work was started in the early fall on Experimental Area No. 2, at Vegreville. This was a typical mixed farming region and believed to be more representative of the average conditions to be encountered in the company's operating territory.

Dominion-International Merger — 1944

One of the highlights of 1944 was a merger which brought International Utilities Corporation back into the picture.

At a board of directors meeting on November 7, E.W. Bowness reported that formal notice had been received that Dominion Gas and Electric Company had been merged with International Utilities Corporation under the terms of an agreement dated July 1, 1944.

International Utilities was again at the helm and considerable additional capital was invested in the Canadian properties during the following summer.

In July 1945, International Utilities subscribed to a further half-million dollars of the common stock of Northwestern Utilities. In December the company offered its existing shareholders the right to subscribe to an additional five thousand shares of the six percent preferred stock at par, although the shares on the market were selling over par. The half-million dollars was raised without difficulty. In the same month the outstanding four and one half percent bonds, amounting to a little over two and one half million dollars, were called for redemption and a new issue of four and one half million dollars in four percent bonds was sold to ten Canadian institutions and one American institution operating in Canada. In summary, about three million dollars of new money was raised. About half of the new money would be used to extend the system to the Red Deer area. The balance would be devoted to expanding the existing plant.

While International Utilities was investing further capital in Northwestern, it increased its common stock equity in Canadian Utilities by a quarter of a million dollars through exchanging two and one half thousand seven percent preferred shares for 74,850 common shares. The preferred shares then outstanding were changed to five percent preferred and in addition to the two and one half thousand shares so exchanged, five thousand preferred shares were sold to the public at par. These operations raised nearly seven hundred and fifty thousand dollars.

Canadian Utilities preferred shares at the time were quoted on the Toronto Stock Exchange at one hundred and two dollars. Existing $2,473,000 five percent U.S. pay bonds were called for redemption and replaced by two and one half million dollars of three and three-quarter percent U.S. pay bonds which were sold at one hundred and three dollars U.S. per bond. In addition a million dollars was issued in four percent Canadian pay bonds at par. In total one million seven hundred thousand dollars was raised for improvements and extensions to Canadian Utilities' properties.

Utility Growth Continues — 1944

I n the Vegreville District in 1944 the demand for electric pumping at oil wells had increased to the point where the district was unable to cope with it, even though George Cummine, the plant operator at Lloydminster, had been running the plant steadily all summer to supplement the power supply available from the grid. With the definite prospect that there would be a further increase in pumping load in 1945, along with further development in the Lloydminster oilfield, the decision was made to raise voltage of the line between Vegreville and Lloydminster to 22,000 volts.

This job required most of the summer and fall since every insulator on the line had to be changed to handle the higher voltage. Bill Spence and his crew from Vegreville made the change-over on November 12 with Ed Kelly in charge.

In Saskatchewan, at Prince Albert, the steam plant was by now so heavily overloaded that the standby units could no longer carry the extra load. Arrangements had to be made with the Saskatchewan Power Commission to supply the Prince Albert District with additional capacity from its plant at Tisdale. A five-mile 13,800-volt line was built by the company between Valparaiso and Tisdale to tide over this emergency.

In gas operations, 1944 was relatively quiet for Canadian Western although more than a thousand new service lines were installed. With wartime shortages of labor and materials at no time during the year was the company able to obtain sufficient manpower to fill its work crews. Much credit was due to the employees who had to pick up the slack.

In small communities, Taber was the area of most activity, with fifty new services to accommodate, due mainly to an influx of oil workers. At Brooks a well was drilled and connected to the plant.

Northwestern felt the pinch for manpower and materials even more than Canadian Western, and on a number of occasions had to borrow men and materials from its sister company.

The main project in new military activity was construction of metering and gas heating equipment at the Wainwright Army Camp. This was designed and installed under the supervision of Wilf Gray.

Hudson's Bay Well No. 1 at Viking was abandoned for the owners by Northwestern. The well caught fire during the operation and the Star drilling machine was badly damaged. It took several months to get parts for the machine, but they were finally obtained and it was practically rebuilt.

It was spruce-up time at Viking and all the buildings at the Viking Field camp were painted. Land for a gravel pit was purchased at Kinsella and this pit supplied sand for sandblasting and gravel for new walks at Viking. The line supplying the town of Viking was replaced with new and reconditioned pipe for a distance of four miles.

End of the War — 1945

By the spring of 1945 the end of the war was plainly in sight. Servicemen were beginning to come back from overseas. Military training was being phased out in Western Canada. Then, on the very eve of the winning of the war in Europe, came the unexpected and sudden death of U.S. President Franklin D. Roosevelt, on April 12.

Northwestern's general manager, Julian Garrett, had been a classmate of Roosevelt's at Harvard University in 1904. Garrett summed up his feeling about the president's death this way:

> *His death is a distinct loss to the cause of world peace. We all remember his policy of "The Good Neighbor" enunciated in his inaugural address in March, 1933.*
>
> *. . . Truly, the world has lost an illustrious statesman, a gentleman of magnetic personality, and one of the foremost humanitarians of all times. His greatness will indubitably be acclaimed by the historians of the future.*

It was a time of mixed joy and sorrow everywhere. For the energy group there was the joy of beginning to see its servicemen and servicewomen come home again and carry on where they had left off. There was the sorrow of having lost some of them.

The joyful announcement of victory in Europe came on May 8, 1945. Then the war with Japan ended on August 14. The world conflagration had at last come to an end.

It is significant to note at this point that the greatest technological breakthrough of the war — the development of nuclear explosives — was destined to have the greatest impact on the peaceful utilization of energy. The atomic bomb heralded the future of nuclear power generation.

Throughout Canadian Utilities' service areas electrical operations continued to expand. Rural electrification experiments were now proceeding full tilt. The test area lines at Vegreville were completed in February, bringing electric power to another forty-five happy farmers.

To complete the rural electrification tests, a third project was constructed at Melfort, Saskatchewan in 1945. This region was chosen because it was primarily a grain growing area and would provide valuable information on what might be expected in this type of farming district.

Although the war was over, it was still difficult to obtain materials to build farm lines. The farmers themselves were having trouble obtaining electrical materials and having their homes and farmyards wired. Deliveries were expected to remain poor for some time, since they were caused by overloaded factory conditions created by the tremendous demand from all parts of Canada for wire, hardware, and poles, after six years of stringent control.

Growth of electrical load and numbers of customers served had been continuous throughout the war. By the end of 1945 nearly twenty-two thousand customers were being served, with total sales standing at almost 41 million kilowatt hours.

On February 23, 1945, with the end of the war in sight, Canadian Western staff gathered at the Palliser Hotel in Calgary for the first annual awards banquet and dance in five years. It was the beginning of getting back to normal after pinching the pennies, buying Victory Bonds, and hoping and praying for an end to hostilities. But it wasn't quite normal yet. Liquor rationing still made it necessary to append the letters BYOL to the banquet invitations.

For Canadian Western 1945 brought a heavy construction program, although much of it was carried out under continued adverse conditions. It was not until the latter part of the year that sufficient labor became available to get back to normal.

During the year the company laid just over ten miles of new main lines in its distribution systems in Calgary, Lethbridge and towns. Houses erected by the federal government under the Wartime Housing and Veterans' Land Act schemes were directly responsible for a large portion of this increase.

New service lines installed during the year were nearly fifteen hundred with prospects for 1946 in excess of two thousand. The company's gas revenue figures for the year surpassed the three million dollar mark for the first time.

While Canadian Western was engaged in all this construction activity in Southern Alberta, Northwestern was engaged in its biggest construction year since 1923.

Two extension crews from April to November, plus a third crew during October and November, were required to install a hundred and fifty-three extensions with the use of a ditching machine.

Service crews started installing services April 15 and by the end of the year over two thousand new services and eighty-one separate garage services had been installed. Ten service crews were required to make these installations. Because of the labor shortage only skeleton crews were working part of the time. In September the main line crew was moved to Edmonton to increase the size of the service crews. Apart from new services a hundred and seventy-nine alterations were made to services on customers' premises.

Out in the field over six miles of sixteen-inch pipe were laid as the first lap of a third and larger line to Edmonton. This new line, from the Kinsella field, supplemented the two lines (ten-inch and twelve-inch) between Viking and

Edmonton, and the ten-inch and twelve-inch single line between Kinsella and Viking. During the coldest days of the 1944–1945 winter these lines were taxed to the limit to supply the demand for gas in Edmonton. "The year of 1945 was a busy one," said A.J. Danes, distribution supervisor, in his summary of the year's activities, "but I think 1946 will see the busiest year this company has ever had."

CHAPTER 6

Post-War Boom

Northwestern's Southern Extension

Following the war, E.W. Bowness, vice-president and managing director, saw the desirability of a significant expansion of Northwestern's service area and found one close at hand in the string of prosperous communities south of Edmonton, from Camrose to Red Deer. Red Deer particularly, he felt, had a substantial growth potential, as it lay about halfway between Calgary and Edmonton and far enough from both to have an important identity of its own.

Bowness felt such an expansion of Northwestern's activities would not only be an economically viable undertaking, but would also be useful in re-absorbing into the organization a good many of the gas companies' technical and administrative personnel who had served in the armed forces.

Money was still tight and funds for capital expansion were hard to come by. It took all of Bowness' persuasive powers to obtain approval for the expenditures from International Utilities, but he finally succeeded and detailed planning got underway in the fall of 1945.

An example of the tightness of funds is seen in the design of the pipeline. Although provision for future load growth was recognized as being important, it was felt that the project could only afford an eight-inch line as far as Ponoka, where the Alberta Mental Hospital provided a major load. From there to Red Deer it would have to be six inches. When the plans were reviewed by the project engineers they suggested that for the modest increase in cost the line should continue at eight-inch diameter all the way to Red Deer, to allow greater capacity to serve Red Deer's future growth. The answer was simply that there was not enough money available.

In later years, of course, this was regretted as Red Deer continued to grow. Additional capacity was provided first by the installation of a compressor at Poe, the inlet of the extension. Eventually, additional gas was fed into the system from the south end, by tapping Canadian Western's 1956 northern extension, which had a new source of gas at the Nevis field east of Red Deer.

Armed forces returnees who went to work on Northwestern's southern extension included Brigadier J.C. (Jim) Jefferson, in charge of administration for the project; Captain B.W. (Bev) Snyder, project engineer; Major E.H. (Tiny) Wright, regulator station and distribution system design; and non-commissioned officer Carl Bo-Lassen, chief draftsman. The team was directed by Northwestern's general superintendent, Barclay Pitfield, and drew on the construction experience of additional men such as transmission foreman Fred Imler and distribution expert Allan Danes.

During the planning stages of the project in 1945 Tiny Wright, Allan Danes and Harold Robbins travelled to Los Angeles and San Francisco to study pipe-laying operations. Those were the days when the gas company was the major pipeline builder in Alberta, and it was important to keep up-to-date on the latest methods and equipment. Pitfield, Jefferson and Snyder visited pipeline projects in Oklahoma, Kansas, Missouri and Nebraska, and placed orders for various items of transportation and construction equipment.

Then the work began. First came the right-of-way survey by air, to help the ground crews dodge obstacles such as lakes and sloughs. Next came the survey on the ground, followed by clearing operations.

About one hundred miles of pipeline were to be built, and it was obvious that Northwestern didn't have enough people to do it all. A crew was brought up from the sister company in Calgary, under the direction of George Kellam, who had served as a captain in the army. The Calgary crew set up its tent camp in the Poe-Camrose section. It was at Poe that the southern extension would branch off the main line. The frost was out of the ground early that spring and the Calgary crew began its ditching operations the first week in April. The Northwestern crew set up its tent camp just east of Bittern Lake, and started a week later. At the same time the mains and service crews started working on the distribution system in the towns.

The tent camps for the crews laying the transmission pipe were provided with as many amenities as possible. One important consideration was that the workers should be able to wash properly. Since Tiny Wright had become familiar with sanitation units during his service overseas, he helped design portable showers for a special shower tent. The water had to be hauled in with a tank truck, and then a pump was used to put the necessary water pressure into the shower heads.

The showers were appreciated more than the cooks. "Our cooks just couldn't seem to satisfy the fellows," Wright reminisced. "We lost several of them, and finally got Pat Smith, who had worked in an army kitchen during the war. Pat worked out all right."

After clearing right-of-way the lengths of pipe were strung along the route. Sections of pipe were welded together like a long sausage, on skids, first by the tack welders and then by the follow-up welders who put on the extra beads which made the welds as strong as the pipe itself. Then came the cleaning and priming machine. A coating machine followed, giving the pipe a coat of coal tar enamel and a wrapping of asbestos felt before it was lowered into the ditch. Finally, behind the back-filling operation, came a clean-up crew.

The early spring was a blessing in 1946, but the early part of the summer was rough. It was said to be the wettest June in history. "Sometimes a cat (bulldozer) would get stuck," Wright said, "so we'd send another cat after it, and it would get stuck too."

But the crews kept working when weather permitted and finished most of the line that summer. By the time they got to Lacombe the frost started setting in, so the remainder of the line had to be finished in the spring of 1947.

Army experience proved invaluable on many occasions, particularly as the crews battled nature's obstacles in the Battle River valley. At Gwynne, where the terrain was so swampy that the ditchers bogged down and couldn't get through, they devised a system of trenching with explosives. The dynamite did such an outstanding job of "blowing" the ditches that the crews had trouble afterwards in finding "enough stuff to cover the pipe!"

At a point south of the Battle River crossing, the concrete foundations for an abandoned pump house were found in the middle of the pipeline right-of-way, adjacent to the CPR Calgary-Edmonton railway and not far south of the railway bridge over the Battle River. The pump-house originally supplied the provincial hospital at Ponoka with water from the river. After securing permission from provincial authorities to remove the obstruction the task was assigned to Tiny Wright with his background of demolition experience in the Royal Canadian Engineers and fresh from his triumphs with the use of explosives in ditching through swampy ground.

Wright accepted the assignment with great delight, calculated the amount of explosive required, placed the charges with care, connected them up and pushed down the handle of the exploder. The concrete foundations promptly disappeared and nothing but a gaping hole remained. It should be noted, however, that Wright's calculations were based on his copy of the manual of military engineering, in which the size of the charge is carefully calculated and then multiplied by two or three to be sure, for no failure can be tolerated in active wartime.

The result was a tremendous bang and a towering cloud of dust and debris which caused considerable consternation among CPR personnel at the Ponoka station, a mile or so to the north. Hearing the noise and locating the dust cloud in the vicinity of the railway bridge, they had the presence of mind to place an immediate stop order on all rail traffic that might be approaching that vicinity. Wright was busy making explanations and reassuring CPR officials as the Edmonton-Calgary passenger train was due to pass over the bridge at about that time.

The pipeline, at various intervals along its length, had to be cleaned and blown out before being finally put to bed. A mechanism known as a pig, fitted with wire brushes, was forced through the pipe under pressure. When it reached the far end, sometimes rather unexpected objects would come shooting out in front of it. At Morningside a whole family of skunks was blown out. Another time there was a woman's corset.

Wild Rumors about Gas — 1945

Back in 1945, when officials of Northwestern Utilities were explaining the benefits of natural gas in Ponoka, Lacombe and Red Deer, someone attending one of the meetings requested an answer to the rumor that "the use of gas in the home would result in all the paper peeling off the walls!"

There were other wild rumors in those days, including queries about "air being pumped into the gas" and whether or not "gas would kill all the flowers in the house." In general, however, a keen interest in the project and an intelligent appreciation of the benefits of natural gas were shown at the meetings.

The thoroughness of the "missionary work" of the company's officials was borne out when the votes were cast in plebiscites. The franchise in Lacombe, for example, was approved by an overwhelming majority of 252 to two. In Ponoka the majority was 204 to three.

The public meetings were held in advance of the plebiscites, but only after initial groundwork had been laid with the councils. One of the humorous highlights of those meetings in the fall of 1945 was an occasion in Red Deer, when Bowness, often referred to as the Father of the Southern Extension, went to Red Deer to explain the terms of the proposed franchise to city council.

When Bowness got to City Hall, the city commissioner had left for the day, and an important document could not be found. Here's how Bev Snyder, writing for the *Courier*, related what happened:

> *Bowness, aided and abetted by a clerk of the city office, descended on the commissioner's office, and in a very short space of time, created a chaos of opened files and strewn papers. The missing document was, of course, reposing all the time in a basket on a table in the council chambers, where it had been placed by the commissioner before his departure, so as to be readily available for the meeting. It is understood that the city office is only now getting back again to normal routine, and that all recent office events are referred to as having taken place "so many weeks after Bowness wrecked the place."*

Bev Snyder was quite familiar with Bowness' negotiations with the councils of the various communities on the southern extension, particularly in the initial approach. Once approval for the necessary capital expenditures was obtained, Bowness' impatience to get started on franchise negotiations would brook no delays. Snyder had just returned to Calgary after obtaining his discharge from the army, when he was met by Bowness, who informed him that the two of them were to leave next morning to visit all the communities on the southern extension.

Snyder demurred on the grounds that he hadn't had the opportunity to unpack his civilian clothes yet, and that he had nothing to wear but his army uniform. That did not, however, deter Bowness, so next morning they started out. The negotiations were conducted by Bowness, with Snyder acting only as a silent observer, dressed in his army clothes. It was long afterward that E.W. admitted that he felt it would do no harm for the various councils to see that Northwestern personnel had "done their duty for their country."

The 1946 program was the largest Northwestern and its sister company had ever undertaken to that time. It cost nearly two million dollars, and was carried out despite postwar difficulties in obtaining delivery of materials. It was part of a planned expansion program undertaken jointly by the two gas companies, to be spread over three years.

The companies commented on this program in an advertisement placed in the *Financial Post* and *Financial Times*: "We're betting five and a half million dollars on Alberta . . . we believe in Alberta and we are proving it in a material way . . . with hard cash."

Gas Turned On in Four Communities — 1946

Gas was formally turned on in Camrose on August 15, 1946, with a flare-lighting ceremony in the parking lot of the old CPR station, now the site of the Camrose Plaza Shopping Centre. "When we finished the distribution system at Camrose we had two turn-on ceremonies," Tiny Wright said. "There was the official one, with the mayor and town fathers presiding, and the unofficial one that followed in the local pub, which was marked by the boys bringing a horse into the bar and feeding it beer!" No one got very upset about the rowdy parties in those days, Wright added, because gas company personnel had a reputation of working hard as well as playing hard.

The turn-on ceremonies in Wetaskiwin took place on August 16, with a flare-lighting at 51 Street, just off the lane between 49 and 50 Avenue.

Gas was formally turned on in Ponoka on October 18, 1946, on a vacant lot at 51 Street and 50 Avenue, where the Treasury Branch is now located. The flare was at a point about in the middle of the present building.

The Lacombe ceremony took place on December 2, with a flare-lighting on the site of the old Love's Flower Shop at 4408 on the Calgary-Edmonton Trail.

When the gas company's southern extension was first proposed, Lacombe did not immediately sign the agreement. A syndicate hoped to drill for gas and oil in the immediate vicinity of the town and had promised the community a better deal. The scheme fell through, however, and when the war ended Northwestern was enthusiastically granted the franchise.

Service to Red Deer and completion of the southern extension was to wait until August of the following year.

Head Office Fire — 1946

A set-back occurred in Northwestern's Edmonton office building early in 1946, when a fire, causing approximately thirty thousand dollars damage, broke out on the main floor on the morning of February 16. Discovered about 7 a.m. by the night watchman as he was about to start on his final round, the fire had gained considerable headway before the fire department arrived. As a result, the commercial and home service departments were left homeless for a time, while the stairway leading to the upper floor and much of the woodwork and walls on the second floor were badly scorched.

Although it was a Saturday morning, practically the entire staff was on hand to help shortly after the news was broadcast at 8 a.m. The women pitched in with dusters and scrub pails, along with the men, to clean up furniture. Temporary quarters for some of the staff had to be obtained at nearby offices of other companies.

Growth in Southern Alberta — 1946

In Southern Alberta the heavy construction programs continued through 1946. Almost fourteen miles of various sizes of main were laid during the year. Nearly twenty-five hundred service lines were installed, representing forty miles of service pipe. With all this construction activity, the company was hampered by continued delays in pipe deliveries and the worst material shortage in its history. Service was only extended where the needs were critical. Garage service lines, for example, were completely halted.

The Canadian Western transmission line construction crew, in addition to helping Northwestern with the southern extension, laid a new line to augment the gas supply to the town of Brooks, the commercial centre of the Eastern Irrigation District, where a canning factory opened that year.

Management Change — 1946

In 1946 H.S. Watts retired. He was then secretary-treasurer of Canadian Western. He had been with the company since July 1913, and a director since

1932. Over the years Watts made many important contributions to the city of Calgary as well as to his own company. For example, he took a leading part in the Calgary tree planting campaign, which helped make the city one of the beauty spots of western Canada. He was succeeded by W.L. McPhee.

Honors for War Service

Several decorations in addition to those already listed in foregoing pages are worthy of particular note at this point. Board chairman Bowness and Yorath, secretary of the three companies, were both made members of the Order of the British Empire (Civil Division). The award to Bowness was in recognition of his work for the Navy League of Canada; and Yorath's in recognition of his management of an elementary flying school.

William N. Reid, Royal Canadian Naval Volunteer Reserve, was awarded the Distinguished Service Medal for outstanding service in a motor torpedo boat flotilla. And there were awards from other countries to Capt. B.W. Snyder, Royal Canadian Engineers, whose work before and during the clearing of enemy troops from the Scheldt Estuary was so admired by the government of Belgium that they made him a Chevalier of the Order of King Leopold II with Palms, and also awarded him the Croix de Guerre 1940 with Palms. The Netherlands government, equally appreciating Snyder's work, made him a Knight of the Order of Orange Nassau with Swords.

Another award which should be mentioned is the St. John Ambulance Association's Service Medal for the years 1939 to 1945, which was presented to Wilf Gray, distribution superintendent and safety engineer. During the war Gray trained classes from the Sea Cadets, Army, Red Cross Corps and civilians.

While various members of the staff received well-deserved military decorations and awards for outstanding community service, it must be remembered that there were many dedicated employees who were constantly going the "extra mile" to help customers and the general public. One small example could be noted. A message was received by the company's night operator one evening:

Will you please call Mrs. Hector at W3753 at 4 a.m. She has a very sick child and is afraid she might go to sleep and not wake up to give her child the medicine that she has to take at that hour.

The lady made this request because she had no alarm clock. Needless to say the night operator complied with the request in the company's usual obliging manner.

New Power Plant at Drumheller — 1946

The year 1946 saw the start of a vigorous post-war expansion program of electrical operations. Drumheller was bursting at the seams with expanding load, and after a great deal of study it was decided to construct a new power plant with provision for future expansion. A start was made in the spring. By the time winter set in the foundation, footings and substructure were in, ready for construction of the main part of the building the next spring.

Along with plant expansion at Drumheller, a new 24,000-volt line was built that year north from Elnora to pick up the communities of Lousana, Delburne and Ardley. This line was continued from Ardley to Erskine to complete a loop so electric power could be supplied in emergencies to the Stettler District via the new line, or directly north from Drumheller by the original 33,000-volt line.

In March the company acquired the franchise for Youngstown, about thirty-five miles east of Hanna, along with a small direct current plant. Dick Gretzinger moved from Kindersley, Saskatchewan, to take over operations. The direct current system was changed over to alternating current, with the installation of a 50-horsepower Cummins diesel engine driving a 38-kilowatt generator. Roy Nurse was in charge of installing the engine and Harry Chamberlain, who had been working most of the winter at Delburne, helped Gretzinger rebuild the town distribution lines.

Jack Bagshaw and farm field supervisor Steve Hawrelak were active during the year with the farm electrification program, carrying out surveys, organizing new projects and holding farm field days to demonstrate the latest in electrical farm equipment to interested groups of farmers.

Farm Experimental Area No. 4, in the Willingdon area, north of Vegreville, was energized on September 15, bringing power to thirty farm homes. An additional twenty farms were to be hooked up as soon as wire and other material, which was in short supply, became available. With the great demand throughout all of Canada for poles and wiring supplies, shortages continued for many months after the war.

By the end of the year, however, almost five hundred farm customers were connected to company lines, an increase of about a hundred and fifty over the previous year. Most of the new farm customers were located in Alberta, although a few had been added in the Melfort experimental area and along existing transmission lines in Saskatchewan.

The head office "floating" construction crew under foreman Slim Hansen was kept busy all year with the construction of various lines, including a twelve-mile extension to serve the village of Marwayne.

Saskatchewan Take-over — 1947

E arly in 1946 the company was advised by the Saskatchewan Power Commission that it proposed to purchase all of the Canadian Utilities' electric properties in the province. This take-over of the electric system by the CCF government in Saskatchewan was not entirely unexpected, as steps had already been taken to nationalize other investor-owned electric utilities operating in the province.

The take-over was unavoidable. Saskatchewan Power had expropriation powers under the Power Commission Act. Ebasco Services Inc., a New York engineering consulting firm, was hired to carry out an evaluation of the company's Saskatchewan properties. At the same time the head office accounting staff was put to work under the direction of T.A. (Monty) Montgomery, preparing the volumes of data required to consummate the transfer of properties.

Some expansion work was going on even at that time. A new 100,000-pound Babcock-Wilcox steam boiler was installed in the Prince Albert plant to help meet the rapidly growing load on that system, and plans were underway to increase the capacity of the plant by a further 7,500 kilowatts.

The other Saskatchewan properties consisted of diesel oil engine plants at Wilkie, Kindersley, Kerrobert, Rosetown, Yorkton and Grenfell, along with almost five hundred miles of 13,200 and 22,000-volt transmission lines. The properties were located in three areas: Indian Head, Yorkton and Prince Albert Districts.

A great deal of midnight oil was burned by Monty and his head office group in gathering the necessary data and statistics. Working with Monty were Tom Cornborough, Milt Irvine, Johnny Payne, Walter Hopson, George Craig, and George Watson.

The Saskatchewan Power Commission paid just over three-and-a-half million dollars for the properties, excluding the diesel plant and distribution system at Lloydminster, Saskatchewan. This was retained by the company as the plant there supplied the Vegreville District with power and formed part of the Alberta system.

The Saskatchewan Power Commission, which came into being in the late twenties, was later (in 1949) incorporated as the Saskatchewan Power Corporation, and is today popularly known as SaskPower.

The effective date of the transfer to Saskatchewan Power was January 1, 1947, but Canadian Utilities agreed to operate the various properties for the commission until March 31. Then at the end of March the take-over was consummated in the office of H.F. Berry, chairman of Saskatchewan Power. Canadian Utilities was represented by B.M. Hill, president and general manager; H.A. Dyde, legal counsel for the company; and Ted Smart, representing the Montreal Trust Company. Berry handed the cheque covering the purchase price to the trust company representative, with the understanding that the company would retire the existing bond issue which was held partly in the United States and partly in Canada.

Following the meeting a few more details were completed in connection with the assets and liabilities and the operation of the properties for the commission during the first three months of 1947. On completion of these details the operations of Canadian Utilities in Saskatchewan officially ended.

Saskatchewan Power agreed to offer employment to all Canadian Utilities' staff then working in Saskatchewan. However, there was much sadness among the staff in both Alberta and Saskatchewan when the time came for the family to split up. President Hill expressed these feelings aptly in a letter to former Canadian Utilities employees in Saskatchewan:

> *The present situation with regard to our Saskatchewan staff takes my mind back to a similar situation in which I found myself at the end of World War I. There were quite a group of us who had worked, played and fought together for some months. We knew each other as well as it is possible after months of close association; the peculiar likes and dislikes of one another; the ability of each to give and take, and in some cases, the dreams and hopes for the future. But our job over there was finished and the association of months, and in cases, of years, had to be broken. It was not easy, but could not be avoided.*
>
> *I think you will all agree that there is a similarity between that situation back in 1918-1919 and the one we are facing now. Many of us have been together for a number of years. We too, have worked, played and — yes, fought together. We have worked to build up our company organization, to improve our service and to impress on our customers the value of electricity in their daily lives. At odd times, when conditions would permit, we have relaxed and played together, getting to know and understand each other by so doing, and we have fought when it was necessary to maintain our position to protect the company's name or reputation. The similarity continues as we are reaching the parting of the ways and some of the close association of past years comes to an end.*
>
> *So my mind goes back again to those 1918-1919 days and I give you all the same sincere wish that was so often heard, "God speed and best of luck."*

The company was able to rehire a few former staff members who found it difficult to adjust to working for the government-owned power commission. Among the people who returned to Alberta in the next few months as jobs became available were Ernie Harrison, line foreman at Prince Albert; Austin Nicoll, serviceman at Yorkton; Fred O'Beirne, former district superintendent at Indian Head; V.G. Bert French, lineman at Melfort; Con Montpetit, serviceman at Indian Head, and Art Collins, plant operator at Kerrobert.

A Hectic Year — 1947

Following the sale of the Saskatchewan properties, all of Canadian Utilities' remaining properties were concentrated in Alberta with the exception of the plant and distribution system at Lloydminster and the isolated diesel plant serving Fort St. John in British Columbia. The company's physical assets for electrical operations were reduced from nearly eight million dollars to less than four million dollars, and customers dropped by half to twelve thousand.

Although the loss of the Saskatchewan holdings was a severe blow to the company, it brought about a concentration of effort towards developing the Alberta properties. The province was entering a boom period with oilfield development programs. Most of the larger cities and towns also expanded rapidly. Urban growth was accompanied by an expansion of the rural electrification program that brought electric power to many farms adjacent to existing power lines. The year 1947 turned out to be the most hectic year in the history of Canadian Utilities up to that time.

First of all, Canadian Utilities, like most other power companies in Canada, was short of generating capacity. The anticipated reduction in demand for electricity once military activities ceased did not occur. Rather, the demand continued to increase.

As the company's plants and lines had become heavily loaded during the war there was little spare capacity to take care of the constantly increasing requests for service. Deliveries of equipment, apparatus and materials were slow and uncertain since manufacturers were in the same difficult position. Along with all this, costs were rising steadily and it was soon found impossible to estimate with any degree of accuracy what a job would cost on completion. In spite of all these difficulties a great deal of progress was made during the year.

By the end of 1947 the new power plant at Drumheller, started in 1946, was practically completed and a reinforced concrete stack, one hundred and sixty feet high, had been built to help draft conditions and to control the emission of flyash. The new 100,000-pound boiler had been installed and was ready for a test run, and a 7,500-kilowatt Parsons turbine, on order from England, was expected early in 1948.

During the year the transmission system was expanded by an additional one hundred and seventy-five miles of line. Many miles of new farm lines were built in all three operating districts, bringing electric service to a further two hundred farms.

In the Drumheller District, a 12,000 volt three-phase line was built some twenty-two miles long. It ran north from Botha to serve the villages of Red Willow and Donalda, along with about fifty farms in the area. The Over-the-Hill Farm Experimental Area No. 6 near Drumheller was turned on in April of the same year, bringing service to another thirty farms in that district.

Slim Hansen's construction crew was busy building farm lines and rebuilding the Three Hills-Trochu line for 22,000-volt operation, while the Drumheller line crew under foreman Tom Manning changed the Drumheller-Swalwell 13,000-volt line loop to 22,000 volts to improve service conditions in the Carbon-Three Hills area.

Radio System Expands — 1947

In late 1946 Bill Marsh went to Chicago and bought a quantity of U.S. war surplus radio telecommunication sets at low prices. This two-way transmitting and receiving equipment was ideal for expansion of the communications system started in the Drumheller District a few years earlier.

The greatly expanded radio set-up proved so successful that it was decided to extend radio coverage to the Vegreville District. The Grande Prairie District on the other hand, did not obtain such a system until 1954 when a greatly improved and more reliable frequency modulated (FM) mode of transmission and reception was installed under the direction of Bill Whitley. The company's entire service area was eventually covered by two-way radio.

At Youngstown Dick Gretzinger and Roy Nurse installed a second Cummins unit in the local plant to bring the total capacity up to 100 kilowatts. Youngstown was the headquarters for the Prairie Farm Rehabilitation Act administration.

In 1947 also, the company acquired a franchise and a small plant in the village of Rycroft, thirty-seven miles north of Sexsmith, which was the nearest point on the Grande Prairie transmission system. The Rycroft station was operated as an isolated plant until 1950, when a transmission line was built to connect this area to the Grande Prairie District system.

Grande Prairie District was also having growing pains. The load on the plant at Grande Prairie jumped by twenty-six percent during the year and the peak could only be handled by putting into service a power plant owned by the federal government that had been used as a standby unit at the airport during the war. Plans were underway to increase the plant capacity, but the installation of a new diesel unit was not completed until October 1948. The new unit brought the total plant capacity at Grande Prairie to 1,470 kilowatts.

Prior to 1947 there was little in the way of farm electrification in the Grande Prairie District. A survey was carried out that summer, and in the fall a 13,800-volt line was extended from Hythe to take in the hamlets of La Glace and Valhalla Centre and a group of about fifty farms in the vicinity. The contractor for the job was Dave Harkness of Calgary.

A great effort by Harkness and company personnel enabled the lines to be energized on Christmas Eve. The *Canadian Press* carried this story on December 25:

> *This is a Merry Christmas for fifty families in the Peace River district of Alberta. Last night the switch was thrown to bring the district of Hythe electricity for the first time. It was probably too late to provide for electric lights on the Christmas trees, but anyway — if they have radios — the farmers can start off the day with Christmas music. The Grande Prairie staff of Canadian Utilities worked all day last Sunday to ensure the farmers electricity in their homes for Christmas.*

Start of Electric Oil Well Pumping — 1946-1947

O ver in the Vegreville District the main cause of concern during the year was the shortage of generating capacity. The electrical load had been increasing rapidly since the end of the war, arising largely from the discovery and development of oilfields in the Vermilion and Lloydminster areas. These fields had been developing since 1943 when private operators found oil in the Vermilion district. By January 1946, there were forty-nine wells pumping oil in the area, with fifteen of them using electricity supplied by the company.

The idea of using electricity for pumping oil wells met with some skepticism at first, but its success was assured by its economy, improved service, cleanliness and centralized control when compared to competitive fuels.

The interest of oil men was later centred on the Lloydminster field where a much larger area had been proven productive. These wells also required pumping and by the summer of 1947 nearly forty wells were being pumped with the expectation of more to follow.

Husky Oil Company built an oil refinery at Lloydminster — the largest asphalt plant in Canada — completed in June, taking up to three thousand barrels of heavy crude oil daily.

The Husky development had a pronounced effect on conditions in Lloydminster, and the community expanded rapidly. The economy of the whole territory was buoyant, and electricity sales reached new heights.

During the summer a contract was let to extend the 22,000-volt line from Smoky Lake to Waskatenau and Radway, where the company had acquired franchises. In September, Canadian Utilities purchased the electrical system and oil engine plant in the village of Bonnyville and also the municipally-owned steam plant and distribution system of Vermilion. The plant at Bonnyville, forty-five miles northeast of St. Paul, was to be operated as an isolated plant until a transmission line could be built to it. This did not take place until 1950.

In acquiring the town-owned electric system at Vermilion the company agreed, as one of the conditions, that on the basis of receiving a twenty-year franchise it would build a new power plant to serve the entire Vegreville district from this point. On July 29 the burgesses of the town cast a decided vote in favor of the sale of the plant and giving the franchise to the company. There were 327 votes in favor, and only 66 to continue town operation of the plant.

Canadian Utilities took over the plant and distribution system on August 1. Plans got underway immediately for the new plant, which was to be built under the supervision of Jim MacGregor, Canadian Utilities' assistant general manager.

The increased load in the district demanded that the plant be built quickly. Delivery time on new steam turbines was about three years, which was totally impractical in view of the urgency. The diesel plant at Lloydminster, with its three small units, was only capable of generating some 380 kilowatts, while the

99

Polar Atlas unit at Vegreville could handle an additional 150 kilowatts of load. In addition, the Calgary Power tie line between Vegreville and Holden had a limited capacity of about 300 kilowatts.

The Vermilion plant itself was run down. If it had a new boiler and extensive repairs it could put out some 500 kilowatts. On top of everything it was forecast that the coming winter peak load might exceed the combined available generating capacity, and serious problems could occur in the event of a breakdown in any of the equipment.

As an interim measure Roy Nurse acquired a Rolls-Royce aircraft engine rated at 500 horsepower and belt-connected it to a 450-kilowatt generator. He and Bill Whitley installed this unit in the Vegreville plant in September to supplement the diesel unit during peak load periods. Roy was able to modify the gasoline engine to run on natural gas. Art Collins, who had been with the company at Kerrobert, Saskatchewan, was hired to operate the enlarged plant.

Generators from Warships — 1947

Meanwhile company officials were checking all available sources to try to find secondhand generating equipment for the Vermilion plant. Finally they heard of two United States naval vessels that were being taken out of commission. This was the answer. They purchased boilers and turbines with their auxiliary equipment from the destroyer escort vessels, the Chase and the Essington. These ships were built in 1943 and 1944, and had short but dramatic histories during the war. The Chase was attacked by a Japanese suicide bomber near Okinawa in May 1945. The plane missed the ship but crashed beside it, the bombs exploding, blowing in six compartments. The Chase was abandoned but later salvaged by another vessel and eventually pulled to port.

The Essington, on the other hand, was loaned to the Royal Navy and used for the protection of convoys. Its most exciting moments came during a four-day battle east of the Azores when it headed an attack on a fleet of enemy submarines. Its depth charges blew an enemy submarine to the surface, where it was destroyed. The convoy reached its destination unscathed.

Four turbo-generators, with their boilers and associated equipment, were taken out of the vessels during the early fall of 1947 and shipped to Vermilion by rail. Andy Duncan, an engineer on the Drumheller power plant staff, went to San Diego and Philadelphia to supervise the dismantling and shipping of the equipment.

Before the generators could be used by the company it was necessary to modify the voltage output. There were two ways of doing this. One was to leave the windings just as they were and install auto-transformers; the other was to have the generators rewound. The decision was to have them rewound. Each machine, after rewinding, had a rated capacity of 2,250 kilowatts. Adapting these destroyer escort generators for use in a power plant was what Ed Kelly aptly described as a case of "beating swords into plowshares."

Each of the boilers was rated at 30,000 pounds of steam per hour at a pressure of 445 pounds. In the navy these boilers were fired with oil. The company modified them to burn natural gas.

The Leduc Strike — 1947

The oil boom began for Alberta when Imperial Oil Limited, after drilling 133 consecutive dry holes, discovered oil a few kilometres to the northwest of the town of Leduc. The first well was brought in on February 13, 1947, and was named Imperial Leduc No. 1.

For Imperial Oil this climaxed a twenty-year search at a cost of almost twenty-five million dollars. It ushered in a new era for Canada. Economists have called the Leduc discovery one of the most important events in the economic history of the country. Previously Canada was an oil-poor nation, importing more than nine barrels of every ten consumed. Since then the picture has reversed, with Canada having achieved the capability of being oil-independent.

The original discovery rig used by Imperial Oil for Leduc No. 1 is now a tourist attraction on the southern outskirts of Edmonton, heralding the message that this is where the oil boom began.

On March 8, 1948, Atlantic Well No. 3 near Imperial Leduc No. 1 went out of control and ran wild, pouring oil over the countryside and finally catching fire on September 6. An estimated one-and-a-quarter million barrels of oil and vast quantities of natural gas erupted before the fire was finally extinguished and the well put into production. Probably this incident more than any other brought to the world's attention the potential of the Leduc oilfield.

The field was subsequently developed with a total of nearly two thousand oil wells, containing two hundred million barrels of recoverable oil and as well became an important source of oilfield gas for Northwestern Utilities. After the initial discovery at Leduc, many new gas and oilfields opened up in Alberta.

Red Deer Turn-on — 1947

The excitement of the Leduc discovery added momentum to the southern extension project. The transmission line into Red Deer and the Red Deer distribution system were completed and natural gas was officially turned on in the city on August 22, 1947. The ceremony marked not only the beginning of gas service for Red Deer, but also the completion of the southern extension.

A banquet was held in the Buffalo Hotel, attended by fifty guests and employees. Guests included representatives from all the major communities served by the new line. Red Deer Mayor H.W. Halladay was one of the speakers, along with J. Cuthbertson of the Red Deer Board of Trade, ex-Mayor E. Hogg, and the gas company's own H.R. Milner. Following the dinner the mayor lit a natural gas flare in the city square.

The *Calgary Herald* noted in an editorial that the turning on of natural gas in Red Deer meant that three-eighths of Alberta's population — about three hundred thousand persons — were now being served by natural gas. "The new service means much more to these centres than improved heating and cooking facilities," said the *Herald*. "Wherever natural gas has been introduced, industrial development has followed. Calgary, for instance, would lose some of its largest industries if deprived of natural gas."

Three different types of river crossings were used on the southern extension. At Ponoka the line was laid under the Battle River; a suspension bridge was used to cross the Blindman River near Blackfalds; and at Red Deer the line was laid on the existing highway bridge.

The design for the Blackfalds suspension bridge was obtained from the Great Lakes Pipe Line Company and was similar to some installed in the United States, although it was Northwestern's first bridge of this kind. Unforeseen difficulties were encountered with this project as the footings for the south tower were in quicksand. The footings were eventually stabilized, however, and the pipeline project continued.

Out of necessity Northwestern and Canadian Western had by now become practically self-sufficient in all aspects of the natural gas business, having pioneered many developments in construction, maintenance and safety procedures related to utility operations. The group was recognized as a model for all of Canada in this regard.

Oil Boom Brings Challenges

T he spectacular growth in population and the demands for gas service placed tremendous strains on the companies to build new transmission and distribution lines to serve more homes, businesses and industries. "Our facilities have been taxed to the utmost," commented Northwestern's vice-president and general manager, Julian Garrett, in his year-end report on the construction activities of the company. During the past two decades the number of customers had grown three and a half times, from just over eight thousand in 1927 to more than twenty-seven thousand at year-end 1947. That year alone nearly four thousand customers were connected. Many applicants for gas service had to be kept on the waiting list as the shortage of steel pipe continued.

During the year the company spent nearly two million dollars on capital works, mainly on the southern extension, and on twenty additional miles of sixteen-inch and the third transmission line from the Viking-Kinsella field. Four new wells were drilled. These, with seven others previously completed, were connected to the field gathering system.

A temporary line, consisting of almost three miles of six-inch pipe, was laid bare on top of the ground from the Edmonton transmission system northward to the site of Imperial Oil's new refinery just east of Edmonton. Plans called for later replacement of this temporary line by a permanent twelve-inch line to serve North Edmonton, Namao Airport, the Provincial Institute at Oliver and Fort Saskatchewan.

Gas service was also extended to the Alberta Hospital at Ponoka, with two regulator stations, although by year-end the gas had not yet been turned on at the hospital.

Name Change at Calgary — 1947

H arry Hunter, general superintendent, reported at the end of 1947 that Canadian Western had had one of the most successful years in its history, with an additional thirty-two miles of gas mains laid and over twenty-eight hundred services installed throughout the system. Coaldale and Barnwell were added to the communities served, and the number of customers passed the thirty-four thousand mark in November.

It was in 1947 that the company changed its name from The Canadian Western Natural Gas, Light, Heat & Power Company, Limited to Canadian Western Natural Gas Company Limited. Dropping the words Light, Heat and Power made the name much less cumbersome, in addition to the fact that the company was not really engaged in the light and power business.

Concern Over Gas Reserves — 1947

I n financial circles there was a lot of talk about exporting oil and gas (particularly gas) to the eastern United States. Despite new finds of oil and gas and the booming economy, Northwestern and Canadian Western officials were worried about the possibility of their sources being depleted by such exports. The concern experienced when Bow Island supplies began to dwindle was still fresh in their memories. The increasing demands in the big cities led to projections indicating that this could happen eventually with Viking-Kinsella and Turner Valley reserves.

President Milner noted in his 1947 annual report to shareholders that the estimated recoverable reserves in the Viking-Kinsella field were about seven hundred billion cubic feet. In 1947 Northwestern withdrew nearly 11 billion cubic feet, more than four times as much as in 1934. At this rate of growth the field might only be good for another thirty-five years. Milner said:

> There has already been invested by this company in plant for the production, transmission, and distribution of natural gas, and by its consumers in domestic and industrial appliances, over twenty-five millions of dollars.

*That amount and the millions more which will be invested in the future must
be fully protected.*

*. . . With so much at stake, every effort should be made to conserve for
Central Alberta our presently abundant reserves of natural gas.*

Turner Valley gas reserves were being exhausted even more quickly than Viking-
Kinsella. The recoverable reserves were estimated at less than half those at Viking-
Kinsella. With more than 18 billion cubic feet being withdrawn annually, the
Turner Valley gas could be exhausted in sixteen years, Milner said.

Severe Winter — 1947-1948

The winter of 1947-1948 was touch-and-go for Canadian Utilities' power plants.
The Vegreville District was not alone in having to worry about its capacity
to handle peak loads. It was the same everywhere. At Drumheller particularly,
with the new plant not yet on stream, the operators had their fingers crossed.
Technically, the boilers and generators should not have carried the load they did,
but chief engineer Blythe Davidson admitted that the engineers just speeded up
the generators and managed to get over the peak, much to everyone's surprise
and relief.

That winter was one of the longest and most severe on record. March 1948,
was ushered in with blizzards, drifting snow and blocked roads. April brought
melting snow and flooding, making travel very difficult.

At Youngstown, in east-central Alberta, country people were isolated for
weeks, and heavy loss of livestock was reported. At Hanna there was a three-
month period during which the highway was open for only five days. Serviceman
Bill Lennon had to ride the freight train on more than one occasion to read meters
and repair lines in the district. Snowshoes and shovels were standard equipment
everywhere.

On April 23, 1948, the Red Deer River overflowed its banks. Country roads
became quagmires, and Ed Kelly had to hire an airplane in Calgary to patrol
the lines in trouble zones. In Drumheller flood waters got into the plant basement causing damage to the heavy motors and creating a power outage of several
hours. It was an exhausting day for the staff, to whom the local weekly, *The
Drumheller Mail*, paid the following tribute:

*Neither flood waters, which for a time completely surrounded the Cana-
dian Utilities plant here, nor fatigue, which came to each of the men in
nauseating waves from overtime labor, stopped the crews at the powerhouse
in their determination to provide power, light and heat to homes in this valley
during the last week's record rampage of the Red Deer River.*

*At one time water seepage in the plant basement reached a height of
four feet, three important motors burnt out and a series of other mishaps,*

*including outside trouble, were faced by the flood-harassed crew and sur-
mounted in turn.*

*That the power was shut off for such a short time despite the magnitude
of the circumstances is in itself a tribute not only to the energetic action
of the powerhouse crew, but to their fortitude in sticking with the job.*

Line Construction Continues — 1948

The completely new plant at Drumheller housing the 7,500-kilowatt Parsons steam turbine went into operation early in October of 1948, as did an additional 600-kilowatt Mirrlees unit in Grande Prairie. At Vermilion the first of the four units in the new plant went into service on November 7. Nearly one hundred miles of 22,000 and 34,000-volt transmission line were built to tie the new plant in with the existing system in the Vegreville District.

The major line construction during the year was the 34,000-volt line from Vermilion to St. Paul, via Derwent and Elk Point, some sixty-five miles long. This was the first such line in the district, and it was the first time the company ever used steel towers. Two were built several years later, to support the span over the lake which had been formed by the dam on the Vermilion River.

There was much activity in the rural electrification program. By the end of the year more than eight hundred farms were receiving service from company-owned lines in nine different experimental areas.

The energy rates for farm customers in test areas (other than the Grande Prairie District where rates were slightly higher) were based on a net minimum of five dollars monthly for the first 20 kilowatt hours, with all energy in excess of 20 kilowatt hours at three cents per kilowatt hour. The company absorbed the cost of building the lines, with the farmer paying only the cost of wiring his yard and buildings. The average cost to the company in the nine test areas worked out to around six hundred dollars per farm.

After the test areas were completed, a study was made of the results. It became apparent that high construction and operating costs, combined with low revenues, would not permit the company to carry out a full-scale program of farm electrification unless outside financial assistance was made available for the construction of farm power lines. The rates which would have to be charged to support these costs would be so high that they would discourage farmers from installing electricity. Calgary Power Limited, the other major electric utility in the province, had been carrying out similar tests and came to the same conclusion.

Obviously the most feasible and economical way to bring about the electrification of the farms in Alberta was on a co-operative basis in which farmers themselves would organize rural electrification co-operative associations, which would finance and own the lines and related equipment. The Alberta government offered to make low-cost money available for this purpose.

The power companies agreed, in turn, to build the farm lines and to operate the farmer-owned distribution systems for the rural electrification associations (REAs). They also agreed to sell electric energy to REA members at special rates to compensate the farmers for their capital investment in lines. This was the farm electrification plan adopted by Canadian Utilities and Calgary Power, with the approval and assistance of the provincial government. Since that time the majority of the farms supplied with electric service in company service areas have been on this basis.

Provincial Plebiscite — 1948

T he year 1948 was an election year in Alberta and public power was a political issue. Saskatchewan had nationalized its power companies the previous year, and there were groups in Alberta who contended that the government should acquire the electric properties owned and operated by private companies.

The government decided to hold a plebiscite on the issue, along with the general election on August 17. The vote, by an extremely small 151-vote majority, was against government ownership.

The Social Credit party was re-elected with its usual strong majority, and being private enterprise oriented by philosophy, accepted the majority decision.

That majority decision, however, was so close (50.027 % to 49.973 %) that some of the advocates of government take-over, among them Elmer Roper, who was at the time a member of the Legislative Assembly and in later years became Mayor of Edmonton, pressed the government for a judicial recount of the votes. Premier Manning's response was that there was nothing to be gained by going to all the expense of a recount, since even if a recount showed a few extra votes one way or the other, the change would still be insignificant and certainly not enough to give the government a clear mandate to go into the power business.

Milner found some interesting comparisons in the tabulation of the results, which he brought to the attention of the premier. He pointed out that if those ridings where the major private companies were not operating were eliminated from the totals, there would be a majority against provincial ownership of somewhere in the order of 2,100. The seven constituencies where the major private companies were not operating were Athabasca, Beaver River, Edson, Grouard, Lac Ste. Anne, Medicine Hat and Peace River. Of these seven, Milner noted that Medicine Hat went strongly for private ownership despite not being served by a private company (more than five thousand voted for private power compared to about twelve hundred for provincial ownership), and if Medicine Hat was eliminated from the group of seven constituencies, the majority for private ownership would be around six thousand.

Specifically, the plebiscite asked voters if they were in favor of the generation and distribution of electricity being continued by the power companies, or whether they would favor the generation and distribution of electricity being made a "publicly owned utility administrated by the Alberta Government Power Commission."

Canadian Utilities accepted the majority decision of the people and the government as a mandate to proceed as rapidly as possible with the extension and development of electric power in Alberta, including provision of service in rural areas.

Wherever it was in the interests of the public that an integration of operations be brought about with Calgary Power, this would be done also. Thus came about the start of a comprehensive provincial electric power grid system. During the years that followed transmission lines were built in various places to enable the electrical output of the two companies to be interchanged on an equitable basis, resulting in overall economics and improved service to the public.

Canadian Utilities Returns to Edmonton — 1948

The highlight of 1948 for the Canadian Utilities' head office staff was moving from Calgary to Edmonton. While the company was operating in Saskatchewan as well as in Alberta there was no particular disadvantage in being located in Calgary, although Calgary never had been central to its operations. But now that electrical properties were spread throughout Alberta the move was a logical one, as Edmonton was much more central to the three operating districts.

For a few of the old-timers the move renewed memories of the first headquarters of the company, in the CPR Building on Jasper Avenue, when it was still known as Mid-West Utilities. But for most of the twenty-five staff members affected it meant pulling up roots, selling homes, leaving friends and relatives, in order to re-establish in the capital city. Eventually, however, the necessary adjustments were made by nearly all the former Calgarians.

The decision to move to Edmonton was made in the fall of 1947, but the move itself did not take place until the end of June 1948. The new head office in Edmonton was located at 10529 Jasper Avenue, over the Seven Seas Restaurant. A second storey had been added to the restaurant while it was under construction on the strength of a ten-year lease which the company took out on the whole upper floor of the building. By July 5 the move from Calgary was completed.

At Northwestern Utilities 1948 brought records in every department. Well over four thousand new services were installed, with more than three thousand of these in Edmonton alone, and nearly a thousand on the new southern extension. Nearly twenty-five miles of distribution lines were put down, the majority in recently built-up sections of Edmonton. Work was carried out by sixteen service crews and four extension crews.

Revenue from gas sales was almost three million dollars. On the other side of the ledger, the company spent more than that in capital works and in maintenance and operation. As business and the number of customers increased, so did the work of the inspection department, which handled nearly twenty-one thousand service calls during the year.

Drilling a Gas Well

R eaders of a 1948 issue of *The Courier* were treated to an informed account of what it meant to drill a gas well, written by production engineer Ray Paterson. Once the site was chosen and the right-of-way acquired, Paterson explained, a licence to drill was obtained from the conservation board. Then a bulldozer moved in and levelled an area to accommodate the derrick and pipe racks, dug the mudpits and cleared a roadway into the location.

The rig builders followed and put up the 122-foot steel derrick with the aid of a power take-off from a truck. Then the crews moved in, working around the clock in three shifts, aided by a Caterpillar diesel, a mud pump, another pump for supplying water from the nearest slough, and an electric generator.

First to be drilled was the rat hole, about forty feet deep, to accommodate a square sectioned length of steel known as the Kelly. Then the mouse hole, about thirty feet deep, to hold the next joint of drill pipe. The drillers' love of animals was further evidenced by a couple of "catheads" and the "dog house" to be found about the rig. "Presumably something had to replace 'bull' and 'calf' wheels of the cable tool driller," Paterson said.

The main hole started with a fourteen-inch bit, drilled to one or two hundred feet depending on the formation. Then casing was run down and cemented in. "Any sounds resembling wailing or gnashing of teeth during this operation are ordinarily found to emanate from prospective home builders as they watch all that cement being pumped into a hole in the ground," Paterson went on.

Two days later, when the cement had set, drilling continued with a nine-inch bit, for seventeen or eighteen hundred feet. Samples of the cuttings were taken every ten feet. Finally the hole got down to pay dirt, or more accurately, the "gas sand," but everything had to be carefully sealed off and kept in place until the well was ready to be brought in. This was accomplished by gun perforating, using steel bullets fired from a specially designed gun capable of penetrating the casing and about four inches of cement. "Next, the initial open flow is measured," Paterson said. "While the main purpose of this, of course, is to determine who wins the sweepstake at camp on the size of the well, the result is also entered in the company records and given to the government, the name of the sweepstake winner being withheld to avoid trouble with the income tax authorities."

River Crossings — 1948-1949

S o much for putting pipe down vertically. By way of major horizontal pipe laying, another twenty-two miles of sixteen-inch transmission line were laid during 1948 by Northwestern Utilities.

Most exciting of all that year was the preparation for the Saskatchewan River crossing, a mile east of Edmonton, near the new Imperial Oil refinery. Nothing like this had ever been done by the company before. The challenge consisted of laying eleven hundred feet of thirteen-inch heavy pipe below the riverbed.

The work had to be completed in winter, so that crews could work from a platform of ice twenty inches thick. In January 1949, the pipe was lowered into the riverbed, hydraulically tested to seven hundred pounds and weighted down with eight-foot casings made of twenty-inch pipe filled with concrete.

River crossings were the big projects for both the gas companies in 1948 and 1949. At Lethbridge, Canadian Western laid two lines across the Oldman River to replace old pipe which had burst.

When the main transmission line was originally laid in 1912 it crossed the river four miles north of the city. The main line was sixteen-inch pipe, but the river crossing was made by two parallel twelve-inch lines, laid below the river bottom and protected by wooden piles.

In 1947 the north branch was reconstructed and relaid as a welded line and buried from four to six feet below the river bottom. Then in April 1948, it developed a leak in the deepest part of the river and had to be taken out of service. Later in the year, during June floods, the south branch broke. The city of Lethbridge and points east had to be supplied with gas from the Bow Island field for about six weeks, until a temporary six-inch line was pushed through the twelve-inch pipe of the south branch and reconnected. High water levels seriously hampered the work. As work progressed it became obvious that the entire length of both the branch lines would have to be relaid.

The north branch was completed and placed in service on October 25, and the south branch was completed about six weeks later. The pipe in both cases was buried from four to six feet below the river bottom and protected by wooden piles driven on the downstream side. It was weighted down by concrete-filled sections of old sixteen-inch pipe to prevent it from floating.

Growth in the South — 1948

S peaking of Canadian Western accomplishments generally in 1948, general superintendent Harry Hunter reported: "The staff of the company has completed the largest construction program in its recent history." The number of customers increased by over eleven percent, and the length of distribution mains increased thirty-one percent. Forty-one miles of new mains were laid in the field.

The conversion of the transit system in Calgary from streetcars to buses necessitated relaying many gas mains and services to allow for paving of the streets. New standards of paving adopted by the city made it necessary to lower gas mains below the normal depth.

Some of the smaller towns were growing considerably, and gas extensions had to be made to keep up with the demand. Of particular note were Taber, High

River, Brooks and Coaldale. A new sugar beet refinery under construction at Taber at a cost of five million dollars, one of the most modern sugar factories on the continent, was designed to use gas exclusively for its operations.

Work in the field included eight miles of sixteen-inch pipe between Pine Creek and the Ogden high pressure station, duplicating the existing sixteen-inch line. Four and a half miles of ten-inch pipe were laid to connect the Turner Valley ten-inch line to the sixteen-inch line near Pine Creek.

The year brought more honors for gas company personnel. In the spring two officials were made Commanders of the British Empire by Governor-General Viscount Alexander. They were A.G. Baalim, a director of Canadian Western, and Brigadier J.C. Jefferson, manager of sales and utilization for Northwestern. The decorations were for outstanding service to the country during the war years.

The year 1948 saw the Calgary Stampeders football club bring home the Grey Cup. One of the members of that team was Canadian Western employee Bob Leathem. The game was played in Toronto, against the Ottawa Roughriders. As soon as the Stampeders won, civic authorities declared a half holiday to welcome home the champions. When the heroes arrived home thousands of fans met them at the CPR station where another company employee, Kitch Elton, led the cheering section.

Milner Appointed Board Chairman — 1949

The annual meetings of three companies on April 28, 1949, brought a considerable number of executive changes. Ray Milner, president of the three companies for seventeen years, became chairman of the companies, filling a position vacated by E.W. Bowness. Although Bowness retired as chairman, he remained on as a member of the board for each company.

F. Austin Brownie, who had been executive assistant to the president of the three companies and general manager of Canadian Western, succeeded Milner as president of the two gas companies, while Bruce M. Hill, formerly vice-president and general manager of Canadian Utilities, became Canadian Utilities' president. He was succeeded by James G. MacGregor as general manager.

Dennis K. Yorath, formerly secretary of Canadian Western and Canadian Utilities, became general manager of Northwestern Utilities, R. Cody McPherson, formerly general manager of Northwestern, became general manager of Canadian Western. Yorath was replaced as secretary of Canadian Western by S.C. Murison, and as secretary of Canadian Utilities by T.A. Montgomery. Montgomery was formerly treasurer of Canadian Utilities, and was succeeded in that post by A.M. Irvine. P.D. Mellon, formerly vice-president of Canadian Western, who had been with the Calgary gas company since its incorporation in 1912, retired but continued as a director as well as a consulting engineer.

The Vermilion Plant — 1949

The year 1949 was another eventful one for the electrical operations. On January 26 the new plant at Vermilion was officially opened. Some three hundred people from the town and district, along with representatives of various government departments, joined the staff and Canadian Utilities' officials at the plant site adjacent to the town in the Vermilion River valley.

The plant was decorated with flags, and over the switchboard was a large map of the Vegreville District transmission system. Each town served by the plant was represented by a colored light bulb.

Mrs. Robert Horne, wife of the chief engineer at the plant, smashed a bottle of champagne against one of the turbines. Dr. J.L. Robinson, Alberta Minister of Industry and Labour, threw the switch to activate the plant, and to add excitement to the event, the safety valve on one of the boilers was blown.

The Vermilion plant was built in record time despite many obstacles. In charge of the operation was the company's general manager, Jim MacGregor. Also involved was Lee Drumheller, who was largely responsible for locating and arranging for the purchase of the U.S. naval equipment referred to earlier in this chapter. The plant was humorously labelled by the staff as the Good Ship MacHeller, after MacGregor and Drumheller. Other staff members who were involved included Roy Nurse, Blythe Davidson, Ed Kelly, Bob Horne, Don McGill, Bob Kelly, Howard Pitts, Ted Fantham and Gus Gudmundson, district superintendent at Vegreville during that hectic period.

Shortly after the opening of the plant the second unit began feeding electricity into the system, and by Christmas all four generators were in operation. The generating crisis was now over, at least for the time being. Excess energy was fed into the Calgary Power system over a new 34,000-volt tie line between Wainwright and the Vermilion plant. This line was built by McGregor Telephone and Power Construction Co. Ltd., on behalf of the two companies, with Canadian Utilities owning the first six miles south of the plant.

An unusual feature of the Vermilion plant was that the machinery was installed on its foundations before the building was erected. Another feature was the large cooling tower for the water passing through the condensers. At full load the plant required some ten thousand gallons of water per minute. Since the Vermilion River could not deliver this flow, a dam was built to form a large storage pond, and a cooling tower erected so that the same water could be used over and over again.

The lake formed by the backwater from the dam was later to be the basis for the Vermilion Provincial Park, with picnic, boating and swimming facilities provided by the government. Many thousands of visitors have enjoyed the amenities of this small oasis over the years.

More Farms Connected — 1949

With the introduction of the new rural electrification policy whereby all farm electrification would be carried out by farmer-owned rural electrification associations (REAs), Jack Bagshaw from head office, along with Steve Hawrelak and Bill Marsh, rural supervisors at Vegreville and Drumheller respectively, and George O'Brien, district manager at Grande Prairie, were kept hopping all year attending meetings, explaining the new policies to interested groups of farmers and arranging for the construction of the lines for the many farmers now clamoring for electric service.

By the end of 1949, fourteen REAs had been organized at various locations in the company's service territories, and lines for eight of these groups had been built.

The Wayne Rural Electrification Association, located in the predominantly Danish area of Dalum, near Drumheller, was the first of the 135 such co-operatives to be served by the company. The lines for the Wayne association were completed on August 11, 1949, bringing electric service to thirty-two farmers in the area. By year-end the company was serving fourteen hundred farm customers of whom some six hundred were members of REAs.

More Line Capacity — 1949

With the rapidly expanding oilfields and the Lloydminster load, it was necessary to provide more line capacity in that part of the province. This required expansion in 1949 of the substation at Vermilion, installation of two outdoor oil circuit breakers, a new 1,500-kilowatt substation at Lloydminster and a new 34,000-volt line from Vermilion to Lloydminster. This gave Lloydminster two sources of electric power supply — a 34,000/22,000-volt line via Derwent and a new 34,000-volt line from Vermilion. The division of the supply from the Vermilion plant provided much better flexibility of operation, as well as greater protection from outages for the customers in the Lloydminster area.

In the meantime, the 22,000-volt line to Glendon and Bonnyville, started the previous year, was also under construction. This line was completed on October 28, enabling the company to shut down the oil-fired plant at Bonnyville. The Vegreville plant also had been shut down and taken out of service earlier in the year.

At Drumheller new line work included extension of a 22,000-volt line, some sixteen miles in length from Coronation to Veteran; the completion of the Forestburg-Rosaline line which was started in 1948; and the building of the first 66,000-volt tie line between the Drumheller plant and the Calgary Power system at Rockyford.

The Calgary Power tie line was capable of exchanging 6,000 kilowatts of power between the two systems. As was the case with the Vermilion-Wainwright tie line, the line ownership was divided between the two companies, with Canadian Utilities owning the first fifteen miles out of Drumheller.

The switch tying the two systems together was closed on September 30. At a luncheon following the switch-closing ceremony, Canadian Utilities president, B.M. Hill, called the interconnection between the two utilities an important step in provincial electrification. "Completion of the whole plan linking all generating units in the province was a gigantic task and a worthy goal," he added.

By the end of the year the Drumheller tie delivered over 12,500,000 kilowatt hours to the Calgary Power system, and provided Canadian Utilities with some seventy-five thousand dollars of additional revenue.

Drumheller took a big step forward in 1949 in modernizing its street lighting system. On October 8, at a ceremony attended by Canadian Utilities and the City of Drumheller, the switch was thrown putting into operation forty-three new steel standards equipped with the latest General Electric incandescent fixtures.

In the Youngstown area, which was still operated as an isolated plant, a thirty-six-mile, 22,000-volt line was built to Oyen, near the Saskatchewan border. Plans called for the eventual spanning of the gap in the high voltage line from Hanna to Youngstown, so that the whole territory east of Hanna would be supplied from Drumheller.

Up in the Peace River country the biggest event of the year was the opening of the bridge across the Smoky River, closing the last ferry on the road between Mexico and Alaska. The bridge was located at Bezanson near Grande Prairie. The ferry had been in operation since 1911. It held only six cars and, with the completion of the Alaska Highway and the heavy settlement in the Peace River area, had become quite inadequate.

Other interesting developments were taking place in the Peace country. Walter Schlosser and Warren DuBois, who had been associated with Canadian Utilities in the early years in Saskatchewan, were now operating Northland Utilities. Northland Utilities was centred mostly in the Peace River country and was destined a few years down the road to amalgamate operations with Canadian Utilities.

DuBois was busy that year bringing gas to Dawson Creek. "That was the first gas to be exported out of Alberta," he recalled years later. "It took us two years of negotiating with the Oil & Gas Conservation Board to get the permit, and once we had the permit it took us only ninety days to get the job done."

The year 1949 turned out to be a very good one for electrical operations and the company continued to grow at a rapid pace. It was now serving nearly nineteen thousand customers in one hundred and eighteen communities. The number of kilowatt hours sold rose to 53 million from the 30 million of the previous year. Revenue was up $330,000 from the previous year to $1,655,411.

In the three years since the company had sold half of its properties to the Saskatchewan Power Commission, the sale of electric energy had grown to the point where it now exceeded the combined sales in the two provinces in 1946. At the end of 1949 more communities were being served in Alberta than were being served in both Alberta and Saskatchewan in 1946. Installed plant capacity in Alberta also exceeded the total 15,957 kilowatts of capacity owned by the company prior to the sale.

Another item of interest was the news that the new general manager of Canadian Utilities, James G. MacGregor, had written another book in his spare time. *Blankets and Beads* was a historical novel based on the early days along the North Saskatchewan River. MacGregor probably inherited his love of the wild from his father, the late James MacGregor, a hardy pioneer who had farmed a homestead at Westlock, Alberta, from 1906 until his death in 1949, at the age of 85. *Blankets and Beads* was the first of many books that McGregor was to write about Alberta and the West.

Northwestern's North Yard — 1949

T he highlight of 1949 at Northwestern was the opening of an operations and maintenance centre called the North Yard. Its opening, on November 9, was timed to coincide with the twenty-sixth anniversary of the arrival of natural gas in Edmonton.

The North Yard occupied a large city block between 112 and 113 Streets, on the north side of the CN tracks between 105 and 106 Avenue. The buildings, of steel, concrete and brick construction, housed distribution offices; garage and repair shop; stockroom; receiving and shipping area; machine, carpenter and welding shops and the meter-testing department. Large stockpiles of pipe were stored outside.

The company's new general manager, Dennis Yorath, asked to summarize his impressions of the year's activities, felt that the hackneyed "growth and expansion" phrases had become inadequate. Northwestern, he said, was "bursting its britches." Here is how he put it:

> *This company burst every seam of its old garments. Like a boy in his early teens, no matter how well the mother plans, she can not alter his "jeans" or buy new ones fast enough to keep up with his stretching limbs. So with Northwestern — despite carefully planned budgets — situations changed so rapidly during the year that plans had to be constantly revised to meet the altering circumstances.*
>
> *It was hectic but it was fun — such terrific expansion brings not only added interest and zest to the operation of a natural gas utility but also a certain amount of glamor.*

President Brownie, in his annual report to shareholders, again stressed the need for taking every precaution to ensure an adequate supply of natural gas for Alberta residents in years to come. The company bought Imperial Oil's interest in the Viking-Kinsella field for two point nine million dollars, which the directors felt was "an extremely fair price," being the equivalent of somewhat less than one cent per thousand cubic feet of the estimated reserves. And Northwestern entered into talks with Imperial Oil with a view to piping Leduc oilfield gas to Edmonton.

Northwestern drilled five new wells during the year, and built a gathering system to tie them together. As an experiment, three of the wells were perforated with a new method known as "jet perforating," with good success. The process puts holes through the casing and the cement which surrounds it so that natural gas can enter the pipe. Earlier methods used explosive charges. Jet perforating employed a stream of fine particles discharged at extremely high velocity.

In the distribution system Edmonton's building boom brought the greatest number of new services since the original construction of the gas system in 1923. About forty-three miles of distribution mains were laid to serve nearly forty-five hundred new customers. The largest extensions were to Jasper Place in the west end and to King Edward Park in the southeastern part of the city. A thirteen-inch intermediate line was laid to the city power plant, where one boiler was converted to natural gas fuel, with plans for further conversion the following year. A sixteen-inch intermediate pressure line was completed across the low level bridge, while a new regulating station was built and larger mains supplied for the downtown area.

On the new line to the southern towns more than twelve hundred new services were installed, including a large extension to serve north Red Deer.

The home service department put out over six thousand items of mail during the year, ranging from welcome letters to recipe books, and held cooking demonstrations and exhibitions in various places. The head office building on 104 Street underwent a general renovation, including installation of air conditioning.

Employees Form Association — 1949

T he staff of Northwestern organized an employees' association in 1949. The idea was wholeheartedly supported by both management and staff. The new association undertook to co-ordinate many projects which formerly had operated independently without sufficient staff communication, including donation drives, for example, and various recreational and social events. At the election in September Ben Banks was elected chairman, Art Lover vice-chairman, and as councillors: Sid Warren, Gwen Mason, Ernie Pidgeon, Ray Dolan, Gordon Chambers, Cliff Gates, Dick Cottrell, Charlie Hallett and Norm Blades.

The year was a busy one, but as Dennis Yorath had noted, everyone had a lot of fun too. August 21 was a great day for company golfing enthusiasts, for it was the first time the Edmonton company defeated Canadian Western to win the intercompany tournament and receive the smart new trophy created that year by Ike Pelletier of Lethbridge.

41,000 Customers Now Served — 1949

"Ⓞne wonders if there will be an end to the record-breaking expansion of this postwar era," commented George H. Benoy of Canadian Western's customer sales and service department in a report on new business.

More than two thousand new services were installed in Calgary during 1949, and more than a thousand in Lethbridge and other communities. The total number of customers served was at a new high of forty-one thousand.

Gas sales increased by more than 800 million cubic feet, and the daily peak load increased from the 120 million cubic feet of the previous winter to 130 million cubic feet. This is the actual amount of gas delivered to the whole system in a twenty-four-hour period. A great deal of work had been done to ensure an ample supply of gas, and at no time during the peak period did the company have to ask any large industrial consumers to cut back, as had been done in some winters.

In Calgary a new wing was added to Canadian Western's West End Shop. The stockroom was remodelled as well. Fred Humphries and his customer service staff shared the basement there with Art Gell and his laboratory. This is where all new gas appliances were tested for safety and reliability. Here, also, instruction was given to customer servicemen and apprentice gas fitters.

The main floor was occupied by the shop office staff under Jimmy Dunn and Art Hodges. Ed Coleman and Tommy Dodds shared a spacious office with Carl Windsor, timekeeper, in the operating and construction department. From the front office the stores ledgers and meter records were maintained.

The West End Shop became the site for more extensive construction in 1950, with a new thirteen thousand square foot warehouse and workshop being built. It centralized the mechanics' repair shop, welding shop, machine shop, blacksmith shop, the automobile parts stockroom, and an office for the mechanical supervisor.

New Calgary Office Building — 1950

Ⓒanadian Western's most exciting project in 1950 was the start of construction on a new head office building. The company had been in its building at 215 Sixth Avenue S.W. since 1914. There had been talk of a new building ever since early 1946, when the company retained the Ebasco Corporation of New York to prepare a set of plans. However, due to rising building costs construction had been postponed.

Then Canadian Utilities moved to Edmonton in 1948, which left room into which Calgary staff could expand. But the company was growing so rapidly that in 1950 it became apparent that it could no longer operate efficiently in its old quarters. Several preliminary plans were drawn in consultation with a local firm of architects, Stevenson, Cawston and Dewar. Then a Canadian Western team spent a week inspecting large utility buildings in Winnipeg, Minneapolis, St. Paul and Des Moines. On the basis of this experience, along with many more management conferences, a plan was finally adopted.

Tenders were called for and a bid by C.H. Whitham Limited was accepted. The sod-turning ceremony to launch the project, at the northeast corner of Sixth Avenue and First Street S.W., was held on October 23. Plans called for a two-storey building plus a basement, with provision for future expansion to six stories. The superstructure would be reinforced concrete, and the exterior finish, black granite and Manitoba Tyndall stone.

Jumping Pound Field — 1950

In May 1950, negotiations between Canadian Western and the Shell Oil Company were opened for a supply of natural gas from the Jumping Pound Field west of Calgary. A contract was signed in July. The contract called for Canadian Western to build, by year-end, a pipeline, measuring station and control equipment to take 20 million cubic feet of gas per day, at a load factor of eighty percent. This meant an average daily take of 16 million cubic feet.

Shell agreed to construct a gathering system and scrubbing plant by year-end to supply the 20 million cubic feet per day at a maximum pressure of seven hundred and fifty pounds.

Studies showed that Canadian Western would need a twelve-inch line, thirty miles long. Accordingly, the pipe was ordered, along with the necessary valves, welding fittings, regulators, welding rods, coating materials, river weights, expansion sleeves, construction machinery and camp equipment. With the necessary easements obtained the bulldozer started preparing the right-of-way.

By the beginning of October the company was ready to begin pipe-laying, but the pipe had not yet arrived. Finally, on October 20, the first loads of pipe arrived. The pipe was unloaded, hauled and strung, and the welding crews started immediately, with help from Northwestern Utilities. Work was completed on schedule by year-end.

Jumping Pound takes its name from a small creek about six miles southwest of Cochrane. The creek has sharp banks forming a natural enclosure. In the early 1800s the Stoney Indians found that by closing off the narrow gorge of the creek they could trap game inside the confines of the banks. In the buffalo hunts the animals were driven over the cliffs, jumping to their death in the natural pound below — hence the name. In 1944 Shell Oil of Canada discovered gas on the boundary of the creek with a very high rock pressure. Since 1950 the field has been a major source of supply for Canadian Western.

Canadian Western sold well over 24 billion cubic feet of gas in 1950, an increase of nearly four billion over the previous year. Such rapid increase in gas consumption made it important that an ample supply, preferably from several sources, be available at all times. With this in mind, more work was done during the year in upgrading gas storage capabilities in the Bow Island field. An indication of the importance of this enormous storage facility was the fact that in January of that year ten percent of the gas used by the company was drawn from this reservoir. The field also allowed the company to close its normal transmission lines when necessary for repairs, and still supply everyone with gas. This procedure enabled the company to supply Lethbridge in 1948 when both transmission lines crossing the Oldman River failed.

In 1950, the company added about forty-four miles of distribution mains and installed thirty-six hundred services. Major improvements in Calgary itself included installing a mile of sixteen-inch intermediate pressure main on Sixth Street S.E., including a line under the Bow River, to augment the gas supply to the North Hill.

In Lethbridge and district low and medium pressure stations were erected and four new medium pressure regulating systems were installed in existing stations. Five outmoded systems of heating gas prior to reduction from high pressure to intermediate pressure were replaced with new heat exchangers.

9,000 New Customers in One Year — 1950

G as companies president Brownie noted that the companies had built seven million dollars' worth of new plant during 1950 and added nine thousand new customers to the systems. He pointed out also in the annual report to shareholders that this was the year in which Northwestern reached out for new gas supplies with construction of a line to the Leduc oilfield.

Northwestern started taking in surplus oilfield gas from the Leduc field in the early summer. The reserves of this field were estimated to be in the order of 600 billion cubic feet. Northwestern's consulting geologist advised that at least 500 billion cubic feet would have to be added to the company's reserves within the next ten years.

The concerns of the companies about exporting natural gas were alleviated, too, when the Petroleum and Natural Gas Conservation Board, after public hearings extending over many months, ruled that not sufficient gas had been developed in Alberta to justify export.

General manager Dennis Yorath had stated in 1949 that the company was "bursting its breeches" with expansion. Now 1950 turned out to be much more exciting, with the successful completion of a four million dollar capital construction program. "Not only did we build that much new plant but we also operated what in our opinion is a pretty efficient natural gas utility," Yorath said.

Eight new wells were drilled in the Viking-Kinsella field and seventy-four miles of new field and transmission lines were laid. The Viking field station was completely rebuilt in a new location.

Gas service was brought to Fort Saskatchewan on October 27, with a flare-lighting ceremony in which the mayor turned the valve and distribution supervisor Allan Danes lit the flame. Along with Fort Saskatchewan, service was brought to the provincial hospital at Oliver.

Distribution construction during the year almost doubled that of the previous year, with eighty-two miles of new distribution mains. The largest domestic extensions were to new subdivisions in Edmonton.

Largest Gas Pipe in Canada — 1950

O ne of the highlights of 1950 was the laying of three miles of large diameter pipe as part of a looping system tying in a new gate station and serving the Edmonton power plant with gas from the Leduc field. Twenty-inch and sixteen-inch intermediate pressure lines were built from the new No. 1 Gate Station on Edmonton's southeastern limits, across the Dawson Bridge to tie in to the main city loop. The twenty-inch line was not only the largest diameter pipe in the company's system, it was the largest diameter pipe used for the transportation of natural gas in Canada at that time.

The pipe for this line was purchased in the United Kingdom, transported by boat through the Panama Canal and unloaded at Vancouver. Several thousand feet of twelve-inch line for the project were ordered from the Page-Hersey Mill in Welland, Ontario.

Jefferson CD Co-ordinator

D uring the year Northwestern's manager of new business, J.C. (Jim) Jefferson, was appointed Civil Defence Co-ordinator for the City of Edmonton through a public service arrangment in which the company made Jefferson available to the city on a "dollar-a-year" basis.

The local media gave unstinted praise to the selection, and to the gas company for making it possible. During the Second World War, Brigadier Jefferson was the man responsible for getting the first Canadian troops across the Seine, winner of the DSO and Bar, Croix de Guerre and CBE. Now he had the job of co-ordinating all civil defence matters in the Edmonton area.

Coal to Kilowatts — 1950

T he year 1950 saw the beginnings of what would eventually lead to mammoth undertakings of converting coal to kilowatts. Natural gas-fueled power plants were all the rage at the moment, but Canadian Utilities foresaw that Alberta's vast reserves of coal could be economically strip-mined and used for generating electricity. Of special interest were the reserves in an area northeast of Drumheller.

Two companies announced plans for large scale strip mining operations in the areas of Halkirk and Forestburg. The overburden would be removed by large electrically operated draglines, and then the coal itself removed with a giant shovel. It was estimated that coal mining operations in the area would have an annual demand of some five million kilowatt hours.

Initially electricity for those projects was supplied from the Drumheller plant, by a line begun in 1950 and completed the following year. Eventually, the power would be supplied from Canadian Utilities' large new Battle River generating station at Forestburg.

Considerable transmission line building took place in the Drumheller district in 1950. Fifteen miles of 69,000-volt line were built to the strip mining area, and forty-five miles of the same kind of line between Hanna and Castor. These provided an additional power source to feed new oilfield and mining operations, along with rural electrification and the growing domestic load in the towns.

Expansion continued at the Drumheller plant. Changes were made in the new generating station in preparation for a second 7,500-kilowatt turbine and boiler, to double the output of the plant. The new generator was scheduled to go into operation in early 1952.

A significant management change took place at Drumheller at the end of October when Lee Drumheller resigned his position to return to the United States, where he was born.

Lee's father, Sam Drumheller, was an early pioneer rancher in the Red Deer River valley, and was the first person to open a commercial mine in the area. Lee himself worked for the old Mines Power Company which later merged with Union Power Company. When Union Power was taken over by International Utilities Corporation and operated by Canadian Utilities, Lee was appointed district manager.

Moving to the position of district manager on Lee Drumheller's resignation was plant chief Blythe Davidson, who had been with the company at Drumheller since 1940. Davidson had worked in power plants at Lethbridge and Vermilion.

Management Changes — 1950

S ome top-level management changes in Canadian Utilities followed the resignation on September 1, 1950 of general manager Jim MacGregor.

MacGregor left the company to open his own hardware business but he was soon back in the power business when the province appointed him chairman of the Alberta Power Commission, a position which he ably filled for many years.

At the end of the year, Canadian Utilities' president, B.M. Hill, announced the appointment of J.C. (Jack) Dale as general manager, replacing MacGregor. Born in Kitscoty, Alberta, Jack Dale graduated as an electrical engineer from the University of Alberta in 1932 and, after three years with Northwestern Utilities, transferred to Canadian Utilities. His career was interrupted for five years when he served with the Royal Canadian Artillery, from which he retired with the rank of Major. Dale eventually became president of Canadian Utilities.

To fill the position vacated by Jack Dale, A.E. (Gus) Gudmundson was promoted to superintendent of construction. He had been manager of the Vegreville District since 1949. The new manager for the Vegreville District was George O'Brien, manager at Grande Prairie since 1944.

Vegreville rural construction supervisor Ernie Harrison was appointed manager at Grande Prairie. Harrison then had more than twenty years of service with the company.

Canadian Utilities employees, like their colleagues in Northwestern, formed their own employees' association in 1950, electing T.K. Cornborough as president and Anna Murphy as secretary-treasurer. Other members of the first executive council were Harry Brown, head office; Eric Holun and Robert Sutherland, Drumheller District; Jim Nicholls and Paul Drolet, Vegreville District; Ralph Klatt and George Ferraby, Grande Prairie District.

1,000 Miles of Lines — 1950

C anadian Utilities built more than a thousand miles of electric transmission lines in 1950. The bulk of this construction consisted of rural lines on behalf of REAs.

In Grande Prairie, plant capacity was increased with the installation of a 1,200-horsepower diesel unit, replacing an older and smaller unit which was moved to Fort St. John, B.C. to help carry the growing load there.

Ducks Unlimited — 1950

S peaking of sports and wildlife, the Vegreville District had an interesting development in 1950. The Morecambe Dam, a joint project of Ducks Unlimited and the company, was built to conserve water in the string of five Vermilion lakes which supply the bulk of the water for the Lower Vermilion river. The river, in turn, supplied the cooling water for the Vermilion power plant.

During normal years the spring run-off supplied sufficient water for all purposes, but during years like 1949-1950, when practically no run-off was obtained, the level of the lakes dropped so low that no water flowed out into the river.

When Canadian Utilities commissioned the Vermilion plant at the beginning of 1949 the company already had a dam in Vermilion. Late that year, however, it became obvious that a second dam would be needed a few miles upstream, to conserve all available water in the lakes and feed controlled amounts into the river. Ducks Unlimited, always interested in conservation of water for duck breeding and feeding purposes, was contacted and it was arranged that Canadian Utilities would assume the responsibility of obtaining the necessary land and other rights where flooding would occur. Ducks Unlimited in turn would build a dam to meet the requirements of both parties.

When completed in 1951 the dam made it possible to raise the level of the lakes by four feet, providing an even flow of water down the Vermilion River, instead of the usual mad rush of water during spring run-off followed by no flow after June or July.

Blizzards, Floods and Fire — 1951

J ack Dale had a rough initiation as general manager in 1951. It seemed everything went wrong that could go wrong. The previous winter was particularly severe with heavy snowfalls, followed by spring rains and flooding. The mud made travel and working conditions difficult, in fact, at times, impossible.

On March 16 southern and central Alberta were hit with a blizzard, blocking roads and generally creating havoc. At Youngstown the driving snow drifted into the attic of the plant and a hole had to be cut into the roof in order to shovel the snow out. The plant was a soggy mess, with Dick Gretzinger and Jake Goodman working around the clock to try to keep the generator and other equipment dry. Main Street had snowdrifts from ten to twenty feet high.

The eastern part of the province served by the CNR between Calgary and Saskatoon was without train service for a whole week. A west-bound passenger train was stranded near Oyen, and when the storm was over it was completely covered by snow. At Vegreville the drifts in front of the office were so high that a tunnel was needed to gain entrance to the building and Bob Kelly, for one, skied to work.

Many areas of the province were without power for long periods of time as poles and wire were unable to withstand the force of gale winds and driving snow. Eva Crummy, home service director, described the trials and tribulations of the service crews in the Drumheller District in their attempts to restore power:

> When the big snowstorm struck Alberta on March 16, the power lines suffered. Trouble calls started coming in from Hanna and other districts surrounding Drumheller. To relieve the situation at Hanna, the power was rerouted through the Castor substation, while men went to work on the line to get it working before the heavy load came on Monday morning.
>
> Canadian Utilities Limited takes a dim view of any of its customers going without lights and also appreciates the difficulty of the farmer whose pump

won't work to supply his family and livestock with water. And it is serious, too, when the stoker is unable to handle the fuel, so necessary at a time like this. Telephone lines are busy co-ordinating the efforts of men in the field.

Roads weren't impassable. They just weren't! The servicemen fought their way through drifts of snow, identifying their location by the presence of the lines, which in places extended only a short distance above the snow. Cars were out of the question. Even sleighs were impractical. But one serviceman commandeered a horse on the way. He got to the source of the trouble, fixed the line and returned the horse when he was through.

Another serviceman climbed aboard a snowplow which was trying to clear the railway.

Even airplanes were called into service. After considerable effort and much telephoning, a plane was obtained at Calgary to look over the lines in the Wintering Hills district. The plane proved its usefulness under such circumstances and detected the trouble on the line. But when it followed back to where the two servicemen were wearily plodding through the snow, it was unable to pick them up.

Notes were dropped to the men below, directing them to the source of the trouble on the line. The disappointed servicemen followed these directions, located the trouble, repaired it, and ultimately found their way back home, using the same method of transportation that they had used on their way out — their own two feet!

Fire in the Plant — 1951

At 11:23 p.m. on April 11 power to the entire Drumheller District had to be cut off due to a fire in the main switchboard feeding the new Parsons turbine. The fire was caused by a faulty insulator.

The men at the plant put the fire out and tackled the repair job immediately, but the smoke was so thick that they had to run outside every few minutes for fresh air. The main switchboard was a mass of twisted and burned metal. One would have thought it would take weeks to get the plant back on the line. The loyal plant, service and line crew staff, however, had the system tied to a Calgary Power line within two hours, and by five o'clock in the morning they had the turbine running again. Two hours later it was feeding 2,000 kilowatts an hour back into the Calgary Power system.

Elements on the rampage were not the only problems in 1951. There was a shortage of poles for power lines. Supplies were delayed because of "cold war" controls imposed by the government. Experienced help, too, was hard to get.

Dale summed the year up this way: "That so much was accomplished in the face of these difficulties is a real tribute to all concerned at our head office and in the field."

More and More Power Needed — 1951

Much of the work on the transmission system in 1951 was rebuilding lines to provide increased capacity to meet the steadily growing demand for electric power. For instance, the old 22,000-volt line from the Vermilion plant to Vegreville, fifty-six miles in length, was converted to 34,000 volts, bringing the entire line between Lloydminster and Vegreville up to this standard.

Two new sections of 69,000-volt line were built in the Drumheller District, bringing better service to Stettler and Castor, and an adequate supply of electricity for the Battle River strip mining operations north of Halkirk.

In the Grande Prairie District the high voltage grid was extended to Rycroft and then to Spirit River, where the company bought the town-owned plant and distribution system.

In the Vegreville district new power lines were built to bring central station electricity to six new communities. By this time the district was operating a small plant at Cold Lake and from this isolated plant service was extended to Grand Centre.

An event of major significance in the district was an announcement from the Department of National Defence that a thirty million dollar Royal Canadian Air Force airport and training establishment would be located near Grand Centre. On November 1 the company entered into a ten-year agreement with the department to supply the station with electric energy from the Vermilion plant. This would involve building about a hundred miles of 69,000-volt transmission line, along with extensive substation work and upgrading of feeder lines. The route was selected, easements obtained and a start made on staking out a portion of the line.

In Drumheller at year-end, work was still progressing on installation of the second 7,500-kilowatt Parsons steam turbine. A second 100,000-pound boiler was brought into use to help provide steam for the turbine.

Six hundred and ten new farm services were provided in 1951, requiring the construction of almost five hundred miles of distribution lines. Along with demands for farm service were demands for industrial use. At Lloydminster there was the large new Sidney Roofing plant and about fifty new oil wells for which electric pumping was installed.

West to Banff — 1951

The adverse weather in 1951 made life interesting for the gas companies as well as the electrical company. This was the year that Canadian Western built a transmission line from the Jumping Pound field west to Banff, serving en route the large Canada Cement Plant at Exshaw.

In February the crews completed the twelve-inch Jumping Pound line to Calgary. This involved an underwater crossing of the Elbow River at Weaselhead, just west of Calgary. The depth of the pipe from the water surface was seventeen feet. The work was performed from an ice platform at a time when the temperature was minus twenty degrees Fahrenheit.

The crews then moved into the mountains to build the line west to Banff, traversing lakes and swamps on the ice. Every kind of weather was experienced that spring — frost, snow, rain and flooding streams.

In the spring the line across the Morley Flats went quickly. At the same time, a crew was put to work on the tricky job of laying a line across the golf course at Banff. This line had to be finished by June so it would not interfere with the golf season, and it had to be done without leaving a trace of ditches or any damage to trees.

The line from Exshaw to Banff was started in July and completed in September. Although many existing swamps had been crossed in the cold weather, Canadian Western's George Kellam reported that "new ones had been formed by the long steady rains, and many small creeks which were formerly dry were now fair streams." He went on to note that "the beavers, our national emblem, caused endless trouble with their construction, and looked with disdain on our job."

While the weather and the beavers were complicating the job of crossing streams, there was one river crossing of which the crews had pleasant memories. That was the Cascade River job, upstream of which Calgary Power had a hydro dam. "When we were all ready, Calgary Power simply shut off the river and we crossed Cascade like the Israelites crossed the Red Sea — dry-shod," Kellam said.

Wildlife Stories

T he stories of beaver dams and hydro dams in Banff National Park can be added to stories of the bears; particularly one overly-neighborly bear encountered by Spud Stordy when he was installing a service in the town of Banff. He was near the area where the bears were in the habit of scrounging leftover food discarded in garbage cans. The story goes that as Spud was engrossed in attaching an awkward elbow on a service line he felt what seemed to be a hand on his shoulder. Thinking it was only his colleague, Pete Loewen, Spud continued working, but the weight of the "hand" kept getting heavier, so finally he reached up to remove it, and found to his dismay the shaggy fur of Mr. Bruin.

The rest of the story, as related in the staff magazine, goes like this:

> Some have asked how Spud comes to have two patches on the knees of a certain pair of his overalls. They need no longer query, for Spud took off on his hands and knees in such a rush that we are surprised that anything remains of said garment at all.

*The good housewife, coming upon the scene and observing Spud's predica-
ment thereupon dispatched the denizen to his forest with a few quick parries
of her broom.*

*We are pleased to say that Spud is now able to sleep again at nights after
his harrowing experience.*

The meter readers were not to be outdone by the bruin story. They countered
it with a bull story, claiming that their Eric Watson was minding his own business
reading meters in Banff one day when he heard a snort behind him. He turned
to see a huge bull moose, ears back and a threatening gleam in his eye, heading
straight for him. Eric in turn headed straight for the nearest house on the double,
where fortunately a kind lady let him in.

Natural gas was officially turned on in Banff with a flare-lighting ceremony
on Friday, October 19, 1951, at the south end of the Bow River Bridge. The gas
valve was opened by J.A. Hutchinson, superintendent of the park, and lit by
Charles Reid, vice-president of the Banff Advisory Council. Five hundred new
customers were now added to the system.

Telemetering — 1951

A dditions were made during 1951 to the company's recently installed system
of telemetering pressure information from strategic points on the transmission lines to a central control board located in the Manchester high pressure station in Calgary. Having pressures recorded simultaneously all at one point, enabled
engineers to check pressures at the extreme ends of the transmission and distribution systems. Thus, if trouble was indicated at any time, a crew could be sent
to the trouble area immediately.

The two gas companies acquired about seven thousand new customers in 1951,
bringing the combined grand total to over ninety-three thousand. Nearly forty-
seven thousand of those were Canadian Western customers. Gas sales by Canadian Western rose twelve percent to 26 billion cubic feet.

Canadian Western was the last of the three utility companies to form an employees' association. At its first meeting in the early summer of 1951 employees elected
the following executive: Chairman, Walt Hopson; vice-chairman, Adam Kaiser;
small towns, Carl Edlund; West End Shop, Bob Thompson; head office, Lou
Benini; Lethbridge, Ron Cormack; operating and construction, George Fawcett;
service inspections, Tom Jordan; fields, Jack Morrison; services, Carl Windsor;
ladies, Marie McCaffary; main line, Bob Dale; and secretary, Nora Geddes.

Changes in Edmonton — 1951

W ork on the new Calgary head office building proceeded throughout the
year, and at year-end was nearing completion. While this was going on

in Calgary, in Edmonton Northwestern converted its 104 Street garage into office space.

Actually, there was talk of putting up a new office building in Edmonton, but prices were high and there was a shortage of structural steel, so the decision was taken to convert the garage into office space for the time being. The vehicles which had been housed here were then temporarily sheltered in a quonset type building.

The front office at 104 Street also received a face-lifting, with installation of three-quarter-inch unbreakable glass doors, new flooring, new display areas, better lighting and improved customer service facilities.

The additional office space was sorely needed, as the company continued its rapid expansion. The next major new community to receive gas service in 1951 was the town of St. Albert, just north of Edmonton.

Service was also extended to the Griesbach Army Barracks and the Namao Airport, north of Edmonton, during the year, and then in the fall the eastern extremity of the system was extended to the Wainwright Army Camp.

Twelve new wells and thirty-three miles of large diameter pipe were laid as part of a fourth transmission line from the Viking field to Edmonton.

Apart from construction challenges, Northwestern wrestled with rate hearings in 1951. President Brownie argued the company was faced with sharply rising costs on every hand, and if it was to remain sound, in order to treat its customers, staff and investors fairly, it could not escape the necessity of raising rates. Accordingly, an application was made on March 15 to the Board of Public Utility Commissioners for rate increases. By year-end, after extensive hearings, approval for increases was assured.

Brownie pointed out in the annual report to shareholders that over a period of fifteen years the company had kept pace with intense growth challenges under difficult conditions, and had in fact made several rate reductions to its customers. Even now, with rate increases, "the average Edmonton domestic user still has an annual gas bill lower than before the war, and lower than it would be almost anywhere else on the continent for the same annual consumption," he said.

More Honors — 1951

The year brought more honors for key personnel of the companies. The Edmonton Flying Club made Dennis Yorath an honorary life member. Northwestern's chief utilization engineer, Graham Dale, was nominated for the Executive of the Year award by representatives of sixty executive associations from Canada, England and the United States. Milner, chairman of the three companies, was honored by two eastern Canadian universities, receiving the degree of doctor of civil law from Mount Allison University in New Brunswick; and degree of doctor of canon law from the University of King's College in Halifax.

J.G. Pattison, an early employee of Canadian Western who was decorated posthumously with the Victoria Cross in the First World War, was further honored by the federal government in 1951. Five mountains in Jasper National Park were named in honor of Canadian recipients of the Victoria Cross. The mountains are all visible from the highway which goes through the park. The first name to appear in the list was that of Private Pattison.

100,000 Gas Customers — 1952

N orthwestern Utilities and Canadian Western both reached a milestone in 1952 as each company installed its fifty thousandth meter.

Among the more than four thousand new customers that Northwestern added to its system during the year were the Canadian Industries plant, with an estimated annual consumption of nearly a billion cubic feet, and Alexandra Brick and Tile, with an annual consumption of nearly a quarter of a billion cubic feet.

The major building project during the year for Northwestern was the construction of the newest and most easterly operating base, the Irma field station. The new utility building housed the office, stockroom and garage. The town agent's house was built for Len Loades and his family, and an additional staff house was built to accommodate a staff of eight.

At the Viking field station, too, a new dwelling was built, along with an eighteen-foot addition to the field office, and landscaping.

Safety First — 1952

T he energy group intensified its accident prevention program in 1952, and the results were encouraging. The accident frequency for the gas companies dropped from forty-three to twenty-six accidents per million man-hours worked, but it still wasn't as low as the accident frequency rate of member companies of the American Gas Association. More work was needed.

The loss of George Duncan was a grim reminder that safety cannot be overemphasized. On September 24 Duncan and John MacDonald were working in a new regulating station when a flash fire occurred, burning both men severely. They were rushed to hospital, where Duncan died on October 3. MacDonald went on to a thirty-five year career with the company.

George Duncan had been popular with the staff. Scottish by birth, he had survived army action in Europe and the Mediterranean in the war, after which he joined the gas company as a truck driver and heavy machine operator.

In electrical operations the need for safety consciousness was brought into sharp focus by the tragic death of young Joseph Hooks, an employee at Stettler, on November 26. Joe was lowering a dead line, mounted on poles, under a live 33,000-volt circuit to allow a high oil rig to pass beneath the line. While he was pulling the dead line down, a wire in an adjacent span snapped up into the high voltage line, causing his death.

Move to New Building — 1952

In the south, the highlight of 1952 for Canadian Western was the move into the new office building at the end of June. An open house was held on Saturday, July 5, when about five hundred visitors were guided through the building by staff members.

The main entrance, through glass doors, brought visitors into the foyer, with walls of polished marble. In the main public area, visitors were impressed by the decor and the feeling of spaciousness. Executive offices and the boardroom were on the second floor. The basement featured a three-hundred-seat auditorium, home service test kitchen, printing room and boiler room. The building boasted a natural gas-fired air conditioning system as well.

In the field, main line crews carried out an interesting project building a pipeline bridge across the Bow River just below the Seebe dam. This was part of a change in the line to Banff. A new road approach from the Banff highway paralleled and then crossed the Canadian Western pipeline. The pipeline bridge was built on the south bank, cables were strung across the river and the bridge was pulled across, sliding on the cables. Then it was lifted into place on its permanent bank seats. The eight-inch transmission pipe was attached to the bridge, crossing the chasm about sixty feet above water level. The temperature at the time was forty degrees below zero, accompanied by high winds.

The town of Banff by year-end was almost at full load, with nearly eight hundred meters in operation. The world famous Banff Springs Hotel was in the process of renovating its heating system to use natural gas exclusively.

Convocation Address — 1952

More honors came to the companies in 1952. Board chairman Milner was made an honorary doctor of laws by the University of Alberta at its fall convocation, and Brigadier Jefferson went to Ottawa to join the national civil defence program.

Milner was chosen to give the convocation address at the university, and chose as his topic the place of the individual in the Canadian economic and political system. Summing up his thoughts at the conclusion of his speech, he said:

> *The case I make today is for the encouragement of the individual and an individualistic outlook. It is an attitude of mind.*
>
> *It fits into no pattern of uniformity. It is prepared in freedom of thought and freedom of action. It is prepared to battle for moral principles, and to stand up and be counted regardless of the consequences.*

129

It was the individualist — the rugged individualist if you like — both great and small, both famous and unheard of, who created the splendor of the Elizabethan age and founded the worldwide power of the Anglo-Saxon. He laid the long enduring basis of our present prosperity. He can be discarded or forgotten at our peril.

We Canadians have the future in front — not behind us. None could be more aware of it than those who live in Alberta. We have prospered as individualists in a society as nearly classless as the world has known. We believe that concentration of power is bad whether vested in government, in business, or in pressure groups. We have no love for the European doctrines of paternalism and state socialism. We expect and want no Utopia, nor have we any wish to be the guinea pigs of Utopian experiments. Government should exist within the proper sphere of its activities as the servant of the people. As individuals, and individualists, we should keep it there.

National Appointment for Jefferson

J im Jefferson was loaned to the federal government as deputy civil defence co-ordinator, and director of operations and training for Canada under General F.F. Worthington, Federal Civil Defence Co-ordinator.

In his capacity as co-ordinator for Edmonton, Jefferson had developed the city's civil defence organization to what was considered a model for all of Canada. "We wish Jim good luck and every possible success in the big job he has undertaken," said the editor of *The Courier* in making the announcement to the utilities staff. "We will look forward to the day when he returns to this company, having placed Canada's civil defence on a sound footing."

Power at Cold Lake — 1952

O ne of the biggest electrical projects of 1952 was the building of a 69,000-volt line from the Vermilion plant to the Cold Lake air force training centre. This hundred-mile line brought central station service to Cold Lake, which until then was served by a small diesel plant located in a log cabin.

Oil developments were projected for the Bonnyville area, where one refinery was already under construction. The long-range need for more generating capacity in the district was becoming obvious. Studies indicated that a unit for peak loads would be the most logical next step, and that it should be located at the Vermilion plant. An order was placed with Brown-Boveri of Switzerland for a gas turbine generator set, capable of delivering 9,400 kilowatts. Shipment was scheduled for February 1954. When installed, it would be Canada's first gas turbine to power an electric generator.

Another major project in 1952 was the installation of the second Parsons turbogenerator at Drumheller. Shipped from England to Churchill on Hudson Bay, the equipment arrived later than expected, all sixty tons of it occupying three flatcars and a boxcar.

Although late delivery put the project severely behind schedule, the Drumheller staff went all-out to get the generator installed by the beginning of December, in time for the peak load period.

The Drumheller District was expanding rapidly. New oilfield and coal field operations were hungry for electricity. To the east the transmission of central station power now extended all the way to the Youngstown-Oyen area, and the local diesel plant at Youngstown was shut down. In the Hanna area service was extended to a strip-mining coal field at Sheerness, the second coal field in the district to employ an all-electric shovel in its mining operation.

The two small generators at Youngstown were shipped to Grande Prairie and Fort St. John to increase generating capacity in the Peace River country and in Canadian Utilities' most northerly plant. Discoveries of oil and gas in appreciable quantities in the Fort St. John area were radically increasing the need for more electric power, and a start was made on a new plant building. The company reached an agreement with the federal government to serve the local airport, so that the Department of Transport, which had been supplying the airport load from its own plant, would retain the plant for standby use only.

Operation Dustbowl — 1953

It was Friday, February 13, 1953. But the day went smoothly and at five o'clock the TGIF (Thank God it's Friday!) Club left Canadian Western's Calgary offices for the Valentine's Day weekend, convinced there was no bad luck.

Then at nine o'clock in the evening an incident occurred which indicated maybe all wasn't well after all. There was something rotten in the gas system, because the Jumping Pound plant "passed a slug of sour gas." When that happens it becomes imperative that the sour gas be blown to the atmosphere before it causes more trouble. This was done. The sour gas was caught in the transmission line before it reached Calgary, and blown out of the line during the early morning of February 14.

Still all was not well. About eight o'clock that evening the telemeters at the Manchester high pressure station showed that the regulator at the Jumping Pound connection near the nitrogen plant was not operating properly. Transmission foreman Joe Wise went to investigate, and found that the regulator was leaking at the packing gland. He adjusted the controls and tried to stop the leak; then went to an adjacent building to phone the office. While he was phoning the regulating building exploded and burned down. Emergency measures were instituted to bypass this station with gas supply for Calgary, and the wreckage was cleared away on Sunday morning.

When the regulator was taken apart in a post mortem at the Calgary West End Shop, it was found to be badly worn because of large quantities of abrasive silica dust. The trouble was not over. Now calls started to come in from customers in the central and northern parts of Calgary. The pilot lights on their appliances were going out, and the flames in their furnaces were burning low. The gas company called in extra servicemen to handle the trouble, and extra men were put on duty for the night.

One of the men who was called in for emergency duty on Sunday evening was H.P. (Ted) Forsey. He was just getting interested in a mystery story on the radio when he was called away to help with what he later dubbed Operation Dustbowl. When he arrived at the main office he found telephone calls were "flooding the switchboard and sending the operators nearly crazy." Forsey, along with Art Smith, Hal Robbins, Fred Humphries and others, set up an emergency telephone system and started dispatching servicemen to handle the complaints.

After 11 p.m., when most people were going to bed, the calls subsided a bit, but at 6:30 in the morning of February 16 it was worse than ever. All servicemen were pressed into duty immediately, along with all the meter readers who had any knowledge whatsoever about trouble-shooting. Extra men were called in from Lethbridge to help. "Calls kept pouring in," Forsey reported. "In all, over eleven hundred calls were completed by fifty-five men during the period from 8 a.m. to 10:30 p.m. creating what must be a record for one day's operations."

It was determined that silica dust plugging the small orifices in gas burners was causing the trouble. Emergency announcements were made on the air and in the newspapers to explain to customers what was happening. Dedicated gas company employees worked many long hours all that week. The girls in the home service department did yeoman service by preparing meals for hungry crews of trouble-shooters.

After the Monday crisis the calls began to taper off, and by the next Sunday, February 22, things were almost back to normal. In total thirty-five hundred calls had been completed during the emergency.

The trouble was traced to an incident at the Shell Jumping Pound scrubbing plant on Christmas Day, seven weeks before the mid-February crisis in Calgary. The plant had passed sour gas and had belched some nineteen barrels of silica beads, each about one-eighth inch in diameter, into the pipeline system. These beads came from a tower which was used for extracting moisture from raw gas before it was fed into the system. A retaining screen in the tower failed because it was a factory-installed copper screen which should not have been used for sour gas service. Once in the pipelines the beads were ground to dust by abrasion as they moved through the lines clogging the system, particularly regulator parts.

Gas Sales at Record Level — 1953

D espite challenges like Operation Dustbowl, 1953 was another successful year for Canadian Western with nearly five thousand new services added throughout the system. Again, as for many years in the past, the company distributed more natural gas than any other company in Canada, volume rising to well over 28 billion cubic feet.

In Edmonton, Northwestern was not far behind in its volume of gas sales with nearly 26 billion cubic feet. But its rate of growth was even more spectacular, with an increase of nearly six thousand customers in 1953. Nearly five million dollars were spent on capital additions to plant, straining the company's financial resources severely. No common stock dividends were paid to shareholders by either of the two gas companies that year, all earnings being retained for expansion purposes. Also, to obtain extra cash for expansion, the companies sold some of their security holdings, including more than one hundred thousand common shares of Anglo-Canadian Oil stocks.

By year-end it was obvious that even though a rate increase had just gone into effect, it would not be long before another one would be necessary to enable Northwestern to meet the increasing costs of doing business.

Vermilion Added to System — 1953

T he major new community added to Northwestern's system in 1953 was Vermilion, where the company acquired the property of Franco Public Service Limited, which had been serving the town with gas for thirteen years from nearby wells.

The acquisition of the Vermilion distribution system was largely due to the depletion of gas reserves in the Vermilion field, hastened by the increasing demands of the Canadian Utilities' power plant which had been converted to gas and tied in to the distribution system some time previously. Vermilion Consolidated Oils, Ltd., the owners of the field, thought they had ample supplies of gas to feed the power plant by extending their field gathering system to tie in a gas well called VCO 4.

This well had an interesting history. When first brought in it had an extremely large open flow and was described as the largest well in the British Empire. At one time it was planned to use this source to supply a pipeline to Saskatoon, but that project died with the outbreak of the Second World War. For lack of markets, VCO 4 remained unconnected until the power plant was converted to natural gas. After being connected, it produced gas at a rapidly declining rate for only five months, when it drowned out due to water encroachment.

In view of all this Franco Public Service was quite receptive to an offer by Northwestern to purchase the town distribution system since the assurance of future gas supplies required the construction of a pipeline connecting the system to the Kinsella field.

In Canadian Utilities' electrical operations in 1953 work was started to enlarge the plant at Vermilion in preparation for the first gas turbine in Canada, due to arrive early the next year. To ensure an adequate supply of gas, Northwestern Utilities ran a gas transmission line from the Kinsella field to Vermilion.

Canadian Utilities, in its twenty-fifth year, had grown from small beginnings in the Vegreville District to a sizeable electric utility, serving nearly twenty-five thousand customers in more than two hundred communities. Northwestern, at the same time, was in its thirtieth year. It was now producing gas from more than one hundred wells at Viking, Fort Saskatchewan and Legal, with one hundred and eighty-six miles of gathering lines, four hundred and eighty-nine miles of transmission lines, and six hundred and two miles of distribution mains.

Although oilfield activities were responsible for much of the continued growth of Canadian Utilities, in the total picture the rural department had the most impressive record in 1953. More than eighteen hundred farms were connected, bringing the total number of farms served to fifty-two hundred. To service them, seventeen hundred miles of line had to be built, bringing the total to forty-two hundred miles of rural electrification association lines served from the company's transmission system.

Northwestern in the Lead — 1954

N orthwestern Utilities stole the show in 1954. This was the year in which its sales of natural gas soared to 33 billion cubic feet, for an increase of twenty-nine percent over the previous year. The company not only surpassed its southern Alberta sister but was now Canada's largest distributor of natural gas.

The company's successes were spectacular. And the esteem in which it was held by the public was never better, as reflected in the fact that early during the year Edmonton city council unanimously agreed to renew the franchise for a further ten years.

The number of customers increased by almost five thousand, bringing the total to well over sixty thousand. This figure had more than doubled in the short span of seven years.

Two additional gas sources were connected during the year, bringing the total to seven. A forty-mile, twelve-inch pipeline costing four and a half million dollars was built from the Bonnie Glen-Wizard Lake fields, to bring an initial 15 million cubic feet per day of oilfield residue gas to Edmonton. A smaller pipeline was run to the Acheson field.

The Canadian Gas Association held its forty-seventh annual meeting at the Banff Springs Hotel that year. Northwestern's general manager, Dennis Yorath, giving his retiring address as president of the association, to the six hundred delegates, said:

> . . . *Our association has got to become a business organization prepared to get out and do a job on behalf of what is about to become one of Canada's major industries.*

. . . If we do not do this, the only alternative is to rely upon the American Gas Association to act for us. I suggest to you that that is impractical, unsound, and unfair to them and us. The two organizations will always be closely associated, and we will always hope to get a great deal of help from them, but if for no other reason than that our governments and legislatures are very different, in my opinion we must speak to Canada for the industry with our own voice.

The Canadian gas industry has come of age — tomorrow it starts treading the road to maturity.

IU Directors Visit Companies — 1954

The directors of International Utilities Corporation, headed by President Howard Butcher III, toured the company's Canadian properties that summer. These properties represented an investment of more than one hundred million dollars.

With Butcher were Eric Butler, vice-president; W.P. Miller, president of the Philadelphia Chamber of Commerce; J. Paul Crawford, vice-president of the New York Trust Company; T.S. Watson, securities broker; Norman S. Robertson, president of the North American Life Assurance Company; F.W. Clark of New York, securities broker; and W.E. Warner of Philadelphia, attorney-at-law.

Butcher told the media he was greatly impressed with the rate of development in Alberta, and that International Utilities expected to continue its program of making capital works expenditures of nearly ten million dollars annually in the province.

Television was just beginning to make its impact on Canada. The gas companies were among the first industries in Alberta to use this advertising medium, sponsoring a series of dramatic half-hour programs entitled Favorite Story, produced in Hollywood and starring Adolph Menjou. The trend-setting commercials on the program were produced for both Alberta gas companies by a U.S. film group, in co-operation with the Seattle Gas Company.

It was a great year for Northwestern Utilities and for Edmonton, topped off by the Edmonton Eskimos bringing the Grey Cup home from the exciting November 27 football classic in Toronto. Northwestern had a float in the Grey Cup parade.

It wasn't exactly an uneventful year for Canadian Western either. Calgary was growing by leaps and bounds. The city annexed surrounding land to accommodate new subdivisions, particularly the Thorncliffe Heights and Glendale areas. In all, gas service was supplied to eight new residential districts in Calgary in 1954.

Forty-two miles of new mains were installed in Calgary and district, an increase of almost twenty percent over 1953 construction. A new pipe coating yard was built in Manchester and a new stores building at the West End Shop.

F.A. Brownie Heads Three Utilities — 1954

A major step in bringing the management of the gas and electrical operations together occurred in 1954 with the appointment of F. Austin Brownie as president of Canadian Utilities, in addition to his position as president of both gas companies. This appointment was occasioned by the retirement of Bruce M. Hill at the age of sixty-five. Hill was one of the early employees of Canadian Utilities. He started with the company in 1928 when it was still Mid-West Utilities, and served it for twenty-six years, five of them as president.

Brownie was forty-six when he assumed the Canadian Utilities' presidency. He was a graduate of the University of Alberta in civil engineering. He joined Northwestern Utilities in 1935, and five years later transferred to Canadian Western as assistant general manager. He subsequently became general manager of Canadian Western, and was appointed president of the two gas companies in 1949.

Brownie's year-end summary of the accomplishments of the three companies noted that thirteen thousand new gas and electric customers were connected to the systems, and the companies spent nine million dollars on capital additions necessary to serve new and existing customers. Fifteen million dollars in new capital was raised to assist in meeting these and future capital expenditures.

Turbine Starts at Vermilion — 1954

The highlight of 1954 for Canadian Utilities was the commissioning of the new gas turbine at Vermilion, on November 26. With production superintendent Roy Nurse as master of ceremonies, Alberta industries minister N.A. Willmore unveiled the control panel and turned the switch which activated the unit.

The turbine started to turn, and Nurse explained to the guests the mechanical sequence which took place as the machine gained speed. When finally up to speed the generator driven by the gas turbine had to be synchronized to the system. The delicate operation of synchronizing fell to general manager Jack Dale. As the synchronoscope dial showed the impulses coming together, Nurse described what Dale was doing, and when the switch slammed into place at precisely the right second, Dale grinned and Nurse called out: "She's on the line — she's making power and she's making money!" Chief plant engineer Jack Kneale and his boys beamed. All the months of hard work were starting to pay off.

In the Peace River country there was further coming together of the energy group in 1954. The company entered into joint operations of a generating station with Northland Utilities at Fairview. This step was taken to use the low-cost natural gas available in the area. In the fall a 1,200-kilowatt natural gas-fired unit owned by Canadian Utilities was installed in the new plant building, which housed other units owned by Northland. In the years that followed a close working relationship with Northland Utilities evolved, leading eventually to amalgamation of the companies.

To tie the Fairview plant into the Grande Prairie system some thirty-two miles of 69,000-volt line were built between Fairview and Rycroft. This line featured the longest power line span in Alberta — thirty-eight hundred feet across the Peace River. The line was energized and the new plant at Fairview commissioned on November 9, with Northland president Walter Schlosser, Canadian Utilities president Austin Brownie, and Jack Dale, Roy Nurse, and Jack Ford in attendance, along with mayors and councillors from towns in the district.

In the Drumheller District, plans were announced for the construction of a new generating station on the Battle River near Forestburg using strip-mined coal for fuel.

Finally, in 1954 Canadian Utilities strengthened its radio communications network, particularly its shortwave radio communications in the Peace River country. The total number of sets was now fifty-eight, including seventeen main or ground stations.

GASCO Players

R ecounting the highlights of the early fifties would be incomplete without mention of Northwestern Utilities' GASCO Players, an informal in-house group which performed skits and musicals at special functions each year, particularly at the annual awards banquet in the spring.

The 1954 awards banquet was a special one, the previous year having been Northwestern's thirtieth anniversary. The GASCO Players put on a show at that banquet, held at the Macdonald Hotel, which they called Musical Memories.

Ten years later the GASCO Players again did an anniversary show, this time for the company's fortieth anniversary, and they called it Life Begins at Forty! Over the years they have done many others, with names such as April in Paris, Magic Carpet Fantasy, Gas Lite Gaieties, and This Evening Has Twelve Months. Canada's centennial year featured a production humorously titled, Canada, Let's Give it Back to the Indians.

In the seventies the shows of the GASCO Players tapered off and for a few years went into limbo, while the company experimented with hiring professional outside talent for its annual events. "Bringing in entertainment simply was not the same as doing our own in-house productions," commented Doreen Barry, supervisor – customer information centre, the costume designer and always one of the guiding forces for the shows over the years. In the eighties Bruce Dafoe, general manager, brought the shows back. Younger people today occupy many of the traditional roles, and the fun of utilizing in-house talent is back.

For many years Al Shanley was producer and director of most of the shows. Bill Wagner was deeply involved, as were Al McGarvey, Cliff Gates, Jack Livingstone, Peter Marples, John Gray, Mills Parker, Les Henderson, Bill Hite, Wally Scott, Cathy Sunderland, Gus Mireault, Ed Matthews, and many others.

Many of the same performers who took part in the GASCO Players productions also took part in the annual Children's Christmas party. The marching band at these parties, with Jack Winters in charge, always went over big with the kids, as did Santa Claus, his helpers and the clowns, all company employees giving of their talents.

CHAPTER 7

The Late Fifties

South to Cardston — 1955

Canadian Western was back in the news headlines in 1955 with its own southern extension — the Raymond-Magrath-Cardston transmission line from Lethbridge. With nearly sixty miles of pipeline, it was the largest single extension since the company's original system was installed in 1912.

The Cardston extension was approved at the beginning of the year. The route was chosen, surveyed, and most of the river, creek and coulee crossings were installed by the end of April. Line construction started in May but was halted by three weeks of rain and snow. Altogether the entire line was installed in nine working weeks.

Crews from Lethbridge and Calgary started construction of the distribution mains in Raymond and Cardston on a wet, snowy April 18. The wet conditions continued for nearly a month, ending in a paralyzing snowstorm on Friday, May 13. It lasted three days, and left twenty-two inches of heavy snow. "Such weather not only brought the gas company crews to a halt," said senior engineer Elmer Provost, "it also grounded the ducks that were foolish enough to enter sunny Alberta a little early."

Despite having to fight mud and snow, the crews made good progress, and it was not long until they were ahead of schedule with the installation of mains and services. The entire project was completed in September.

The turn-on ceremony for the southern line was held in Lethbridge on August 24. Among the fifty guests were Mayor E.P. Tanner of Magrath, head of the franchise negotiating committee; Mayor Frank P. Taylor of Raymond; Mayor Henry H. Atkins of Cardston; Mayor William N. Hogenson of Stirling; and Harold Long, managing editor of the Lethbridge Herald.

The mayors were high in their praise of the efficient and courteous manner in which the gas company executed its construction program, and expressed appreciation that the company hired local labor, relieving seasonal unemployment.

Following a banquet the guests were taken to the compressor station near the Lethbridge airport. There the four mayors turned the valve to mark the official opening of service.

Canadian Western spent more than three million dollars on capital works in 1955, with about half the money going into the Cardston extension. While this extension was the longest job in terms of miles of pipe, the most difficult job of the year was replacement of the company's lines crossing the Oldman River, just north of Lethbridge. The pipeline crossing required a trench twenty-eight feet deep, as engineers anticipated a future shift in the river's course.

Well over five thousand customers were added to the system in 1955, bringing the total to nearly sixty-four thousand.

The Canadian Western team worked hard that year. They played hard, too, at the first annual intercompany curling bonspiel in Red Deer on February 20. Eight rinks were sent from Canadian Western and Northwestern. As the last rock came to rest it was found that Canadian Western had won the F.A. Brownie Trophy by twenty-one points. The trophy was presented to Walt Hopson by Bruce Willson, director of administrative services.

Export Permit

B ruce Willson was in the news in the spring of 1955 when he spoke at the annual convention of the Canadian Gas Association at Niagara Falls, Ontario. TransCanada Pipelines had a permit from the Alberta Petroleum and Natural Gas Conservation Board to export gas from the province at a rate of 540 million cubic feet per day, and Willson commented on it:

> . . . This is a very substantial daily quantity and equivalent to the capacity of many of the cross-country pipelines of the U.S.
>
> It may come as a surprise to some of you to learn that in Alberta, the capacity of the systems of the two major utility companies is approximately 450 million cubic feet per day, or over eighty per cent of that proposed for TransCanada.
>
> These systems have been developed and expanded to meet the growing market requirements of the province and while this local natural gas development has taken place rather quietly, it has been, nevertheless, substantial.
>
> Rather than being only distributing companies, the Alberta utilities own, operate and maintain five producing fields together with widespread

transmission facilities. Coupled with the fact that the companies carry out their own pipeline construction, the past ten years have been ones of substantial activity in all departments.

However, the integration that exists under these circumstances has made possible numerous economies and even though the major plant expansion has taken place during periods of high cost, the companies are proud of the fact that the rates charged for natural gas service are on the average within five percent of those of 1939.

There was a growing interest right across Canada in Alberta's abundance of natural gas. This was particularly obvious in the number of visitors from other provinces who went through the gas companies' display areas at the Calgary Stampede and the Edmonton Exhibition that year. The displays depicted "fifty years of progress" in commemoration of Alberta's fiftieth anniversary. At the Calgary Stampede alone, with its record-breaking crowd that year, an estimated two hundred thousand persons passed through the display under the grandstand. The central area of the display, called The Hall of Flame, contained seating accommodation for one hundred guests who were entertained by Canadian Western's Ted Forsey at the organ.

The Northwestern display in Edmonton featured a major appliance promotion in connection with the Golden Dream Home which had an all-gas kitchen.

New Shop Building — 1955

N orthwestern's construction program and the growth of the company continued their record-breaking climb in 1955.

The number of customers had passed the sixty-five thousand mark by year-end, payrolls were getting close to two and one half million dollars and there were more than four hundred employees.

Major additions to the system were Spruce Grove and Stony Plain, west of Edmonton, served from the Acheson field, also west of the city. To the east a distribution system was started to serve the new townsite of Campbelltown, initially with more than one hundred houses. This community later became Sherwood Park. The largest industrial and commercial loads acquired that year were Inland Cement Company, Premier Steel Mills and Westmount Shoppers Park.

The early freeze-up in the fall came at the peak of distribution construction programs and created some problems. It became necessary to thaw the ground by burning straw and coal along the ditch lines. Ironically, for a time the gas company became one of the best customers for coal in central Alberta. Cold weather is always good for gas sales, though, and that year the company's gas sales revenue came close to the ten million dollar mark.

Northwestern's new meter repair shop and office building on 112 Street was officially occupied on October 3. It housed portions of the distribution department, technical services department and sales and service department, in addition to a shop designed to handle the reconditioning of about one hundred gas meters per day.

A two-hundred-and-fifty-seat auditorium on the second floor was the feature of the centre. It was ideal for cooking demonstrations and other gatherings, with its stage and fully equipped kitchen.

Finally, another step forward was heralded by the acquisition of new property south of Jasper Avenue on 104 Street, with plans to lay the foundation the next year for a new office building. At the same time Canadian Western announced that six storeys would be added to its downtown Calgary office building.

Battle River — 1955

The most spectacular project in Canadian Utilities' electrical operations in 1955 was the start on the coal-fired electric generating station on the Battle River, eleven miles southwest of Forestburg. Tenders for the seven million dollar plant and transmission lines were called in the early spring. The general contract was awarded to Mannix-Gill Limited.

A dam thirty feet high was built across the river at a point due north of Halkirk. Four hundred acres of valley land were cleared for a reservoir, which would be ten miles long and a mile wide when full. Water from this man-made lake was to be used for condensing steam in the powerhouse.

The boiler was purchased from Combustion Engineering Limited, to be installed the following year, and the turbine-generator purchased from Brown-Boveri Limited of Switzerland. Initial output was to be 32 megawatts, with plans for additional generating units to be added in years to come. The nearby open-pit mines were to supply the coal for fuel.

While this work was going on the new gas turbine at Vermilion was purring away. It put in sixty-five hundred hours of operation that year, converting 700 million cubic feet of gas into 34 million kilowatt hours of electricity, but soon it would be overshadowed by the giant coal-to-kilowatts plant to the south. Already thirty miles of a 138 kilovolt tie line to the Battle River station were completed, with another fifty-two miles to be built the next year.

Grande Prairie — 1955

In Grande Prairie on June 2, 1955, J.H. Vollans, assistant supervisor of Northern Alberta Railways, arrived on a special train with a very special load — the biggest internal combustion engine in Alberta. The natural-gas-fueled, internal combustion reciprocating engine was thirty-eight feet long, sixteen feet high and fifteen feet wide.

It had sixteen cylinders and was capable of developing 3,700 horsepower. It cost one hundred and ninety thousand dollars. In the Grande Prairie plant it was to drive a 2,500-kilowatt generator, purchased from English Electric at a cost of ninety-seven thousand dollars.

The base for the engine had been poured earlier, and as soon as the engine and generator were moved into position, a steel building was erected over them. It was officially commissioned on December 12, by Alberta's industries and labor minister Ray Reierson.

Large-scale generation of electricity was new for Grande Prairie, and there were a few problems, particularly fires. One occurred in December 1954, that caused considerable damage. Another fire in November 1955, started in some new electrical equipment. The entire staff turned out and fought the blaze for about an hour and a half before they brought it under control. Two months later, however, after some building repairs and replacement of three switch panels, everything was back to normal.

Grande Prairie was booming. North Star Oil Company Limited announced plans to build a twenty-five hundred barrel per day oil refinery at a cost of two and one half million dollars. There was also Peace River Pipe Line Company, which wanted power as soon as its pipeline from Valleyview to Edson was completed. This required construction of a 69-kilovolt line from Clairmont, six miles north of Grande Prairie, to the oilfield south of Valleyview, a distance of seventy-seven miles.

Speed was of the essence. The line was started in mid-August. Despite numerous problems, including bad weather and the necessity of scrounging heavy duty transformers from other districts, it was in service by the end of the year.

Punch Card Billing — 1955

C ustomer billing was becoming more voluminous year by year and was crying for a more streamlined system. A survey carried out by Peat, Marwick, Mitchell and Company recommended major changes to the utility companies.

The survey indicated the companies were now serving enough customers that "punch-card" billing would be economical. It was recommended that an International Business Machines system be adopted. The eighteen-month conversion program started on September 6, 1955 and brought the companies into the computer age, marking the beginning of an ongoing process destined to revolutionize not only billing procedures, but accounting, payroll, inventory control and a host of other tasks.

F. Austin Brownie

E arly in 1956 a sense of deep sadness descended on the companies. President F. Austin Brownie died in Calgary on January 23, at the age of forty-seven.

The esteem in which he was held by all who knew him, and the sense of loss felt by employees of all three companies, is reflected in the following tribute in the staff magazine:

> *With Brownie's passing we have lost a most capable leader; one who guided our organization through its greatest years of expansion, with skill and ability. With his passing, too, we mourn the loss of a fine gentleman, and a friend to all . . . a quiet, gracious man, with a sympathetic regard for the feelings of others.*
>
> *A tireless worker, Brownie spent long hours at his desk, directing the affairs of our companies with little thought for his own health. He carried the burden of responsibility for the company's welfare, and his thinking and direction, his feeling of what was right and good for our organization, our customers and for the employees, will surely be remembered.*
>
> *Had he lived — this year Austin Brownie would have received his twenty-year service button. And he would have worn it with pride, for our late president gave service to this company in generous measure.*

Frank Austin Brownie was born in Montreal. The family moved to Calgary when he was a boy. There he received his primary and secondary education. In 1931 he graduated from the University of Alberta with a BA and a year later he received his BSc in civil engineering.

In 1935 he joined the staff of Northwestern Utilities as an assistant engineer. Four years later he was transferred to Calgary as assistant to the general manager of Canadian Western. He was appointed general manager in 1948. The following year he became president of the two gas companies and in 1954 became president of Canadian Utilities as well.

He was past president of the Canadian Gas Association and past director of the American Gas Association; past president of the Association of Professional Engineers of Alberta, and a member of the Engineering Institute of Canada.

Management Changes — 1956

A t an emergency meeting of the board of directors of the companies, held on January 27, H.R. Milner was appointed acting president, pending the annual board meeting later in the year. Milner had been president of the three companies from 1932 to 1949, when he was succeeded by Brownie. At that time he became board chairman of the companies, a position he continued to hold as well as that of acting president.

At the annual meeting held in May, Jack Dale was appointed president of Canadian Utilities, and Dennis Yorath president of the two gas companies. Milner continued to hold the office of chairman of the Canadian subsidiaries of International Utilities.

Other executive changes included the appointment of Cody McPherson, general manager of Canadian Western, as senior vice-president of the two gas companies; Fred A. Smith as vice-president, finance, of the three companies; K.L. McFadyen as comptroller; and the election of Bruce Willson to the board of both gas companies. H.W. Francis, a director of Northwestern, was also elected to the board of Canadian Western.

The Battle River Dam — 1956

It was Friday, April 13, 1956 — three years and two months after Canadian Western's Operation Dustbowl in Calgary, and eleven months to the day after a paralyzing May storm struck Alberta and dumped twenty-two inches of heavy snow on the countryside. The men working on construction of the Battle River station kept telling themselves there was no bad luck on Friday the 13th. In fact, it brought good luck to a few of them who had bet that this would be the day when water from the man-made lake would rise high enough to start flowing over the spillway at the new damsite.

The water went over at 9:45 a.m. There was a reservoir of cooling water ten miles long and a mile in width — a beautiful lake dotted with islands — a massive dam and a sturdy-looking concrete spillway.

The runoff kept coming. In less than a week it was three feet deep over the spillway. Then on April 21 a little water showed up on the downstream side of the dam. This was the wrong side for water! The crew tried to plug the hole in the dam but the water kept coming. The trickle turned into a stream and the stream turned into a flood. Then half the spillway broke away and swept down the swollen river.

Unless the spillway was rebuilt immediately there was no hope of getting the new power plant on stream that year. The men decided if Lady Luck had anything to do with this they would meet her more than halfway by working harder than ever. By the end of October they had the dam repaired and sufficient water impounded to allow the plant to go into operation in November. "The assumption was made that it could be done and with the co-operation of all concerned it was," said Jack Dale at the end of the year. "While there are still some finishing touches needed, the Battle River plant was fired up and came on the line in November in time to carry its share of the peak load."

Southern Division Formed — 1956

The biggest single line-construction project during 1956 was the completion of the 138-kilovolt line tying together the Battle River and Vermilion plants. Forty miles of this "H" frame line were built during severe winter conditions and the remaining twelve miles completed during July, which was exceptionally wet for cross-country construction.

In the fall E.W. Edge King was placed in charge of the building and operation of lines, as transmission and distribution superintendent. King had formerly worked for the East Kootenay Power Company and then with McGregor Telephone and Power Construction Company Limited. Over the years which followed he advanced rapidly in the company, eventually becoming president of all of International Utilities' Canadian subsidiaries.

With the Battle River Station going on the line in the fall, the Drumheller and Vegreville Districts were now interconnected, and would have to be more closely co-ordinated. Together they became known as the Southern Division, and George O'Brien, who had been serving as Vegreville District manager, became division manager. He was succeeded at Vegreville by Gordon H. Parker as district manager.

At Drumheller Harold E. Davies, who had been with the company for almost twenty-two years, was promoted to the position of district manager, and Blythe Davidson became steam operation superintendent for the South Division. At head office, the chief electrical engineer, Jack Ford, was made manager of operations.

Roy Nurse and Wilson Sterling spent considerable time in the Valleyview area in 1956, getting ready for a new power plant with a Brown-Boveri turbine installation similar to the one at Vermilion. The site selected for the plant was beside the Little Smoky River, nine miles south and three miles east of Valleyview. This was to be known as the Sturgeon plant.

Sterling designed the plant and supervised its construction. By the end of the year the foundation was laid, with steel work planned to start in the spring. The turbine — a 10-megawatt unit — was scheduled for delivery the following May 1957.

Over in B.C. the company's property in Fort St. John was taken over by the B.C. Power Commission in 1956 after a year of negotiating. It had been a promising area and it left a hole in Canadian Utilities' operations. Despite having to dispose of its assets at Fort St. John on July 1, for slightly over half a million dollars, the company's overall operations showed substantial gains over previous years. Energy sales increased by twenty-one percent. Six million dollars in capital additions to plant now brought the company's total assets to more than thirty-one million dollars.

Northern Extension — 1956

The Canadian Western expansion plan continued to unfold dramatically in 1956 as the company's service area moved north to Red Deer, bringing gas service to Carstairs, Didsbury, Olds, Bowden, Innisfail and Penhold, plus the Bowden Institution and the Penhold RCAF station. Later, negotiations were completed to provide service to Airdrie and Delburne. Gas for these communities

The Early Days
1908 - 1938

Canadian Western
Natural Gas Company

"The First 30 Years"

Eugene Coste, president of
Canadian Western from its
founding in 1911 until 1922.

The discovery well, Old Glory, struck gas in the Bow Island field east of Lethbridge in 1909,
proving there was a field large enough to supply most of southern Alberta. The well flow was
8.5 million cubic feet a day — the largest in Western Canada to that time.

The drilling crew that brought in Old Glory poses with the founder of Canadian Western. From
left: W. R. Martin, H. Gloyd, Eugene Coste, G. W. Green (who later became general
superintendent of Northwestern Utilities) and A. P. Phillips.

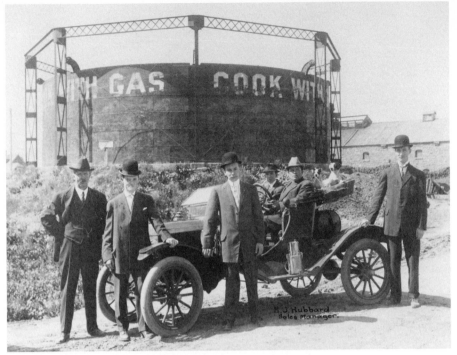

Until 1911, Calgary's first gas system served 2250 customers from a manufactured gas plant and some 30 miles of mains. Engineer and manager A. I. Paynes (far left) and sales manager E. J. Hubbard (far right) pose with other staff of the Calgary Gas Company.

By 1914, interest in oil and gas was in full swing in Calgary, as shown by this view of Centre Street West between Seventh and Eighth Avenues. The low cost of shares on the signs indicates the intensity of the promotional drives generated by this first oil boom.

When this photograph was taken in 1912, the company had not yet acquired motor vehicles and still used horse-drawn carts to transport gas meters.

Modern times arrived for the Calgary meter department in the fall of 1915, when this meter truck was first used. Tom Cavanaugh is at the wheel.

Horse and mule-drawn teams were an important part of early pipeline construction. Four-horse teams hauled the 16-inch pipe used to build the Bow Island-Calgary line, while eight-horse teams were used for backfilling.

This coal-fired trenching machine provided steam power for construction of the Bow Island-Calgary pipeline.

Although hand labor and relatively primitive construction methods were used to build the pipeline from the Bow Island field to Lethbridge and Calgary, the 170-mile line was completed in only 86 working days.

Early transmission pipe was coated by hand, using hot tar and a "granny rag" as shown here.

Early employees stand inside the compressor station built at Bow Island in 1930. These compressors were used for underground storage of natural gas.

W. ISLAND GAS REPRESSURING PLANT
UNDER CONSTRUCTION JUNE. 25. 1930
W. V. RING. CALGARY.

Line surveyors in 1912 take a break for the cameraman.

The Bow Island repressuring plant is seen here under construction in 1930, when the Bow Island field was converted to a reservoir where gas was stored to meet peak load requirements in winter.

A welder, pipe wrappers (inset) and a drilling rig crew (bottom) are photographed on the job in the days before hard hats and welding masks became standard safety equipment.

As dusk fell on Calgary on July 17, 1912, some 12,000 citizens lined Scotsman's Hill to watch the lighting of the inaugural flare which marked the arrival of natural gas from Bow Island.

Eighth Avenue S.W. in downtown Calgary is seen here in 1912 — the year that natural gas arrived from the Bow Island field. At the height of the pre-World War I boom, this was the busiest thoroughfare in the city.

Canadian Western occupied these premises at 215 Sixth Avenue West in Calgary from 1913 to 1952. Note the entrance to the company auditorium to the left.

Harold E. Timmins (seated) and Arthur S. Kruger are photographed in 1914 at Sixth-Avenue office.

Calgary staff show off their fleet of service vehicles and (inset) a new Ford roadster in 1929. The vehicles feature the original Canadian Western crest, developed by general superintendent Fred Heuperman.

This early construction crew poses with a promotional sign: "Cook with gas — better results, less cost."

Lethbridge employees in the late '20s pose in front of the Canadian Western office, next to the Marquis Hotel.

Natural gas service expanded rapidly to communities in southern Alberta, keeping crews such as these busy throughout the '20s and '30s.

Carl Edlund leaves the Fort Macleod office in 1930. Carl was agent for Fort Macleod and Granum from 1928 until 1960.

Canadian Western's Taber office and compressor station is shown here in 1938.

Secretarial staff, dressed in the business attire appropriate to the late '40s, work at their desks in the company's Calgary head office.

Billing machines were introduced in Calgary in 1927, replacing hand-written bills. This represented a tremendous labor-saving advance at the time. From left, Bill Reid, Neil Howell and Ray McDougall as shown here in the late '40s. (Inset) Early hand-written gas bills such as these were replaced by the new technology.

Parade floats with employees on board were often used by the gas companies to promote the use of natural gas in Edmonton and Calgary. This 1929 Canadian Western float displayed the services available to the homemaker.

Cooking demonstrations have been a popular feature of Canadian Western's home service department since its inception in 1929. These employees, in their nurse-like uniforms, were photographed in 1935 at the demonstration kitchen located in the Calgary head office.

The Early Days
1914 - 1939

Northwestern Utilities Limited

"The First 25 Years"

The Viking News

"THE PAPER THAT IS MAKING VIKING FAMOUS."

VOL. II. - NO. 25. VIKING, ALBERTA, THURSDAY, OCTOBER 29, 1914. SUBSCRIPTION PRICE $1.00 PER YEAR

GAS STRUCK AT THE VIKING WELL

War Situation Remains Satisfactory to the Armies of the Allies

Come Out to the Patriotic Meeting Next Monday Evening

Hallowe'en Dance in Hillikers Hall, Friday Evening, October 30

Drillers Strike Gas at a Depth of 2193 Feet

Gas was struck at the Viking gas well early last Saturday morning. The crew had no anticipation of the impending strike and came onto it suddenly during the midnight hours.

The flow while not heavy at first, kept on increasing in volume and pressure and on Saturday was capped.

The news was phoned to Edmonton and the Sunday morning train brought fifteen members of the Edmonton Industrial Association to Viking. They were Pres. W. J. McGrath; Jas. Brodie, gas engineer; Dr. P. H. Vanderwoort; W. A. Milne, Secretary of the Association; Mr. and Mrs. W. J. McNamara, mayor of Edmonton, and wife; Alderman Jas. East; Alderman Rice Sheppard; J. F. Philip, G. T. P. city passenger agent; F. G. McDermid, of the McDermid Engraving Co; Mr. Robinson, a capitalist; Messrs. C. J. Robinson, R. T. Campbell, H. H. Hull, W. A. Riggs, R. C. Chown, E. J. Mahar and Jas. W. Adair, all representative business men of Edmonton.

The entire party went out to the gas well, armed with testing apparatuses and other gas machinery. The pressure on Sunday was found to be 25 pounds and on Monday it increased to 120 pounds. The amount of volume of the flow was 67.9 and it promises to be of sufficient quantity to be of commercial use. The gas was piped and set afire and the flames shot high in the air. The burning well was photographed by the official photographer of the association while a large crowd gathered round.

The gas drillers are of the opinion that they have struck a branch of an immense area of gas, and if drilling should continue, something is in store for this district. The contract for drilling terminated at 2200 feet, and as that depth has been reached, drilling is at a standstill at present. A meeting of the Edmonton Industrial Association, promoters of the Viking gas well, is being held in Edmonton today and they will decide whether to drill deeper or not. Pres. Magrath stated last Sunday that in all probability they would. It is simply a matter of financing it.

The Allies Are Slowly But Surely Gaining Ground

This week's war news has been of a highly encouraging character. It is evident that the morale of the German troops has been seriously undermined. No longer are they the invincibles they were taught to believe they would prove when arrayed against the soldiers of other nations. In vain have they been hurled against the Allied line in France and Belgium. That barrier of steel has proved invulnerable even to the fiercest assault. Have we not here another proof of the superiority of mind over matter? The machine-prepared masses of Germans are no match for the living, thinking and acting units who compose the armies of the Allies. Every man in the latter knows exactly that for which he is fighting.

Fighting has begun on the front in Eastern Prussia. The Russians have repulsed fierce German assaults and have taken hundreds of of prisoners.

The Indian troops turned a German victory into defeat yesterday. The Germans had poured into the British trenches near Lille a relentless fire which made the British "Tommies" retreat. All went well for the Germans until they met the British reserves who happened to be the Indian troops. For a moment there was a wild scrimmage and then with a whoop the Sikhs and Ghurkas fell onto the German lines with their famous knives and in a short time 20,000 of the enemy were cut up into shreds. Never has there been such slaughter on any field.

The German Press are trying to belittle the Canadian contingent which is at present training in England, but we venture to say that when our boys get into action against the modern Huns, they will think otherwise.

Magazines.

Large line of Magazines for sale at News office for 15¢ each.

Cook Found Not Guilty.

T. G. Cook charged with the murder of W. B. Crawford at Wainwright on May 14 last, was discharged by Justice Ives last Friday afternoon. The jury was instructed by the Judge to bring in a verdict of not guilty and after a short deliberation they came into the court room with their decision.

His Honor then addressed the accused: "Thomas Gilbert Cook, you are discharged from custody. You have been compelled to undergo severe strains, not only at your trial but during the weeks previous and when you were in custody and you will feel that you are certainly above all suspicion."

T. G. Cook intends to remain in Wainwright where he is general manager of the Imperial Lumber Company.

This is a Queer World.

The Board of Trade Meeting called last Tuesday afternoon to confer with representatives of the Edmonton Industrial Association in regard to an exhibit of the district to be placed in the Industrial Hall at Edmonton, was poorly attended. It seems that the Viking merchants are so busy the year around that they can't get together once a year, while their city brothers, who have bigger business interests come together every Thursday noon for a luncheon to discuss problems that confront the city. This is a queer world.

Flour Mill Practically Completed.

The Viking flour mill is practically completed. That is, as far as the building is concerned. The carpenters expect to finish the work early next Saturday forenoon. The machinery is on its way to Viking and the freight may bring it here any day, possibly this week. A meeting of the donators is called for next Tuesday afternoon at three o'clock.

Public Meeting.

A public meeting will be held in Hilliker's hall on Monday Evening November 2, at 8:30 P. M. for the purpose of organizing a branch of the North Alberta Patriotic association at Viking. This is a province wide movement for the purpose of obtaining help for the dependents of our brave Canadian lads who are at the front. Hon. Chas. Stewart, Minister of Public Works, John Blue, Provincial Librarian and others will deliver patriotic addresses. A short musical programme will also be given. Everybody is welcome and respectfully requested to turn out to this meeting.

The regular meeting of the Women's Institute has been postponed from the first Friday in November to the first Friday in December. On that date a lecturer from the Department of Agriculture will be present to give a lecture to the ladies.

Patriotic Concert.

The Viking Progressive Bachelors Club have arranged for a patriotic concert to be given in aid of the Canadian Patriotic Fund in Hilliker's hall Monday evening, November 16. It will be full of patriotic sentiment throughout. Several choruses, songs, musical and vocal solos, a tableau, addresses and selections. The proceeds of the evening will go to aid the wives and children of soldiers who are fighting our battles. Tickets will be on sale early next week and everyone should avail themselves of the opportunity to help in this great cause.

Special to the News

Just as we go to press we receive a message from the Edmonton Industrial Association stating that the work on the Viking gas well is to be continued.

Notice of Meeting.

A meeting of the donators to the Viking flour mill will be held in the sample room of the King Edward Hotel Tuesday afternoon November 3rd, at three o'clock. All interested are requested to be present.

: BLACK-LEG :

(Third of a series of Articles by M. M. McLeod, V. S., of Viking.)

This disease also under the names of black-quarter, quarter-ill, symptomatic anthrax, murrain and various other terms in different districts, is mainly confined to young cattle and sheep. It has been observed occasionally in animals more than two years old, but principally affects those between six and eighteen months. It is usually fatal, although cases of recovery are not unknown. Generally the best of the herd are the ones that are attacked.

Cause—The cause is known to be a rod shaped organism, the bacillus of Black-Leg. This organism is what is known as spore forming, that is, when not under favorable conditions for multiplying, it forms into spores and has the power to resist heat or cold to a considerable extent. In this condition they can live in the soil for upwards of 20 years and up to that time if taken into the animal economy can produce the disease.

The disease is spread by the infected animal from the discharge from its mouth and nostril, but principally from dogs, wolves, crows, etc., eating off of the carcass of an animal dying from Black-Leg and depositing the germs miles from where the animal died.

Symptoms—The onset is so sudden that it may be unobserved, the first intimation being that the owner will find one or more of the young cattle dead in the field. If anything is noticed it is usually in the form of sudden illness with loss of appetite, dullness, high fever and lameness in one leg. Closer examination reveals a swelling, at first hard, and afterwards crepitating (crackling) in the muscles of the neck or affected limb, this crepitating, crackling sound is produced by the presence of gas in the tissues and muscles and is absolutely diagnostic.

As the disease progresses the patient manifests signs of dull, worrying pain and is unable to stand, eventually becoming comatose (unconscious.)

Treatment—Various remedies have been tried as curative means in the treatment of black-leg, but no drug has yet been found which can be considered to be specific. The only method of combating the disease is Prophylactive (preventative). This is done by vaccinating. There is on the market today several good reliable vaccines, which, when properly used, produce an immunity against an attack. The federal government has taken this subject up and have put a black-leg vaccine on the market at a minimum cost, namely 5 cents a dose. This is the one I would advise you to use as it is the most reliable.

The proper place to vaccinate is just behind the shoulder. Clip off a small patch of hair, disinfect the skin with a solution of carbolic acid or other disinfectant; then with the vaccinating instrument insert the vaccine under the skin.

The proper time to vaccinate is the spring and fall. Why I say twice a year, is because there is a lot of black-leg throughout the country and by vaccinating twice a year, will give your stock double immunity against the disease. After vaccinating it takes from 12 to 20 days before the stock are immune, and the immunity lasts for one year. Calves between the age of 6 and 18 months are the proper age to vaccinate. Those vaccinated at two to four months of age have to be revaccinated in one month's time.

Next week I will take up temperature and respiration as regards diagnosis in disease.

M. M. McLEOD, V. S.

ROCKERS

Bedroom Rockers $1.75 and $2.00

Arm Rockers $2.50 up to $7.50

We will repair free of charge or replace any of these rockers that do not give satisfaction.

Alberta Furniture & Undertaking, Co.

Now Is The Time.

to put in a supply of No. 1 Winter Apples. We have some boxes left yet but they are going like hot cakes in January.

Come and get your share to-day—Look at these prices:

Single Box Lots	$1.65
Five " "	1.60
Ten " "	1.50

J. A. ROBINSON, Prop.

The Viking Land Co.

Real Estate - Loans - Insurance

GRAIN INSURANCE

If you are contemplating holding your grain for higher prices why not insure it against loss by fire until such time as prices warrant you disposing of it. Below are our rates for short term Grain Insurance.

Per $100.00:

For 1 Month,	18 cents;	with prairie fire protection 30c
For 2 Months	27 "	45c
For 3 "	36 "	60c
For 4 "	45 "	75c
For 5 "	54 "	90c
For 6 "	63 "	1.05

W. McATHEY, Manager.

The October 29, 1914 edition of The Viking News proclaimed the discovery of natural gas in the Viking area, under the headline, Drillers Strike Gas at a Depth of 2193 Feet.

Dignitaries gather for the sod-turning ceremony for the Viking No. 1 well on March 11, 1914. It would be nine years before gas from this area was piped to Edmonton.

This photograph of the Viking No. 1 well shows a wooden rig typical of the type used then.

This crew working on the Viking No. 2 well included (far left) Karl Klentsche and (far right, kneeling) W. R. Martin. The photograph was taken in the late teens.

Downtown Edmonton in 1925, with streetcar tracks running down Jasper Avenue, and the Macdonald Hotel, overlooking the north Saskatchewan River.

Pipe is unloaded from the Canadian Pacific rail line in south Edmonton (then the city of Strathcona) in 1923.

Northwestern construction crews work on the first natural-gas pipeline to Edmonton in August, 1923, at a location about eight miles outside the city. The crew manhandled the pipe into position and lowered it into the trench with the aid of log trestles.

A ditching machine works on the Viking-Edmonton pipeline in 1923.

This "bucketwheel" ditching machine was used in the 1923 construction of the transmission line from the Viking field.

These natural-gas distribution lines are being laid in south Edmonton in 1923. Note the dresser couplings along the pipeline, the precursor of today's welded joints.

Northwestern Utilities crews lay the gas main down 100th Street, north of Jasper Avenue, on August 1, 1923. The building on the left with the clock tower is the old main post office — a location now occupied by the Westin Hotel.

Northwestern's Edmonton warehouse and vehicle storage building is seen here in 1923.

Serviceman Shorty Livingston (right) poses with Northwestern's first customer service truck in the early '20s. The picture was taken in Edmonton's university area, in front of the home of Dr. Eardlay Allin.

Northwestern staff members stand in front of their new office building. This was the first section of the 104th St. building (located north of Jasper Avenue), built in 1928.

The company's vigorous promotional efforts included storefront displays such as this one on Jasper Avenue in 1925.

The Corona Hotel, photographed here in 1912, stood at the corner of Jasper and 106th Street in Edmonton. The hotel was destroyed 20 years later in a gas explosion and fire that posed serious financial challenges for the company during the '30s.

The "clean heat" neon sign on top of the Agency building (next to the Capitol Theatre) was a downtown Edmonton landmark for many years. This photo shows Jasper Avenue between 100th Street and 101 Street in the mid-'30s.

Northwestern decorated its Edmonton head office building on 104 Street (north of what is now the Cecil Hotel) to celebrate the visit of King George VI and Queen Elizabeth in 1939.

The main floor of the head office building, photographed in 1937, housed Northwestern's office clerks and cashiers as well as an appliance display. Note also the public water fountain.

The company began promoting the use of natural gas even before gas arrived in Edmonton. This "rest and relax" tent was a popular feature of the 1923 Edmonton Exhibition.

A home-heating display at the 1935 Edmonton Exhibition.

This Northwestern Utilities float won first prize in its category in the Edmonton Exhibition parade of 1925.

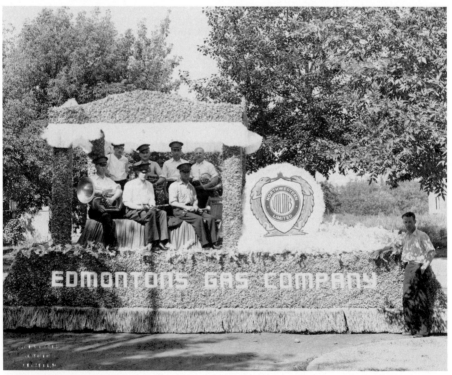

The company's float in the 1936 exhibition parade featured an employee band. Members included Stan Shedden (bottom row, centre) and Danny Salzl (to his left). Standing at right is Shorty Livingstone.

Company service vehicles have taken many forms over the years. The snowplow (top photo) was operated by Northwestern during the winter of 1936-37, before the city had a snow-removal fleet of its own. Bottom, the lack of paved roads was hard on vehicles used for pipeline construction and maintenance.

The Early Days
1927 - 1947

Canadian Utilities Limited

"The First 20 Years"

Union Power was purchased by International Utilities in 1927 — the year this photograph was taken — and its assets were acquired by Canadian Utilities in 1935. Union Power supplied power from this generating plant to Drumheller and nearby coal mines.

The Drumheller plant (photographed here in 1947) remained an important source of power for Canadian Utilities throughout the 1940s and '50s. The coal-fired plant became the basis of a transmission grid that served south-eastern Alberta.

In 1928, Canadian Utilities built the first mobile rail-car generator in Canada. The diesel-fired unit was used to provide emergency power. Thirty-seven years later, the company pioneered the use of mobile units mounted on truck-trailers.

Early company offices were turned into showrooms for electric appliances as part of the merchandising program, which lasted for some 35 years and was only phased out in the mid-'60s.

This early construction crew includes Nick Hrushka (far left) and Con Monpetit (third from left). Installing power lines called for a great deal of manual labor — workers using the old "bar-and-spoon" could dig only four or five holes a day in hard or rocky ground.

Charlie Ouellette stands beside an early Canadian Utilities service vehicle, photographed in Grande Prairie in 1931.

Early power plants such as this one in Grande Prairie generated electricity from small, diesel-fired units. As the transmission grid grew, small, local plants in each community gave way to larger, more cost-effective plants.

Ernie Harrison (right) and a co-worker repair a transmission line near Prince Albert in 1940. Ernie subsequently became manager, first of the Grande Prairie District and then of the Vegreville District, before retiring in 1974.

A crew strings conductor cable across a slough during construction of the Prince Albert-Melfort line in 1931. Before the Saskatchewan government nationalized electric utilities in 1947, Canadian Utilities served an extensive area of that province.

Drumheller servicemen repair a power line in the early 1930s.

Drumheller serviceman Bill Goodwin changes a street light in 1939.

Canadian Utilities scraped through the Depression years with an agressive program to build demand for power. This travelling demonstration van, photographed in 1936, was loaded with appliances to whet the customers' appetite for modern conveniences.

Staff gather outside the Drumheller plant in 1947 during the sod-turning for an expansion to the facility. The 7500-kilowatt generator installed as part of the expansion was the first in Western Canada to burn pulverized coal instead of lump coal.

This photo shows the boiler control panel for the old Drumheller plant, with the mill which pulverized coal in the foreground. (Below) Drumheller staff show off their fleet of service vehicles during the 1930s. Standing in front of truck in right foreground is Lee Drumheller (after whose family the community was named), Drumheller District manager during the '30s and '40s.

A post-hole digger is used to set power poles in the Lloydminster area in 1946.

Farmer Claude Webb ceremonially buries his kerosene lantern at the official opening of Alberta's first experimental farm electrification area in 1944. The system brought electricity to 78 farms and a cheese factory in the Swalwell area near Drumheller.

Guests gather for the official opening of farm experimental area Number 2, near Vegreville, in 1945. At the end of the war, fewer than 100 farms in the company's service area received electricity. Within the next decade, that number grew by 5200.

One of the earliest power plants in Fort McMurray was housed in this log building, built in 1940 on a site near the Hangingstone River. A modern standby unit occupies the site today.

Saskatchewan-based Dominion Electric built electric plants in the Peace River area, such as this one in McLennan. The company's Alberta facilities were bought by two employees, Walter Schlosser and Warren Du Bois, and became Northland Utilities.

Ray Cordell (left) moves diesel units with the help of a U.S. Army vehicle. Construction of the Alaska Highway in 1942 spurred electric development in the north. Ray joined Northland Utilities when it took over the Dominion Electric System in 1945.

The Yukon Electrical Company Limited brought electricity to Whitehorse in 1901. The company was acquired by Canadian Utilities until 1958. This photo shows an early view of Whitehorse's Front Street, looking south.

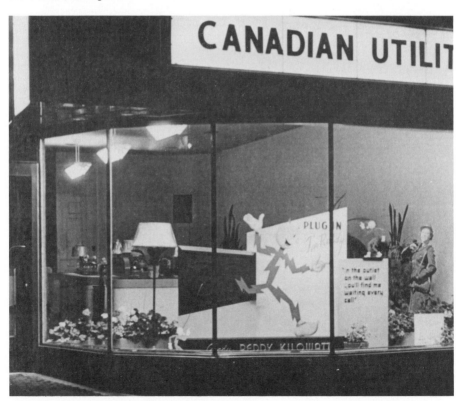

Canadian Utilities adopted Reddy Kilowatt as a promotional symbol in 1942. The perky character — a lightning flash for his body, a light-bulb for his nose — had already been adopted many U. S. investor-owned utilities to symbolize "your electric servant."

Earl Griffen stands beside a camp trailer used to house the transmission construction crew during the 1950s. The crews lived a nomadic life and the trailer housed six or eight people.

The company's float in a parade marking the opening of the Elk Point bridge featured a safety display. The display, warning people about the dangers of using electricity improperly, travelled extensively throughout the company's service area.

Bob Kelly installs a control panel at the Vermilion plant in the late 1940s. Bob, the son of Canadian Utilities' pioneer Ed Kelly, played an important role in the development of the electric company.

A new neon sign featuring Reddy Kilowatt, with the slogan "at your fingertips" is installed at the Vegreville office.

Northland Utilities built the Astoria hydro plant near Jasper in 1949 to supplement the diesel-fired units then serving the town. Today, Astoria remains Alberta Power's only hydro installation and Jasper remains isolated from the provincial grid.

Felix Lamarre (left) works on the wood-stave pipeline that served as the penstock for the Astoria hydro plant.

The Boom Years
1945 - 1975

**An All-Companies Look at the
30 Years that Followed the War**

The Vermilion plant was an important source of generation for Canadian Utilities' customers throughout the 1950s. (Inset) Canada's first natural gas-fired turbine travels to the Vermilion plant in 1954. Owing to severe post-war shortages of equipment, the first four units at the plant consisted of reconditioned turbines from two U.S. Navy destroyer escort Vessels.

Dignitaries and staff gather for the official opening of the Vermilion plant's third unit in 1954.

The Sturgeon generating station was commissioned in 1958 to provide much needed generating capacity in the northern part of the company's service area. The generating units made use of a unique source of energy: sour gas from nearby oilfields.

The first "wishbone" structures appeared on company lines in 1963, and have since become characteristic of 144-kilovolt transmission lines. The distinctive structure, developed by company engineer Don Peterson, is unique to Alberta Power.

Employees pose during a training school for linemen.

Over the years, Canadian Utilities acquired a number of specialized vehicles for building and maintaining power lines in difficult terrain. (From left): Harold Trenaman, Dick Pony and Steve Nazar stand in front of the company's first Bombardier snowmobile.

An internal-combustion engine — then the largest in Alberta — travels to the Grande Prairie plant in 1955 to drive a 2500 kilowatt generator. This was the last expansion to the plant, which was phased into a standby role in 1958.

Premier Ernest Manning poses with the 1964 recipients of Alberta Junior Citizen of the Year awards. Alberta Power has co-sponsored the awards program — which recognizes the contributions of young people to their communities — for the past quarter-century.

This photo shows the first two units at the Battle River generating station. The first unit (30 megawatts) was commissioned in 1956. The plant now has five units, the most recent being the 375 megawatt addition commissioned in 1981.

Canadian Utilities moved its head office from Calgary to Edmonton in 1948, into office space above the Seven Seas Restaurant on Jasper Avenue. This remained the electric company's head office until the Milner Building was completed in 1959.

Workers haul a 20 megawatt gas turbine unit out of Deep Creek in 1966. The equipment was en route to the new Simonette plant southwest of Grande Prairie. The truck carrying it bogged down in the creek and an unexpected flood capsized the unit.

The 1972 Grande Cache flood destroyed — among other things — a railway bridge and section of track. Company employees worked 20 hours a day for a week to repair damage to the electric system, which included a mile-long section of line destroyed by the flood.

Lightning set the Fairview substation on fire in 1973.

Yukon Electrical operates this small hydro plant near Whitehorse. However, most of the electricity needed to serve customers in the territory is generated from facilities now operated on behalf of the territorial government by Yukon Electrical.

Yukon Electrical celebrated its 70th anniversary in 1971 by distributing 70,000 "Yukon Booster" litter bags.

This aerial view shows the site of the Fort McMurray plant as it was in the late 1950s. There has been a generating station on this site since 1940. The house to the left of the plant houses Alberta Power staff to this day.

(Inset) Bob Duncan became the driving force behind the electric company's development in Fort McMurray in 1957, after Canadian Utilities purchased the system then serving 230 customers.

Engineers Al Keeler (left) and Urban Stang survey construction on the H. R. Milner generating station near Grande Cache in 1971. By the mid-1970s, Alberta Power had assembled a team of employees capable of managing the large construction projects needed to meet growing electric demand.

Crews lay natural gas transmission line from the Jumping Pound field west of Calgary to the town of Banff in 1951.

A Northwestern crew installs an intermediate pressure distribution system in Red Deer. Note the animated flame character on the signs — the predecessor of today's gas genie symbol.

The right-of-way for the Grande Cache transmission pipeline, laid in 1969-70, went through northern Alberta muskeg.

The arrival of gas service in Alberta communities has traditionally been marked by flare-lighting ceremonies such as this one, held in Trochu in 1960. Mayor John Stankiewich hailed the end of hauling in coal and hauling out ashes as a result of the new service.

Construction of the Milner building began with a ceremony on April 30, 1957 during which Ray Milner turned the first sod. From left: H. R. Milner, Q. C.; D. K. Yorath (president, Northwestern); J. C. Dale (president, Canadian Utilities); and mayor William Hawrelak.

The Courier, the employee magazine of the gas companies, marked its 40th anniversary in April, 1967. The cover photo included two long-time employees: Cy Metcalfe of Northwestern (left) and Phil Heather of Canadian Western.

The Ellerslie camp housed construction crews building Northwestern's southern extension. This photo, taken in June, 1950, shows the office tent to the left and stock tents on the far right. From left: Ken Stewart, Ken Dunkley, unidentified, Nick Baker and Bob Haycox.

The Viking field house (left) housed workers during the boom construction years.

Northwestern's No. 1 regulating station at Red Deer was photographed in 1949. The "Clean Skies" billboard became a landmark between Edmonton and Calgary.

A popular service of Northwestern's Blue Flame Kitchen has been the daily broadcast, Problem Corner on radio station CJCA. Station announcer George Payne and Northwestern's home service director Joyce Pearson are seen broadcasting live.

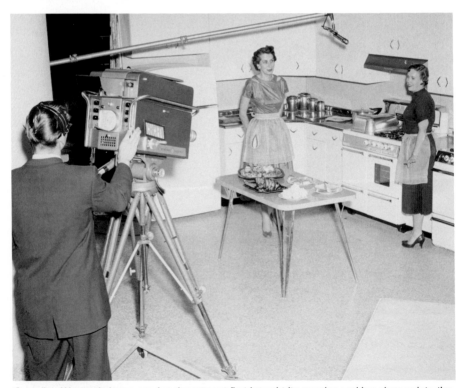

Canadian Western's home service department first brought its popular cooking classes into the home via television in the late '50s. Here, Evelyn Erdman (left) and Marilyn (Day) Sangster — who later joined Northwestern's Blue Flame Kitchen — are televised live.

Northwestern arranged tours in June, 1955 for employees to see the company's outside operations, including this ditching machine. From left: Ernie Pigeon, Ben Hoeffstetter, Bob Breen, Craig Moon, Phil Crawford, Bill Hite, John Belter, Ron Gibbons, Renee Betts, Donna Webber, Marty Couper, Derry Weir, Paul Gauvreau, Vern Wilson, Frank Lylock, Chuck Moore, Doug Johnston, Norman Olson, Bob Trudel, George Baril (operator), Jack Kimmitt, Fred Bradshaw and Gib Slocombe.

This building at 140 Sixth Avenue West, in Calgary, served as corporate headquarters for Canadian Western from 1952 to 1982. In 1957, another six storeys were added to it.

Operating a control station in Calgary during the 1960s required operators to keep an hourly log on pressure, temperature and volume of natural gas flow. Joe Clitheroe was a control station operator when this photo was taken.

The Clean Air Fleet was introduced in 1970, when Canadian Western began a conversion program that would allow service vehicles to run on either gasoline or natural gas.

This display home in southwest Calgary in 1972 served as a showcase for Canada's first experimental natural gas fueled energy cell.

Starting in the early 1960s, Canadian Western and Northwestern became industry leaders in the installation of plastic pipe for rural service.

The Men and Women at Work and at Play

An Employee Profile Over 75 Years

The West End Shop was the workplace for hundreds of Canadian Western employees for more than 50 years. The shop staff in 1921 included (front row, from left): F. Bigelow, A. Whyte, O. J. Doten, N. D. Mackinnon, C. Spencer, F. Humphries, W. Mickens, W. L. Bletcher, A. J. Shrubsall. Middle row: R. Cunliffe, N. Carter, C. Barraclough, H. G. Webb, H. McDonald, G. Wrathall, T. Cavanaugh, W. Lindsay, J. Carnegie. Back row: C. S. Murison, C. G. Fawcett, C. W. Brown.

These two unidentified Canadian Utilities' line crews were photographed in Castor (top) and Stettler (bottom) in 1929.

Canadian Western's hockey team in 1924-25 included (back row, from left): Jimmy Dunn, Charlie Spreadbury, A. E. Heighton, George Wrathall, Clarence Murison, Ike Pelletier and Ernie Briggs. Front row: E. G. Clarke, Harold Timmins, Eddie Wait, Phil Heather, W. E. Gray and I. Hunter.

Northwestern's hockey team of 1926 included (back row, second from left): Ernie Bell; (centre row, from left): John Whelihan, Claude Ferrier and Harry Hind; and Ray Dolan (front row, far left). The remaining members are not identified.

Canadian Western employees gather for the company picnic in Calgary on Labor Day, 1914.

The Canadian Western Glee Club was formed in 1932 and won many awards in city and provincial music competitions. This 1935 photograph includes (back row, from left): B. T. Banks, P. E. Heather, G. Harbour, J. Chase, P. McNeill, D. Davies, J. Johnston, G. Benoy and H. E. Timmins. Front row: J. Gillespie, H. Forsey, A. S. Whyte, J. Walker (conductor), C. W. Leans, W. J. Gray, A. Smith, A. Gell and M. C. James.

Section A of Edmonton's Commercial Bowling League in 1931 included the following Northwestern employees (back row, identified according to the number on the photograph): Alf Garner (1); C. H. Spencer (2); Dave Airth (3); Claude Ferrier (4); and Shorty Livingstone (5).

Members of Canadian Western's cricket team in 1935 included (back row, from left): M. H. Walters, Hal Robbins, R. J. Stringer, Bev Snyder, S. Webster. Front row: R. G. Paterson, Cy Metcalfe, S. Baldwin, Ben Banks, Phil Heather, J. S. Higgins, F. A. Smith. Cy Metcalfe and Ben Banks subsequently transferred to Northwestern.

Calgary and Edmonton employees for the two gas companies gathered in 1950 for the inter-company annual golf tournament, held at the Red Deer Golf and Country Club.

Canadian Western's hockey team won the 1941-42 Big Six Commercial League championship in Calgary. The team included: L. Wilson, G. Whitfield, L. McPhee (coach), H. Meadows, G. McDougall, V. Ferguson, G. Crawford, P. Snell, V. Collison, W. Tarnou, R. Frolerik, J. Willis, J. Gilkes and V. Steer. Also in the photo are league officials G. Crawford and W. Williams.

This 1956 baseball team, made up of Canadian Utilities and Northland Utilities employees from Grande Prairie, included (standing, from left): Jed Sunderman, Ken Callies, Bill Sinkewich, Ron Stang, Jim Haiste, Ross Hogg, Alex Gorrie, and Ralph Klatt. Kneeling: unidentified, Reid Scouville, Harry Sykes, Al Murchie and Lorne Beaupre.

Fishing clubs such as this Canadian Western group have been popular through the years. Accepting their trophies are (front row, from left): Len Marshall, Ken Guinn, Lou Mackie, Peter McCulloch Jr. Back row: Ray Bodman, Harold McFadyen and George Dixon. Far right is Les Smith.

This Canadian Utilities rink won first place in the St. Albert curling championship in 1971. From left: Lawrence Svitich, Hugh Campbell, Harold Lewis and Larry Gullion.

Ray Olenik (left) accepts the Northland Utilities trophy from Henry Bandura. The trophy is presented to the winning team in the annual Alberta Power golf tournament.

Kay McCarthy of Northwestern Utilities operates a billing machine in 1953. A typical residential customer's bill of the period is seen in the inset.

Northwestern's accounting department in the renovated 104th St. office in 1952. From left: Karen Neilson, Graham Dale, Lura Hall, Ray Rowsell, Frank Wilkins, Pauline McHugh, Ken Stewart, Herb Moore, Ben Banks, Ed Shiels, Mary-Kay Dea, Cathy Van Beem, Fred Lewis and John Whelihan (company treasurer).

Moving into the Milner Building on April 17, 1959. Central records staff include (from left): Joan Millman Tebbutt, Cathy Carr, Bernice Griffith, Adeline Jacula, Carol Matheson and Doreen Barry.

To aid the World War II effort, Canadian Western formed the Calgary Girl's Knitting Club.
Back row, from left: L. Mitchell, N. Macartney, C. Strick, I. Moore, M. Jackson, and H. Yeo.
Front row: T. Walker, Mrs. Pattison, M. Burgoin, H. Davies, J. Ellis, G. Halsall and O. Mayo.

Employees have had a long tradition of involvement in community projects and festivities. Here, a Northland Utilities float featuring Reddy Kilowatt takes part in a 1966 parade in High Level.

From left, Canadian Utilities employees Lorne Ross, Ted Edey and Bob Harle serve a buffet meal during the 1954 official opening of a new unit at the Vermilion plant.

The electric companies' annual banquet to recognize employee service is a tradition dating back to the 1930s. Pictured here are guests at Canadian Utilities' banquet in 1952.

Canadian Western employees are honored at the company's annual long service awards banquet, held in 1958 at the Palliser Hotel.

Members of Canadian Western's West End Shop Club performed many comedy skits in the 1930s and '40s, and were noted for their outlandish costumes at company gatherings such as this one in 1933.

Alberta Power has hosted Christmas parties for the children of its employees in locations throughout the company's service area since the company was founded.

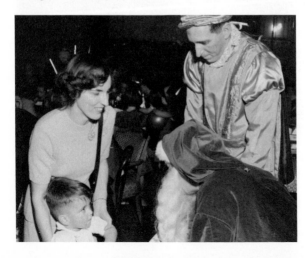

Santa meets Dale, son of Canadian Utilities employee Austin Nicoll, at the 1953 head office children's party.

Northwestern's 1955 banquet featured a French theme. The employees appearing in this production, April in Paris, include (from left): Ken Wolsey, Larry Arcand, Verna Swanson, Sharon Dolighan, Andrey Lawrence, Mabel Chapman, Irene Wallace, and Dorothy MacRae.

Two of Northwestern's favorite performers, Cliff Gates and Al McGarvey, present their version of "How You Gonna Keep Them Down on the Farm", at the Cafe La Flamme Bleu. Seated, from left: Rosemary Lundhal, Doreen Barry and John McFarlane.

Northwestern's stage productions grew over the years. Seen in the Gasco Players' 1979 production, Salute to Service, are (from left): Myra Baloun, Eric Eisner, Carol Whiteman, Janis Powelske, Darryl Wagner, Cam Ross, Bill Wagner, Maria Viverois, Purvis Kinney, Larry Maslyk, Arlynn Hrabec, Peter Marples, Les Henderson, Sharon Turner and Des O'Neill.

This Canadian Utilities survey crew, photographed in the 1950s, included: from left: Phil Beaupre (now administrator, properties); Lorne Beaupre (now senior serviceman in Beaverlodge); Don Flory (retired from the lands and property section); and Art Smythe.

Employees in the Milner Building in Edmonton formed a cross country ski club in the mid-'70s. Here from Northwestern are (left to right): Purvis Kinney, Brenda Meier and Mills Parker, in Hawrelak Park.

Alberta Power, Canadian Utilities and Northwestern staff celebrate Edmonton's Klondike Days in the Milner building in 1979. The event included beer-drinking contests, dancing girls, Klondike Kate and Klondike costumes.

Canadian Western pensioners and their partners enjoyed a bus trip to the Kananaskis area west of Calgary in the summer of 1984.

The Canadian Western employee fishing club was organized in 1952. Pictured here are participants in the 1958 fishing derby held at Seebe. Back row, from left: Earl Purdy, Jim McDonald, Charlie DeRycke, Dave Coupland, Jim Jimpson, Tom Jordan, Bill Spence, Harold McFadyen, Alex Riddell, Pete Vaughan and Bob Nobes. Front row: Murray Ross, Mel Portfors, George Bedu, Dave Thornton, Jerry Peters, Fitz Fitzpatrick, Dick Walton, Bill Lanham, Bob Snyder and Joe Clitheroe.

Retirement gatherings have been an important employee function in all companies. Blythe Davidson (right) receives a congratulatory handshake from Wilson Sterling at Blythe's retirement party in 1971. Blythe was an important figure in developing Canadian Utilities' coal-fired plants during the 1950s and 1960s.

CU Centre employees hit the streets for their regular lunch-hour run. This 1985 group included (from left): Ross Hewitt; Doug Smith; their friends Sandy Daly and Bill Gilroy; Owen Edmonson, Gerry Fisher, Adele Bannerman and Lynne Taylor-Ryan.

Canadian Western employees have actively supported Calgary Stampede activities over the years. Getting into the western spirit at the Sixth Avenue office are Richard Benedictson and Brenda Roeke.

Curling has always been a popular company sport. This rink at an ATCOR employee bonspiel in Calgary included (from left): Betty Gee, Paul Wyers, Glen Fischer and Brenda Fischer.

The Modern Era

**A Colorful Look at the Companies
in the mid-1980s**

A cross section of company facilities is shown in this fold-out color picture section, including:

1. Canadian Western Centre, Calgary.

2. Natural gas district service centre, Calgary.

3. Underground natural gas storage, Fort Saskatchewan.

4. Remote meter reading.

5. Canadian Utilities Centre, Edmonton.

6. Control panel, Sheerness Generating Station.

7. Sheerness Generating Station.

8. Coal-handling facilities, Battle River Generating Station.

9. Natural gas control centre, Edmonton.

10. Ethane extraction plant, Edmonton.

11. Borealis office building, Fort McMurray.

10

borealis building

11

8

9

was supplied through an extension to a gas processing plant at the Nevis field, east of Red Deer. There was also an inter-connection to Northwestern's southern extension at Red Deer.

Temporary offices were set up at Olds and Innisfail, and construction was started in these towns on May 1. Little progress was made at first as crews and machines fought surface mud and subsurface frost which combined to keep the ditching operations at a slow crawl. Soon, however, warm Alberta sunshine thawed the ground and the work proceeded quickly.

More than one hundred guests gathered in Red Deer on September 28 to help Canadian Western mark the arrival of natural gas in the communities on the company's northern extension. Guest of honor was Alberta Premier Ernest Manning, who addressed the gathering and later officiated at the turn-on ceremonies at the metering station two miles southeast of Red Deer.

Although the official turn-on for the northern extension was held at Red Deer at the end of September, it was not until the end of November that service was finalized in some of the communities along the way. By the time the winter cold set in, however, they were all enjoying the comfort and the advantages of having switched over to natural gas as their fuel supply.

At Lethbridge in the early summer a ten-mile, eight-inch line was built to Picture Butte to serve the town and the sugar factory there, and the communities of Shaughnessy and Diamond City. At the same time Lethbridge crews built a six-mile, three-inch line to Nobleford.

The gas company hockey team deserves special mention for 1956. It captured the Calgary industrial league championship for the fifth straight season when it defeated the fire department in the best of three final series. Playing coach was Roy Kelly and team manager was John Kell.

Twelve Communities Added — 1956

Northwestern Utilities added twelve communities to its system in 1956. The towns of Mundare, Chipman, Hilliard, Lamont and Bruderheim were served from a transmission line from the Beaverhill Lake area, east of Edmonton. Josephburg was served by a stub from the Fairydell-Fort Saskatchewan line. Further south, Sylvan Lake was served through a line from Red Deer; Mulhurst from the Texaco absorption plant at Bonnie Glen, and Millet from the Bonnie Glen transmission line.

To the west Onoway was supplied from the Mid-Western Industrial transmission line serving the new Calgary Power plant at Wabamun; Edson and Old Hinton were served from the North Canadian Oils Limited transmission line to the pulp mill at Hinton.

President Yorath noted in his year-end message to the staff that Northwestern for the first time found itself serving towns not connected to a company-owned transmission line and with gas that it was buying at the town gate rather than at the field or supplied from its own reserves.

This was true of Edson, where gas had been officially turned on October 24. The people in Edson turned out to watch the mayor open the valve and light the ceremonial flare on main street. Some said it was the largest crowd Northwestern had ever had for its turn-on ceremonies. Following the official turn-on, about four hundred people packed the Legion hall for a demonstration by the home service department on cooking with gas.

It was a record construction season for the company. At its peak there were nine mains crews and twenty-five service crews at work throughout the system. Everywhere pipe was being laid — all sizes, from two-inch to twenty-inch. The large pipe was required for the fourth transmission line to Edmonton from the Viking-Kinsella field. This line had to go under the Fort Saskatchewan River near Beverly. That job was done with the help of Fulton Banister, a pipeline company familiar with such challenges.

The installation of more than seven thousand new services in 1956 brought the grand total of customers served to more than seventy thousand and revenue from gas sales exceeded ten million dollars for the first time.

The money was coming in but it was going out even faster. Wages were going up, the cost of materials was high, and capital works projects alone that year ate up nearly five and a half million dollars. This meant issuing many more shares. The wires of the brokerage houses hummed as brokers sold the company's securities. The gas business in Alberta was a sound investment.

Fort McMurray — 1957

As with the Saskatchewan properties, the loss of the British Columbia electric properties of Canadian Utilities was quickly offset by additional acquisitions in Alberta. One of those that would have a large impact on the company and on the province was the purchase of McMurray Light and Power Company Limited. It was serving three hundred customers at Waterways and McMurray in northeastern Alberta.

These towns were in the area of the Athabasca oil sands, with almost limitless petroleum resources waiting to be developed. Negotiations for the the electric power franchise were carried on all summer and completed in November. A purchase price of one hundred and sixty thousand dollars was agreed upon and Canadian Utilities took over operations on January 2, 1957.

Bob Duncan moved from Grande Prairie as superintendent of the new Fort McMurray District. Duncan was an old-timer in the north country, having worked in Yellowknife for six years prior to taking charge of the Fort St. John District for Canadian Utilities in 1942. He had moved to Grande Prairie in 1953 as line superintendent.

Duncan did some research on the history of power at Fort McMurray and found that the first commercial generating plant had been installed in Waterways in 1933. It was operated by a man named McNeil with power from a 10-kilowatt engine. McNeil sold out to a storekeeper named Boisvert, who supplied power only from dusk to midnight with the exception of day service for the traditional Monday wash.

In 1937 a J. Durocher, who had been operating a plant in Lac La Biche, sold out and moved to McMurray where he installed a one-cylinder semi-diesel 25-kilowatt unit, which has since been placed in the Fort McMurray museum. He put in a small 2,300-volt single-phase distribution system and charged twenty-five cents a kilowatt hour on an evening schedule. Bob Duncan commented thirty years later: "Today's rates represent a 'modest' ninety percent reduction from that original figure!"

In 1940 Durocher built a plant at a new location on the Hangingstone River, about midway between McMurray and Waterways. On this same spot Canadian Utilities subsequently built its plant. The early plants were all housed in log buildings.

With the arrival of United States military forces in 1942, a three-phase line was built between the power plant and McMurray and Waterways and a 170-kilowatt three-cylinder unit was installed. In 1954 Durocher sold out to a G. Sandulac who operated the business for three years, increasing the generating capacity with a 90-kilowatt unit removed from a Fort McMurray salt plant that had closed. In 1957 Canadian Utilities bought the plant and distribution system from Sandulac, who moved to Edmonton to go into the motel business.

Another major acquisition completed in 1957 was Slave Lake Utilities Limited, which served a group of communities along the south shore of Lesser Slave Lake. The company acquired distribution rights in Kinuso and Faust on October 1, 1956, followed by Smith, Slave Lake, Wagner and Canyon Creek in the spring of 1957. Canadian Utilities crews began immediately to tie the system together with an upgraded power line and centralized generating equipment. The area was then tied into the main transmission grid in the Peace River country.

Across the Saskatchewan border Canadian Utilities made a two-year deal to supply Saskatchewan Power Corporation with electricity to help serve the area between Lloydminster and North Battleford. This was an exchange deal, using a connection established earlier at Lloydminster with which Saskatchewan Power could supply the town with power in case of a Canadian Utilities outage. The connection was now reversed to feed electricity to Saskatchewan Power, enabling Saskatchewan to defer for two years the capital expenditure of a transmission line into the North Battleford area.

Milner Building — 1957

The year 1957 saw the start of construction of "Edmonton's most modern office building," the twelve-storey Milner Building that would tower higher than any other office building in the capital city.

The project was to be named in honor of company chairman, Ray Milner. Despite the fact that Canadian Western was adding six floors to its Calgary office building, and Northwestern recently had moved into its new meter repair shop and office building, the energy group was growing so quickly that some long-range facilities planning was needed.

Canadian Utilities was beginning to spill over into other buildings besides its quarters above the Seven Seas restaurant. It was common to see offices accommodating two desks when they were designed for one.

The start of construction on the Milner Building took place April 30 when the company persuaded Milner himself to turn the first sod. The site — 10040 - 104 Street — was on the west side of the street, half a block south of Jasper Avenue.

Dennis Yorath chaired the sod-turning ceremony, attended, among others, by Edmonton's Mayor William Hawrelak. "This is an important occasion for Milner," the mayor said, "for he has been connected with the gas company since its inception. The new building is indeed something of which we can be proud." Canadian Utilities' president Jack Dale presented Milner with a chrome-plated shovel to turn the first sod.

The building, designed by architects Rule, Wynn & Rule, cost six million dollars and featured a heated sidewalk and driveway and a gas-fired air-conditioning system.

In Calgary that spring, Canadian Western moved into the six-storey addition to its office building, the new floors to be shared with the Shell Oil Company and various other tenants. The eight-storey Natural Gas Building was perhaps the first in Canada to use natural gas for both summer and winter air conditioning. The building was cooled by a Carrier automatic absorption refrigeration machine which uses heat rather than a motor-driven compressor for the refrigeration cycle. The Milner Building, too, was designed to be heated and cooled by natural gas.

Gas for California

One of the tenants in the new portion of the Natural Gas Building in Calgary was Alberta and Southern Gas Co. Ltd., which was seeking a permit to export gas to California. Northwestern and Canadian Western entered into a long-term contract with this company to enable the Alberta gas companies to purchase gas to augment their own supplies and give the Alberta companies a prior right over the export company's requirements.

The principals in the three hundred and thirty million dollar Alberta and Southern pipeline project were the Pacific Gas and Electric Company, Canadian Bechtel Limited and the Alberta gas companies.

The group was seeking permits from the various Canadian and American governmental bodies involved, and was hoping that these permits would be obtained in time to enable the project to be completed and initial deliveries of four hundred million cubic feet per day to be made in 1960.

Exports to Eastern Canada — 1957

Meanwhile, gas started flowing east from Alberta in July 1957. Alberta Gas Trunk Line fed gas from three southeast Alberta fields into the Trans-Canada pipeline for delivery to Regina and Winnipeg. Alberta Premier Ernest Manning turned the valve which started the gas flowing in the trunk line system. "It is only the beginning of an era in the gas industry that will eclipse anything we ever thought or dreamed of," he said. TransCanada President N.E. Tanner said gas was expected to be delivered to prairie cities by early September.

Yorath told the golden anniversary meeting of the Canadian Gas Association meeting at Jasper Park Lodge that summer that pipelines such as the trunk line and the proposed California line, along with new plant expenditures and drilling programs, would see expenditures of capital in the order of two billion dollars attributable to western Canada natural gas over the next five to seven years.

He went on to emphasize that the primary concern of Canadian Western and Northwestern had always been its Alberta customers and its relationships with export groups would always be governed by that primary concern. He cited some figures on recent growth in Alberta. The number of customers served by the two companies had more than doubled in ten years to almost one hundred and forty thousand, while the annual volume of gas sales had nearly tripled to ninety billion cubic feet.

At the same time as all this rapid expansion was taking place, the average rate charged by both companies was "lower today than in 1939." On the Canadian Western system the average rate was twenty-seven cents per thousand cubic feet, down three and a half cents from 1939. Northwestern's rates were even lower, for an average of twenty-four cents per thousand cubic feet as compared with thirty-one and a half cents in 1939.

Yorath said, however, that the increased cost of materials, equipment, labor and money was making it necessary for the companies to ask for rate increases.

Canadian Western made the move first, in the fall of 1957. It went to the Board of Public Utilities Commissioners with an application for a rate increase. There was no question it was needed. Despite the company's customers increasing by nearly five thousand that year, and its gas sales passing the ten-million-dollar mark as Northwestern's had done the previous year, the company's net income had actually decreased from the previous year.

Harold E. Timmins

In 1957, the gas companies mourned the loss of Harold E. Timmins, who died in Calgary on October 30 at the age of sixty-three. For almost half a century Harold Timmins was known to a host of people in Alberta as Mr. Gas.

Timmins began his career in the gas industry in 1912 as a junior clerk in the Calgary office of Canadian Western. At his death he was director of new business for both the gas companies, as well as being on the board of Canadian Western.

More Communities Served — 1957

Northwestern had a busy year in 1957 as well, taking on nearly seven thousand new customers. Service was extended to many new communities, including Evansburg, Entwistle, Wildwood, Glenwood, Gainford, Seba Beach and Niton Junction, served from the North Canadian Oils transmission line between Wabamun and Hinton; Islay, served from the company's Lloydminster line; Lavoy, Ranfurly, Innisfree and Minburn, served by a transmission line from the Viking field; and Drayton Valley, with the gas supply to come from a conservation plant in the Pembina field. In addition, Northwestern purchased the Athabasca Valley Utilities distribution system at Hinton, serving nearly three hundred customers.

Northwestern's safety program was paying off with a dramatic decrease in accident frequency. Lost time per million man hours worked was less than half of what it had been the previous year.

The gas companies were becoming more mature, to be sure. It even showed in their advertising program. With the conclusion of Douglas Fairbanks' television film series in Edmonton and Calgary, the companies embarked on sponsorship of cooking demonstration shows, which proved popular.

The companies that year won several awards from the Public Utilities Advertising Association, in competition with major American utilities.

In sports news Norm Haynes, assistant agent at Black Diamond, was in the limelight in 1957. He was a member of the team which won the gas company's championship chuckwagon trophy at the Calgary Stampede, presented that year by Canada's new prime minister, John Diefenbaker.

Yukon Electrical — 1958

The year 1958 brought a significant northern reach on the part of Canadian Utilities with the acquisition of the electric companies then serving the city of Whitehorse, capital of the Yukon Territory. In April Canadian Utilities purchased all the outstanding shares of The Yukon Electrical Company Limited and the Yukon Hydro Company Limited.

Whitehorse, with a population of over four thousand, was an important distribution and communications centre for the mining industry of the territory. The city is on the Alaska Highway and is the terminus of the narrow gauge White Pass and Yukon Railway, giving access to coastal shipping at Skagway, Alaska.

Edge King, Canadian Utilities transmission and distribution superintendent, was promoted to the position of general manager of Yukon operations and moved to Whitehorse.

The Yukon Electrical Company Limited had been incorporated in 1901, shortly after the Klondike Gold Rush of 1896. The archives of the company had some reminders of the cost of electricity back in those early days. There was a clipping from *The Weekly Star,* for example, of a company advertisement placed in the May 28, 1908, issue. It read:

Commencing June 1 meter rate of electric light has been reduced from the maximum rate of ninety cents to fifty cents per kilowatt hour. A corresponding reduction has also been made in the price of wiring and supplies.

When Canadian Utilities acquired the new subsidiary the rate was six and a half cents per kilowatt hour. The system consisted of a diesel generating plant with a capacity of 700 kilowatts and distribution lines serving sixteen hundred customers in the Whitehorse area.

The Yukon Hydro Company, a much smaller operation than The Yukon Electrical Company, was incorporated in 1950 and operated two hydro plants with a combined generating capacity of 1,600 kilowatts, selling power to the electrical company.

During this period, the federally owned Northern Canada Power Commission was building a hydro power plant at the Whitehorse Rapids on the Yukon River. The first 7,500-horsepower unit was scheduled to go into operation later in 1958. Although no agreements had been signed between the NCPC and the privately owned electrical companies, it was anticipated that future power requirements would be obtained from the new government-owned plant.

Following the purchase at Whitehorse, Canadian Utilities built a plant to serve the community of Haines Junction, one hundred miles farther northwest on the Alaska Highway, where construction of an oil refinery was in prospect.

The northward reach continued in Alberta as well with installation of a generating plant at Fort Chipewyan on the shore of Lake Athabasca about one hundred and fifty miles north of Fort McMurray.

Turbine Plant Starts Up — 1958

O ver in the Peace River country, the Sturgeon gas turbine plant south of Valleyview went into production at the beginnning of 1958. The generator used sour flare gas from the Sturgeon Lake oilfield and in turn supplied power to pump the oil from the same wells and push it into a pipeline to Edmonton.

The first full load tests at the plant were completed on January 21, supervised by Brown-Boveri engineers and under the critical eyes of Roy Nurse, Canadian Utilities' production superintendent, assisted by Glenn Martin. The success of the tests exceeded all expectations for smooth running. Soon the plant was feeding power to the hungry systems of Canadian Utilities and Northland Utilities in the Grande Prairie and Peace River area as well as the newly acquired group of communities along the shore of Lesser Slave Lake. The connection with Northland was another important step towards the ultimate integration of that company's operations.

The Sturgeon plant and the recent addition of the Fairview plant, the latter operated jointly by Canadian Utilities and Northland, provided much greater efficiency and economy of operation so that the Grande Prairie plant could be gradually phased out into a standby role.

In 1958 Grande Prairie became Alberta's tenth and most northerly city. The new city, with a population of seven thousand, put on three rollicking days of whoop-up, February 13 to 15, with full participation by the Canadian Utilities staff under Ernie Harrison, district manager.

During the year, Canadian Utilities continued to build major transmission lines and connected a variety of new loads. A temporary diesel plant was built at Swan Hills to serve oilfield activities there. To the southeast the Kaybob oilfield and Fox Creek were connected to the company grid.

The appointment of Jack N. Ford as general manager of the electric company was announced in October by president Jack Dale. Ford was a graduate of the University of Alberta, having received his degree in electrical engineering in 1934. He entered the electric utility field in 1934 when he joined a power company in Regina as serviceman. Two years later he joined Calgary Power and served as distribution and transmission engineer. In 1951 he was appointed chief electrical engineer for Canadian Utilities and five years later was named manager of operations.

H.W. Mike Francis

At the intercompany level, the energy group lost H.W. Mike Francis, director of purchasing for the three companies, in Calgary on February 19, 1958. Although he was 69, his death came as a shock to his many associates and friends for he had not been in ill health. He had been purchasing agent for the companies since 1928.

Francis was an ardent lover of horses and the game of polo. He was born in London, England, and educated there and at Cambridge University. Here, in part, is a tribute paid to him by gas companies' president, Dennis Yorath:

He was reputed the most popular purchasing agent in Canada and possibly on the continent. This is indeed a tribute, as purchasing agents, for some unknown reason, apparently are not the most popular breed in the world and generally are regarded as being colder than bankers and tougher than pipeliners.

No one was more friendly, more sympathetic, more warm in his approach — to salesman and tycoon alike — than Mike, who will be long remembered for what he contributed to the life and atmosphere of Calgary — for his preservation of the finest of British traditions and behavior — for his intense loyalty to everything and everyone of which and of whom he was fond.

More Gas Sources — 1958

For the gas companies, 1958 went down in history as the year in which major steps were taken to ensure that Albertans would always have ample supplies of natural gas. In February the companies made a submission to the Royal Commission on Energy, taking the position that when an export permit is being considered, the exporter should be required to establish that in addition to any quantities requested for export there is first a sufficient supply to meet provincial requirements for a rolling period of not less than thirty years, and that this gas is available to residents of Alberta at costs not in excess of those paid by the exporter.

The two gas companies reiterated this policy before the Oil and Gas Conservation Board at hearings held on applications of TransCanada Pipe Lines Limited, Westcoast Transmission Company Limited and Alberta & Southern Gas Co. Ltd. to export gas.

Canadian Western's measures to ensure ample supplies of gas for the immediate future, particularly for peak winter loads, began right at home in its original source of supply, the Bow Island field. The company installed a new compressor in the field station, doubling the capacity of the plant. The 800-horsepower compressor, weighing almost fifty tons, enabled the station to handle up to 30 billion cubic feet of gas per year and on a daily basis could compress and store up to six million cubic feet.

Next, Canadian Western built fifty-eight miles of sixteen-inch pipeline to connect its system to the reserves of the Carbon field, northeast of Calgary. Six wells in the field were purchased and two more were drilled, making the field an important source of additional gas for peak load requirements. This project took a major portion of the company's eleven million dollar capital expenditures in 1958. The peak demand on the Canadian Western gas system in 1958 occurred on December 6, amounting to 213 million cubic feet.

At the end of the year Canadian Western's estimated recoverable reserves connected to the system stood at well over a trillion (a thousand billion) cubic feet. Negotiations were under way with various producing companies for the purchase of even more supplies.

The company also entered into an agreement with Westcoast Transmission Company Limited, which had applied for a permit to export a trillion cubic feet, giving Canadian Western first call on 50 million cubic feet per day from the East Calgary field.

Thirteen Thousand New Customers — 1958

T he year 1958 was one of record expansion for the companies. Service was begun to a number of communities adjacent to the Alberta Gas Trunk Line system, the first of which were Vauxhall and Enchant in the Canadian Western areas, and Oyen, Consort and Monitor in the Northwestern areas. The gas supply for these towns was purchased from TransCanada Pipe Lines Limited.

Over the entire systems of both gas companies a record number of nearly thirteen thousand new customers was connected, bringing the total served by the year-end to eighty thousand in fifty-three communities for Canadian Western, and nearly eighty-four thousand in sixty communities for Northwestern.

Both companies entered into an agreement with TransCanada, which had permits to export five and a half trillion cubic feet of gas to eastern Canada. This agreement was similar to the one already entered into with Alberta & Southern Gas Co. Ltd. whose application to export gas to California was before the Oil and Gas Conservation Board. The TransCanada agreement gave the two gas companies priority over TransCanada's export requirements.

15 Sources of Supply — 1958

N orthwestern's major connection of 1958 was a transmission pipeline between Edmonton and the Pembina oilfield, some seventy miles west. This line was completed in the fall with gas flowing into the system in October. This new source of base load gas was very valuable, enabling the company to conserve the dry sweet gas fields required to meet the rapidly increasing peak demand, and also to bring about a number of operating economies throughout the system.

Northwestern's peak winter demand by this time was nearly 300 million cubic feet a day. The largest customer was the city-owned Edmonton power plant, which installed its first gas turbine that year. The plant used nearly nine billion cubic feet of gas during the year, for an average of 23 million cubic feet per day.

By year-end the company had a total of fifteen sources of natural gas supply available to meet the requirements of its customers. Recoverable reserves were estimated at nearly three trillion cubic feet connected to the system, including about a trillion cubic feet available but not at that time under contract.

Consolidation — 1959

T he year 1959 was one of consolidation for the International Utilities group of companies. It was a year of adjusting to the spectacular new developments of the late fifties — new office buildings, new power plants, new fields from which to extract gas and new pipeline companies from which to buy gas. It was now nearly half a century since the dream first began to unfold on the banks of the South Saskatchewan River. It was time to adjust to new phases of the dream, to consolidate what had been achieved and to prepare for the new and greater challenges which the sixties and seventies would bring.

There were a lot of things that were new — even new rate schedules. Both gas companies had been forced by rising costs to ask the Board of Public Utility Commissioners for a review and upward adjustment of their rates. For Canadian Western this was pretty straightforward. The board approved the proposed new rate schedules on May 27, 1959, and they were put into effect at the beginning of June. They represented an average increase in rates of sixteen percent, so that on a full-year basis the company would receive an average of thirty-four cents per thousand cubic feet of gas sold.

It was a sizeable increase, but Canadian Western rates were still among the lowest on the continent. Gas was still the best bargain in the household budget.

Opposition to Rate Increase — 1959

Things were a little more complicated for Northwestern Utilities. It was about mid-year 1959 when the board approved the company's proposed new rate schedule, and the rates were put into effect on September 1. They were designed, with the board's approval, in such a way that over a period of the next four years Northwestern would recover, in addition to the revenue requirements for that period, one million seven hundred thousand dollars, which the board found to be the deficiency in revenue received during the first eight months of 1959. They were also put into effect on the basis of a "purchased gas adjustment clause," which meant they could be varied upwards or downwards depending on what it cost the company to buy its gas, particularly from oilfields.

This would have been all right, except that Edmonton politicians claimed the gas company was unfair in asking the people to have that lost revenue for 1959 made up, and at the same time asking to have its rates subject to the cost of buying gas. So the city's lawyers challenged the board's rulings and got the city of Red Deer and two towns to join them in the case. The Supreme Court of Alberta agreed to hear the appeal the following year.

Meanwhile, in view of this appeal, the gas company was forced to ask the board to approve a further increase in rates, which the board granted on November 6.

A brief explanation of what was meant by the "purchase gas adjustment clause" might be useful at this point. For many years the company followed the practice of trying to make good use of oilfield residue gas which, if not used, would simply be burned off in giant flares similar to the flares that burned millions of cubic feet of gas in the Turner Valley field when the oil boom first started there. This kind of gas was too useful to be wasted and the gas companies bought it to use for heating people's homes in the winter and cook their food and energize the wheels of industry. The electrical operations of the energy group were also buying this residue gas. The new Sturgeon plant, for example, was converting sour oilfield gas to power.

In Northwestern's case, in 1959, about three-quarters of its total gas supply came from oilfield sources. Why not use this gas, the company reasoned, and conserve the gas in the Viking-Kinsella field for future use?

But the bargain prices, and the amount of oilfield gas which was actually available at any given time, fluctuated wildly, depending on how much crude oil was being moved out of the oilfields. This unpredictability was why the company wanted an adjustment clause in its rate schedule.

Billing by Therms — 1959

There was another interesting development in 1959 which made history. North-western switched to therm billing. As long as the gas was coming almost entirely from the Viking-Kinsella field billing customers by volume was acceptable. But now Northwestern was getting gas from as many as sixteen sources, and not all the gas from these sources had the same heating value per cubic foot. An instrument called a calorimeter is used to obtain the heating value of the gas.

A therm is a unit of energy equal to one hundred thousand British Thermal Units (BTUs). One BTU is the quantity of heat required to raise the temperature of one pound of water one Fahrenheit degree.

Use of the therm as a basis for the new rates was adopted by Northwestern so that all customers would pay the same per unit of heat. Until then a customer, for instance, in Red Deer receiving Nevis gas with a heating value of perhaps eleven hundred BTUs, was paying the same rate as the customer in Wetaskiwin receiving Viking-Kinsella gas with nine hundred and sixty BTUs.

The Pembina field southwest of Edmonton was a good example. In 1959 almost half the gas sold by Northwestern came from this large field. On a volume basis, a house supplied with a dry gas would pay ten to twelve percent more than one using Pembina gas, because of the difference in heating value.

More Communities Served — 1959

During 1959 Northwestern connected ten new communities to its system. Five of these — Thorsby, Breton, Warburg, Buck Creek and Sunnybrook — were served off the line bringing gas from the Pembina field to Edmonton. The Thorsby, Breton and Warburg turn-on ceremonies starred ladies who were old-timers in the communities turning the valve, assisted by the mayors of the communities.

Murray Stewart, who had become general manager of Northwestern in 1956, had a pleasant surprise at Breton when a pretty little girl, Barbara Larson, presented him with a bouquet of flowers on behalf of the community. Stewart responded by giving them to Mrs. Mindy Anderson, who turned the valve to light the flare.

Northwestern's other five new communities in 1959 were Provost and Cadogan, served from the Provost field; and Alix, Mirror and Bashaw, served from the Alberta Gas Trunk Line system. It was fashionable that year to have ladies turning the valves for turn-on ceremonies. Not to be outdone, Mirror's mayor, Mrs. H. Simpson, did the honors herself.

Canadian Western, likewise, started service to ten new communities in 1959. Acme, Beiseker, Carbon, Irricana and Strathmore were served from the transmission line connecting the Carbon field to Calgary. The other five — Barons, Carmangay, Champion, Kirkcaldy and Vulcan — were served from a line laid by the company to connect with the pipeline of Alberta Gas Trunk Line just north of Lethbridge.

At Vulcan, Mayor William Munro described the turn-on as "the thrill of a lifetime." The people of the community had long "looked forward to natural gas," he said. "Canadian Western has co-operated in every way possible, and has gone to a great deal of trouble and expense in making it possible for residents of Vulcan to enjoy natural gas."

All in all, Canadian Western led the way in 1959 with the greatest number of new customers added to its lines. Its total of more than seven thousand compared with almost six thousand for Northwestern and about two thousand five hundred new electrical customers for Canadian Utilities.

Main Line Camp Retired

T he end of the fifties brought an end to one of the most colorful aspects of pipeline work with the retiring of the main line camps. These tent camps were used for many years in construction work in the years before the oil boom, when almost all pipeline work was done by company crews. The tent camp was a very practical, portable board and room facility.

Over the years the tent camps were used each summer for a variety of projects. For example, Northwestern's southern extension in 1946-1947 was built with crews housed in a miniature tent-town complete with mess tent, washrooms and administration office. Canadian Western's camp was used in servicing of the sixteen-inch line to the Bow Island field, where each year a mile or two of line would be taken up, sand-blasted, primed, coated, wrapped and put back down.

Northwestern's main line camp went into storage in the early 1950s and was eventually disposed of.

The last two major projects for Canadian Western's main line camp were the line to Jumping Pound in 1950 and the Carbon line in 1958. George Kellam, one of the men who was in charge of the camp, recalls that it did not seem practical to continue using tents after the Carbon line project. The large-scale construction projects which were carried out by the company's own crews were now mostly completed, and there was a trend, too, to contracting out projects in the years that followed. Kellam put the tents in storage, where they stayed for nearly two years and then the company sold them. It was the end of an era.

Move to Milner Building — 1959

I n Edmonton the highlight of the year was the move to the Milner Building on 104 Street. The move for the staff of Northwestern and Canadian Utilities was made over a weekend, beginning on Friday, April 17, 1959.

On the last morning, the last coffee was served in the old Northwestern lunchroom. For nine years Mrs. Prather had served almost three hundred cups every working day — or almost seven hundred thousand cups in that period. In a gesture of fun, Ken Currie withdrew an old sock from the last pot. This was claimed to be the secret ingredient of Mrs. Prather's fine brew!

As the older books which recorded company activities were brought out of storage and readied for moving, entries from their faded pages brought memories to senior employees, and provided those with lesser years' service with information about the early days of development. The projects undertaken and completed through the years, the sports and social functions, the revered names of those no longer there — all were woven into the heritage of the gas company.

Down from the upstairs hall came a framed front page of *The Viking News* extra, dated November 5, 1914. The headline read: GAS STRUCK. In a bottom corner advertisement, apples were offered at a dollar fifty a box.

In the back storage room, Peter Podhaniuk found a picture of early construction showing a trainload of pipe being unloaded on to horse-drawn wagons. A service truck in another photo appeared to be a Model T Ford of early twenties vintage.

For the first time in twenty-eight years the big safe in the main floor vault was moved. The castors needed oil, and the movers needed strength. The five thousand pounds of dead weight was handled efficiently, though slowly, by MacCosham's Moving & Storage.

It was not only moving time for Northwestern, it was moving time for Canadian Utilities as well. For the first time in the history of the two companies they would now be together under one roof. The old quarters above the Seven Seas restaurant were by now becoming unbearably cramped, and it was a happy day when Canadian Utilities staff, along with Northwestern, moved to the sparkling, spacious new Milner Building.

Moving day for the company was much the same as Northwestern's. Company secretary T.A. (Monty) Montgomery was in charge of the move, and Monty pitched in with everyone else, helping to carry an endless number of boxes out of the old quarters to the new building.

The whole move went without a hitch, which required considerable advance planning. The billing department, for example, which operated on a close day-to-day schedule, brought its work up a day in advance and made the move without a moment's loss of time.

For both Canadian Utilities and Northwestern, the Milner Building brought a totally new look. The pneumatic mail tubes, for example, by means of which mail could be sent almost instantaneously from all twelve floors of the building to the centralized mailing room was a feature so modern it seemed almost like a luxury. The glass-enclosed central switchboard area on the main floor, too, was another innovation.

The cafeteria in the basement provided an atmosphere of "togetherness" for employees. There were not only conveniences for employees, but also for the public, particularly customers. A drive-in wicket on the north side of the building meant customers could now pay their bills without stepping out of their cars!

The main floor also featured a street-level, walk-in appliance sales and display area, where Edmontonians could now buy gas appliances from Northwestern, as the gas company moved into the appliance selling field. The merchandising department's official inauguration of appliance sales featured week-long cooking demonstrations to launch the new services in the Milner Building. The test and demonstration kitchen on the main floor gave the home service department a new look and it became known as the Blue Flame Kitchen.

Northern Developments — 1959

C anadian Utilities had an interesting and exciting year in 1959. Northern developments were again in the forefront. The new plant was completed in the historic northern Alberta community of Fort Chipewyan. It is largely an Indian settlement, a Hudson's Bay post and the location for various government agencies, including administration offices for Wood Buffalo Park. It is also the departure point for boats to Uranium City and Fort Fitzgerald.

Further south, work continued to increase service in the Fort McMurray area. Cities Service Research and Development Company engineers began setting up a plant at Mildred Lake, twenty-five miles north of McMurray, which they hoped would uncover an economical way of extracting oil from the Athabasca tar sands. They called on Canadian Utilities to provide a temporary diesel generator for their power requirements.

The request for service was made on March 25, and prompt action was required to get the equipment to the site before spring break-up, as the unit would have to cross an ice bridge which was rapidly failing. Canadian Utilities hustled the equipment together — even made up a switchboard to go along with it — in record time. It was the last piece of equipment to get into the site before the ice bridge went out at the end of March.

Hydro Project Proposed

U p in northern B.C. there was more excitement. The progress of the Peace River Power Development Company became a matter of particular interest to Canadian Utilities, and the company bought a block of two hundred and fifty thousand shares. H.R. Milner was appointed to the board of directors of the new development company.

Preliminary studies of the Peace River power development project indicated it was feasible to develop the world's largest hydro project on the Peace in the vicinity of the Rocky Mountain Trench. Potential production of power was estimated as high as eight million horsepower, and the cost of development would be about half a billion dollars.

Canadian Utilities bought the generating plant and distribution system in the hamlet of Hudson Hope, which was adjacent to the site for the proposed main dam. The plant was enlarged and the distribution system improved immediately.

Still farther north, Canadian Utilities purchased a small plant and distribution system at Watson Lake on the Alaska Highway in the Yukon, and built a new plant to serve the growing community.

Swan Hills Muskeg — 1959

T hen in the Alberta oil patch there was Swan Hills, and that was an adventure. A transmission line was started from the Sturgeon plant into this bush and muskeg country where grizzly bears still roamed. Glenn Martin and Steve Nazar commented on their trips into Swan Hills for the company's new staff magazine, *The Transmitter*. They claimed a good way to describe working in such an area is "mud, sweat and tears."

Before the power line from the Sturgeon Plant was complete, a temporary plant had to be built with several small generators. Each was quite literally dragged through the mud to its plant location.

The road into the temporary plant, if one could call it a road, was lined with abandoned vehicles ranging from passenger cars to bulldozers. There were piles of materials, even groceries, where trucks had either spun out or broken their axles and drive shafts.

The roads were confusing and if you didn't know your way around you might start on a gravel road and wind up on a deteriorated bulldozed slash through the trees, leading to some oil well, with quagmire in the depressions and steep slopes on the greasy hills.

Nazar and Martin claimed the trees were so close together that even the deer and moose had difficulty getting their horns through them, and it was a common occurrence to have trees fall on power lines. "The generator of our number one unit burned out due to one of these trees."

"Many of our desk-bound colleagues express envy at our periodic holidays in the Hills," Nazar and Martin said. "To them, we extend the warmest welcome to join us on our next trip. But we urge them to bring their own Eaton's catalogue and other survival necessities!"

Finally, back in civilization, Canadian Utilities again scored another first in the power generating field in 1959 when it completed arrangements for the purchase of another gas turbine, the first to be made in Canada.

Canadian Westinghouse was awarded the contract to build and install the new turbine in the Vermilion plant. It would embody all the latest technological features and was designed to burn either gas or oil for fuel. Rated at 20,000 to 30,000 kilowatts, it would replace the original 8,500-kilowatt turbine, which was to be moved to the new Sturgeon plant to strengthen the generating capacity in the Grande Prairie district.

CHAPTER 8

The Industrious Sixties

Shares for Albertans — 1960

As the fifties were ushered out and the industrious sixties ushered in, Albertans were becoming aware of the opportunities open to them for investment in their own industries. Albertans began to take a keen interest in the International Utilities group of companies from the standpoint of increasing local ownership in the energy business.

Canadian Western led the way in accommodating this interest by making common shares available to Albertans. The company offered one hundred and eighty thousand ordinary shares to the public, aimed primarily at the residents of this province, in March 1960. The shares were put on the market at $16.25 per share and sold like hotcakes. Over half a million shares were applied for. When the three million dollars' worth of shares were all allotted, Canadian Western had more than three thousand new shareholders, most of them residents of Alberta.

The experiment was so successful that Northwestern began making plans to prepare a similar offering of shares. The two offerings were the first with common shares; although three years earlier, in 1957, Canadian Utilities made a start in this direction by issuing six million dollars' worth of convertible debentures to the public.

Prior to Canadian Western's issue of common stock to the public, almost ninety-eight percent of the company's common stock was owned by International Utilities. The 1960 offering brought the proportion owned by the general public up to eleven percent.

Canadian to the Core

The matter of domination of Canadian industry by foreign capital, particularly those industries based on natural resources, came under considerable fire in the media in 1960. Critics included James Coyne, governor of the Bank of Canada, who raised the issue at a meeting of the Canadian Chamber of Commerce in Calgary.

Actually, an analysis of the share structure of International Utilities showed that while the corporation owned most of the common stock of the Alberta energy companies, the common stock of International Utilities itself was quite widely held. Only fifty-two percent of its common stock was owned by United States residents. The remainder was held in Canada, Great Britain and other countries. The shares of International Utilities were listed on the New York and Toronto Stock exchanges.

International Utilities had a board of fifteen directors of whom four were residents of Canada and one of Great Britain. But the Alberta energy companies also had their own boards of directors. Each had eleven directors, all of whom, except one, were residents of Alberta. The exception was the president of International Utilities.

Dennis Yorath commented on local control and management in a message to the staff:

> . . . As you well know, our staff consists entirely of Canadian citizens, all Albertans, each with a stake in the communities in which they live. None of them has been brought here from the United States. Our people regard Alberta as their home, and I know their children do also.
> . . . In the thirty-six years that I have been with our organization I have never experienced any interference or dictatorship by International Utilities in the operation of these companies, and I do not anticipate any.
> . . . The point which I wish to make is that while we are largely owned by an American corporation, that company in turn is almost fifty percent Canadian-owned, and operationally we are Canadian to the core — no one can truthfully say otherwise.

Despite this, the criticism that the companies were financially controlled from New York kept appearing in the press. And there was the fact too, that the government of Canada enacted tax legislation which made it more attractive for Canadians to invest in Canadian companies.

The upshot of all this was that International Utilities decided to establish itself as a United States corporation resident in Canada. The actual move didn't come about until the following year, but it was precipitated mainly by events in 1960. The move was of considerable benefit to the Canadian shareholders of International Utilities. Among other advantages they would now be entitled to a twenty percent tax credit on dividends.

Service Highly Regarded

A long with their efforts to encourage more ownership of common shares in Alberta, the companies accelerated their public information programs in general in 1960. A public opinion survey indicated among other things that Northwestern, in particular, was coming under more criticism than before on the matter of increased rates for gas sevice.

One gratifying result of the opinion survey was that regardless of whether people thought Northwestern was charging too much for gas, or whether they favored a municipal take-over of the company, the company's standard of service was highly regarded.

Another public information project that year was the release of a new film on the operations of the gas companies, titled, The Turn of a Valve. The twenty-minute sound-color motion picture was a successor to the 1955 production Meet Your Gas Company. The film dealt with the high cost of finding and developing gas sources and the investment by the gas companies in facilities to serve the public. This investment had amounted to some eighty-five million dollars in gross plant additions by the two companies in the short span of ten years.

Commenting on the industry, Carl O. Nickle, publisher of the Daily Oil Bulletin, said Alberta, which had long been Canada's largest consumer of gas, had the lowest cost of gas in North America. He said: "Alberta now has more than two hundred thousand consumers, the hungriest in Canada in all categories."

A New Growth Record — 1960

C anadian Western added nineteen communities to its gas system in 1960. Fifteen towns, villages or hamlets were served with gas purchased from TransCanada Pipelines Limited and transported by Alberta Gas Trunk Line Company Limited, and four communities were served from the company's pipelines. This is the largest number of communities that the company had ever added to its system in one year.

Almost four million dollars were expended on additions and improvements to the system and in bringing gas to the more than five thousand new customers added that year.

In Calgary, gas service was extended to forty-seven new shopping centres, eighteen office buildings, fifty-three apartments, two university buildings, a sports stadium, and a hospital extension among many large loads.

Communities added to the Northwestern system in 1960 included the town of Rimbey and the village of Bentley, in the picturesque valley of the Blindman River between Sylvan Lake and Gull Lake in central Alberta. On hand for the turn-on ceremonies in these communities were Alberta highways minister Gordon Taylor and industry & development minister Russell Patrick.

Patrick noted that forty-eight new industries had established in Alberta during the past year. "While not all communities in Alberta are able to attract industry, the availability of natural gas is an important plus factor," he said.

Industrial Sales Promoted

T he gas companies were very much aware of this. Industry was good business. Large industrial loads helped to keep domestic rates the lowest on the continent. If the company did not have a substantial industrial load, the portion of its costs which is properly borne by industry would have to be carried by residential and commercial customers.

With this in mind they created a sales and industrial development department in 1960, with one of its basic functions being to encourage new industry. So the industrious sixties brought not only a desire on the part of newly prosperous Albertans to own voting shares in their energy utilities, but the energy utilities themselves promoted industrialization as a means of diversifying their markets and loads.

This was true of the power company as well as the gas companies, "As to the future, it remains our basic challenge to intensify industrial diversification, thereby reducing our dependency on one major segment of our economy," said Canadian Utilities president Jack Dale.

The oil industry continued to be an important industrial load, particularly in new areas like Swan Hills. A transmission line from the Grande Prairie district grid was extended to Swan Hills during the year, and the two diesel units which had been operating in the temporary local plant were sold to the Yukon company.

Growth in the Yukon — 1960

U p in the Yukon things continued to move right along. General manager Edge King announced that two more communities were receiving power. On August 27, 1960, an isolated diesel plant and distribution system went into operation at Carcross, forty-five miles south of Whitehorse. This community derived its name from the two words "Caribou Crossing." It was here, at the outlet of Lake Bennett, that the huge herds of caribou gathered to cross the river.

A similar plant and distribution system went into operation at Carmacks in late October. Located a hundred miles north of Whitehorse, this community was named for George Carmacks, who touched off one of the most exciting eras in the annals of the north when he discovered gold in the Klondike.

Not far from Carmacks was the only operating coal mine in the Yukon, and about one hundred and fifty miles farther away was the United Keno Hill Mine, the largest silver mine in the British Commonwealth.

Edge King was moved to Edmonton in 1960 for increased responsibilities at head office. He retained, for the time being, the title of general manager of the Yukon companies, while James A. May, who had been transferred to Whitehorse in 1959, was appointed resident manager. Jim May first joined Canadian Utilities in May 1946, to work with the construction crew. In 1949 he launched some contracting projects of his own, but returned to the company in 1955 as construction supervisor and went on to become manager of the company's North Division.

Power Generation Expansion — 1960

S mall generating units were installed during the year in the Simonette oilfield and at Anzac in northwestern Alberta. At Hudson Hope, where the company had hopes of becoming increasingly involved in the huge B.C. hydro project on the Peace River, more work of a minor nature was done on the small generating plant. Financially, however, Canadian Utilities' involvement was not so minor, as the company acquired a large block of shares in the Peace River Power Development Company Limited, bringing its holdings to four hundred and forty-two thousand shares.

In Fort McMurray a new steel building was erected for the power plant, replacing the former log building. The big news, however, was still the Battle River station in Canadian Utilities' South Division. A power supply study was carried out by production engineer Wilson Sterling. Based on this study a second steam generating unit similar to the one already installed in the plant was ordered from Brown-Boveri (Canada) Limited. The target date for commissioning the new unit was the fall of 1964. This, and the new 30-megawatt gas turbine generator for the Vermilion plant, was all part of a five-year program of capital works started in 1959, expected to cost in the order of fifteen million dollars.

Another first occurred in 1960 when Stettler became the first community in Alberta to adopt a street lighting conversion program. The three-year program would see every streetlight in the town converted to a mercury vapor lamp, providing much brighter illumination than the former incandescent lights.

Northland Utilities — 1961

O n January 10, 1961, a joint statement issued by Howard Butcher III, president of International Utilities, and A.U. Anderson, president of Northland Utilities Limited, announced that International had taken steps to acquire control of Northland Utilities by means of a stock exchange arrangement between the two organizations. Northland accepted the offer, which became official at its annual meeting of shareholders in Edmonton on June 19.

At that time Northland was supplying electric service to thirty-one communities in Alberta, the Northwest Territories and northern Saskatchewan, and natural gas service to seventeen communities in Alberta and British Columbia.

The communities served with electric power were Athabasca, Berwyn, Blue-sky, Brownvale, Colinton, Dixonville, Donnelly, Enilda, Fairview, Falher, Fort Vermilion, Girouxville, Grimshaw, High Level, High Prairie, Hines Creek, Jasper, Jean Cote, Joussard, Hotchkiss, Lac La Biche, Manning, Meanook, McLennan, Nampa, North Star, Notikewin, Wabasca and Whitelaw in Alberta; Hay River, Northwest Territories; and Uranium City in Saskatchewan.

Those served with natural gas were: Berwyn, Bluesky, Brownvale, Clairmont, Fairview, Grande Prairie, Grimshaw, High Prairie, Jasper, Peace River, Spirit River, Rycroft, Sexsmith, Whitelaw and Woking in Alberta, and Dawson Creek and Pouce Coupe in British Columbia.

The major portion of Northland's gross revenue was derived from its electrical properties, which in 1960 totalled one million seven hundred and seventy-five thousand dollars. Its natural gas revenues for the same period were almost one million five hundred thousand dollars.

Jack Dale was named president of Northland in addition to serving as president of Canadian Utilities and its subsidiaries in the Yukon and at Fort McMurray. Dale had become president of Canadian Utilities in 1956, and by this time was also on the board of directors of International Utilities and Northwestern.

Northland had been founded almost fifteen years earlier. Prior to the formation of the company, Dominion Electric Company operated a small electric system in the Peace River area in Alberta along with similar operations in Saskatchewan and Manitoba with headquarters at Estevan, Saskatchewan. The general manager of Dominion Electric was Walter H. Schlosser.

When the Saskatchewan Power Corporation was established in 1946, Dominion Electric was dissolved and Schlosser purchased the company's interests in Alberta. The new company was named Northland Utilities Limited. Schlosser was joined in the new venture by William Sullivan and N. Warren DuBois, who also were previously employed by Dominion Electric.

By 1961 Northland was supplying natural gas service to more than eight thousand customers, mostly in the Peace River country. The number of electric customers by this time had risen even higher — to ten thousand. The company had a staff of one hundred and thirty-five. About one hundred were located in the various service points and the others at the head office in Edmonton, at 10042 - 109 Street.

Northland joined the rest of the utility group in the Milner Building on October 14. The new location provided improved working conditions and greater efficiency in intercompany communication.

Greater efficiencies were brought about in the service areas as well. A 69-kilovolt transmission loop was completed, interconnecting the generating plants and main substations of Canadian Utilities and Northland. Studies to determine the most economical method of operating the integrated systems resulted in a generating program that minimized production costs throughout the Grande

Prairie-Peace River service area. Joint use of generating and transmission facilities was brought about wherever possible. Joint purchasing of supplies, in larger quantities, brought about better unit prices. Northland's billing was converted to the punch card system.

Reddy Kilowatt

The little man with a lightning flash for a body, a light bulb for a nose and an electric outlet for an ear, first became associated with Canadian Utilities in 1942. In 1961 this symbol of electricity, called Reddy Kilowatt, also became the symbol of Northland. Reddy Kilowatt was an international trademark available only to investor-owned power companies, and the Canadian Utilities group was the first to introduce him in western Canada.

Reddy was born in 1926 when Ashton B. Collins, an employee of the Alabama Power Company, attended a convention in Chicago. On his way home by train Collins was meditating on the notion that there should be a way of personalizing the usefulness and readiness of electric service.

As he gazed out of the train window a sudden thunderstorm developed and a brilliant stroke of lightning illuminated the sky. A clear picture materialized in Collins' mind — a many-handed electric servant ready to work at the push of a button.

It took a while for the symbol to catch on. In 1934 Philadelphia Electric Company adopted him, and after that he became the symbol of one private company after another, until he was adopted by more than two hundred power companies in the U.S. and Canada and twenty foreign countries.

Changing trends in advertising have taken their toll on the use of Reddy Kilowatt, but it is a symbol fondly remembered by many in the industry.

Changes in the North — 1961

Jim May was recalled from Whitehorse in 1961 to take over the management of the Drumheller District, as Gordon Parker returned to head office as transmission and distribution superintendent. Appointed to take Jim May's place in the Yukon was R.H. (Bob) Choate, a graduate in electrical engineering from the University of Alberta, who had been with the company since 1952.

Then there was Fort McMurray. While not as far north, in many ways it was as challenging and exciting as the Yukon or points on Lake Athabasca. Those were the days before Fort McMurray had an all-weather road to Edmonton. District superintendent Bob Duncan was also president of the Fort McMurray Chamber of Commerce and a leading advocate for a good highway to the south.

Duncan and Bill Hrushka of head office moved a 100-kilowatt diesel unit to Fort McMurray by truck on February 21. The seven-ton unit was the first such shipment of freight to make the trip by road. The last lap of the three hundred and fifty-mile trip — more than two hundred miles of winding forestry trail beyond Lac La Biche — was the challenging part. It was snowing heavily and they passed other vehicles stalled on icy hills but arrived at their destination safe and sound. Duncan hailed the trip as a milestone in Fort McMurray's quest for highway access to the outside world.

Milner Becomes IU Chairman — 1961

International Utilities' move to set up its principal office in Toronto came about in 1961. H.R. Milner was appointed chairman of the board. The announcement was made by International Utilities' president Howard Butcher III on August 3 following a board meeting. Butcher also announced the appointment of Jack Dale and Dennis Yorath as vice-presidents of International Utilities.

Establishing International Utilities as a United States corporation resident in Canada considerably enhanced the corporation as most of its properties and operations were in this country. Not only were most of the directors for the corporation Canadian, but the latest list of shareholders showed there was now a larger number of common shares held in Canada than in the United States.

Of the common shares, there were thirty-six hundred Canadian and about three thousand United States shareholders. Moreover, of the total outstanding preferred and common shares, forty-seven percent were held in Canada and forty-six percent in the United States. The remaining shares were held chiefly in Great Britain.

Milner was a national figure in many respects. Earlier in the year, at the end of February, Prime Minister John Diefenbaker had announced Milner's appointment to the twenty-five-member National Productivity Council. Members of the council represented primary industries, commercial establishments, labor and agricultural organizations and the general public. It was set up by the Canadian government to provide advice and information on the problems of raising productivity in Canadian industry and meeting the challenge of the technological era. Milner was the only Albertan on the council.

Milner's other public service activities at this time included his being chancellor of the University of King's College in Halifax, governor of Trinity College School and chairman of the Edmonton Advisory Board of the Salvation Army.

Expropriation in B.C. — 1961

On August 1, 1961, the province of British Columbia took over B.C. Electric Co. Ltd. in a sudden and unexpected move.

While there had been rumors for some weeks as to what Premier W.A.C. Bennett had in mind, few suspected that the move was imminent. It appears his own MLAs knew nothing of the legislation they were going to be asked to approve until they had taken their seats in the legislative chamber for the special session on August 1. But the bill was passed quickly and unanimously. Even the directors and officers of the company said they had no knowledge of the government's intentions.

While the legislation was being considered, the staff of the utility company was attending the funeral of their chairman and chief executive officer, Dal Grauer. It was not until after the funeral that they learned what had happened. Premier Bennett said he was greatly concerned over the coincidence of the timing, but Grauer's personal friends claimed it was merciful he had been spared the news.

The president of the Investment Dealers Association of Canada said: "It seems inconceivable in a democratic society that any government can expropriate the properties of others on its own terms without provision for appeal."

Some business and industrial leaders, and newspaper editors as well, said that calling this move "expropriation" was too mild; it was "confiscation." An English newspaper described the move as "one of the most shattering blows to the cause of international investment for a long time."

Dennis Yorath said: "It is frightening to realize that, in a country such as Canada, the property of any corporation or individual can be seized by the stroke of a pen without any previous discussion or negotiation with the owners, or even arbitration proceedings, and without any subsequent appeal to the courts of law."

The *Lethbridge Herald* said: "If governments can and should take over power companies, why not other industries? If private enterprise in the field of power is expropriated by the government when it is successfully built up and proven profitable, how safe is private enterprise in anything else?"

Premier Ernest Manning said that in Alberta: ". . . it is in the best interests of the public to leave the operation of utilities to private enterprise. No advantage could accrue to the people of this province through public ownership that is not available to them through power development by private ownership as carried on today."

Rate Schedule Upheld — 1961

A highlight of 1961 for the natural gas industry was the Supreme Court of Canada's upholding of the Public Utilities Board's decision of 1959 on Northwestern's rates, which had been challenged by the cities of Edmonton and Red Deer. A unanimous decision handed down by the Supreme Court confirmed the jurisdiction of the Public Utilities Board. In effect, the position taken by the company was upheld.

New developments for Northwestern during the year included extension of service to the town of Rocky Mountain House and the villages of Eckville and

Clive. These communities were served with gas purchased from gas export companies and transported to Alberta Gas Trunk Line.

Sales to large industrial users continued as one of the major concerns of Northwestern. Large loads helped to hold down the average cost of gas, especially for the domestic customer. But now, for the first time, independent brokers were trying to sell quantities of gas to industrial markets in Edmonton and central Alberta in competition with Northwestern.

The Swan Hills area was an example. Several competing projects for the conservation and marketing of casinghead gas produced in this oilfield northwest of Edmonton were being promoted. Two of them went to the Oil and Gas Conservation Board as applications. This meant Northwestern had to go to the board and reiterate its position that it was in the long-term best interests of the Alberta consumer to have such residue gas marketed through the facilities of the gas company.

Eventually a compromise was reached. Northwestern offered to purchase from three producer applicants, but only one — Federated Processing Ltd. — was prepared to negotiate a definite contract. As a result a contract was signed with Federated and a start was made on a Northwestern Utilities pipeline from Swan Hills to Edmonton.

Canadian Western Anniversaries — 1961 - 1962

The year 1961 was the half-century point for Canadian Western as a corporation. On July 19, 1911, the company was incorporated with the cumbersome name, The Canadian Western Natural Gas, Light, Heat and Power Company, Limited.

The company came into being as the result of natural gas discoveries made by Eugene Coste in the early 1900s. By 1961 most of the old-timers who knew Coste personally were gone, but the name was still familiar to most Calgarians because of the Coste House in the Mount Royal district, a large French chateau type residence he built and in which he and his family lived for a number of years.

Construction of the one hundred and seventy-mile pipeline from Bow Island had started on April 22, 1912, and was completed on July 19. A few days later gas was turned into the Calgary and Lethbridge systems. Most of the golden jubilee celebrations took place in 1962, when the company had actually completed fifty years of service to the people of Southern Alberta, rather than dating the celebration from the time of incorporation of the company in 1911.

Observing the golden jubilee in 1962 was doubly significant since 1962 was the year the company passed the hundred thousand mark in customers served. From fewer than seven thousand customers in the original five communities, to one hundred thousand in eighty-five communities with a combined population of almost four hundred thousand people, was an imposing growth record.

In 1913, the first year for which complete figures are available, the company sold just under four billion cubic feet of gas, with the revenue totalling about eight hundred thousand dollars. At the end of 1962 the comparative figures were in excess of 46 billion cubic feet, with the revenue totalling nearly seventeen million dollars. Between 1912 and 1930 total production from the Bow Island field was nearly 34 billion cubic feet — about equal to what the company's customers were using in nine months in 1962.

Average rates, too, were interesting. In 1913 the average rate per thousand cubic feet was twenty-one cents. It climbed to a high of forty-six cents in 1925, and at the fifty-year mark was just over thirty-six cents. Gross tangible assets of the company in 1912 were about five million dollars. At the end of 1961 they stood at almost fifty-seven million dollars.

A revealing comparison can also be found in taxation figures. The first year for which a figure was available on federal, provincial, municipal and other taxes was 1926, when they totalled forty-one thousand dollars. In 1961 they were nearly two and a half million dollars.

From its early Bow Island beginnings as a source of energy primarily for heating and cooking, natural gas progressed to where fifty years later it was being used in innumerable ways commercially and industrially as well as domestically — generating electricity, powering sugar beet factories, energizing pelletizing plants for cattle feed, driving pumps for irrigation systems, providing fuel for breweries and canning factories, running machinery in oil refineries and cement plants, heating metal and melting glass in manufacturing processes, cooling huge office towers in the summertime through gas-fired air conditioning, and providing the raw materials for petrochemical developments — to mention just a few of its many applications.

In Calgary the occasion of having completed fifty years of service was marked by a commemorative ceremony at which Mayor Harry Hays unveiled a plaque in the Canadian Western office on July 24. Three days later Mayor E.C. Lonsdale of Lethbridge unveiled a similar plaque in that city. Special tributes were paid to customers who had been with the company continuously through its fifty-year history.

The Calgary mayor noted that among cities of more than one hundred thousand people, the city received natural gas service more reasonably than any other on the North American continent, and suggested that if the company continued to give the same sort of service for the next fifty years as it had in the past fifty, it would still be operating in the next century.

The mayor of Lethbridge told the luncheon crowd there that the fifty years of association between Canadian Western and the city was a "shining example of how private enterprise and the people work hand in hand." Here are some of Lonsdale's comments:

175

I want, on behalf of the city, to congratulate the company and all those people who have contributed in the early and more trying years. Today I think that the level of service that we all enjoy is a measure of how the company has developed.

I would just like to point out the fact that all of these things that look like sure-fire deals today, basically when they started out they were a high-risk proposition. Somebody decided to take that risk and I think we, whatever level of the world we may be in, should restrain ourselves from being too envious and too quick to try and move into that field.

Quarter-Million Customers — 1962

Canadian Western and Northwestern both passed the one hundred thousand customer mark in 1962. In just ten years, from 1952 to 1962, the number of customers had doubled. The new associate company, Northland Utilities, added nearly ten thousand gas customers, bringing the total number of gas customers of the three companies to more than two hundred and ten thousand.

The Canadian Utilities electrical operations passed the fifty thousand mark in 1962, up two thousand from the previous year. Northland had more than eleven thousand electrical customers by now, giving the electrical operations of the energy group a total of more than sixty-one thousand customers. This put the number of customers served by the group past a quarter of a million.

The half-century mark was the occasion, too, for bringing about a new look in the companies' corporate identification program. The traditional crests of the two gas companies were retired and replaced by a modern graphic symbol which has been used extensively in all company publications, on company stationery, buildings, vehicles and equipment, and is even flown on a company flag. Among its many benefits was that it was to be used by both Canadian Western and Northwestern, giving them a common identity and making gas company recognition much easier.

The symbol is a stylized form of the letters "N" and "G", for natural gas, incorporating also the blue flame of gas. Its development took place over a period of several months and was designed by Len Gibbs, at that time creative director of the companies' advertising agency, James Lovick & Co. Ltd. of Edmonton. Gibbs in later years left the advertising field to become a fine artist and several of his works are represented in the company's corporate art collection.

Shortly after the gas companies introduced their symbol Canadian Utilities came out with a new company symbol featuring the stylized letters "C" and "U", incorporating a lightning stroke as a symbol of electricity.

Willson Becomes President — 1962

H.R. Milner retired as chairman of the board for the two gas companies at the annual meeting in February 1962. Dennis Yorath was elected chairman of both companies. Milner remained on the board of directors and was made honorary chairman of both companies. Bruce F. Willson was appointed president.

Milner continued as chairman of the board and as a director of International Utilities Corporation of Toronto. He also remained as chairman and a director of Canadian Utilities.

By this time Milner was one of Canada's most prominent business leaders. In addition to being senior partner in the law firm of Milner, Steer, Dyde, Massie, Layton, Cregan and Macdonnell, he was a director of numerous companies, including The Royal Bank of Canada, Canada Cement Co. Ltd., Page Hersey Tubes Ltd., North American Life Assurance Co., Burns & Co. Ltd., and Northwest Industries Ltd.

The gas companies' new president, Bruce Willson, had joined Northwestern in November 1945, following active service in the Canadian Army. He held a number of engineering appointments and in 1953 was appointed assistant general manager. Late in 1954 he was transferred to Calgary as director of administrative services for the two gas companies. In 1956 he was appointed vice-president operations and, in 1958, executive vice-president.

Gas as Total Energy Fuel — 1962

Northwestern's industrial sales showed a healthy upswing in 1962, amounting by this time to about forty percent of the company's total sales. The sales and industrial development department put forth every effort to keep the gas company in the forefront of industry, and it was successful at it. For example, that year it held a two-day seminar at which more than a hundred consulting engineers and architects met to take part in discussions on natural gas utilization in heating, air conditioning, refrigeration, the gas fuel engine, the gas turbine, and incineration.

One of the highlights of the seminar was an address by Dana Price, a consulting engineer from Houston, Texas, on the "total energy package," a concept which utilizes natural gas as the sole fuel source for the generation of power, heating and air conditioning of buildings.

The gas companies were beginning to think in terms of such concepts, in fact, as the use of natural gas as the sole source of power not only in large industries, commercial establishments and educational institutions, but even in homes. Conventional methods of converting fuel to electrical energy, said company engineers, had peak efficiencies of about forty percent. New power sources, on the other hand, had potential efficiencies of sixty to eighty percent and could also utilize waste heat to generate electricity.

Costs of transporting and distributing energy in the form of natural gas, the companies claimed, were far below those of electricity. So they dreamed about all-gas homes that would in future receive electricity from a fuel cell tucked in the basement. Industries would have their own MHD converters. MHD stands for the jaw-breaking name magnetohydrodynamic. An MHD converter employs a high temperature gas stream moving as a conductor between powerful magnetic poles.

Construction Activity — 1962

In the Pembina oilfield, near Drayton Valley, the company built a gas interchange system by means of which gas was transported from the field to Alberta and Southern Gas Company Limited. The gas was fed into the thirty-inch Alberta Gas Trunk pipeline south of Lodgepole.

In the southwestern part of the province Canadian Western extended service in 1962 to the communities of Blairmore, Bellevue, Frank and Hillcrest, located in the Crowsnest Pass, and to the community of Cremona, southwest of Red Deer. Service became economically feasible for these communities as a result of the construction in 1961 of the foothills system of The Alberta Gas Trunk Line Company Limited. Gas for these communities was obtained under Canadian Western's contracts with the owners of the gas transported through that system.

During construction of the Canadian Western transmission line in the Crowsnest Pass it was necessary to lay eight thousand feet of pipe in the bed of Crowsnest Lake. For the project the company constructed a barge out of old telephone poles, with barrel floats and a plank deck on which an electric welder and four to five men worked during the operation.

When the pipe was laid it was placed under pressure and a diver sent down to check the line for damage. It was an interesting all-company operation. Even the boat used to tow the pipe and the barge was, in a way, a gas company boat. It belonged to Canadian Western's Ernie Elvey, who was its captain during "Operation Crowsnest Lake." As for the barge, the crew claimed it was a mighty fine piece of workmanship, and when they were finished with it they donated it to a church summer camp located on the lake.

In general, the energy business in Alberta kept pace with the prosperous business climate of the province. Canadian census figures showed that on a percentage basis Alberta's population increase was higher than any other province.

Investor Versus State Ownership

Canadian Utilities lost its last existing foothold in power generation and distribution in British Columbia in 1962 when the government-owned B.C.

Hydro and Power Authority purchased the small diesel plant and distribution system at Hudson Hope, near the proposed Peace River power development.

The provincially-owned hydro company was formed by the B.C. legislature in 1962, being an amalgamation with the old B.C. Electric Company which the provincial government had acquired the previous year. The former investor-owned B.C. Electric began its hydroelectric and electric-railway operations in the province in the late 1890s, and many businessmen were shocked when it was expropriated by the B.C. government in 1961.

With the energy business going great guns in the prosperous province of Alberta, some people were advocating that the government should be in the power business here as well. Canadian Utilities' president Jack Dale commented on this in a speech to the Alberta Weekly Newspapers Association.

Quoting from a pamphlet on electric power published by the Dominion Bureau of Statistics, Dale produced figures showing that the fixed asset costs per kilowatt of installed capacity were twenty-three percent higher in government-owned electric utilities than in investor-owned companies. The fixed asset investment per customer, too, was higher for government utilities, by almost thirteen percent.

The figures showed that employees per thousand customers numbered twenty-four percent more in government utilities, and the government paid twenty-two percent more than investor-owned utilities in salaries and wages per customer served. Finally, the cost per kilowatt hour sold to the customer was seventeen percent higher in government-owned electric utilities.

Looking at what some other countries were doing, Dale noted that in the United States, for example, private enterprise served seventy percent of the population with electric power. In Sweden, one of the most highly socialized countries in the world, fifty-eight percent of the electrical service was provided by private enterprise.

Some countries were reverting to private enterprise after trying state operation of power systems. In Japan the huge state monopoly was replaced almost completely by nine private companies, each operating in its own territory under the supervision of a state control board. In West Germany a large industrial complex, including major power companies, was being denationalized.

Income Tax Rebates — 1963

C orporate income taxes were another aspect of the ownership of gas and electric companies not faced by government-owned utilities. Here the investor-owned utilities were at a disadvantage. Jack Dale and Bruce Willson both made submissions on this subject in 1963 to the Royal Commission on Taxation.

The Canadian Utilities' brief urged that all electric utilities be taxed uniformly regardless of ownership. "In the year 1962," Dale said in his brief, "our income taxes amounted to one million three hundred and sixty thousand dollars. We know of no other industry which has such a high tax component in its commodity sales price."

If it was necessary to tax utility companies to obtain federal revenue, he contended, then customers of government-owned utilities should pay taxes in the same manner and at the same rate as customers served by investor-owned utilities.

The long and difficult fight to obtain income tax rebates for customers was led for the Canadian Utilities group by its vice-president of finance, Kenneth L. MacFadyen. He worked in co-operation with the Canadian Gas Association to present a united front on behalf of the gas industry.

The efforts of Canadian Utilities and other investor-owned gas and electric utilities were successful, to a considerable extent, in convincing the federal government that inequities did exist. The wheels were set in motion to rebate income taxes paid by the utility companies to the appropriate provincial governments. The government of Alberta, in turn, decided to pass the money on to the utilities for a rebate to their customers. It was not until the fall of 1969 that this finally came about. The income tax rebate still appears on Alberta utility bills today.

Bigger Generators, More Power — 1963

C anadian Utilities continued to move toward supplying electricity from large centralized power stations in 1962 and 1963. The 30-megawatt Westinghouse gas turbo-generator was completed in the Vermilion plant, and remote controls were installed so that it could be operated from the Battle River station.

At Battle River meanwhile, work continued on schedule towards installation of the second 32-megawatt unit, the commissioning target date being 1964.

The owners of the nearby Diplomat Coal Mine introduced a giant shovel to speed production and bring about new economies in coal mining. At the time this was Canada's largest mechanical shovel, capable of moving thirty-six yards of overburden in one scoop. The shovel, powered by electricity from the Battle River plant, was bought from the Peabody Coal Company in Indiana. To move it to Alberta by rail required forty flatcars. When assembled, the machine weighed nearly three million pounds.

Most of the electricity for the south division was now generated from the Battle River plant, and the Drumheller plant was used mainly for meeting peak load power. The two General Electric steam turbine generators in the old Drumheller plant were retired. They had served the district well for many years, generating the bulk of power used in the area between 1927, when the first unit was installed, and 1948, when the new plant went into operation.

However, the usefulness of these generators did not cease with their removal from the plant. The smaller unit was donated by the company to the Southern Alberta Institute of Technology in Calgary for use in the power engineering courses. The 2,500-kilowatt turbo-generator, in service since 1929, went to the new Northern Alberta Institute of Technology in Edmonton for the same purpose.

The Grande Prairie power plant underwent considerable change in the spring of the year. The four Polar Atlas diesel units were removed and the old switchboard was dismantled and at two o'clock in the morning of August 28, 1963, Canadian Utilities engineers put the finishing touches on a new 72-kilovolt tie line to make the Peace River country a part of the Alberta provincial grid.

The operating tie was made at the Sarah Lake substation near Swan Hills from which an eight-mile transmission line had been built to the Calgary Power line from Whitecourt. The new tie line replaced the 24-kilovolt oilfield line built in 1960 to tie the two systems together at this point. The Peace River system could now operate in parallel with the provincial grid.

The construction of a second and still heavier transmission line between the district and the provincial grid also got underway in 1963. It featured a new type of 144-kilovolt single-pole-transmission structure known as a wishbone. These structures, the first of their kind in the province, improved electrical reliability and provided good mechanical strength at reasonable cost. By year-end about half of the fifty-five-mile line from Fox Creek to Valleyview was completed.

Canadian Utilities' electrical operations were moving along well. In the period of a decade, energy sales had increased almost three hundred percent. During that period the company expended more than thirty-five million dollars to expand its power systems.

The most rapid expansion, on a percentage basis, was taking place in the north. The Yukon companies, from the time they were acquired in 1958, tripled energy sales and doubled their revenue by the end of 1963. The Fort McMurray Power Company showed similar growth. From the time it was acquired in 1957 it tripled its energy sales and almost doubled its revenue.

Then there were Northland's operations, mainly in the Peace River country. A plant was completed at Worsley, additional generating facilities were installed at Fort Vermilion, High Level, La Crete and various microwave sites were installed along the Mackenzie Highway.

On the gas side of the business, Northland received franchises to serve McLennan and Donnelly with gas by means of an extension from the Peace River transmission line. A pipeline was built from Worsley to Fairview, bringing additional gas to Fairview for power generation.

Computers Speed Accounting Change

GASCO 1962 was an acronym which had a special meaning for the accounting department at Canadian Western. It stood for General Accounting System Change-Over, and it meant some burning of the midnight oil for the people who were intimately involved in streamlining the system. General accounting procedures were changed from the old hand posting system to punch card data processing.

At the same time the system of accounts was converted to the new Canadian Gas Association classification, and a new system of responsibility accounting was introduced. In the commercial and machine accounting section the delinquent system was completely revamped with the emphasis on automation.

All this was part of an intercompany program which has become increasingly more sophisticated over the years. By today's standards those early installations would appear as pieces of rather ancient and inefficient hardware, yet at the time they enabled the companies to begin gearing their entire operations for the electronic age.

People who watched the federal election results on television in the spring of 1963 were impressed by the way the CBC used an IBM 1401 computer to process data with lightning speed and predict the final outcome of balloting across the country. Shortly afterwards president Bruce Willson announced that the gas companies would soon be installing the same models of computers in Calgary and Edmonton.

No major reduction in staff was involved in the change-over. Employees who might have given up routine tasks to the computer were given new job opportunities as the companies continued to grow and expand. "Computers are part of the move towards progress and efficiency," Willson said. "If we are to discharge our responsibility to our customers to provide the lowest cost service possible, then we must take whatever steps are necessary to improve efficiency and reduce unit costs."

The Swan Hills Line — 1963

For Northwestern in 1963 the largest project was the building of a four million dollar pipeline from Swan Hills.

The pipeline, one hundred and twenty miles long, brought new natural gas supplies to Northwestern's markets from a vast complex of oilfields to the north and west of Edmonton. The main supply came from the processing plant operated by Imperial Oil at Judy Creek. This supply helped serve the needs of one of Northwestern's major customers, Canadian Industries Limited, in northeast Edmonton.

The twelve-inch line from Swan Hills went through all kinds of terrain, and involved the crossing of numerous sloughs, swamps, creeks, roads, railways and three large rivers. At the start, trenching through Swan Hills muskeg presented its own kind of challenge. The soil here is frozen like cement in winter and soggy as a soaked sponge in spring and summer. In some areas of this virgin country access roads called shooflies had to be cut from the main road at various points to facilitate movement of men and equipment. Then there was the rolling terrain in the Calahoo area where almost every pipe joint had to be shaped to the contours of the ditch by a hydraulic pipe-bending machine.

The project was largely an Alberta undertaking, with pipe manufactured in Edmonton by Alberta Phoenix Tube and Pipe Limited; construction by a local contractor, Banister of Edmonton; pipe enamel from the Husky refinery at Lloydminster and wrapping from the Peace River Glass Company plant at Fort Saskatchewan.

Gas Reserves — 1963

At the end of 1963 the recoverable reserves of gas in the fields connected to the Northwestern system were estimated to be more than three trillion cubic feet. Similar reserves in the fields connected to the Canadian Western system were estimated at more than one trillion cubic feet. During the year one-third of the total gas requirements of the Northwestern system was produced from the company's own properties. Most of the balance was purchased from gas processing plants located in the major oilfields in the Edmonton area.

The proven reserves for the entire province at the time were considered to be about thirty-four trillion cubic feet, with a considerable amount of this already contracted for, or allocated to specific markets. TransCanada Pipe Lines, for example, had approval from the Oil and Gas Conservation Board (which administered the Gas Resources Preservation Act controlling gas export) for the export of six and a half trillion cubic feet. TransCanada in 1963 filed an application for the export of an additional three trillion cubic feet.

This application by TransCanada was followed by another submission to the board from the gas companies, similar to submissions made some years earlier, urging caution in authorizing export of gas. One rule set by the board was that the estimated provincial needs for a period of thirty years should be set aside before additional export was authorized. "We feel quite strongly that the full thirty-year needs should be available in the form of economically located proven reserves, without placing any reliance on possible future discoveries, before further export is authorized," Bruce Willson stated in a message to the gas companies' staffs. "We have filed a submission to this effect with the conservation board."

"Total Energy" Development — 1963

Exciting new developments continued to take place in 1963 in the utilization of natural gas promoted by the sales and industrial development departments of the companies. One of these developments was the "total energy" concept in which the natural gas supply to a building or plant is the sole source of energy for heating, lighting, air conditioning and power purposes. An outstanding example of this was the recently-completed Hillcrest Junior High School in west Edmonton. A compact, windowless building of circular design, the school was the first total energy school in Canada. Its unusual design created great interest among school authorities.

Another example was the station of No. 43 Canadian Forces Radar Squadron, east of Penhold. Generators powered by natural gas-fired turbines provided all the power requirements on this important air defense installation.

The air conditioning of commercial buildings was a large load for the companies. There was the new Northern Alberta Institute of Technology, for example, with a structure covering an area of more than fifteen acres, making it the largest building in Canada to be fully air-conditioned with natural gas.

Fortieth Anniversary — 1963

In the fall of 1963 Northwestern celebrated its fortieth anniversary. The company could look back on a proud service record during those years. Gas sales were now seventy times what they were in 1924, the first full year of operation. Revenues were fifty-three times as high as they were in 1924. And the average gas rate was only thirty-two cents per thousand cubic feet, twenty-four percent less than the average rate in the first year. By now nearly half a million people in eighty different communities depended on the company for their fuel needs.

Times were buoyant, but they had not always been that way. There had been difficult struggles just to stay in business in the twenties and thirties. Except for a small dividend in 1930, no dividends were paid on the common stock until 1938. A sizeable portion of the company's plant had been built using funds raised by the sale of preferred shares and in both 1934 and 1935 the net income was not equal to the dividend requirements for those shares. Then the war years presented their own challenges, including shortage of manpower, materials and capital. But employees of the gas company worked with dedication and without fanfare, and the company pulled through.

From one supply line serving fewer than two thousand people in 1923, the Northwestern system over four decades grew into a network of more than twenty-seven hundred miles of transmission and distribution pipelines connected to seventeen major sources of supply.

Battle River Doubles — 1964

In 1964 the second 32-megawatt generator was commissioned at the Battle River station, doubling the plant's capacity. The new unit cost more than four million dollars.

Before the second Battle River unit was on line, engineering studies were well under way on the next phase of development for the plant. It was decided to proceed with a third unit, to be commissioned in 1968. The proposed unit would boost the capacity of the plant by 75 megawatts. However, demand was growing so rapidly that before plans for the third unit were completed the decision was made to double its capacity. It was evident additional capacity would be needed eventually. In the meantime, any excess capacity would be sold to Calgary Power.

Jack Ford, general manager of Canadian Utilities, estimated the cost of enlarging the plant and installing the new generator at twenty-two million dollars. This included the cost of providing for future enlargement of the plant, so that in years to come it would be able to accommodate 600 megawatts of generating capacity. Commissioning date for the third unit was set for June 1969.

Battle River was now well established as the central station for east-central Alberta, but it was too far from the Peace River country and the far north to serve that area economically. Additional generating capacity in the form of another gas turbine would be needed in the north prior to the commissioning of unit three at Battle River. The gas turbine would be installed somewhere in the northern part of the system, possibly in the Worsley area, which was served by Northland Utilities.

Meanwhile, the growth of the provincial transmission grid, reflecting increased co-operation among the electric utilities in the province, made some major strides in 1964. Three new tie lines were established between Canadian Utilities and Calgary Power. First, the Valleyview-Fox Creek line, begun the previous year, was completed in October. Second, a thirteen-mile 138-kilovolt line was extended from Vegreville to Holden where a switching station, jointly owned with Calgary Power, with major carrier and control equipment was completed. The third tie, consisting of twenty miles of combined 25 and 72-kilovolt line was built south of Empress in the Drumheller District.

In other transmission work, a line was completed from Slave Lake to Smith, so that the isolated Smith plant could now be dismantled.

Inside the Arctic Circle — 1964

In 1964 the Canadian Utilities group became the first investor-owned utility company providing electric power service north of the Arctic Circle. Early in the year an agreement was reached between The Yukon Electrical Company and the Yukon Territorial Government for the company to supply power to Old Crow, about six hundred miles northwest of Whitehorse and about eighty miles inside the Arctic Circle.

Under the agreement the operation would be reviewed in a year's time, and then the company would either turn it back to the government or make a long-term arrangement for the supply of electricity to the community.

Old Crow over a period of years became endeared to readers of *The Edmonton Journal* and other newspapers by the inimitable column of Edith Josie, starting with Here are the News. This community is located on the Porcupine River, a tributary of the Yukon. It is three hundred and fifty miles from the nearest road at Dawson City, and accessible only by air or by water.

The plant was to consist of three diesel units, of which two were to be held in reserve. It would supply government, RCMP, the mission, and native customers. Maintenance would be carried out from Whitehorse, using charter aircraft. Building this plant and distribution system was no routine matter because of the extreme isolation of the community.

Electrical engineer Glenn Mead, in charge of the installation for Yukon Electrical, wrote a report for Canadian Utilities' staff magazine, *The Transmitter*, of his trip to Old Crow and the construction of the plant. "Building a power plant in Old Crow was one of the most interesting jobs The Yukon Electrical Company has ever undertaken," Mead said. "Always before, when we built a plant, it had been possible to return for something that was forgotten, or to take it in on the next trip. But at a cost of four hundred dollars to charter a plane it had to be a one-shot deal with nothing forgotten. It would have been impossible to do this if it were not for the extensive experience and knowledge our employees here have in construction of small diesel plants. Even so we checked, double-checked and re-double-checked lists of material that was sent on a barge which left Dawson City on July 9."

On July 8, 1964, Bob Choate, Angelo Andolfatto and Don Joe flew to Old Crow on a regular scheduled flight which went once a month from Dawson City. Choate staked out the location of the plant and made a few last-minute arrangements, then flew out on the same plane, leaving Andolfatto and Joe behind to build the plant. Before the barge arrived with the generators they had the floor laid, consisting of gravel and local logs. They finished erecting the plant on July 20.

That was the day Bill Kerr, Vern Finster, Steven Esteves, Nels Madsen and Glenn Mead left to commission the units. They arrived in Dawson City in the evening, but couldn't get a plane to Old Crow until the next evening. It was a strange experience to take off at 11 p.m. and watch the sky getting lighter from then to midnight as they flew into the land of the midnight sun, over rugged mountains known as the Ogilvie Range. They landed on a gravel bar four miles upstream from Old Crow at 12:30, and as soon as they had unloaded their gear the plane took off again. "It was, of course, broad daylight," Mead said, "so the mosquitoes had no difficulty in locating us and nearly ate us up by the time the RCMP boat arrived to pick us up. We stayed in tents, and tenting has its own set of disadvantages that do not need description here. We were fortunate that the department of public works was building a new building for the RCMP in Old Crow and we made arrangments to eat at their cookhouse. It was a bit of a shock to us to have to walk half a mile for our meals. We soon gave up coffee breaks."

The nearest settlement to Old Crow is Inuvik, one hundred and eighty miles to the east. The isolation of the people living there is indicated by their reference to places like Dawson City as "outside."

The barge carrying the last of the equipment arrived in Old Crow at midnight on July 27. Two days later the crew was ready to return to Whitehorse and radioed Connelly-Dawson Airways for a plane. The plane, however, developed engine trouble and had to make an emergency landing on a lake about seventy miles south of Old Crow. The weather was terrible, and it took all day to get the pilot, one passenger and some freight flown into Old Crow. It was nearly noon on July 31 when the utility crew finally left for Dawson which looked like a metropolis to them, to say nothing of how Whitehorse looked after they motored the three hundred and forty miles back to home base.

Fred Wittlinger, who had been managing a small plant in Old Crow for the Northern Canada Power Commission for three years, transferred to Yukon Electrical and agreed to stay in Old Crow another year to train a local man to operate the plant.

Service in the North — 1964

O ther communities in the Yukon and northern B.C. to which electric service was extended in 1964 included Burwash, Stewart Crossing, Swift River in the Territory and Lower Post in B.C.

Northland Utilities reached still farther north in 1964 when it purchased the distribution system in Fort Providence, Northwest Territories, from the Department of Northern Affairs and National Resources, and built a power plant. Fort Providence was strategically located at the Mackenzie River crossing on the new Hay River-Yellowknife highway.

The plants at Hay River, Fort Vermilion and Jasper were enlarged that year. And as the Great Slave Railway pushed farther north, new areas were opening up, one of which was High Level. Northland established a new 1,350-kilowatt plant there in 1964. Northland also extended gas service to the town of Beaverlodge and the village of Hythe.

In Canadian Utilities' northeast area there was more good news in 1964. Great Canadian Oil Sands (GCOS) launched its two hundred and fifty million dollar project to extract oil from the tar sands of the area. The new plant was located twenty-five miles down the Athabasca river from Fort McMurray, adjacent to the Cities Service development at Mildred Lake. At the opening ceremony on July 2 Alberta Premier E.C. Manning officially launched the GCOS project.

The rapid influx of construction workers increased the demand on the company's system that year by sixty-five percent over the 1963 load. Bob Duncan, Fort McMurray District superintendent, knew this was only the beginning!

Plastic Pipe Speeds Rural Gas Service — 1964

The most far-reaching new development in the gas companies in 1964 was the introduction of plastic pipe natural gas lines on a large scale for irrigation, especially in southern Alberta, and for gas distribution in rural areas. As an outgrowth of this technological breakthrough, the companies embarked on an aggressive program of extending gas service to thousands of customers previously beyond economic reach of existing pipelines.

On those irrigation applications requiring only small-diameter pipe, a product made from polyethylene, unwound from huge wooden reels, was used. In the larger sizes which had to accommodate the high winter heating loads, pipe made from polyvinylchloride (known as PVC) was used. Continued developments in plastic pipe and improvements in physical properties eventually led to further refinements and changes in piping materials.

Pumping water by means of natural gas-fired engines was the most economical way of supplying energy for irrigation. The energy cost using gas ranged from one-half to one-quarter of the cost using diesel fuel, propane or gasoline. Another advantage was that the pipe was underground, assuring dependable, uninterrupted service.

By mid-summer two hundred and sixty-five quarter sections were under contract for natural gas service for irrigation fuel needs. Farmers were so enthusiastic that the installations were as much as six weeks behind orders.

Gas-powered systems were installed to provide irrigation for over three hundred quarter sections during 1964. Natural gas service was also provided to one hundred and sixty-eight new farm customers by Canadian Western. At the same time, Northwestern laid a test section of PVC plastic main west of Drayton Valley to serve twenty-four rural customers.

Public Ownership Again Debated — 1964

The question of provincial and municipal ownership, as opposed to investor ownership, of utility companies continued as a highly controversial issue in 1964. The City of Edmonton, led by Mayor Ivor Dent, a socialist of long standing, made ominous rumblings about investigating the possibilities of purchasing Northwestern's Edmonton system. This was an option the city always had under the terms of the franchise, although it was exercisable only at the time of franchise renewal.

Northwestern's general manager, Murray Stewart, was most outspoken on the issue. "Investor ownership is a lot closer to being public than is government ownership under any conditions," he stated in a speech at the University of Alberta. "Government in our society has grown to be something above and beyond every other force, and yet there are some people who believe that somehow government ownership will get them closer to the working of a utility, will somehow give them more control over the activities and any changes, particularly of rates. Nothing could be further from the truth as the people of B.C. are finding out. B.C. Hydro is making a lot of unilateral changes, subject to no authority but their own. Under B.C. Electric the local authorities had an opportunity to oppose and to be heard and to influence the decisions of a regulatory authority. This is now long gone."

Northwestern survived quite handily the efforts of the advocates of municipal take-over, just as Canadian Utilities survived the controversy occasioned by the Liberal Party of Alberta in the early sixties when the party espoused the policy that the province should enter the power business as the government of B.C. had done.

New Control Station — 1964

Among the major developments in Canadian Western's day-to-day operations was the completion, in 1964, of the new control station in southeast Calgary at the intersection of 58 Avenue and the Blackfoot Trail. The building replaced the old Manchester high pressure station.

The new station was of a circular design, and the impressive panel of instruments on the wall, with telephone and radio communications at arm's length, was a far cry from the original control room with only two pressure gauges. In the new control room, by comparison, there were twenty-two gauges and charts which gave readings on the various lines throughout the system.

Chief operator George Kirkaldy recalled work at the old Manchester station when it was out on the open prairie with nothing but the Burns & Company horses and cattle nearby. The duties of the operator at that time included being gardener. The grass had to be trimmed and flowers planted around the station to make it attractive. The cattle used to stick their heads through the fence to eat the flowers. The operator coming on night duty would have to walk half a mile from the trolley line through waist-high grass. On a rainy night he would be soaked by the time he reached the building.

A significant project completed the previous year was the construction of a new service centre at the corner of 11 Avenue and 10 Street SW. Built as a facility for construction, operating, maintenance and service personnel, the two-storey structure was the first major expansion at the company's West End Shop area since 1950, when a machine and vehicle repair shop had been erected.

Below Zero Emergency — 1964

A striking test of the companies' gas systems, as well as the endurance and ingenuity of its service people, took place at mid-December 1964. It was the coldest day of the year — thirty-five degrees below zero Fahrenheit, with

A RECORD OF SERVICE

winds gusting up to forty miles an hour, giving an equivalent temperature in still air of ninety-five below.

On this day, of all days, an automatic valve failed at the Nevis inter-connection of Alberta Gas Trunk Line and Canadian Western lines. It was designed to open when gas from the Nevis gas plant, was insufficient to meet demands. This morning it failed to open.

It was four o'clock in the morning when the Red Deer servicemen received their first indication of the pressure drop. In Edmonton Dave Collier, manager of production and transmission, and Bill Brander were called out about 4:30 a.m. by operators at the No. 1 Gate Station because of the general concern with the cold weather.

While at the station they saw the pressure drop on the Nevis supply line. Hugh McAllister was contacted at Wetaskiwin and drove immediately to the station at the Trunk Line inter-tie.

Calgary was contacted at 6:30 a.m. where Elmer Provost, manager of production and transmission, was at the control station. Provost didn't leave the station that day, or that night. Both he and Stu Gell were to spend more than thirty hours there before they felt the situation was in hand. Similar surveillance was maintained in Edmonton by Collier and Brander.

To assist McAllister, a crew from Calgary and Carbon was sent on its way. Everything depended on repair of the malfunctioning valve, as the gas supply from the Nevis plant was insufficient for the two company systems, and nine towns along the line, from Airdrie in the south to Camrose in the north, would be affected by the emergency.

When McAllister arrived at the station he found the door locked. He broke it down and located the trouble in the control panel. No gas was flowing! Neither McAllister nor another employee with him was familiar with the station and they had to size up the situation quickly. They tried to activate the controller manually but this failed.

Now the ingenuity of the two gas men came through. They proceeded to cut off some tubing from the immobilized equipment, straightened it out and installed it in such a way as to bypass the controller.

Would it work? It did! This action made enough pressure available to activate the diaphragm and the regulator opened. Gas was flowing again into the transmission line.

But the crisis was not over yet. The bitterly cold blizzard conditions meant that gas was consumed by the furnaces of thousands of customers as fast as it was going into the line, and pressures in the system therefore were not being restored.

Scores of experienced men worked all day and all night helping customers through the worst crisis that had been experienced in many years. Many of these men worked with no sleep for twenty-four, thirty or thirty-six hours. News announcers on the air were urging people to turn down their thermostats as much as possible. Wherever large loads could be put on reduced emergency fuel supplies this was done.

Back at the Nevis connection there were now four employees. They kept constant watch during the bitter cold. The heater in the regulator station had gone out. The recording clocks and ink were frozen, so no gauges were recording. The men worked in shifts — two in the station, and two in cars to keep warm. The cars were kept running constantly to provide some heat.

Ever so slowly the pressures climbed back to normal. The gas companies had weathered another crisis and managed to keep it from turning into a disaster.

The companies experienced their peak demand for the year on this bitterly cold December 15. Northwestern delivered a twenty-four hour total of 427 million cubic feet of gas, and Canadian Western 328 million cubic feet.

To round out the highlights for the gas companies in 1964, Canadian Western was connected to an additional source of supply, Canadian Pacific Oil and Gas Limited's plant at Horseshoe Canyon, near Drumheller; Northwestern added Whitecourt and Wabamun to its service area and opened its Klondike Inn on the Edmonton exhibition grounds, visited by more than sixty thousand people during Edmonton's Klondike Days.

IU Buys Coachways — 1965

An interesting venture in 1965 was the purchase by International Utilities of the controlling interest in Canadian Coachways Limited.

Coachways was the largest bus line in Western Canada. It was affiliated with Alaskan Coachways Limited which gave the company extensive operations in Alberta and B.C., and on into the north, including Yellowknife, Whitehorse, Dawson City, Fairbanks and Anchorage.

Canadian Utilities' president, Jack Dale, was named chairman of the board of Coachways, with Coachways president M.R. Mickey Collins continuing for some time as president in an advisory capacity. Gordon Cameron was named vice-president and general manager. Later Cameron was appointed president.

There was a convenient tie-in with Canadian Utilities' northern operations. Telephone and telex facilities, for example, were used jointly by Canadian Utilities, Northland and the Coachways system.

Aside from public transportation, part of the Coachways purchase was a twin-engined Beechcraft Baron aircraft with designation CF-CCL. It was used by all the companies until 1969. It carried a pilot and four passengers and cruised at one hundred and ninety miles per hour. Bill King and Molly Reilly were part-time pilots. In 1969 the Baron was traded in on a Beechcraft Duke (CF-WVF) — a twin-engined pressurized six-seater that cruised at two hundred and forty miles per hour. In the fall of 1978 the company sold the Duke and bought a Piper

Cheyenne II (CG-CUL). This is a twin turbo-prop eight-seater which flies at altitudes up to twenty-five thousand feet at three hundred miles per hour.

The diversification into bus transportation in 1965 was a normal outgrowth of trends already established in the parent company. A shipping firm, Gotaas-Larsen, in which International Utilities had the controlling interest, operated transoceanic oil tankers and bulk carriers. In addition, International Utilities administered a sizeable investment portfolio weighted towards U.S. railroad securities. Costing twenty-two million dollars, the portfolio had a market value of nearly twice that amount by the beginning of 1965. Even steel processing was attracting International Utilities, which by now was into steel scrap and slag operations in Pennsylvania and New Jersey. In 1965 the company invested half a million dollars in an Edmonton-based venture called Peace River Mining & Smelting Company.

At International Utilities' annual meeting in February 1965, board chairman H.R. Milner retired and turned the chairmanship over to Howard Butcher III. The directors, out of appreciation for Milner's contribution to the corporation over the years, elected him honorary chairman. Jack Seabrook, who had been vice-president for five years, moved up to the presidency.

There was a significant shift in the ownership and control of International Utilities, particularly after the corporation opened its principal office in Toronto. By 1965 seventy percent of the parent company's ten thousand five hundred shareholders were Canadian, owning fifty-eight percent of the outstanding shares. The shares were widely distributed, with owners in every Canadian province, throughout the United States and in nine other countries. Eight of the fourteen directors were Canadian, including Jack Dale and Dennis Yorath, both of whom were vice-presidents.

With International Utilities' expansion in the northwest, particularly the acquisition of the Coachways system, the corporation's directors met in Edmonton for the first time in the summer of 1965. Following their meeting they flew to Fort McMurray, Prince George, Prince Rupert and Whitehorse to tour some of the properties.

One of the areas of particular interest to the group was Fort McMurray where Great Canadian Oil Sands was well under way with its oil extraction plant. Canadian Utilities' subsidiary, the Fort McMurray Power Company, almost doubled its sales of electricity during that year, mainly as a result of the influx of workers on the GCOS project.

Storm Causes Power Paralysis — 1965

The electric system had a temporary setback in 1965, on May 16, when a severe ice and windstorm hit central Alberta, causing extensive damage. At the height of the storm power transmission lines were coated with ice to a diameter of three inches under wind conditions gusting to seventy-five miles per hour. More than a thousand power poles were broken or knocked down, and the service outage affected an area of some thirty-five hundred square miles.

Staff, with the necessary equipment, was drawn from all districts of the company. Their determined efforts restored service to all major urban centres within twenty-four hours and to the most remote rural area within a week.

The storm, most severe in the Stettler-to-Consort area, was the worst in the district's memory. Editorial comments by two newspapers serving the area illustrate the appreciation of local residents for the way Canadian Utilities employees worked to restore service.

The *Consort Enterprise*, in the May 20 issue, said:

> *In the face of very adverse weather, the Canadian Utilities men performed miracles. Out of the tangles of lines, broken poles, smashed insulators, they picked up the pieces and brought order to the chaos. Minutes after the storm hit, the linemen were on the job and they haven't stopped yet. Averaging two or three hours of sleep, working in round-the-clock shifts and grabbing a bite to eat when they can, these men are deserving of unstinting praise.*

The *Stettler Independent* commented:

> *Just as people were resigning themselves to another bone chilling night in darkness, the blessed lights came on. Canadian Utilities' workmen had labored around the clock under most adverse conditions of high wind and cold. It seemed almost a miracle that they could do so much in so short a time. Three extra crews were brought in to work with the local men who bore the brunt of the storm.*

Work Continues at Battle River

T he year 1965 saw further preparations for new plants, including preliminary work at the Battle River station's third unit. Preliminary work was also done on construction of a 20-megawatt gas turbine plant to be located in the Simonette oilfield in northwestern Alberta. The plant, which would burn residue gas from oil-producing wells in the field, would be operated by remote control from the Sturgeon Lake plant.

Canadian Utilities spent another two and a half million dollars during the year on building new transmission lines and upgrading existing lines and substations. One of the projects was seventy-seven miles of 138-kilovolt line to increase capacity to the Grande Prairie-Peace River areas from the central Alberta grid.

Bursary Program

T he energy companies have contributed educationally and culturally to their service areas over the years.

There were internal programs as well. One of these was the scholarship program aimed at encouraging children of staff members to acquire a university education.

The bursary program was instituted in 1958 by Dennis Yorath when he was president of the gas companies. The companies had traditionally held annual social get-togethers for staff members on the day before Christmas, with food and refreshments. An evaluation of this event was carried out, and it was felt that the money spent on it could better be spent on helping staff members with education of their children. The fund was instituted accordingly, and the social event discontinued.

In the years that followed the scholarship and bursary program of the group continued to expand. From 1970 to 1987 more than fifteen hundred bursaries, valued at a total of nearly eight hundred thousand dollars, were awarded to the children of employees of the companies.

The program's original objective has remained over the years: "To encourage children of the companies' employees to continue their education by attendance at a recognized institution at the post-secondary level."

Murray Stewart, who became president of the gas companies in 1965, commented on this program:

> In an age when the world's total knowledge will double in less than ten years, merely keeping up with your own field of knowledge becomes a never-ending task.
>
> . . . The funds set aside by the companies for these scholarships are in my opinion serving a purpose second to none.
>
> These scholarships are a tangible evidence of the commitment of the companies, and of the employees of these companies, to higher education.
>
> I urge you to impress upon your children the importance of getting all the education and training they can handle. There are few things indeed that you can do for them that are more important.

Initially, scholarships of five hundred dollars a year for three years were presented to students who had an average of at least sixty-five percent in grade twelve. Canadian Utilities had a similar program for children of staff members in the electric operations.

There were other community-support programs. For example, in 1962 Canadian Utilities had become a joint sponsor with Calgary Power of the Alberta Junior Citizen of the Year awards presented annually at the convention of the Alberta Weekly Newspapers Association. This program recognizes achievement in good citizenship by young Albertans.

The energy group also actively supported the Junior Achievement program, encouraged by Chambers of Commerce and sponsored by numerous industries and business enterprises. Under Junior Achievement, groups of young people set up miniature corporations to produce marketable items and sell them as an educational experience in the free enterprise system.

First Generation Computer — 1965

A n important step into the future for the energy group took place in 1965 when the first generation computer was installed in the Milner Building. Responsibility for its operations was attached to the intercompany comptroller's department. "It was a matter of outgrowing our old IBM punch card equipment," said George Sommerville, assistant comptroller, systems and procedures. "There was too much work for it to handle, and when we made the plunge we went to a computer somewhat larger than the one we have used in Calgary for the past year."

The computer in Calgary was a card system with four thousand bytes (units) of storage, while the new system in Edmonton used magnetic tape with twelve thousand bytes of storage. It could handle at least three times the volume of work performed by the Calgary computer. "We are now into true computer operations," Sommerville said. "We anticipate many changes during the years to come, which could have far reaching effects on our operations."

The months and years that followed did bring many changes as the computer system was continually upgraded.

Other modernization measures included the installation of a radio communication network, remote control operation of valves, electronic telemetering of gas flow information, more sophisticated methods of leak detection, improved safety procedures and more efficient metering devices, to name a few.

Stewart Becomes President — 1965

T he appointment of Murray Stewart as president of the gas companies in 1965 was occasioned by Bruce Willson leaving the companies to become president of Canadian Bechtel Limited, the Canadian subsidiary of Bechtel Corporation of San Francisco.

Stewart had been with the companies since 1949. He was a graduate, B.Sc. civil engineering, of the University of Alberta, and also of the University of Toronto, MBA. He became superintendent of technical services for Northwestern in 1953 and in 1956, at the age of thirty, was appointed general manager. Upon his appointment as president of the gas companies, he was replaced as general manager of Northwestern by David Collier. John E. Maybin, vice-president, engineering and gas supply for the two companies, was appointed executive vice-president for both companies.

New Sources Connected — 1965

A mong capital expenditures on new projects in 1965, Northwestern crews laid a pipeline to the Beaverhill Lake field, forty miles southeast of Edmonton, tying the field to Northwestern's Viking-to-Edmonton transmission lines. The field would make deliveries of one hundred and twenty million cubic feet per day when fully developed. It was the first major company-owned field to be connected in more than ten years. After a decade of development this large new field, mainly company-owned, was an important new gas source, particulary for peak load deliveries.

In the late fall about a million and a half dollars were spent on a pipeline connecting the Paddle River gas field, about seventy miles northwest of Edmonton. The new line connected about one hundred and seventy-five billion cubic feet of additional gas reserves to the system. This gas field became the eighteenth source of supply for Northwestern.

Red Deer Service Centre — 1965

F or some time, it was evident that operating headquarters for Northwestern's southern extension would have to be relocated from Wetaskiwin to the rapidly growing centre of Red Deer. It was therefore decided to centralize the transmission and distribution facilities in Red Deer.

At year-end 1965, just before Christmas, a new Service Centre building in Red Deer was opened. Located in the industrial area of the city, on the west side, the building served as the operations centre for Northwestern in the area.

Red Deer's mayor, R.B. Barrett, said: "This fine new building will be a credit to the city of Red Deer and to the thousands of customers in this area who have recognized a close association between good service and the gas company."

The words of praise from the mayor of Red Deer were only one example of the many compliments the gas company staff was receiving for its dedicated service. Another was an editorial in the *Bashaw Star*, December 1 issue, after a truck demolished Northwestern's regulating station and interrupted service for a time:

> *Although natural gas service to the town of Bashaw was cut off by an accident last Thursday morning just after 3 a.m. the greatest story to come out of the whole affair was the devotion to duty by the staff of Northwestern Utilities and the excellent organization that they showed from the first phone call telling of the damage.*
>
> *Whatever else might be said of the various angles involved in the story the greatest was that they placed service above self-interest. The first inclination of all the crew was to see that their customers were kept in warmth and with cooking facilities.*

Sometimes in the course of administration of big companies this matter of full and immediate service to the end customers is not what it might be, but in this case no one had anything but good to say.

Growth Continues — 1965

Meanwhile in Calgary, Canadian Western continued to forge ahead with unabated vigor. The city of Calgary was growing by leaps and bounds, and the gas company was moving right along with it. Calgary's sixteen percent growth in 1965 was the greatest percentage population increase since 1961 of any metropolitan area in Canada.

Aggressive load-building activities, and leadership in industrial development activities in southern Alberta, were paying off. For example, Calgary by now was the leading city in Canada in the use of gas absorption air-conditioning. Canadian Western installed this kind of air-conditioning in five new buildings in 1965, providing a total of three thousand tons of refrigeration. Included was the largest single installation in Western Canada, a thousand-ton unit in the new biological science building at the University of Calgary.

Another major commercial load added in 1965 was the city's new twenty-six million dollar Foothills Hospital, which at the time was the largest completely new project of its kind constructed in North America. The thirteen-storey hospital, built to care for nearly eight hundred patients, was designed to use natural gas for space heating, air-conditioning, cooking, water heating, clothes drying, incineration and power generation.

Still another important load was the new twenty-four million dollar Western Co-operative Fertilizer Limited plant in Calgary. It used natural gas as a feedstock for the production of ammonia and as fuel for two 3,500-horsepower compressors. It was the company's largest industrial user and the second fertilizer plant on the system. At maximum production it would use nine million cubic feet of gas per day.

Finally, a flare-lighting ceremony at Big Valley, forty miles northeast of Trochu, marked the arrival of natural gas in the eighty-fifth community to be served by Canadian Western.

Largest Burner Ever Built — 1966

The 1966 Canadian Petroleum Exposition, a twenty million dollar oil and gas show at the Calgary Exhibition and Stampede, was dominated by a mammoth gas burner designed and built by Canadian Western.

When gas company engineers received the assignment to "design a burner that will produce a colored flame twenty feet high and five feet wide operating at twenty pounds pressure," they had to start from scratch because no burner of this size had ever been built.

The team consisted of Donald J. Taylor, utilization engineer; Douglas R. Fenton, assistant utilization engineer; and James R. Clachrie, senior customer serviceman.

Sketches and plans soon resulted in a scaled-down model, and then after many tests the full-scale burner was constructed. The finished burner stood more than fifteen feet high, and the top, where the flame came out, was nearly six feet across. It was mounted atop a derrick, one hundred and fifty-four feet from the ground.

New Building for Lethbridge — 1966

A nother highlight of 1966 was the construction of a new service centre in Lethbridge at 410 Stafford Drive.

Canadian Western's Lethbridge offices had been in the downtown Sixth Street building for twenty-seven years. The new building, an impressive addition to Lethbridge's north side, now housed the company's customer service, engineering, meter reading, distribution and business office departments. Improved facilities centralized in the one location permitted service to customers in Lethbridge and district with increased efficiency.

The building was the centre for service in the Lethbridge area, covering some thirty-six communities in addition to the city itself. It featured a drive-in wicket, roomier front offices, a larger and brighter auditorium, larger stockroom, garage and yard facilities. Business started from this new location on Monday, October 24.

Moving the company offices to the north side did not seem to inconvenience customers. In fact, more than half the homes in Lethbridge were now on the north side, making the new location more convenient for many homeowners. And for those who might have found the downtown location handy for payment of bills, arrangements were made for bill payment at any chartered bank without charge to the customer.

Thousands of pounds of equipment, supplies and records were moved to the location without a hitch in service. The old property was sold to Oland Construction Company Limited and the building was torn down.

The new building was the fifth home for Canadian Western in Lethbridge since a giant gas flare marked the start of service fifty-four years earlier, in 1912. Company offices at that time were in the Hull Block. Later they were moved to 620 – Seventh Street South. In 1926 they were moved to Fourth Avenue, and then came the move to the Sixth Street building.

Some of the employees who had been with the company at the time of the move to the Sixth Street building were still with the company for the move to the new building. They included Jack Anderson, foreman of distribution services, and Ron Clifford, supervisor of customer service and utilization.

With new office buildings in both Red Deer and Lethbridge, another highlight of 1966 for the gas companies was a decision of the boards of directors for both companies to meet for the first time in cities other than Edmonton and Calgary. The Northwestern board met in Red Deer on October 12, and the Canadian Western board met in Lethbridge on November 2.

The meeting in Lethbridge was timed to coincide with the official opening of the new building. The directors, headed by A.C. Anderson, Lethbridge alderman and later mayor for many years, joined company officials as hosts at a reception to civic dignitaries, town officials and local business leaders.

Dennis Yorath, Murray Stewart, Kenneth McFadyen, John Maybin and Harry Hunter were among the senior company personnel who hosted the reception with John Fisher, superintendent of Lethbridge and district.

Jumping Pound Line — 1966

If the Bow River could talk, it would probably give a painful account of how it feels to be ripped apart by blasts equalling twenty-one thousand pounds of dynamite. The river blasts opened a deep trench in the hard-rock riverbed twenty-two feet below the water surface to accommodate almost a thousand feet of new sixteen-inch transmission line.

The river crossing, fifteen miles west of Calgary, was part of the construction in 1966 of the twenty-two mile line from the Jumping Pound plant of Shell Canada Ltd., to Canadian Western's Meadowfield Station in southeast Calgary. There were also eleven major highway crossings and five railway crossings.

A critical point in construction occurred at the Bearspaw crossing where the Bow River had to be trenched. Used for the first time in Canada, the blasting system consisted of stringing a series of explosives on the riverbed about three feet apart.

Laying of this line was a follow-up to the signing of a new twenty-five-year contract with Shell Canada to more than double Shell's natural gas supply to the Canadian Western system, including gas from the new field of Jumping Pound West.

Outstanding Safety Record — 1966

It was a year of progress for the gas companies. Business in 1966 showed a healthy increase, there were more sophisticated ways of doing hard work, and gas company personnel were becoming more safety conscious. At a Canadian Western safety dinner held that year, eighty-nine drivers, representing a total of nearly eight hundred years of safe driving, were honored. Awards included five drivers who reached the ten-year plateau, a milestone in safety circles.

Northwestern Utilities employees in the East District reached the twenty-five hundred days mark without a disabling injury. That's over six and three-quarter years. The East District was the third in Northwestern to achieve this record, following Viking-Kinsella and the South District.

Northwestern's continuing expansion during 1966 added more than four thousand new services to the distribution systems. The addition of the new communities of Mayerthorpe, Sangudo, Cherhill, Glenevis, Rochfort Bridge, Lisburn and Villeneuve accounted for nearly five hundred new services and required the laying of seventeen miles of mains including transmission stubs from the Paddle River line.

Power Growth Economic Yardstick — 1966

The electric power operations also showed healthy growth in 1966. The growth of the power industry, in fact, was considered a yardstick of the province's economy. "Kilowatt hours of electricity are a more reliable index of economic growth than dollars, which are subject to inflation," J.E. Oberholtzer, deputy minister of industry and development, told delegates to a Northwest Electric Light and Power Association conference held in Jasper that summer.

Oberholtzer went on to say the demand for electric power in the province was showing a consistent increase of ten to twelve percent per year.

Generator in the Oilfields — 1966

The Simonette plant, Canadian Utilities' newest generating facility was a 20-megawatt gas turbine generator located in bush country seventy air miles southeast of Grande Prairie. Along with the Sturgeon plant near Valleyview, it supplied base load requirements for the Peace River country. A forty-mile transmission line connected the plant to the Alberta grid system at Little Smoky, twenty-five miles south of Valleyview. Total cost of the project, including the transmission line, was nearly three million dollars.

The construction story of the Simonette plant unfolded rapidly. The site was chosen in November 1965, and gravel was hauled in over the winter. Clearing commenced in the spring and construction of the station began in July 1966. November 2 saw the first run-up of the turbine under its own flame, and it went on line exactly one month later.

Not that the time between was without problems. The isolated plant was distant from a rail line, and a setback occurred when the turbine was being transported to the plant site by trucks. The trailer carrying the ninety-ton turbine assembly bogged down while fording a shallow creek, more than two miles from the plant. Subsequent rains converted the gentle stream into a rushing river which overturned trailer and turbine, giving both an unwelcome bath of muddy water. This delayed the project about four weeks. Later the generator crossed the stream without incident.

The Simonette plant operates unattended, sending information by microwave radio to the Sturgeon Plant near Valleyview, and receiving its instructions from that plant by the same means.

Like the two turbines at the Sturgeon plant, the Simonette turbine burned residue gas from oil wells in the area. In fact, the location of these two plants was determined by the availability of this low-cost sour gas.

Oilfield activity accounted for much of the growth of the power companies in 1966. And in the far north there was increased mining activity in the Yukon.

In Uranium City, served by Northland, there was a renewed search for uranium ore that sparked an influx of local and foreign exploration groups. And farther south, Fort McMurray continued to grow by leaps and bounds.

Centennial Year — 1967

The year 1967 was Canada's centennial year, inaugurated in Alberta by the lighting of a gas flare in the Centennial Flame Courtyard on the grounds of the Legislative Building in Edmonton. The torch was lit on New Year's Eve by Lieutenant Governor Grant MacEwan and dedicated by Premier E.C. Manning. Taking part in the ceremony on behalf of the gas companies, which had donated and installed the gas torch, was president Murray Stewart. "We live in a proud, prosperous province and are quite aware that much of our prosperity has come from underground in the form of petroleum resources," Stewart said in his public address on that occasion. "It is, therefore, particularly appropriate in Alberta that a natural gas flame should be used to mark the beginning of the centennial year."

A similar flare was lit in Ottawa. Natural gas flames were, in fact, quite common as centennial projects. A gas flame dominated Expo 67's Place des Nations at Montreal. Also, at the World's Fair, Canadian Western and Northwestern were two of the Canadian gas companies which sponsored the Natural Gas Hospitality Pavilion.

In southern Alberta the Lethbridge branch of the Royal Canadian Legion and local Army, Navy and Air Force Veterans club joined together in a centennnial project — an eternal flame dedicated to members of the armed forces who had been killed in action. The torch was mounted on a marble monument.

In the city of Camrose, Alderman Rudy Swanson decided to put a gas light on his front lawn as a centennial project. He talked to some of his neighbors along Forty-fifth Street and they decided they wanted to do the same. The result was that Northwestern installed seventeen lights on either side of this residential street for the people who banded together for this unique centennial project.

There were, of course, many other kinds of projects. For example, Canadian Western employees collected six thousand dollars in one week to save Advance Industries, a branch of the Canadian Association for Retarded Children, from going out of business. This organization helped a group of mentally handicapped people to learn simple operations with the hope that some day they would be placed in industry. They did not have a government grant for their work and the building they occupied was condemned.

Another project, on a smaller scale but of a similar nature, was the adoption by Northwestern's plant records and sales social club of a nine-year-old boy in Hong Kong through a foster parents plan to help needy people in other countries.

History a Resounding Success

The company's centennial project launched in 1965, was the publication of a book titled *Alberta — a Natural History.* Dr. W. George Hardy, well-known author and former head of the classics department at the University of Alberta was retained as editor-in-chief. The idea for the project was conceived by Dr. Brian Hitchon, associate research officer with the Research Council of Alberta. One of the participating authors was J.G. MacGregor, former Canadian Utilities general manager and then chairman of the Alberta Power Commission.

The book combined under one cover the entire field of natural history as it related to the province of Alberta. The authoritative manuscript, written and edited by thirty of the province's leading authors and scientists, and the hundreds of illustrations complementing the text, combined to produce a book which received virtually unanimous praise from critics, educators and the general public.

The project was co-ordinated for the patron companies by W. Mills Parker, information officer with the two gas companies. There was an initial run of twenty thousand copies of the three-hundred-page book. The book went on to become a Canadian best seller — with five printings totalling seventy-five thousand copies. The *Toronto Globe and Mail* rated the book as Canada's fastest selling centennial book.

In addition to subsidizing the cost of the first printing, and directing the planning and publication of the book, the patron companies donated copies to schools, libraries, institutions, and weekly and daily newspapers throughout the province.

Centennial Year was a milestone from another standpoint as well. It was the year that Northwestern added the one hundredth community to its system while extending gas service to eight new communities — Clyde, Vimy, Benalto, Darwell, Hardisty, Lindbrook, Nisku and Norglenwold. Virtually all major communities in the province now enjoyed the advantages of natural gas.

Canadian Utilities' Fortieth Year — 1967

Centennial Year was a milestone for Canadian Utilities too. It was the year the company celebrated its fortieth birthday. Among the fourteen employees

202

who received long service awards that year were two who had been with the organization during its entire forty years. They were Eric Butler, vice-president and secretary of International Utilities, and Bill Spence, assistant to the district manager of Canadian Utilities at Vegreville.

From its unobtrusive beginnings at Vegreville in 1927, Canadian Utilities had come a long way in the span of forty years. The company now was serving nearly fifty-five thousand customers with electric power with sales well in excess of 500 million kilowatt hours per year. Generating plant capacity totalled about 175 megawatts and work was progressing well towards almost doubling this with the new unit at Battle River.

During its first four decades the company scored many firsts in Canada. In 1929, for example, it owned the first mobile railcar generating plant in Canada. In 1935 the company initiated the first Better Light — Better Sight campaign and about the same time imported the first tri-light lamps in Canada.

In 1936, under the direction of Bill Marsh, who later became rural superintendent, Canadian Utilities became the first utility company in Canada to operate a mobile radio communications system. The system began with a base station and several mobile units at Drumheller, and grew over the years until in 1967 company personnel were operating one hundred and fifty-seven mobile sets, sixty-seven base stations and twenty repeater stations, on three frequencies. The three channels were truck-to-truck (also known as mobile to mobile), local and all points. Contact was possible even in the event of a power failure, as each repeater station was equipped with an automatic-start, gasoline-powered motor-generator set.

In 1944 Canadian Utilities electrified the first experimental farm area in Alberta, and that same year the company electrified the first oil wells in the west, at Borradaile.

After the war, at Vermilion, Canadian Utilities pioneered Canada's gas turbine power generation. As for generating power with coal, the company's history at Drumheller dates back to the twenties. Later, at Drumheller, the company was the first in Alberta to use powdered coal to generate electricity.

Continued Growth — 1967

C entennial year saw continued expansion for Canadian Utilities and its affiliate, Northland, which continued to build high voltage transmission lines in northern Alberta, shutting down isolated diesel plants as central station power from the Alberta grid moved all the way to Meander River within seventy miles of the province's northern border.

Oilfield development in the Rainbow-Zama Lake area continued to stimulate the economy in northern service areas. Work started in 1967 on a plant to accommodate the 30-megawatt gas turbine generator which would soon be moved from

Vermilion to the town of Rainbow Lake where it would use natural gas produced at Banff Oil's Rainbow processing plant. A 144-kilovolt transmission line was under construction to serve the area.

Yukon operations showed a huge increase in power sales with sales of electricity up thirty-eight percent in 1967 over the previous year. Mining activity in the territory was the major factor in economic expansion. New plant and equipment included extension of service to New Imperial Mine, Swift River and construction of a line to Arctic Mining near Carcross. A new office building was constructed in Whitehorse.

At its Battle River station, Canadian Utilities moved right along in 1967. Some three thousand tons of steel, including four forty-ton coal bunkers and a thirty-ton boiler girder were heaved into place.

Work was started on a forty-mile, 240-kilovolt steel tower transmission line from the Battle River plant to a point near Nevis where it would connect with the Alberta grid. This was the company's first transmission line designed to operate at this voltage.

Grande Prairie Renews Franchise — 1967

In gas operations Northland extended service in 1967 to the town of Fox Creek with gas purchased from Alberta and Southern Gas Co. Ltd. At Grande Prairie the city attempted to buy Northland's natural gas system, but when the ratepayers refused to approve the necessary by-law, city council approved a ten-year franchise renewal for the company.

Edmonton and Calgary Booming — 1967

For the second consecutive year Edmonton led all cities in Western Canada in building permits, setting an all-time high of one hundred and forty-one million dollars in 1967. Calgary had an all-time high of one hundred and thirty-seven million dollars. Calgary's skyline was changing dramatically with the addition of such structures as the 613-foot Husky Tower (supplied with air conditioning by Canadian Western); and the Mobil Tower and Royal Bank Building, both exceeding thirty stories in height.

The Husky Tower, later renamed the Calgary Tower, with its revolving restaurant and observation deck, was the tallest structure of its kind in North America in 1967. It provided a breathtaking view of southern Alberta for more than fifty miles in all directions. It had the distinction also of being served by the tallest natural gas line in Alberta. Some fourteen natural gas appliances ensure maximum comfort and convenience throughout the tower.

In Edmonton, Northwestern signed a contract in 1967 to supply a new gas-fired power generating plant to be built by Edmonton Power on the eastern outskirts of the city. Plans called for the first of two 165-megawatt units to be installed in early 1970. The company also contracted to supply the new fifty million dollar fertilizer plant being built by Imperial Oil in the Redwater area, northeast of Edmonton.

Not only cities and towns but also farm areas were targets for unprecedented growth. The two gas companies launched the most ambitious rural service program in their history. Ron Dalby, director of marketing, announced that during the next five to eight years the companies planned to service up to ten thousand new rural customers, requiring the installation of about four thousand miles of plastic pipe for distribution systems and service lines at a cost of eight to ten million dollars.

Since 1964 when Canadian Western was the largest installer of plastic pipe in North America, installing over a million feet, the companies continued as world leaders in this method of bringing natural gas to rural areas at reasonable cost.

Initially Canadian Western was Canada's pioneer in ploughing in coiled polyethylene pipe. In 1966 the company took a further step toward improving the economics of rural service by ploughing in coiled polyvinylchloride as well as the flexible polyethylene pipe.

In 1967 Canadian Western announced the appointment of David B. Smith as general manager, following the retirement of Harry Hunter after forty years of service. Smith was born and raised in Edmonton, graduated in engineering from McGill University, and took his master's degree in science at Massachusetts Institute of Technology.

Gas for Oil Sands Plant — 1967

In the summer of 1967 one of the most unusual gas delivery projects ever to be undertaken in Alberta was completed — the reverse flow of gas through a two hundred and sixty-six-mile pipeline from Edmonton to the Athabasca oil sands plant at Fort McMurray.

The two hundred and thirty-five million dollar plant, designed and built by Canadian Bechtel Ltd. for Great Canadian Oil Sands Ltd. (GCOS), for a short period ranked as one of the largest gas consumers in Canada, with deliveries of natural gas reaching as high as thirty-five million cubic feet per day.

By the time GCOS started production in the fall a total of about three billion cubic feet (enough gas to supply fifteen thousand Alberta homes for a year) had been delivered to the plant by Northwestern.

The pipeline to Edmonton had been built earlier for eventual delivery of oil from the GCOS plant. But first there was a need for large quantities of oil to activate the plant, plus natural gas to generate power, and GCOS contracted with Northwestern for a supply of natural gas for start-up operations.

In August 1966, delivery began of one hundred and forty-eight thousand barrels of oil from Edmonton to Fort McMurray. Natural gas pressure was used to drive the oil through the line.

Then in October, deliveries of natural gas began at a daily rate of flow from three to four million cubic feet. By the spring of 1967 the flow was averaging ten million cubic feet a day, increasing to thirty-five million cubic feet a day during plant start-up operations.

The gas was delivered into the GCOS pipeline at a pressure of 425 pounds, sufficient to send the gas on its two hundred and sixty-six-mile journey to Fort McMurray without further compression. Deliveries ceased when the plant went into full operation after which GCOS used gas, oil and coke produced from the Athabasca oil sands.

McMurray Gas Franchise to Northland — 1968

While Northwestern was delivering gas to the oil sands plant, Northland was looking into the possiblity of supplying gas to the town of Fort McMurray. At first it seemed Northland would have to pipe gas to the town by means of a line up to a hundred miles long. But with the development of the GCOS separation plant twenty miles north of the town, the Albersun Oil and Gas Company began laying a line from Lac La Biche. This meant Northland could purchase gas from Albersun instead of building a long transmission line of its own.

The franchise to serve the town received its initial approval on March 5, 1968 when Northland's proposal was selected over two others presented to the board of administrators. Less than a month after the franchise was granted, trench-digging operations were in full swing.

In mid-May Bev Eastman, Northland's senior customer serviceman at Grande Prairie, was moved to Fort McMurray as gas agent. Marketing representative Scotty Gilliland was transferred temporarily from the Peace River office to conduct a survey of all potential customers.

On August 28, 1968, H.A. McCormick, chairman of the board of administrators for Fort McMurray, touched a flame to a large gas torch outside the Peter Pond Hotel to mark the official turn-on of natural gas for the new town. Although the official ceremony came just three months after the beginning of construction, the first five hundred and twenty-five customers had actually been connected nearly two months earlier, and by now there were more than eight hundred.

Krisa Earns President's Award

At the 1968 Awards Banquet employee Ronald Krisa received the first President's Award to be bestowed on a Canadian Western employee. The award recognized his presence of mind in saving the life of one-year-old Donna

Maria Swansten on October 16, 1967 by successfully applying mouth-to-mouth resuscitation.

Among Top Ten in Canada — 1968

T he year 1968 brought extensive top-level changes in the energy group. These changes were sparked by a major diversification of International Utilities that nearly doubled the size of the company and paved the way for what would eventually evolve as local ownership and control for the energy group in Alberta.

International Utilities acquired the assets of a company known as General Waterworks Corporation. The consolidation of General Waterworks into International Utilities, which took place on March 1, changed the corporation into one with total assets of eight hundred million dollars, annual sales of four hundred and fifty million dollars, net income of more than thirty million dollars and net worth of two hundred and seventy-five million dollars.

International Utilities now ranked in assets among the top ten Canadian industrial companies and among the first hundred U.S. industrials, with more than thirty-five thousand employees in twenty-four countries. Already diversified with shipping, trucking, bus, steel, petroleum, oceanography and mining operations, the company now entered the operation of water, sewer and heating utilities in the United States, plus communications services, additional industrial companies and a dairy products company.

Howard Butcher III, International Utilities' board chairman, resigned from the boards of the Alberta utility companies. International Utilities president, Jack Seabrook, asked for the services of gas companies' president, Murray Stewart, as president of the newly-acquired waterworks corporation, with the president's office to be located in Philadelphia. "The invitation to become president of General Waterworks came as a surprise to me and at a time when things seemed to be relatively stable," Stewart said. ". . . I am looking forward to the challenge of the new job but naturally all of the Stewarts are reluctant to leave Edmonton and Canada."

It was expected at the time that Stewart would serve in Philadelphia for two or three years and then return to Alberta for new responsibilities.

Maybin Heads Gas Companies — 1968

I n Alberta the gas companies held their board meetings in March 1968, and following those meetings board chairman Dennis Yorath announced that John E. Maybin had been appointed president. This made Maybin the ninth president of Canadian Western and eighth for Northwestern. Stewart, who had been president since May 1965, was re-elected to the board of directors of the two companies, and was also appointed vice-chairman of each company.

Maybin was born in Regina and received his early education in Calgary. During the war he served with the Royal Navy in England, and then returned to Alberta to resume his formal education. He graduated from the University of Alberta in 1948 with the degree of bachelor of science in engineering physics. He then went on to Princeton University where he received his master of science degree in mechanical engineering.

He joined the gas companies in 1949 in Calgary as an engineer in the special projects department. On January 1, 1957, he took on the management of the newly-formed intercompany gas supply and contract division. In 1963 he was appointed a vice-president of both companies in charge of engineering and gas supply matters, and continued as head of the gas supply and contract division.

In May 1965, Maybin was appointed executive vice-president of both gas companies. He was a director of the Alberta Gas Trunk Line Company Limited and the Canadian Gas Association.

With Maybin assuming the presidency, five other members of the companies' senior management were appointed vice-presidents. They were: David B. Collier, vice-president and general manager, and a director, Northwestern Utilities; David B. Smith, vice-president and general manager, and a director, Canadian Western; Ronald N. Dalby, vice-president, marketing, Canadian Western and Northwestern Utilities; James H. Pletcher, vice-president, gas supply, Canadian Western and Northwestern; and Beverly W. Snyder, vice-president, engineering and rate administration, Canadian Western and Northwestern.

Alberta's Clean Air Touted

M urray Stewart's move to Philadelphia made the gas companies in Alberta more conscious of what was going on elsewhere in the world, and more grateful for the clear skies over Alberta. Philadelphia was not so lucky. The eastern American city was plagued with smog, and the Philadelphia gas company pointed out in its newspaper advertisements that residents could face the risk of dangerous respiratory ailments if the level of air pollution continued to increase. "One way to reduce air pollution is for industry to change to a fuel like natural gas, a non-pollutant," stated the ads. "Philadelphia Gas Works has encouraged this change by reducing gas rates to large users twice within recent months."

Northwestern's public relations department received a copy of an advertisement which ran in the *Philadelphia Enquirer*, and took the opportunity to get in a plug for natural gas heating. A letter was sent to the gas company in Philadelphia noting that in Edmonton the city's power plant burned seventeen billion cubic feet of gas the previous year, virtually in the centre of the city, and one could well imagine the incidence of air pollution were coal used in the plant.

In a good-natured exchange of letters a tin of "fresh Alberta air" was sent to the Philadelphia gas company with instructions that it be opened when next they had an air pollution alert.

Edge King Elected President — 1968

The extensive upper-echelon changes in the energy group were not confined to the gas companies in 1968. Canadian Utilities and Northland felt the impact as well. Milner, who up to this time had continued to serve as chairman of the board for the two companies, retired. In recognition of his outstanding service to the companies, he was named honorary chairman, and president Jack Dale became chairman and chief executive officer.

Dale had been president since 1956 and by now was also chairman and a director of the Coachways System; president and director for Vancouver Island Transportation Company Limited; vice-president and director for International Utilities; and a director of Northwestern Utilities, Peace River Mining & Smelting Ltd., Echo Bay Mines Ltd., and The White Pass and Yukon Corporation Limited.

Replacing Dale as president of both companies was Egerton Warren King, known to all as Edge. At the time he was general manager of Canadian Utilities and vice-president of Northland. King was also named to the board of directors of Canadian Utilities, succeeding G.E. Kelly, who became an honorary director.

Edge King was born in Calgary. A 1942 engineering graduate of the University of Alberta, he began his career in the electrical industry as a test engineer for Canadian General Electric, Peterborough. From 1943 to 1945 he served as a lieutenant with the Royal Canadian Navy, with overseas service on landing craft, and at naval headquarters, Ottawa.

King entered the utility field in 1945 as an electrical engineer for East Kootenay Power Company Limited at Fernie, B.C. Ten years later he became manager of McGregor Telephone & Power Construction Company Limited, Edmonton. He joined Canadian Utilities in 1956 as transmission and distribution superintendent. In 1958 he was appointed general manager for the company's subsidiary operations in the Yukon.

He returned to Edmonton in 1961 as executive vice-president of Northland and became general manager of Canadian Utilities on January 1, 1966, when Jack Ford was appointed vice-president.

Remote Meter Reading

The companies continued to experiment with new technology being introduced to its industry, including everything from computerized accounting to meter reading. Canadian Western scored another first in 1967-1968 with the installation of two hundred experimental remote meters. These were believed to be the first such gas meters in Canada. With this equipment in place, the meter reader could plug an instrument into a receptacle on the outside of the house to read the gas consumption without having to enter the house. "Most noticeable advantage is the time element," said George Dixon, one of the meter readers. "In some cases I can read two or three meters in the time it would take to go into a basement and get a reading."

Going into basements to read meters always required caution in any case. No one knew this better than meter reader Jim Hill in Edmonton whose "beat" included the home of Robert Evans. The Evans home was reputed to have only a cat as a house pet, but the cat happened to be a hundred and fifty-pound jaguar that Evans kept in the basement. The jaguar, whose name was Tory, was the size of two German shepherd dogs and his diet was four to five pounds of raw meat every day. Tory was born at the Calgary Zoo and his owner planned eventually to return him to the zoo after he had finished writing a book on jaguars. Meanwhile, meter readers were not inclined to venture into the basement unless the man of the house was around to keep Tory in a good mood.

Remote meter reading, computerized operations, and other forms of automation were by now winning for Calgary and Edmonton a reputation as cities of the future. A well-known trade magazine claimed Calgary had "the greatest concentration of computer power per capita in the world." Seven data centres and a dozen computer facilities owned by oil companies in the city represented an investment total of about twenty-four million dollars. As for Edmonton, for the fifth consecutive year the city set new construction records. With its population increasing faster than any other city in Canada, building permits reached a total of one hundred and sixty-six million dollars in 1968.

Capital investment in Edmonton and Calgary was second only to Toronto. More than a hundred and fifty new industries located in the province that year, bringing an investment of three hundred million dollars.

Battle River Work Continues — 1968

The year 1968 was an active one for the power companies as well. The largest project was unit three at Battle River. The civic works, stack, boiler and coal handling plant were now installed, and the electrical and piping work well underway. Work on the installation of the turbine itself was proceeding well.

The forty-mile, 240-kilovolt steel tower transmission line from the Battle River plant to Nevis was energized at a preliminary 144 kilovolts in mid-October, representing another major tie into the provincial power grid. Another tie added to the grid that year was a sixty-mile 240-kilovolt line connecting the Slave Lake area at a point near Barrhead.

In Rainbow Lake the gas turbine transported from the Vermilion plant was installed and placed in operation on August 7.

A sixty-six-mile transmission line was started to serve developments at the McIntyre-Porcupine mine and the future town of Grande Cache. The company began investigating the possibility of building a 150-megawatt steam plant in that area to burn waste fuel from a mining operation set up to furnish two million tons per year of metallurgical coal to Japanese industry.

Coal Industry Revives

Old King Coal was making an amazing comeback in Alberta. After the war, the coal industry had declined for more than a decade to the point where some people thought it was finished as a major industry. Everyone knew the coal was there — an estimated forty-seven trillion tons resting under seven hundred thousand square miles of the province's surface.

Coal started making its comeback, mainly in the electric power industry. By the late sixties thermal electric plants were consuming nearly half of the nearly four million tons mined annually in the province.

In Saskatchewan, too, coal was popular for generating power. "Perhaps the best known industrial market for coal lies in the generation of electric power," said a publication of the Saskatchewan Power Corporation.

Then the metallurgical industry came along as a big coal user in 1968, particularly in Japan. Deals and prospective deals for shipping coal to Japan totalled nearly a billion dollars. Right across the northwest, including the United States, the use of coal for refining steel and other metals was growing.

Lower Rates in Yukon — 1968

In the Yukon various kinds of mining operations, from copper to gold, were the major factor in healthy growth for the power companies. The sale of 60 million kilowatt hours of electricity in 1968 was up forty-four percent from 1967, and revenue was up twenty-eight percent. Yukon Electrical's largest customer was New Imperial Mine, about fourteen miles south of Whitehorse. Others included Arctic Mines and Venus Mines.

In 1901, when The Yukon Electrical Company was originally incorporated under ordinance of the first territorial government, power sold for a dollar for the first kilowatt hour and forty cents for each additional kilowatt hour. By 1950 the rates had dropped to 10.7 cents, by 1955 to 6.5 cents. By 1968 Canadian Utilities, of which the Yukon company was a wholly-owned subsidiary, had brought the rates down to where the residential rate was 1.6 cents per kilowatt hour.

This inspired the editor of the *Whitehorse Star* to comment:

> *Yukon Electrical is looking like one of the best things that have happened to this territory since overproof rum. The firm has brought reliable and efficient services wherever it has strung wires and has shown a consistent policy of cutting rates wherever costs and consumption warrant such a happy move . . . Nice to see the company taking this action on its own initiative without pressure from anyone outside the firm.*

Executive Changes — 1969

On April 18, 1969, Horatio Ray Milner, Q.C., officially stepped down from active business association with Canadian Utilities, Northland, Canadian Western and Northwestern Utilities. In recognition of his long and distinguished career, the companies appointed him an honorary director and honorary board chairman.

Milner's retirement was in keeping with a new resolution of the companies to the effect that directors who had passed their seventieth birthday would not be re-elected to the board the following year. Among the individuals who were instrumental in the founding of the companies, Milner was the only one who was still actively associated with all of them.

Milner's retirement was marked by a party held in his honor in Edmonton attended by more than three hundred business associates from Alberta and across the country. His outstanding business record included having been chairman of at least eleven companies, a director of more than two dozen, the president of seven or more and the principal officer of two. He had received honorary doctorates of law from three universities and was named chancellor of one. In Edmonton he had participated in almost every worthwhile money-raising campaign conducted in the city, including his having been the first president of the Community Chest.

That summer International Utilities' chairman John M. Seabrook announced a series of promotions and executive appointments that had the effect of further consolidating the operations of the four companies under one executive team.

Dennis Yorath assumed the new post of chairman of the executive committee of International Utilities. After more than forty-five years of service, he retired as chairman of the two gas companies, but continued to serve as a director and a vice-president of International Utilities and as a director of all four of the Alberta companies, along with his new responsiblity of chairing an intercompany executive committee. This made him the senior Canadian officer of International Utilities, listed by Fortune Magazine as one of the 500 largest industrial corporations on the continent.

John Maybin, president of the two gas companies, was promoted to the position of chairman and chief executive officer of the four Alberta companies. At the same time Edge King, who had been serving as president of Canadian Utilities and Northland, became president of all four companies.

Jack Dale, a director, a vice-president and member of the executive committee of International Utilities, was appointed vice-chairman of all four utility companies, as well as serving as a director of the four companies.

Kenneth L. MacFadyen, former vice-president and comptroller of the gas companies, became senior vice-president of finance for the four companies. Ronald N. Dalby became senior vice-president of the two gas companies and a vice-president of Canadian Utilities and Northland. David B. Smith became senior vice-president of operations for the gas companies, and A.J.L. (John) Fisher became general manager of Canadian Western.

Senior appointments for Canadian Utilities and Northland included Robert H. Choate to the position of vice-president and general manager; Jack E. Bagshaw, vice-president, marketing; George D. O'Brien, vice-president, public information; Keith J. Provost, vice-president, electrical engineering; and Wilson G. Sterling, vice-president, production.

Grande Cache — 1969

The most spectacular developments in the energy group in 1969 were related to coal. There was the completion of the new coal-fired generator at the Battle River station, which had the effect of doubling Canadian Utilities' generating capacity; and there was the begining of work on a new 150-megawatt generating station in the coal mining area of Grande Cache in northwestern Alberta.

"The Grande Cache development with its several years of studies and negotiations is one of the most interesting projects undertaken by this company in recent years," said Keith Provost. Prospects for this giant plant became a reality with the signing of a contract by McIntyre Porcupine Mines to supply coal to Japan.

During 1969 work progressed well on the plant, due for commissioning in 1972. Work started also on a 240-kilovolt line and a 144-kilovolt line, a large substation, sub transmission lines and an underground distribution system for the new town of Grande Cache. Work on the high voltage transmission line began early in the year but was considerably hampered by rough terrain and extremely cold weather followed by an early spring break-up.

Even the gas companies got into the act with the McIntyre Porcupine mining developments. Bringing gas to the coal mines may have seemed like the proverbial bringing coals to Newcastle but it happened! Northwestern built a pipeline to the coal complex, following the Canadian Utilities' power right-of-way, through sixty-eight miles of extremely rough terrain at a cost of more than two million dollars, to supply natural gas for the coal mine. The gas was used for drying the coal after it had been washed to remove impurities. Initial annual sales of gas for this purpose were forecast at nearly two billion cubic feet.

Battle River Unit 3 Starts Up — 1969

When Edge King threw the switch that officially put Battle River generator No. 3 on the line in the fall of 1969, it marked not only a tremendous stride in the company's progress but also a foretaste of things to come. While finishing touches were still being put on the twenty-eight million dollar unit, work was already under way on the Grande Cache plant. It was to be named the H.R. Milner Generating Station. A second generator for Rainbow was on order as well, and long-range plans were initiated for a 300-megawatt addition to the Battle River plant.

Over the short space of four years Canadian Utilities had experienced an increase in electric demand of fifty-four percent, and it was anticipated that over the next five years the demand would almost double the 1969 figure.

The Battle River plant, with unit three in operation, now consumed about eight hundred thousand tons of coal per year from a field with estimated reserves of nearly two hundred million tons.

Advances in Computers

The operations of the energy group were becoming more sophisticated as the sixties drew to an end. The computer system in the Milner Building had its own high priests who tended it, communicated with it and knew how to interpret its messages to the rank and file. In Calgary Canadian Western replaced its card system computer with a disk system. Right off the bat the new system reduced the time required to produce a billing register to about half of what it had been under the old system.

Canadian Western's new computer — an IBM 360 Model 25 — was one of the first of its kind in Canada and the second one installed in Alberta.

First Rate Increase in 43 Years — 1969

The north again was reporting the fastest growth in energy consumption. Northland showed an impressive increase for 1969 of more than thirty-five percent in its kilowatt-hour sales. The fifty-three-mile, 144-kilovolt transmission line between Rainbow and Zama, started in 1968, was completed to replace mobile generators used in that area. Oilfield demand continued strong. New substations and major additions were built at Rainbow, Zama, Valleyview and Jasper.

Despite increases in power consumption, however, Northland's net earnings were down. Increased costs of operation more than offset the revenue gains. The company had no alternative but to go to the Public Utilities Board for a rate increase.

Northland was not alone. Inflationary pressures were mounting in Canadian Utilities as well. Increased operating expenses and cost of capital forced the company to apply to the board for its first increase in power rates in forty-three years of operation. The board's review approved a seventeen percent increase in allowable revenue to cover these increased costs and allow a return of eight and a half percent on an approved rate base.

Tax Rebates — 1969

I nvestor-owned utilities were by now beginning to receive income tax rebates, thanks to federal tax concessions initiated several years earlier by the energy group in Alberta. But certain sections of the federal government's new white paper on tax reform, relating directly to electric, gas and steam utilities, caused a great deal of concern on the part of all utility shareholders when the report was issued in the fall of 1969. The effect would be to deny any tax credit for dividend income to shareholders of utility companies. Board chairman John Maybin commented on this in the annual report of the companies:

> . . . This has created a difficult financing situation for which the only apparent solution, if the proposals are adopted, is one that leads ultimately to higher costs to the consumer. Strong representations are being made on a company and industry-wide basis to resolve the situation by obtaining the same tax credit treatment for utility shareholders as for investors in any other enterprise.

More Growth — 1969

W hile power consumption in the north was increasing fastest on a percentage basis, the companies on the whole experienced healthy increases in customers and load. Canadian Western added six thousand new customers to its system in 1969, the largest annual increase in customers in ten years. Lethbridge, along with Calgary, was expanding in all directions. Among other projects, plans were going ahead for construction of the University of Lethbridge.

In Calgary a twenty-four-inch gas line was installed, the largest ever by the companies. The project was made necessary by the construction of a city roadway interchange at Sixty-six Avenue and the Blackfoot Trail.

Edmonton reached another milestone in its growth on July 30 when the gas company installed the one hundred thousandth natural gas service line within the city. The city's population had multiplied four-fold since the discovery of the Leduc oilfield in 1947.

On a system-wide basis Northwestern was now serving one hundred and seven communities throughout north-central Alberta with more than one hundred and thirty thousand service lines. The Edmonton power plant was its largest user, and the Imperial Oil fertilizer plant at Redwater, which went into production that spring, was the second largest single customer. The fifty million dollar plant, thirty miles northeast of Edmonton, uses natural gas in the manufacture of nitrogen fertilizer.

Severe Cold in January — 1969

A nother plus for the gas companies in 1969 was their excellent performance during a cold snap early in the year — one of the longest and most severe spells of extreme sub-zero weather on record. It lasted from January 7 to February 1. The average temperature in Edmonton in January was fifteen degrees Fahrenheit below zero while the normal temperature for that time of year would have been six degrees above zero. Calgary, where the normal average would have been fifteen above zero, averaged thirteen degrees Fahrenheit below zero.

Through it all customers of the gas companies remained cozy in their homes and offices as natural gas service continued uninterrupted. Such was not the case with other utilities. In Calgary the water department had problems with frozen and broken water mains. City crews were unable to keep up with the breaks and had to have help from private contractors and the gas company. Canadian Western sent five crews with compressors and diggers to help in a situation that lasted several weeks.

A sidelight of the cold spell was the number of cars stolen from the parking lot at the Milner Building in Edmonton when many employees left their cars running to keep them warm. One such theft was written up in the *Edmonton Journal* which reported that Al Shanley's car was borrowed by a gentleman who immediately drove it to the police station. There he checked himself into a cell block in order to have a warm place to spend the night. He got the free night's lodging plus an additional seven days in jail as a bonus.

Fire in Red Deer — 1969

In other news that year, the companies had a setback in the spring when a fire of unknown origin destroyed Northwestern's natural gas high pressure station in north Red Deer on March 29.

A local resident who noticed the station on fire at eight o'clock in the morning turned in an alarm to employee Al Barber. District foreman Hugh McAllister and a Northwestern crew immediately rushed to the scene along with the Red Deer fire department. It was three hours before the fire was brought under control. Thanks to quick action on the part of the distribution department, gas service to the city was sustained and only a few homes in the immediate area were affected.

A secondary casualty of the fire was a billboard on company property, a landmark in Red Deer. The sign proclaimed "Look Up — the Cleanest Sky in the World is Above You. Natural Gas Keeps it So." For many years this "Clean Skies" billboard was a familiar sight to motorists travelling Highway 2.

This fire was a reminder of an explosion which had occurred nearly a year previously in Edmonton, costing two lives and the destruction of a building known as the Dunston Apartment Block. That was the first serious explosion related to natural gas in the area in a great many years, but the company felt nevertheless that it should ask for an outside opinion as to whether its safety procedures were as good as they should be. John Maybin commented:

We brought in a firm from Chicago. They checked us over and assured us that our inspection procedures were far more rigorous than most other gas companies. Within the last few days I have received a 10-year summary of the safety record of practically all the areas served by natural gas in the United States. During that 10-year period the record in the areas served by our companies is far better than the average for the industry as a whole.

We can be proud of our record over the years. We can't in any way be proud of the experience in Alberta in the past year. Let's do our utmost to get the industry record back on the track . . .

Booklet Reprinted in U.S.

In a more normal vein, the gas companies received an encouraging pat on the back in 1969 when the American Gas Association reprinted a booklet created by Canadian Western, titled Facts about Discoloration in the Home. It was first published in 1964. It was developed over the years as the company pointed out to its customers that natural gas had nothing to do with discoloration of walls, and for that matter it had nothing to do with a variety of other problems in the home for which it was sometimes blamed, ranging from sick animals to rheumatism. The AGA expressed its appreciation to Canadian Western for allowing the association to reprint and distribute the material all over North America.

Finally, on the electrical side of the business, companies' president Edge King was elected president of the international Northwest Electric Light and Power Association (NELPA) at its sixty-second annual meeting in Spokane, Washington in September.

CUL Power Company Publications

George O'Brien entered the ranks of the company's pensioners in 1970 after forty-two years of continuous service, the longest record in the electric company. His contributions to the company, particularly its public relations program, established a sound pattern for the future.

O'Brien became director of public information for Canadian Utilities and Northland in the spring of 1962. He played a leading role in both external and internal communications, as his department included the publication of the employee magazine, called *The Transmitter*.

In the early years Canadian Utilities relied largely on *The Courier* for news, on an intercompany basis. Then in the mid-fifties it instituted a small employee periodical of its own, concentrating on electrical operations, called *The Spotlite*. It was published anywhere from six to nine times a year, depending on the need for disseminating news.

As Canadian Utilities' electrical operations continued to grow, in the fall of 1957 it introduced an expanded magazine and christened it *The Transmitter*. Its first editor was Dick Clements, a former farm broadcaster from CFCW in Camrose. He was succeeded a year later by Walter Mandick, former editor of the Castor weekly newspaper.

The Transmitter continued to flourish under George O'Brien's supervision through the sixties, and continues to this day as Alberta Power's staff magazine.

CHAPTER 9

The Seventies

Protecting the Environment

The utility companies entered the seventies with a determination to respond to a heightened public awareness of the need for conservation. D.B. Smith, senior vice-president of the gas companies, announced that the companies would divert a significant part of their public relations and advertising budgets towards creating more public awareness of the need to maintain clean air and water, to preserve the natural beauties of the province and to protect wildlife.

A start had already been made in this direction with the sponsorship of the centennial natural history book, *Alberta — A Natural History.*

The environmental program of the companies was intensified through the Alberta Wildlife Foundation of which the companies were major sponsors. President of the foundation was Edgar T. Jones with whom the companies worked in producing a television series on ecology. The board of directors included inter-company supervisor of public relations and advertising, W. Mills Parker, who had served as co-ordinator of the company's history book project.

The companies' environmental series on television was reinforced by the presentation of nature and wildlife films to the Alberta department of education for use in schools.

In 1970, President Edge King announced the appointment of Gordon R. Cameron as co-ordinator of environmental planning with responsibility to ensure that the companies' operations were conducted in such a way as to minimize environmental disturbances.

A positive way in which the gas companies could contribute to keeping the atmosphere clean was through promoting natural gas as a fuel, not only for indusrial processes but even for automobiles. The companies embarked on a program of encouraging the use of compressed natural gas as a vehicle fuel, which would have the effect of reducing air pollution from that source by about seventy percent.

Natural Gas for Vehicles — 1970

C anadian Western was one of the first companies in Canada to use compressed natural gas for its vehicles. The program began in late 1969 under the direction of Roy Nourse, director of special projects.

By mid-November 1970 the companies were ready with their first demonstration model of a dual fuel car that could burn either natural gas or gasoline. A simple pull of a dashboard lever converted operation to gasoline for travel in areas where natural gas fuel was unavailable.

Natural gas was stored in compression tanks in the vehicle's trunk. Much of the development of the vehicle had been done in conjunction with companies in California where smog problems were sometimes acute, particularily in Los Angeles. The car had the additional advantage of economy since natural gas is less expensive than gasoline.

November of 1970 was a good time for demonstrating a natural-gas-powered car. The previous month, down on the salt flats of Utah, the Blue Flame rocket car streaked to a new world land speed record of six hundred and twenty-two miles per hour. The engine was fueled by a combination of liquefied natural gas and hydrogen peroxide with a propulsion system similar in design to the one used to take the first men to and from the moon. The Blue Flame was sponsored by forty-eight companies in the United States and Canada — most of them natural gas utilities.

Actually, the gas companies' demonstration car was not quite the first of its kind in Alberta. Back in the forties William H. Thornton, a Northwestern employee, converted a vehicle in Edmonton to run on natural gas. The fuel tank was rather bulky, consisting of a huge rubber bag covered with canvas mounted on top of the car. The bag contained fifty cubic feet of natural gas, enough for about eight miles of driving. But it was one solution to the gasoline shortage of the day.

Environmental Concerns

T he environmental program included special measures to minimize atmospheric and water pollution at power plants. Much had already been learned at the Battle River station, and now at the Grande Cache location the companies had a head start on environmental planning. Both Battle River and Grande Cache were assigned university students to gather and record data on the air and water in the vicinity of the plants.

At the new H.R. Milner plant at Grande Cache, Canadian Utilities installed a combination of mechanical and electrostatic dust collectors that would eliminate ninety-seven percent of the fly ash, the dust particles in the exhaust gases. The mechanical equipment used centrifugal force to throw the dust out of the airstream, then the electrostatic precipitators attracted the particles towards the electrodes.

By the late seventies the power company was spending millions of dollars a year on environmental upgrading of plants. At the Milner plant a dry ash-handling system was installed at a cost of nearly four million dollars. It handled about fifty tons of fly ash per hour blown through pipes to a silo which stored up to two thousand tons. Before the ash is transported by truck to a dump site it is mixed with water to a damp-sand consistency. Trucks move up to one hundred and fifty tons of ash per hour to the dump.

The plant also has a fabric dust collector system, sometimes called the baghouse system, which replaced the original electrostatic precipitator. The H.R. Milner plant was the first generating plant in Canada to be equipped with such a system.

Fabric dust cleaners, which operate on the same principle as a vacuum cleaner, have been used for many years to collect dust from air and gas streams in industrial processes. It has only been in the last few years, however, that they have been applied to boilers and even more recently to utility boilers.

Since the ash produced by the coal used at the Milner plant is extremely difficult to collect by more commonly used electrostatic precipitators, the fabric system becomes a practical alternative. More than five thousand fabric bags are in service at one time. Each bag is about six metres long and fifteen centimetres in diameter.

In the town of Grande Cache the company eliminated the problems of power poles and overhead wires by installing an underground distribution system. Due to increased environmental concerns, renewed emphasis was placed on strict clearing specifications for transmission lines with a view to preserving the natural environment. The program of creating parks with the artificial lakes at dam sites was stepped up, and coal companies supplying strip-mined coal for producing electricity were encouraged to engage in complete land reclamation on spreads which had been worked over.

Home Service Celebrates 40 Years

Northwestern's home service department celebrated its fortieth year in 1970. It was March 1, 1930, when the department first opened its doors, under the direction of Kathleen Esch, to help promote goodwill, enhance customer satisfaction and demonstrate the many advantages of natural gas to the Alberta homemaker.

In 1931 a demonstration kitchen opened on the lower floor of the company's main office on 104 Street. The seating capacity was fifty, and the home service staff "packed 'em in" with all kinds of classes and demonstrations. Three years later they were up to their ankles in sawdust at the Edmonton Exhibition, participating in appliance demonstrations and displays of various kinds.

Over the years the department put on popular cooking shows in almost every community served by the company. In more recent years demonstration auditoriums were built into the North Yard Service Centre, finally the Milner Building and in the new Canadian Utilities Centre.

As the department celebrated four decades of home service it was well established in the care of five home economists. A fifteen-minute radio program, Problem Corner has been featured weekday mornings on radio station CJCA for over twenty years.

Out-of-town demonstrations included a wild game cooking show, a barbecue show, school demonstrations, budget planning and babysitting courses. In the 1970s a live stage presentation known as the Magic Suitcase demonstrated in an entertaining fashion the various modern-day products made from natural gas.

Jack Dale to Pakistan — 1970

Jack Dale, who had been in the electric power industry in Alberta for four decades, resigned from the energy group in the fall of 1970 to accept a position with the World Bank and Acres International Limited to organize and administer the electrical industry in Pakistan. Eleven countries were donating power plants to Pakistan.

Apart from being an authority on the electrical industry in Alberta, Dale had another qualification he claimed was useful to him in Pakistan. "You have to be either bald or have white hair to work over there," he said. "The people don't respect you and listen to you if you don't." So the silver-haired vice-chairman of the energy group accepted his new job in Pakistan, even though his employers warned him that the normal weather over there is like the storm season in eastern Canada.

He had a two-year contract. They were two stormy years for the Dale family. Over a period of six months they had a variety of hair-raising experiences, beginning with a cyclone and tidal wave, followed by a violent civil war. Finally they got out of East Pakistan with little more than their lives and one suitcase each. After spending time in Europe and the Far East, they returned to Canada. Dale carried out several more consulting jobs, and then retired. He died in 1981.

Another retirement in 1970 was that of Canadian Utilities' vice-president Jack Ford. It was forty-one years since Ford started in the electrical industry with

Montreal Engineering, later Prairie Power Company, in Regina. Next he joined Calgary Power, and then Canadian Utilities in 1951 as chief electrical engineer. He became vice-president, administration, in 1968.

In 1970 J. Herb Hughes, land manager for the gas companies, became president of the four-thousand-strong American Association of Petroleum Landmen International. He was installed at the association's annual meeting in Los Angeles, with the distinction of being the first Canadian elected to the top executive post.

New Trademark — 1970

U nder the direction of the public relations department, Canadian Utilities introduced its new corporate electrical symbol in 1970. The symbol was designed to provide a strong, modern visual identification for the electrical operations. The company colors chosen in connection with the new logo were blue and ochre, which were subsequently embodied in the design of stationery, literature, advertising and on vehicles, equipment and buildings. The new logo depicted an electric plug framed by a circle and was similar in shape to the gas companies' logo.

Underwater Repairs — 1970

B y way of human interest, a Canadian Utilities employee's scuba diving hobby saved the day at the Vermilion power plant in the spring of 1970 when a critical leakage problem was discovered. Steve Nazar, building co-ordinator, donned his diving gear to descend into the underwater darkness of the plant's cooling water reservoir.

The cooling waterline to the plant was leaking. The hole in the pipe was creating enough suction to draw a whale through it. The hole had to be plugged until company engineers could find a more permanent solution. It required two attempts before the plug was installed, and another dive was required for final adjustment.

Re-organization — 1971-1972

S weeping organizational changes took place in 1971-1972. Through a corporate restructuring approved by the shareholders, on January 5, 1972, Canadian Utilities became the holding company and parent of Canadian Western, Northwestern, Northland, and a new company, Alberta Power Limited, incorporated federally October 26, 1971 to assume the electrical operations of the new holding company.

The gas assets of Northland Utilities were subsequently transferred to North-western, and the electrical operations to Alberta Power, while Northland went into voluntary liquidation.

The re-organization had the effect of making Canadian Utilities one of the largest investor-owned utilities in Canada, with net assets of three hundred and twenty-eight million dollars and total annual revenue in excess of one hundred million dollars. It was the only such Canadian company with significant operations in both gas and electric service. Canadian Utilities, as the holding company, adopted the abbreviation CU.

With John Maybin as board chairman and Edge King as president, the seven additional executive officers were Ken MacFadyen, senior vice-president, finance; Ed Ringrose, vice-president, administration; Ron Dalby, vice-president; Andy Anderson, controller; Bill Sullivan, secretary; Harry Bottomley, treasurer; and Harry Brown, assistant secretary and assistant treasurer.

In the previous two years the companies as a group had capital expenditures of more than fifty-five million dollars for additions and improvements to meet the demands for increased service. Now the companies were embarking on the largest construction program in their history, requiring estimated capital expenditures of one hundred and sixty-two million dollars over a five-year period.

Board chairman John Maybin commented: "It will be easier to raise the money for future expansion of each of these systems to keep up with the continuing growth of the population living in the areas now served, and to supply new industries locating there, by making the financial arrangements through one company rather than in four separate pieces as we have been doing in the past. The restructured organization will provide a central company through which all such arrangements can be made."

During the previous five years the companies carried out eight debt financings together with an issue of preferred shares and an issue of common shares. With the new structure, Canadian Utilities could do the financing, and in turn finance the requirements of the subsidiaries.

Shares of Canadian Utilities were already trading on the Toronto Stock Exchange. With the re-organization, application was now made to list them on the Montreal Stock Exchange as well.

International Utilities Returns to U.S. — 1971-1972

While all this was taking place, International Utilities took another step towards its ultimate phasing-out of ownership and control of the Canadian Utilities group. The corporation reverted to U.S. residency, ending a unique eleven-year status as a dual corporate citizen of the United States and Canada.

International's decision was taken at year-end 1971 with the unanimous approval of the board of directors, which traditionally had six members from

Canada, four from the United States, and one from the United Kingdom. The announcement was made jointly by John Seabrook, chairman and president, and Dennis Yorath, chairman of the executive committee. The board had come to the conclusion, they said, that it could no longer justify the exposure of the corporation to the many risks inherent in remaining subject to the increasingly sophisticated taxing and regulatory powers of two sovereign nations.

The rapid growth of the corporation's income from sources outside Canada in the late sixties made it apparent that the tax advantages of Canadian residency had been dissipated, Seabrook said. The corporate office was relocated to Wilmington, Delaware, at the beginning of 1972.

Shortly after the move John Maybin, chairman of the Alberta group, was appointed group vice-president — utilities, for International Utilities. In this capacity he assumed responsibility over all gas, electric and water utility operations of International and also became chairman of General Waterworks Corp., which operated water utilities in eighteen states. He continued to hold the position of chairman of Canadian Utilities in its new role as holding company for International's Canadian utility operations, but was succeeded by president Edge King as chief executive officer of the Alberta companies.

Maybin's appointment filled a vacancy left by Murray Stewart who was appointed president of International's Hawaiian agriculture and land development subsidiary, C. Brewer and Co. Ltd.

Energy Resources Conservation Board

While this was taking place in Canadian Utilities, change was occurring in the Alberta government as well. The Oil and Gas Conservation Board became the Energy Resources Conservation Board (ERCB) in 1971. The Alberta Power Commission ceased to exist as the new board took over most of its functions. The enlarged board also assumed responsibility over the coal industry.

Canadian Utilities' president, Edge King, commented:

. . . The establishment of the new Energy Resources Conservation Board is a recognition of the growing inter-relationship of all forms of energy and of the need to consider the provincial energy needs, and the conservation of available resources, in their entirety.

. . . In the early years of our companies, the energy forms with which we are concerned were merely useful and intriguing conveniences. They have grown in importance until now they are vital and indispensable in every modern community. Not only has the efficient supply of this energy brought increasing responsibilities on the companies, it has also brought a high degree of public interest.

The creation of the Energy Resources Conservation Board is a manifestation of this interest, and we are confident it will prove to be a significant

225

forward step in ensuring the best use of the tremendous energy resources of this province in the years ahead.

New Well Roars into Service — 1971

On the morning of June 28, 1971, in the middle of a rolling green field, beside a tiny lake just southwest of the hamlet of Partridge Hill, Northwestern's newest gas supply, Fort Saskatchewan well no. 10-12-54-22, came into production with a throaty roar.

The final stages of drilling of this well were done with compressed air. Air drilling as opposed to conventional methods prevents polluting the production sand with drilling mud or water.

The well had an absolute open flow potential of 78 million cubic feet per day, the largest of any well in Northwestern's dry gas fields. It would be used to help meet peak winter requirements of the gas company.

The gas companies added nearly fourteen thousand new customers to their systems in 1971, the largest annual increase in ten years. A good number of these connections were new farm customers. Business was good in the industrial sales sector as well. At Edmonton the Gulf refinery completed its eighty-four million dollar expansion to bring production to 80 thousand barrels a day, making it the largest refinery west of Sarnia, Ontario. Imperial Oil disclosed plans for a new 140 thousand-barrel per day refinery, to cost more than two hundred million dollars.

The petroleum industry was good for the whole energy group. More than one-fifth of the group's electric revenue was from the sale of power to more than one hundred oil companies in some seventeen hundred locations.

In the southern part of the province Canadian Western contracted to install and operate a major storage scheme in the Carbon field for TransCanada Pipelines for a twenty-year period. This scheme involved the drilling of several additional wells and the installation of about forty-five hundred horsepower of compression facilities. Plans called for storage of twenty billion cubic feet of TransCanada's gas each summer to be delivered to TransCanada during the following winter.

A new vehicle and equipment maintenance depot was completed the previous year by Canadian Western south of Calgary's McCall International Airport. Covering almost twenty-three thousand square feet, it was planned and built after much study of other such depots so that the best of the ideas could be incorporated in the new building.

Yukon Electrical Anniversary — 1971

The Yukon Electrical Company marked its seventieth anniversary in 1971. General manager Andy Morin kicked off the celebrations by presenting a batch of I'm a Yukon Booster plastic bags to the local Chamber of Commerce — the first of seventy thousand which Yukon Electrical employees distributed.

The original company started in 1901 when the territory was a turmoil of gold rush activity and the population was pushing over forty thousand. The first power plant burned down in 1905 along with the greater part of Whitehorse. It was quickly rebuilt, with the new fire hall as part of the new power plant, but the demand for electricity declined as the gold rush fizzled out.

By 1910 the territory had about nine thousand people left and for the next quarter century little was heard about the Yukon. In 1939, shortly before the war, there were about four thousand in the Yukon. Then came the war and construction of the Alaska Highway. It was boom time once more. After the war there were surplus generators and distribution systems that later served government and private concerns for many years.

Canadian Utilities bought the company in 1958, and from that time on expansion was continuous, systematic and healthy. Celebrating the seventieth anniversary were fifty-three employees with a modern central office building, serving eighty-three percent of all power users in the Yukon.

By the mid-seventies there were ominous signs that the company's properties in the Yukon might be in jeopardy, occasioned by repeated rumblings from Ottawa to the effect that in future all generation and distribution of electric power north of the sixtieth parallel would come under the jurisdiction of the government's Northern Canada Power Commission. Once again Canadian Utilities had visions of being forced to sell some of its properties to government. Negotiations with the Northern Canada Power Commission concerning the sale of company assets in the Yukon and Northwest Territories, however, broke off in 1976.

During its seventy-fifth anniversary celebrations in 1976, The Yukon Electrical Company sponsored staff member Linda Church as one of the seven contestants for the title of Sourdough Queen. Linda and the company's Queen's Float in the parade both took first place in the Yukon's annual Sourdough Rendezvous which rivals Edmonton's Klondike Days.

Power Plant Expansions — 1971

The first submission before the newly formed ERCB was an application by Alberta Power for installation of another 150-megawatt unit at the Battle River station to be built by 1975. The application was approved, subject to certain environmental criteria being satisfied.

While plans were being made for Battle River Unit No. 4, work on the H.R. Milner plant at Grande Cache proceeded on schedule. Capital expenditures on the project in 1971 were nearly twenty million dollars. Construction also started on a ninety-mile 144-kilovolt line from that plant to Grande Prairie to complete another important interconnection in the province-wide power grid system.

During 1972 the company's engineering department installed a unique remote control system between the Sturgeon station east of Grande Prairie and the Rainbow Lake station in the extreme northwest corner of the province, spanning a distance of more than three hundred miles. The system permitted the two 30-megawatt gas turbines in the Rainbow station to be entirely controlled from the Sturgeon plant.

The Grande Cache station went into operation and construction got under way on Unit No. 4 at Battle River. Footings for the four hundred and fifty-foot stack were poured, designed to support more than four thousand tons of concrete and steel lining. The design of the stack took special account of environmental concerns. Not only was the plant equipped with the most modern in electrostatic precipitators, but the existing stacks were removed as part of a ten-million-dollar program to meet more stringent standards.

The new Battle River unit would be completed in 1975 at a cost of fifty-two million dollars. Already on the drawing boards were preliminary plans for Unit No. 5 with a capacity of 375 megawatts and a price tag of two hundred and forty million dollars, to be operational in 1981. The long range need for that unit was determined through the company's participation in the province-wide Electric Utility Planning Council. The generator, as part of the provincial grid system, would at first supply considerable power to other members of the grid until such time as the company's own customers required it.

Sheerness in Planning Stage

With electricity generated from coal now being fed into the system on a massive scale from the Battle River station, the older gas-fired generating plants at Vermilion and Fairview were taken out of service. But even more coal development was on the horizon. Plans began to materialize for building two 375-megawatt units at Sheerness, eighteen miles southeast of Hanna in southern Alberta.

Sheerness coal development plans began in 1972, calling for possible commissioning of the first unit in the late 1980s. Then came a bombshell from the Alberta government: the decision not to approve a mammoth 2,250-megawatt Calgary Power coal development at Camrose-Ryley. This immediately placed pressure on all the power companies in the Alberta grid to find alternative ways of generating electricity. Sheerness plans jumped two years closer overnight.

In the fall of 1975, the Alberta Cabinet approved the Sheerness project in principle.

The Sheerness project would involve mining almost fifteen thousand acres over the thirty-year economic life of the plant. More than three hundred acres of land a year would undergo surface mining by two mining companies. The plant would consume about three and a half million tons of coal per year.

Since the plant site is an area with limited water resources, a twenty-five-mile pipeline would bring water from the Red Deer River to a thirteen hundred-acre cooling pond adjacent to the plant site. Included in the construction were items of special equipment to prevent adverse effects on the environment.

Gas Companies' Anniversaries — 1972-1973

In 1972 Canadian Western observed its sixtieth anniversary followed in 1973 by Northwestern's fiftieth. As a public service project timed to coincide with the two anniversaries, the companies jointly sponsored an hour-long film documentary on pioneer western photographer Ernest Brown.

The production won two first place awards in the 1973 Yorkton International Film Festival. The following spring it received eleven awards at the Alberta Film Festival, including Alberta Culture's Celestial Visitor award for best overall film.

In the mid-seventies the companies sponsored another film, The Birds in Winter, marking the hundredth anniversary of the arrival of the North-West Mounted Police in Alberta. It was narrated by Canadian actor Leslie Nielsen, and premiered at Alberta's Jubilee Auditoriums in Calgary and Edmonton.

Anniversaries are always a time for reminiscing. For Canadian Western the sixtieth was a time of looking back over the years during which the company had been led by a series of ten presidents, beginning with Eugene Coste. Over those years the company had progressed and now was serving more than half a million Albertans.

Northwestern's celebrations the following year featured staff buttons proclaiming Fifty Nifty Years of Serving You. A flare-lighting ceremony was held in Sir Winston Churchill Square, recalling the ceremony on November 9, 1923 when natural gas service first arrived in the city. Among the dignitaries present was Eric Duggan, son of the late Mayor D.M. Duggan, who lit the flare in 1923.

Following the public ceremonies the official party moved to the new Edmonton Public Library, where an engraved mural of the old downtown post office, by Alberta artist Meredith Evans, was presented to the city and the public library, also marking its fiftieth anniversary that year.

Fuel Cells and Clean Cars

In the early seventies Canadian Western continued to lead the way in various kinds of research, particularly the fuel cell. In 1972 the company entered into a contract with Engineered Homes Limited under which Canada's first experimental fuel cell power plant went into a new home in the Oakridge section of southwest Calgary. It provided all the home's electrical needs for a sixteen-week test period.

229

Fuel cell power plants produce on-site electrical power directly from natural gas by electrochemical reaction. They were first installed for the Apollo moon mission space craft by the United Aircraft Corporation.

The power plant in the show home was opened on August 28 by Alberta Telephones and Utilities minister L.F. Werry. Also present was George Govier, chairman of the Energy Resources Conservation Board, who remarked: "The fuel cell is a further step in the conservation and efficient use of Alberta's natural resources."

The two demonstration fuel cell units were a little larger than a washer-dryer combination. Direct current generated in one unit by an electrochemical reaction using natural gas and air was converted to alternating current in the other. The developers claimed the process is about twenty-five percent more efficient than thermal plants and emits only non-pollutants. During the sixteen-week test period more than ten thousand people viewed the units in operation. Inquiries were received from across Canada as well as from other parts of the world requesting information about the fuel cell power plant concept.

Fuel cells for homes may still be in the future, but the idea had some practical applications in Canadian Western's service areas. On Plateau Mountain, eighty-two hundred feet above sea level, the company had a mobile repeater station which needed electricity. It was not practical to run a power line so the company installed two thermoelectric generators, which are similar to fuel cells. These are solid state generators with no moving parts, which produce electricity on the principle of a temperature difference across thermocouples.

Canadian Western and Northwestern continued to promote natural gas vehicles, a program they started in 1969. Demonstrations were held in cities and towns by both gas companies to groups of students, municipal groups, trade fairs and private fleet operators.

Not to be outdone by the gas companies, Alberta Power engineer Don Peterson built his own electric car, or rather modified an Austin Mini and equipped it with an electric motor. With three series-connected batteries the unit had a cruising speed in excess of thirty miles per hour and could be recharged overnight from a standard electrical outlet. Total cost of the vehicle, including a hydrometer for checking the battery fluid, was just under a thousand dollars.

Instant Pipelines

The ploughing in of plastic pipe in rural areas continued to be another specialty in which Canadian Western led the way in the seventies. With the help of a Big Al, a specially designed plough, the company was laying plastic pipe underground at the rate of about two miles an hour. "Instant" pipelines were now a reality. Pipeliners had come a long way since ditches were dug by hand and pipe was coated by hand before being buried.

Big Al was handling two and three-inch pipes like garden hose, laying them forty-four inches below the surface at a speed about as fast as you can walk, with little or no evidence of soil disturbance. Standing nearby, scratching his head in disbelief, is Farmer Brown with his seeder, ready to seed the right-of-way.

Canadian Western acquired another machine in the mid-seventies — the first in Western Canada — a computer which specializes in calculations pertaining to volumes of gas, called an electronic integrator. It was demonstrated at the Canadian Petroleum Show in Calgary.

New Control Centre — 1972

While all those exciting things were going on in southern Alberta, a great deal was happening in Edmonton too. Northwestern's new Natural Gas Control Centre in southeast Edmonton was officially opened October 21, 1972.

The sleek new building, featuring tinted glass and steel with bronze, gleaming in the afternoon sun, was now the hub of Northwestern's operations. It provided a sharp contrast to the first station built half a century previously, which was a small underground vault south of the city in contact with the gas field staff at Viking only by telephone.

By the early seventies it became clear the existing control and dispatch system soon would be unable to cope with the system's growth. The answer: a new building with fully automated gas dispatch and control.

The gate station controlled the flow of gas from pipelines originating from fields in Viking-Kinsella, Pembina, Devon, Bonnie Glen, Paddle River and Beaverhill Lake. In the mid-seventies about five hundred million cubic feet of natural gas would pass through the gate station during a typical cold winter day when demand was near its peak.

The heart of the new and highly sophisticated system of controls was a minicomputer that received signals from key points on the company's far-flung system covering more than three hundred thousand square miles. These signals gave such vital information as pipeline pressure and flow rates, which arrived at the center by radio and leased telephone lines. Data gathered in the field was converted into electrical signals at five remote terminal units located at Redwater, Drayton Valley, Viking, Poe and Bonnie Glen. From these locations the signals were transmitted to the control center's microwave radio.

Computerization Advances

In keeping with technological developments and the new consolidations of the companies' business procedures, the computer center in the Milner Building was upgraded by an IBM 360 Model 40 system. The new central processing unit was more powerful and sophisticated with a much larger information storage capacity.

It was fussy and hypersensitive, too. It demanded a controlled environment where humidity and temperature were carefully regulated. This required a special application of insulation to all exterior walls in the computer room on the second floor of the Milner Building in Edmonton. It caused some envy on the part of staff members who claimed the machine was receiving more attention than they were.

All consumer billing, payroll, inventories, general accounting and dividends were now being handled by the computer centre in Edmonton. For personalized service, however, Canadian Western established a Customer Information Centre at the Calgary Service Centre where all enquiries pertaining to gas accounts, meters, moves and adjustments of appliances could be dealt with.

With data stations set up in both Edmonton and Calgary, processing vast amounts of information and relaying it to other offices took only minutes. The Calgary employee wishing to transfer information keyed the data onto a diskette, then contacted the Edmonton computer center on a special telephone line. The Edmonton operator prepared to receive the data and on a given signal the information was instantaneously transmitted and received. The Edmonton diskette was then inserted in the computer. The same procedure in reverse was used to transmit the new processed material to the Calgary office.

Microfilm was another example of technological advance. In 1975 a two-month record of billing and accounts receivable registers could be stored on a microfilm tape about the size of a wallet.

The tapes were stored in chronological order for easy and immediate reference. A customer enquiry about previous gas bills could be handled in seconds by retrieving the tape, inserting it in the Dietzgen microfilm reader, and jotting down the pertinent information which appeared on the large, easy-to-read screen.

Northwestern began computer billing in 1956, and because of this compact method of storing information, now maintained almost twenty years of billing data in two medium size filing cabinets.

Power load dispatching on the provincial grid system was greatly assisted by computers. Electricity can't be stored, but has to be used as soon as it is generated. The process by which each generating plant is assigned its share of the electrical load is called dispatching. In 1975 engineers installed a new computerized system that improved the methods used to dispatch energy. All pertinent information is supplied to a dispatcher at the push of a button.

Outside Gas Meters

After 1975, it was no longer necessary to have a natural gas meter as part of the basement decor. After an exhaustive study lasting nearly two years, the gas companies' standard practice committee approved the installation of outside meter sets.

All residential and small commercial meters with a maximum capacity up to 415 cubic feet per hour could now be installed outside. These meters are compensated to register accurately despite variation in temperature.

Meter reading showed promise of becoming even more highly automated as Northwestern entered into a joint test program with the city of Edmonton's water, electric and telephone systems and Alberta Government Telephones, for taking meter readings automatically by telephone. Some thirty homes were used in this pilot project, using a device called a transponder attached to the meters and connected to telephone leads coming into the test homes. When the time came for the meters to be read a computer made a connection through the telephone line to the transponder which sent the meter reading back.

Nature on the Rampage — 1972

The year 1972 brought some severe strains to Alberta Power with floods in the spring and hoarfrost in the fall.

Nature went on the rampage in the Grande Prairie district in mid-June. Torrential rains in the foothills brought down tons of melted snow water and creeks flooded to the size of rivers. Highway 34 to Edmonton was closed with some six feet of water flowing across it on both sides of the Smoky River bridge. Both the Northern Alberta Railway and the Alberta Resources Railway went out of commission because of landslides and washouts resulting from the high water.

Alberta Power was hit hard. The 144-kilovolt line feeding Grande Cache and the McIntyre-Porcupine mines was washed out as the normally peaceful thirty-foot wide Sheep Creek became a half-mile-wide torrent. Damage took four days to repair using planes, helicopters, and tracked vehicles to haul men and materials over mud and water. Men were working twenty hours a day.

A damaged section of the power line had to be bypassed with a temporary line, and permission was obtained from the CNR to use its railroad bed for this purpose. Since no heavy equipment could be brought into the isolated site, the repair crew had to use hand tools aided by dynamite to dig six-foot holes in tightly-packed gravel. A helicopter was used to help erect the power poles on the temporary line, while a second chopper operated a shuttle service bringing in men and equipment. Company pilot Molly Reilly lost many hours of sleep as the company aircraft, too, was pressed into service between Edmonton, Grande Prairie and Grande Cache.

At Grande Prairie the power went out when the 144-kilovolt line across the Smoky River could not stand the pressure and went down. A quick switch, however, to the 72-kilovolt transmission line saved the day.

The weekend of November 10, 1972, brought another kind of catastrophe. With temperatures hovering around the freezing point, linemen and serviceman in the Drumheller District were all set to enjoy the long weekend. The lines had been collecting some frost, but nothing to worry about. Then on Friday night ice and frost began to gather at an amazing rate. "For the next four days and nights wires fell, poles broke and utter chaos befell large sections of our lines," said Drumheller's Bill Lennon. "It soon became apparent we were facing a major catastrophe, and the machinery was set in motion. Servicemen and linemen were quickly summoned from homes, meetings, movie houses, or wherever they had planned to spend a pleasant evening. They hurriedly changed clothes and reported for duty."

Phones rang frantically as men and trucks were dispatched to trouble areas. Then as the night wore on the phones were silenced as telephone lines were brought down by the hoarfrost. There was still the radio system, but the airwaves were so jammed that it became hopeless to try to communicate. Each crew realized it was on its own.

For seventy-two hours the ice build-up continued. It was three to four inches thick on the lines. Repair crews were at the point of exhaustion when finally the hoarfrost stopped accumulating. Slowly but surely things got back to normal, but it took about a month to restore the lines to their former condition.

Machines go Berserk — 1971-1972

Bad weather was not the only problem in the early seventies. There was an explosion at the Battle River station in the fall of 1971, which caused nearly a million dollars in damage.

The explosion occurred in the deaerator surge feedwater tank. The thirty-foot-long steel plate tank was crumpled like a popcorn bag as it was torn from its mounting, ripped a hole through the wall and landed about forty feet north of the plant.

The deaerator tank is used to remove oxygen from condensed steam to prevent corrosion of the boiler. It was believed to have been carrying too much pressure as a result of an oversupply of condensate when it exploded. Fortunately most of the repair work was covered by insurance, but it was not until the following April that Unit No. 1 at the plant was put back into service.

At Grande Cache the new power plant, costing nearly thirty-five million dollars, went into production in the fall of 1972. It was luckier than Battle River, but not entirely without complications. The worst of these occurred when one of the four large fans at the top of the water cooling tower broke away from its moorings and tore out a number of supporting wooden beams. The damage was quickly repaired and the plant was back in service.

All in all, despite nature's rampages and the need to repair some large and very expensive machinery, Alberta Power survived the early seventies well. As 1972 went out and 1973 came in the generators and the high voltage transmission lines were humming peacefully.

CU Engineering Limited — 1973

A new non-utility subsidiary of the parent company, CU Engineering Limited, was formed in 1973. It was organized to provide consulting services to both electrical and natural gas clients outside Canadian Utilities and was originally a wing of Northwestern's marketing department.

CU Engineering took its first step by making available the expertise of Northwestern and Canadian Western to rural communties outside the service areas of the companies. The Alberta government had a new policy aimed at bringing gas service to as many people as possible, on a co-op basis similar in some respects to rural electrification associations. Many rural areas were now in the market for specialized utility engineering services.

CU Engineering's first manager was J.R. (Jerry) van der Linden. His staff included Phil Murray, Don Ible and Dennis Havrelock in Edmonton and Gerry Welsh and Don Fawcett in Calgary. They offered rural co-operatives a total package of services ranging from cost estimates to construction supervision, operation and maintenance. The first co-operative to contract these services was the Gull Lake natural gas co-op, west of Lacombe. CU Engineering began operating their system September 1, 1973. Actually, CU Engineering did not have the personnel to operate systems but made the necessary arrangements with Northwestern and Canadian Western, acting as agent for the co-ops.

In 1976 Don Murray left his position as manager of Northwestern's marketing department to become general manager of CU Engineering. The company ceased operation in 1982 when it was amalgamated into new intercompany enterprises.

Arctic Gas Study — 1973

The northward reach of the gas companies went even farther than that of Alberta Power in the early seventies. In 1973 Canadian Western and Northwestern participated in a twenty-seven-company consortium that was working out ways and means of building a twenty-six hundred-mile pipeline along the Mackenzie River Valley to bring gas from Alaska and the Canadian Arctic to Canadian and American markets. It would be the largest pipeline system in the world, costing five billion dollars.

Closer to home, about seventy-five percent of Alberta's population was now being served by Canadian Western and Northwestern, with Edmonton and Calgary as the major growth centres.

Northwestern announced plans for a three million dollar, twenty-four-inch line, twenty-five miles long, with the capacity eventually to deliver 600 million cubic feet of natural gas per day into Edmonton from the Homeglen-Rimbey field.

Northwestern built a new heavy equipment repair centre in 1973, as part of the development on a fifteen-acre site in southeast Edmonton selected for future expansion of the company's operations. The repair centre provided twelve twenty-by-forty-foot repair bays and an equipment cleaning room, vehicle hoist, machine, tool, stockroom and welding areas associated with the repair and servicing of the company's heavy equipment.

A ten-ton travelling crane was installed to aid in the operation. Staff facilities were provided on the mezzanine of the building. Several customer service and distribution crews also operated from depots within the building.

More Floods and Fires — 1973

W eather caused more excitement and some round-the-clock service emergencies at Swan Hills and in the Peace River country. In mid-July 1973, thunderstorms and winds wreaked havoc at Swan Hills with lightning strikes blowing eleven power line fuses and fallen trees knocking out twenty-six lines.

Then in mid-August, a three-day freak snowstorm in the Peace River country flattened crops and knocked down trees and power lines. Farmers in the Hythe, Beaverlodge and Spirit River areas were without power for up to thirty-six hours as the heavy snow knocked trees over power lines.

Northwestern crews were kept busy answering no-heat calls and repairing a gas main which broke when the snow melted and the earth around it settled.

A flood at Old Crow, eighty miles north of the Arctic Circle in the Yukon, occurred in mid-May when a serious ice jam developed on the Porcupine River. Flood waters ran into the village, threatening the airstrip and putting telephones out of service.

At the power plant Donald Frost and his brother Stephan were Yukon Electrical's heroes during the emergency. At the height of the flood there was four feet eight inches of water in the plant buildings. When the water began to recede the two brothers worked feverishly to drain the oil out of the diesels and replace the filters. They did this while there was two feet of water in their own homes, working until they had restored electrical service to the community.

Finally, in the Lesser Slave Lake area of Alberta, there was another story in 1973 — a typical story which is repeated every once in a while in rural areas. A cat, which presumably had already lived most of its nine lives, gambled with fate and lost. This handsome-looking lynx climbed a power pole and tangled with a 25-kilovolt line. The lights in Kinuso and Lakeshore went out momentarily, and the cat was later found dead at the foot of the last pole it ever climbed.

Fire, Line Breaks at Jasper — 1974

A lberta Power suffered a setback at Jasper in 1974 when a fire destroyed five generators and almost the entire power plant, causing more than a million dollars' damage.

The fire started at 2 a.m. on February 20, as diesel fuel was being unloaded from a tank truck into a ten thousand-gallon storage tank. The fire was started by fuel escaping from a broken hose. It was 6:30 a.m. before the fire was brought under control and thirty-five hundred residents woke to find their homes cooling off as forced-air furnaces stopped working.

Fortunately a 600-kilowatt mobile generator at the plant was blackened but unharmed by the fire. It was quickly pressed into operation, restoring minimal power to the hospital, a block of the downtown section, and a few homes. Employees worked non-stop through the night, helped by volunteers. Less than twenty-four hours after the fire, nearly all residents had power again. In thirty-six hours full power was back — even to the ski areas.

The day after the fire two mobile generators left Hay River for Jasper by truck, with part of the route being led by a snowplow. Another two mobile units left Edmonton. B.C. Hydro promised a mobile trailer unit and a 1,000-kilowatt unit on rails later in the day. The RCAF responded to Alberta Power's call and by late afternoon one of two skid mounted diesel generators was aboard a Hercules transport and on its way to Jasper via Namao air base. With all this help the Jasper area soon was back on full power.

In late summer work was started on a new natural-gas-fired power plant, using gas supplied by Northwestern Utilities. The plant, along with installation of twenty-eight miles of transmission lines, cost almost three million dollars.

Alberta Power gave careful consideration to the alternative of supplying Jasper with power from a connection to the provincial grid at Hinton. However, an overhead line would run some twenty-seven miles along a well travelled valley within the national park. The gas line was underground and inconspicuous and was felt to be a more desirable alternative. The decision was made with the understanding that should the price of gas escalate to a point where an electric transmission line to the grid was considered necessary, a power line might still be built in future.

There were more problems at Jasper that summer. On July 24 there was a break in the gas transmission line under the Athabasca River about five miles inside the park gate at a location appropriately called Disaster Point. The changing course of the river at this location had caused problems on several occasions over the years.

Northwestern quickly put a propane-air mix unit into service. Crews from Edmonton and Edson laid nine thousand feet of three-inch line to bypass the break. Normal gas service was restored to the community within three days.

On October 28 there was more trouble at Disaster Point when the river current bared a section of the line. Emergency measures were again instituted, including using gas from storage tanks and rushing the propane air-mix unit into service. The town of Jasper certainly had more than its share of gas and electric service disruptions in 1974.

North Division Leads in Growth

A lberta Power's North Division, with the fastest growth rate of the company's three major divisions, by the mid-seventies accounted for nearly two-thirds of the sales of the total interconnected system. The company did lose one northern community in 1974, the plant and distribution system at Uranium City, in northern Saskatchewan. It was sold to Saskatchewan Power Corporation and more than five hundred customers were given up in that transaction.

Industrial accounts were more than half of the company's total load, and the petroleum industries accounted for about three-quarters of the industrial load. One of the newest industries was the seven hundred and fifty tons per day pulp mill built by Procter & Gamble Cellulose at Grande Prairie. And Fort McMurray, of course, was booming with multi-billion-dollar oil sands activity. It was the strongest growth centre in Alberta Power's service areas. The town's building permits in 1974 multiplied almost seven-fold over the previous year, to forty-one million dollars. By 1976 the total more than doubled again, to nearly ninety million dollars.

Until 1976 Fort McMurray was the largest community in Alberta to be served entirely by a local power plant. Now, with the completion of Alberta Power's new transmission line, it was on the Alberta grid. The line was energized at 144 kilovolts and increased to 240 kilovolts.

Largest Gas Line — 1974

N orthwestern's major construction undertaking in 1974 was the completion of the first section of the twenty-four-inch line from the Alberta Gas Trunk Line's export facilities at Homeglen-Rimbey. The largest diameter transmission line in Northwestern's system, it would carry new volumes of natural gas to Edmonton.

The extent of the growing market for natural gas in the service area of the two gas companies was indicated by the continued growth of Alberta's two largest cities in 1974. Edmonton's building permit total of three hundred and sixty million dollars was almost double the total issued the previous year. Calgary's building permits increased to two hundred and seventy-three million dollars.

Construction began on Edmonton's fifty million dollar rapid transit system and the first stage of the one hundred million dollar Edmonton Centre project. In Calgary, construction began on a one hundred million dollar commercial complex. Calgary's thirty-two million dollar downtown convention centre opened during the year.

The year 1974 brought special honors to Molly Reilly and Dennis Yorath who were both inducted into Canada's Aviation Hall of Fame at Edmonton. Mrs. Reilly, Canadian Utilities' company pilot, and her husband Jack were the only husband-and-wife team named to the Hall of Fame. Dennis Yorath had been associated with aviation for many years. He was president of the Calgary Flying Club 1942-1948 and president of the Royal Canadian Flying Clubs Association 1947-1949. In 1949 he was awarded the McKee Trans-Canada trophy in recognition of his service in the advancement of Canadian aviation.

OPEC and World Prices

T he early and mid-seventies brought significant changes in the international energy picture. The greatest single factor was the emergence of the Organization of Petroleum Exporting Countries (OPEC), drawing largely from Arab countries in the Middle East, but including Venezuela in the western hemisphere.

In 1973, there was a great deal of unrest in the Middle East, particularly hostilities between Arab countries and Israel. This led to a hold-back of oil production and sales on the part of Arab countries — a move often referred to as the Arab oil embargo. The friction continued in 1974 as the OPEC countries demanded increasingly higher prices for their oil. In the west, the United States was seriously affected as it had relied quite heavily on the Middle East for petroleum supplies.

In a short time world oil prices had doubled. Many critics called OPEC an international cartel that was holding the world at ransom by forcing up prices.

As the world prices for oil and gas rose dramatically, the petroleum industry in Alberta sought to bring its prices in line with world levels. At the same time the government of Alberta tried to shield people in this province from being forced to pay unnecessarily high prices. A boon to the gas customers of Northwestern and Canadian Western in 1974 was the government's Natural Gas Rebates Act, which sheltered Alberta consumers from the full impact of international gas price increases.

Small residential and commercial customers particularly were shielded, through the rebates plan, from the impact of gas field prices in excess of a provincial support price of 16.7 cents per thousand cubic feet. Large industrial users, however, were only partially shielded.

Natural Gas Rate Hearings — 1974-1975

I nflation hit everybody during the seventies. If it was hurting the ordinary homeowner, it was hurting the energy group just as much. Increasing energy costs, together with the rising costs of labor, materials and capital, were paramount concerns of the companies. They had no alternative but to go to the Public Utilities Board to ask for higher rates. "To support the necessary new financings in the months and years ahead will require a continuing demonstration of financial integrity on the part of the company," said President Edge King. "At the same time, the inflation which is occurring in every element of operating

239

expense, which shows no sign of abatement, is eroding the earnings essential to this demonstration."

The gas companies were granted upward adjustments in 1974. Northwestern had not had a rate increase in fifteen years.

Submissions to the Public Utilities Board by the gas companies continued in 1975. The board disallowed what it was costing the companies to take part in Gas Arctic studies stating it was not a legitimate expense for rate base calculations. This forced the companies to withdraw from the Northwest Project Study Group, which was working towards building a gas pipeline from the Arctic.

Despite the fact that the gas companies connected nearly twenty thousand new customers in 1975, it was tough sledding. Inflation, and worst of all, the field price of gas as determined by world markets, was going up too steeply. All this had the effect of doubling gas rates for customers in the short space of one year from 1974 to 1975.

The Alberta government's support price shielded domestic and commercial customers to some extent. In 1973 the government raised the support price to 28 cents per thousand cubic feet. The next support price jump the following year, when the field price was up to 73 cents per thousand cubic feet, was to 56 cents.

In 1975 the rebate program protected the gas companies' customers from a total of more than sixty million dollars in gas supply costs, but that was only a partial solution to a much bigger problem — inflation. As an example, a residential gas regulator in 1971 cost $8.39. By 1973 the cost had gone up eighty-nine cents. By 1975 it was $13.30. Steel pipe was another example. From 1971 to 1973 it went up more than fifteen percent, but by 1975 it had risen by an additional forty-four percent.

There was widespread public discontent, but in the final analysis most gas customers believed their utility was trying its best to provide the best possible service at the lowest possible cost. That is why communities kept renewing the franchises of both gas companies. The City of Edmonton, the largest of all the companies' communities, renewed Northwestern's franchise for another ten years in 1975.

The companies continued to urge on various government agencies the importance of ensuring that an ample supply of natural gas be guaranteed for home use and that exports of this non-renewable resource be limited accordingly.

With this basic concern in mind, the companies continued to enter into contracts for many billions of cubic feet of additional supplies. In 1975, for example, they contracted for an additional 330 billion cubic feet of reserves in the Arrowwood and Dixonville areas, in addition to having the previous year contracted for almost 400 billion cubic feet of new supplies in the Sedalia, Paddle River, Opal-Redwater and the Hairy Hills areas.

240

Generating Capital

F inancing the activities of the energy group is a gigantic task which, like many other functions of the companies, was becoming more centralized and more sophisticated. Generating power was one thing. Generating capital was another. It was a job all of its own, and it required the best efforts of some key people.

Once the re-organization of Canadian Utilities as a holding company had taken place, it didn't take long for the company to swing into action performing its major role of raising money. On the morning of March 1, 1972, a phone call to the office of President Edge King confirmed the transfer of thirty million dollars to the company by the Royal Bank of Canada in Edmonton. The money represented proceeds from a debenture issue to provide funds for capital expenditures for the associated companies.

A portion of the money was applied immediately to retire outstanding bank loans incurred by the companies to cover, in part, costs of expansion during the previous year. The balance was immediately invested in a series of short-term securities with varying due dates related to the periods during the year when the money would be required to meet major capital expenses.

The transaction was typical of the function intended for Canadian Utilities. Under the previous organization structure it would have been necessary for each of the companies to raise money on their own which would likely have meant higher interest rates and a more complex procedure all around.

Maybin Becomes CU's New CEO — 1974

T wo years later Canadian Utilities' board chairman John Maybin established an office in Toronto. He returned from Philadelphia, relinquishing the title of vice-president — gas, electric and water services for IU International to become chief executive officer of Canadian Utilities.

In Toronto, Maybin planned to concentrate his activities in the fields of corporate development, long-range planning and relations with the financial community. He was also appointed to the ten-man board of directors of the Alberta Energy Company, established by the Alberta government to give the public the opportunity to invest directly in oil sands, petrochemical and other industrial developments in the province.

CU Ethane Limited Formed — 1975

P etrochemicals created major news headlines in 1975. Using natural gas as the basic building block, the petrochemical industry was a natural for the energy group. The gas companies particularly saw it as an important new dimension through which they could participate in Alberta's development.

The groundwork was laid for the formation of CU Ethane Limited. Canadian Utilities and Dome Petroleum announced a joint venture to build and operate a twenty thousand-barrel-a-day ethane extraction plant located at Edmonton. This forty million dollar project would be an integral part of the ethane-ethylene-based chemical complex visualized for the province. The CU-Dome agreement followed government approval of plans by Alberta Gas Ethylene Company Limited, Dow Chemical of Canada Limited and Dome to establish a one and a half billion dollar world-scale petrochemical manufacturing complex in Alberta.

The joint venture with Dome called for expansion of Dome's existing Edmonton gas plant on the Calgary Trail on the southern outskirts of Edmonton. Gas to be processed at the plant would be supplied by Northwestern Utilities.

Public Utilities Board approval was sought for a plant designed to process 315 million cubic feet of natural gas per day yielding 20,600 barrels per day of ethane and 4,600 barrels per day of propane. Ethane is used to produce ethylene, an intermediate petrochemical building block which, in turn, is used in the manufacture of a host of products including synthetic rubber, plastics, solvents and fertilizer.

The plant went into operation in the summer of 1978, with a staff of about thirty people. Agreement was reached with Imperial Oil Limited to process natural gas from the Golden Spike oilfield, with CU Ethane and Dome sharing the construction costs of a five-kilometre pipeline from the field to the plant site. The companies also installed special facilities to extract natural gas liquids (propane pluses) from the liquid-rich Golden Spike gas before it entered the main processing stream.

About half the ethane produced at the plant is used as feedstock for the manufacture of ethylene in Alberta and the other half exported via the Cochin pipeline for sale in eastern Canada and the United States.

H.R. Milner Dies — 1975

Times were changing. Old-timers were passing on. H.R. Milner died at his B.C. summer home on May 24, 1975, at the age of eighty-six. Dennis Yorath said:

> *Horatio Ray Milner was a man possessed of all the ability, brilliance and understanding that a really great man should possess.*
>
> *His business acumen was often uncanny, few if any problems were unsolvable in his hands. His contributions to the development of Alberta and Canada have been many and have even overflowed into international areas.*

Milner was a company pioneer in the truest sense. His passing brought back many memories. In the early depression and war year crises, when the companies were sometimes on the verge of bankruptcy, his bulldog determination, financial acumen and legal brilliance provided inspiration to everyone with whom he was associated. Then in later years, as the companies became more financially secure, Milner continued to improve corporate measures and programs which made every staff member proud to be part of the team.

Not the least of these programs was the Group Sickness and Accident Fund, which he was instrumental in establishing. Thanks to Milner, the Canadian Utilities group is today acknowledged as one of the pioneers in North America for the way it has provided its own internal employee health and medical coverage — a system which was working long before the government instituted medicare. What is unique about the company system is that it was internally financed from the start, and provided staff members with a sense of security which is no doubt one of the reasons for the company's outstanding number of long service employees.

Capital Projects Abound

H aving connections in central Canada was important for Canadian Utilities, but the economic picture was changing. Alberta's performance compared to Canada as a whole was outstanding. By the mid-seventies capital investment in the province was advancing at an annual compound rate of sixteen percent. A particularly significant gain — thirty-three percent — was made in 1975 in the utilities sector.

As a result, Canadian Utilities' offices in Edmonton, under the direction of President Edge King, continued to expand. More space became necessary than was available in the Milner Building, so the companies rented the third and fourth floors of the nearby Manulife Building.

Much of the impetus for capital spending came from natural resource extraction and upgrading projects such as the Syncrude and Great Canadian Oil Sands developments, along with the even more recent petrochemical complexes.

During the year the governments of Canada, Alberta and Ontario became partners in the two billion dollar Syncrude oil sands project, assuring its continuance following the withdrawal of one of the original partners. The construction work force on the Syncrude site near Fort McMurray had been growing steadily and was expected to peak at about sixty-six hundred employees in mid-1976.

Also, Imperial Oil Limited continued to expand its pilot project to test in situ recovery methods for heavy oil deposits in the Cold Lake area. Other smaller pilot projects in this part of the province were initiated or announced.

The company's capital requirements were met in part during the year by the issue of more than a million new common shares, which went on the market at $9.25 per share to raise a total of ten million dollars in new capital. Earlier in the year there had been a thirty million dollar issue of 10.25 percent preferred shares.

More Money Raised — 1976

T he next year, 1976, brought the largest debenture issue in the company's history, raising fifty million dollars in new capital. "With capital expenditures exceeding seventy million dollars a year, the raising of money has become a major task," commented Ken Biggs, Canadian Utilities' senior vice-president — finance, who took a leading part in the financing program.

That fall Canadian Utilities made another major issue of common shares available to the Canadian public. In November the sale of two million shares at $12.25 provided net proceeds of twenty-three million dollars and added more than two thousand new shareholders, many of whom resided in Alberta and were customers of one or more of the energy companies. About a third of the shares purchased by individuals were sold in Alberta.

At the end of 1976 the company had 5,867 common shareholders, of whom 2,275 were Alberta residents and more than three thousand were other Canadian residents. Shareholders outside Canada numbered only fifty-three, but it must be borne in mind that one of those shareholders was IU International, with a huge block of shares that still gave it the controlling interest in Canadian Utilities.

The shareholder base, however, was expanding, and the increased number of common shares available ensured a ready market at values which were now less inhibited by limited trading volumes. Altogether, three external financings totalling more than one hundred and fourteen million dollars were made to the Canadian public during the year.

During the five years since Canadian Utilities had been re-organized as the parent company of the energy group, net assets (all assets less current liabilities) doubled to five hundred and sixty-nine million dollars, and earnings from operations available to common and convertible preferred shareholders increased sixty-five percent from almost fifteen million dollars in 1972 to more than twenty-four million dollars. However, in terms of dollars invested in the company by the common and convertible preferred shareholder, earnings per dollar involved were about the same in 1976 as they were in 1972 — fourteen cents per dollar invested.

In 1976, for every dollar of revenue the company received, about forty-seven cents was used to purchase natural gas and coal; eleven cents was paid directly to various levels of government as taxes and royalties; twenty-six cents to cover labor and other costs of operation; and eight cents to pay interest and dividends to those who supplied the company with debt and preferred equity capital. Of the remaining eight cents about half was paid to the common shareholders as dividends and the balance re-invested in the business.

The late seventies brought some pressures from the federal government with respect to earnings and taxation, which again discriminated against investor-owned utilities. The major one was an attempt by then federal finance minister Jean Chretien to put an end to the income tax refunds that the energy group had been receiving and passing on to its customers. This would have saved the government about fifty million dollars a year.

Following vigorous protests by the industry and others concerned, the federal government agreed to continue refunds but at the reduced rate of fifty percent rather than the previous ninety-five percent. "The logic of penalizing consumers served by investor-owned utilities is unclear and, in the company's view, requires further re-examination by Ottawa," Canadian Utilities officials stated in the company's annual report to shareholders.

Ferguson Honored for Bravery — 1976

The President's Award was introduced in the two gas companies in 1967-1968 by Murray Stewart. Also known as the president's medal, in the years that followed it became the company's most prestigious award. It was designed to recognize employees who perform unusual acts of bravery, show special initiative or provide outstanding service not only within the company but within the community in which they live.

A recipient of this award in the spring of 1976 was Palmer Ferguson, natural gas district agent in Jasper. On December 15, 1975, Ferguson heroically saved the lives of two Jasper residents when an explosion demolished a building next to where he was repairing a broken service line in the downtown area.

The explosion rocked the building and blew heavy glass blocks out of the windows. Ferguson immediately jumped from the open ditch in which he was working, and seeing a senior resident — Allan McDonald — in the basement of the building, rushed to his aid. He pulled McDonald out through a window, and then risked his life by climbing back down and making his way some distance into the apartment to help Mrs. McDonald to the window, where he lifted her into the waiting arms of A.K. McIntosh, manager of the Scotia Bank in Jasper. The explosion had emptied the building of oxygen, but while Ferguson was rescuing the elderly couple, gas and oxygen were pouring in for another explosion which minutes later virtually levelled the building.

Ferguson could easily have been killed. Recognition from fellow employees came almost immediately, followed by the President's Award in March. But public recognition was slow in coming. Certain segments of the mountain community tried to blame the company for the explosion, and specifically Ferguson as agent. If Ferguson was heroic for going beyond the call of duty to provide help in need, he was even more heroic for the way he stood up to interrogation during the lengthy court hearings which eventually absolved him and the company of any blame for the accident. The Life Insurance Company of Alberta, more than a year after the accident, decorated Ferguson with its silver medal, presented by Lieutenant-Governor Ralph Steinhauer, and later that year Governor-General Jules Leger pinned one of Canada's highest awards for bravery, the Star of Courage, on his lapel.

Similar records of achievement or valor could be told of the other recipients of the President's Award whose names are listed in the appendix of this volume.

Fifty Years of Electric Service —1977

T he electrical operations celebrated a fiftieth anniversary in 1977. It was half a century since Canadian Utilities was founded and began buying up a few isolated generating stations, the first of which was at Vegreville. As the company celebrated its fiftieth anniversary it was particularly significant that it passed the one hundred thousand-customer mark. More than seven thousand new customers were added in 1977, bringing the total to almost one hundred and seven thousand at year-end. Included in the total were nearly twenty-two thousand farm customers, most of whom were members of rural electrification associations.

Energy sales were well past the two billion kilowatt hours per year, and revenues from electric operations were getting close to one hundred million dollars a year. The aggregate population of Alberta Power's service areas was about three hundred thousand, including Fort McMurray, which now surpassed twenty thousand to become the largest community in the electrical service territory.

Courier Fifty Years Old

T he Courier was fifty years old in 1977, and the anniversary was highlighted in the May issue that year. The staff magazine was founded by Dennis Yorath and his father C.J. Yorath in 1927.

An interesting sidelight to its publication was the long association it established with a printing family in Calgary. It was printed continuously from the beginning by a group known as Commonwealth Press in Calgary, with Claude Mitchell in charge of the typesetting and print department. There was a hiatus from 1940 to 1945, while Mitchell, along with many gas company personnel, served in the military. When he returned from overseas in 1945, he started a company called Kellaway Printing, in partnership with Bob Kellaway, and together they looked after The Courier until the early sixties, when it was taken over by the companies to be done partially in-house and then printed in Edmonton.

The printing group in Calgary, however, continued to work for the energy group, and to this day still prints the annual reports of the gas companies as well as Canadian Utilities, the parent company. The printing group today is known as Ronalds Western Limited and is part of a Canada-wide group owned by Bell Canada.

Tobe Mitchell, director of operations for Ronalds Western Limited, Calgary Division, joined his father in the firm in 1950, and recalls the many changes in technology which have occurred in the ensuing years, from the old Linotype machines and hot lead processes to today's highly sophisticated computerized typesetting and automated lithographic printing process.

"In the early days *The Courier* used to arrive from the gas company in a shoe box, with a bunch of pictures and a bunch of copy," Mitchell recalls. "It was quite different from today's carefully pre-formatted magazine which is all put together by modern methods."

Growth of Company Art Collection

A lberta Power's anniversary celebrations, like the gas companies' a few years earlier, also featured works by artist Meredith Evans, commemorating historic sites in the six original communities served by the company.

In recent times Evans' works for the company have been displayed in many places. These works included the famous energy mural which graced the lobby of the Milner Building for years, depicting the evolution of man's use of energy to mechanize his world, and a popular pen-and-ink color wash drawing of Edmonton's historic post office, produced as a commemorative project for Northwestern's 50th Anniversary celebrations in 1973.

The Canadian Utilities art collection has grown considerably over the years. Art inventory and acquisitions today list more than two hundred pieces in the company's art catalogue. These works range from limited edition prints of modest value to prized originals in oil and watercolors. Most Alberta artists of note are represented in the collection.

In the early years, the twenties and thirties, Ray Milner began acquiring art work for company office buildings. One of his favorite themes was paintings of Indian chiefs by Nicholas de Grandmaison, which gave rise to a special preference for Canadian art by the Canadian Utilities group. Works by other Canadian artists followed. A large oil painting by Roland Gissing, for example, hung for many years in Northwestern's Viking field staff house, and an early watercolor by W.J. Phillips is one of the valued pieces in the collection.

Another artist of note who received encouragement from the company in more recent years was Len Gibbs. He was a commercial artist with James Lovick & Company, an advertising agency. When Gibbs left the agency and began making his living as a fine artist, things were not lucrative for him to say the least. To help him get established, the companies gave him some historical photographs from their archives, which he used as the subject matter for four acrylic paintings which are now in the executive offices on the twentieth floor of the CU Centre. Those early paintings brought Gibbs about two hundred dollars apiece. His paintings today are in the five to six-thousand-dollar range.

Each item in the company art collection has its own story to tell. Two-dimensional art, in acrylic, oils, watercolors, fabrics, pastels, pencil, serigraph, zinc, etching, pen-and-ink, silk screen, drybrush, plexiglass, graphite, stain on cotton, aquatint etching, and tapestry are all part of the collection.

In addition to these, there is three-dimensional art in the form of sculptures, including outstanding Stampede trophies by Charles Beil sponsored by Canadian Western. Sculptures commissioned by Canadian Utilities range from commemorative bronze castings by Canadian artist John Weaver to works by Roy Leadbeater and Garry Jones of Edmonton.

$100 Million in Capital Works — 1977

C anadian Utilities spent nearly one hundred million dollars on capital works in 1977. The upsurge in growth was phenomenal. In a three-year period, from the end of 1974 to the end of 1977, total plant and equipment in the energy group increased from five hundred and thirty-nine million dollars to seven hundred and eighty million dollars.

The ability to attract new shareholders was particularly gratifying. As a result of the broader distribution and greater interest by investors, 1977 brought more trading activity in common shares than the total trading of the previous two years combined.

The board of directors of Canadian Utilities was strengthened with the addition of three new members — Ronald D. Southern, president and chief executive officer of ATCO Ltd., Charles N.W. Woodward, chairman of the board and chief executive officer of Woodward Stores Limited, and Kenneth A. Biggs, senior vice-president, finance, of Canadian Utilities. Ron Southern, particularly, was destined to bring about far-reaching changes in the company over the next few years.

Canadian Utilities' capital expenditures totalled one hundred and eight million dollars in 1978 with predictions that over the next five years they would exceed two hundred million dollars a year, particularly with massive new generating units in the offing.

More Exploration — 1977

E xploratory drilling for oil and gas experienced an upsurge in 1977, and there were encouraging discoveries of new reserves.

With more than half the total energy supply in Alberta coming from natural gas, Canadian Western and Northwestern stepped up their own exploration programs. One of the incentives that made this possible was a government-assisted border-flow-back fund. All Alberta gas producers received a pro rata share of extra revenues generated by the differential in price between gas exported to the U.S. and that marketed in Canada. The Public Utilities Board agreed in principle with the companies that these funds could be used to cover the costs of unsuccessful exploration for natural gas.

Success rates were encouraging. Canadian Western took part in the drilling of thirteen wells in 1977, all of them successful. Northwestern was involved in the drilling of forty wells of which twenty-eight were successful. The following year Canadian Western participated in the drilling of twenty-one wells of which twenty were successful. Northwestern participated in thirty-nine wells of which twenty-five were successful.

CU Resources Limited Formed — 1976-1977

A new subsidiary for the energy group was created in 1976-1977. CU Resources Limited was formed to hold and develop certain non-utility resource properties owned by Northwestern and Canadian Western. During 1977 the new company completed an eighteen-well drilling program on properties located near Viking, Alberta. All but one of the wells proved successful with total production of about four hundred barrels a day.

Meanwhile, the other two recently-formed subsidiaries, CU Engineering and CU Ethane, continued to move ahead. CU Engineering completed one of its first large contracts — construction management of a hundred and seventy-mile gas pipeline from gas fields in the Lac La Biche area to the Syncrude site near Fort McMurray. The sixteen-inch line had to be constructed while the ground was frozen since half of it was built in muskeg. It was built to carry some 65 million cubic feet per day to service Syncrude's power plant and oil recovery facility. Tie-ins to the Alberta Gas Trunkline sources serve as a backup supply.

Conforming to the "corridor concept," the pipeline was built close to other gas and oil lines serving the area so that nearby farms experienced a minimum of disturbance.

In addition to work performed for a number of municipalities and rural gas co-ops, CU Engineering undertook to convert existing utility plans to the metric system and carry out some power studies for the federal and provincial governments. Its range of activities broadened to include water system and sewer design and construction management, and assisting clients in the preparation of submissions to regulatory bodies.

Gigajoules and Kilopascals

When Albertans had to start thinking in terms of kilometres per hour in order to avoid speeding tickets, and when even the horses at the racetracks were clocked in metres rather than miles, some people thought this was carrying things too far. But when the gas company began talking about gigajoules instead of thousands of cubic feet of gas and measuring the pressures in the pipelines in terms of kilopascals, some Albertans were convinced the whole world had gone crazy.

The companies' metric conversion committee was headed by Ted Neumann and Rob Churchill who conducted day-long training sessions. "We have to cover most company staff to make it completely effective," Neumann said, while Churchill insisted that practical exercises make the SI units — a name derived from a French term for an international system — easier to grasp.

For the gas companies, conversion meant changing from cubic feet to joules to measure volumes. The metric system's basic measurement of energy is the joule, abbreviated J. Large amounts of energy are now recorded in the company's annual reports in gigajoules, abbreviated GJ and meaning billions of joules; tera-joules, TJ, trillions of joules; and petajoules, PJ, quadrillions of joules. A peta-joule is approximately a billion cubic feet.

There was less resistance in the electric operations of Canadian Utilities. By now everyone knew that a kilovolt was a thousand volts and a megawatt was a million watts, but people were confused by the thought of buying gasoline for cents per litre.

Three Million Dollar Computer — 1979

Times were really changing. Not only were the seventies coming to an end as they succumbed to the metric system, computers continued to take over as well. The three million dollar IBM 3032 arrived at the Milner Building during 1979 and five days after it arrived it was in operation.

The computer room had to be enlarged to accommodate the machine with its auxiliary equipment — two motor generators, three air conditioning units and a water chiller. Some of the equipment, which took hours to lift by crane through a computer room window, weighed more than three thousand pounds per unit.

The new computer had five times the processing speed of its predecessor. In an earlier demonstration, a Northwestern billing run that previously took more than five hours to process was completed in forty-five minutes. Engineering jobs that ordinarily would have been sent to a computer service bureau could now be processed in the company data centre. Such projects include planning of gas supply, sales and revenue forecasting, load estimation and pressure flow analysis.

In the fall, computer terminals were placed in key company locations, providing an immediate link to current customer file information. Terminals were initially planned for installation at Lethbridge, Red Deer, Fort McMurray, Grande Prairie, Peace River, Vegreville, Calgary and Edmonton.

Two printers in the computer centre each had a capacity of two thousand lines per minute. Disks and tapes each could store billions of characters of information to which the computer had direct access. Tapes, if laid end-to-end, would have stretched between Edmonton and Vancouver with each foot of the tape containing up to seven thousand characters of information.

The computer centre went into service around the clock, five days a week. The system was maintained by a staff of forty, under the direction of data centre manager Gordon Anderson.

A Blue Chip Investment — 1979

A s the seventies drew to a close Canadian Utilities was a blue chip investment. It was no longer a struggling little company that had difficulty raising capital. It was a long-established utility providing essential services in a
market that was growing by leaps and bounds.

With ATCO president Ron Southern now on the board of Canadian Utilities,
new horizons were about to open for the company.

Southern's ATCO Ltd. had been in business for thirty-three years, having been
founded in Calgary in 1946 with a four thousand dollar investment. It had
become a giant, having expanded from the original trailer business into large
construction and land development enterprises and then on into petroleum
resource development. It now appeared to be ready for a major acquisition and
more diversification.

Meanwhile, IU International bought another block of Canadian Utilities common shares — almost a million of them.

From the time that Canadian Utilities was re-organized in 1972 it had issued
a total of nearly eleven million new common shares and more than seven million
of these shares were purchased by Canadian investors. All of Canadian Utilities'
borrowing and share financings were now being accomplished through issues
offered in Canada.

Canadian Utilities now had more than four thousand employees and nearly
eight hundred of them applied their savings to acquire ninety-one thousand of
the company's shares in 1979. Through introduction of a savings and stock purchase plan the company was encouraging employees to participate as shareholders. At the end of the year no fewer than fifteen hundred employees were
enrolled in a savings plan which would provide the opportunity to acquire over
two hundred thousand shares in 1981.

Total assets passed the billion-dollar mark in 1979, which was more than double what they had been five years previously. Net earnings per common share
were now well over two dollars.

Board chairman John Maybin said:

> . . . With a number of multi-billion dollar resource projects on the horizon,
> and assuming sufficient political stability in Canada to achieve orderly
> resolution of oil pricing and taxation agreements between governments, the
> prospects for continued growth in Alberta should be the brightest of any
> region in North America. That outlook would seem to ensure another dou-
> bling of the company's asset base within the next five years.

Syncrude was now well established and the next project of this kind was on
the drawing boards, with Alberta Power slated to serve it as well as the town
that would be associated with the development.

251

Capital Investment Risk — 1979

A lberta Power's expenditures for additions to property, plant and equipment during 1979 were a hundred and eleven million dollars — more than double the 1978 level. The new generator at the Battle River station took up much of this. Alberta Power signed an agreement with the City of Edmonton to sell, on a five to seven-year basis, one-half the output of the new unit when it would go into operation in 1981.

Preliminary work moved forward, too, on the Sheerness development near Hanna. The target dates at that time were to commission two 375-megawatt units in 1985 and 1986.

The gas companies added a record thirty-two thousand customers to their systems in 1979 as Northwestern Utilities passed the quarter-million mark in total numbers of customers served.

Capital expenditures in natural gas developments rose thirty-four percent over the previous year to nearly sixty-five million dollars. Outlays were mainly for expansion of transmission and distribution facilities. The largest single project was a twelve million dollar, sixty-four-mile pipeline capable of bringing 300 million cubic feet of gas per day from the Viking area to industries in and near Fort Saskatchewan and to meet increasing peak demand in the Edmonton area.

The Mill Woods Emergency — 1979

T he Mill Woods crisis on the weekend of March 2-3, 1979, brought out the best in Northwestern. When a propane pipeline ruptured and fire forced the evacuation of twenty thousand residents from this south Edmonton subdivision, Northwestern employees helped control the emergency. Shifts stretched as long as thirty-six hours straight as the Northwestern people manned telephones, shut off and restored natural gas service, tested gas samples and patrolled the evacuated area. "I'm very impressed with how quickly and smoothly our staff organized to meet the emergency," said general manager Bruce Dafoe, who himself worked overnight in the customer information centre and at city hall.

The crisis started when a truck driver unwittingly drove through a vapor cloud of propane escaping from a ruptured pipeline, igniting an explosion and fire. The driver, who suffered third-degree burns, was the incident's only casualty.

Propane quickly spread through sewer lines as manhole covers popped and minor explosions occurred. After gas samples were taken from the bottom of sewers, Northwestern's lab was the first to identify propane as the gas responsible for the explosion. Although the explosions were not Northwestern's responsibility, natural gas had to be shut off because of the fire risk.

Throughout the weekend emergency, more than a hundred operating staff worked seventeen hundred hours of overtime while supervisors logged three hundred hours.

Seventy customer service and distribution employees, including recruits from Fort Saskatchewan, Camrose, Stony Plain and Wetaskiwin, were assigned to three-man teams with a policeman and fireman. Together they went door to door, checking with combustible gas indicators and advising homeowners to evacuate.

They patrolled their areas throughout the night, regularly checking manholes for propane readings. When the evacuation ended, teams covered their areas again, turning on gas appliances where help was needed. George Brown, customer service manager, and Jerry Manegre, public relations supervisor, co-ordinated the company's activities with officials at city hall. Brown provided advice on propane and gas while Manegre helped keep the news media informed and had leaflets printed on how to restore natural gas service. As residents re-entered the evacuated area, volunteer amateur radio operators handed out the leaflets.

At the Milner Building the main switchboard was flooded with calls as operators experienced their busiest time ever. The customer information centre was kept humming from Friday afternoon to Saturday evening with more than seventeen hundred calls.

When the evacuation was first announced residents called the gas company to confirm that they should shut off the gas and leave. They not only called about natural gas and propane, they asked about locations of emergency shelters. Husbands telephoned asking where they could find their families. "They just assumed that we knew these things," said Bruce Dafoe, "that we'd not only know our business, but would be involved in all aspects of responding to the emergency."

Mayor Cec Purves summed it up this way in a letter of thanks to the gas company: "Your entire efforts were first class. Your assistance is gratefully acknowledged."

Employee Associations

As the seventies drew to a close the *esprit de corps* of fifty years earlier was there as much as ever. And there was a stability about the energy group that gave each staff member a sense of security. On the outside there were signs of troubled times ahead — labor unrest, more inflation, economic crisis. On the inside, however, there was a quiet confidence, a feeling that the ship was built strongly and could weather many more storms if necessary.

Collective bargaining, for example, was going smoothly, thanks to the joint efforts of the employee   associations and management. These associations — one for each of the three utilities — had grown from their early beginnings shortly after the Second World War when they first came together simply as a means of facilitating better communications. As the years went by they became registered and accredited for bargaining purposes.

The somewhat different needs and working conditions among employees other than office staff have given rise to the organization of office and plant units. Recognition dinners put on each spring by the associations themselves provided a means of paying special tribute to the many dedicated people who have put forth extra effort to make the associations work so well.

Today the employee associations are a model being studied by other companies envious of their success and efficiency. (For a more complete history of the employees associations, see appendix.)

By the end of the seventies it was no longer feasible to hold annual staff meetings in the same way as they were held in earlier years. This meant the employee associations had to help bridge some of the gaps which came about through the normal growth in numbers of people. The last of the old traditional staff meetings took place at St. Basil's Church Hall in Edmonton, with about eight hundred employees attending on each of two days.

CU Pensioners Association

Another association which is typical of the *esprit de corps* in the company is the CU Pensioners Association. With an active membership of almost three hundred, the association has a northern and a southern executive. Canadian Utilities sponsors a variety of activities for retired employees on a corporate basis, particularly the annual dinners which are put on specifically for the association. The pensioners enjoy numerous social and sports activities through the association, and are able to keep in touch through the association newsletters. (A more detailed history of the pensioners' associations is contained in the appendix.)

CHAPTER 10

Recession and New Challenges

ATCO Buys Out IU's Share — 1980

During the years between the First and Second World Wars it was almost impossible to get people in Alberta to invest in something like a local utility company. There wasn't a great deal of money around to be invested, and much of what was around was still going into the development of family farms or industries related to agriculture.

To raise large amounts of money, financiers usually went to major world centres like London and New York. It was not surprising, then, that the controlling interest in the Canadian Utilities group had been held by a U.S. corporation, IU International, for more than half a century.

In the spring of 1980 ATCO Ltd. of Calgary bought out IU International's fifty-eight percent interest in Canadian Utilities. It was a startling, yet not totally unpredictable move for ATCO, as that company had already begun a transition from a multi-industry conglomerate based on manufacturing, to a group concerned primarily with the development of energy and resources. This transition occurred as a result of a 1978 policy decision and the execution of this mission began with the changing of the holding company's name from ATCO Industries to ATCO Ltd.

The three hundred and twenty-five million dollar CU share acquisition culminated a remarkable success story for the Calgary-based firm. ATCO had, over a period of three and a half decades, risen from being a small trailer rental business into a diversified billion-dollar corporation which was not only one of Canada's industrial giants, but had a solid reputation as a builder in countries around the world. (For a more complete history of ATCO Ltd., see Appendix.)

With ATCO as major shareholder, Canadian Utilities became virtually one hundred percent Canadian owned and ATCO's president and chief executive officer, R.D. (Ron) Southern, assumed the chairmanship and ATCO's senior vice-president of finance, C.S. (Cam) Richardson, was made vice-chairman. ATCO's senior vice-president and chief operating officer, N.W. (Norm) Robertson, along with W.L. (Bill) Britton, a partner in the Calgary law firm of Bennett Jones and an ATCO director, also became members of the board.

Edge King remained on the board as president and was additionally appointed chief executive officer. He commented on the change of ownership in Canadian Utilities' annual report to shareholders.

. . . This event marks the conclusion of a very long association between Canadian Utilities and IU International Corporation. CU and its associated companies have benefited significantly from the encouragement offered by that corporation and its representatives dating from the pioneer days of gas and electric services in western Canada and continuing over a span of fifty-six years.

Calgary Power Bids for Control of Canadian Utilities

After ATCO obtained controlling interest in Canadian Utilities, Calgary Power offered to purchase, at a premium price, the forty-two percent of Canadian Utilities common shares which ATCO did not own. The shareholders accepted the offer and by June 23, Calgary Power had received more than forty percent of the Canadian Utilities shares.

ATCO then made an offer for fifty-one percent of Calgary Power's outstanding shares. Calgary Power directors recommended that shareholders reject ATCO's offer and initiated a number of legal actions which were intended to discourage the take-over.

In the spring of 1981 Calgary Power, now operating under its new name of TransAlta Utilities Corporation, owned enough shares of Canadian Utilities to seriously reduce ATCO's flexibility in managing Canadian Utilities through such actions as blocking special resolutions, etc. The situation gave TransAlta a limited veto over ATCO's management of the company and reduced the effectiveness of ATCO's control position.

In the summer of 1982 this situation changed and ATCO's position was greatly enhanced when Nu-West Development, a giant real estate development company which owned twenty-three percent of TransAlta's shares, was faced with a very serious cash flow problem. Canadian Utilities helped Nu-West solve this problem by buying the TransAlta shares for one hundred and seventy million dollars in cash and three and a half million shares of Canadian Utilities common stock worth nearly seventy-five million dollars. This transaction between Canadian Utilities and Nu-West had the effect of diluting TransAlta's holding of Canadian Utilities stock to thirty-one percent of the total shares outstanding, while giving Canadian Utilities a significant ownership position in TransAlta.

The standoff between ATCO/CU and TransAlta Utilities which featured each trying to gain controlling interest in the other included legal hassles which went all the way to the Supreme Court of Canada. The battle finally wound down in August 1982, when the two companies agreed to gradually dispose of each other's shares.

Recession Hits Alberta

The seventies went out with spiralling inflation, and the beginning of the eighties brought an economic recession. Companies with heavy debt loads were bankrupted by high interest rates, and companies that were fully staffed for expansion were forced to lay off thousands.

Alsands, a thirteen-billion-dollar oil sands plant planned for Fort McMurray that had promised to pump new life into the economy, folded. The federal Liberal government's national energy program imposed punitive taxes that had the effect of driving a great deal of investment and technical know-how out of Alberta.

Could the energy group survive? "We've done it before, and we'll do it again," came the answer from a new team of leaders imbued with the same spirit that carried the energy pioneers through the dirty thirties and the war years.

Canadian Utilities' president Edge King called on management to "examine your operations so as to avoid beyond question any redundancy in the use of personnel or equipment. The need for new hiring is to be critically examined and similarly all operating costs are to be reviewed to determine if they may be postponed, reduced or eliminated."

"We pride ourselves in the efficient manner in which we operate but it is imperative that not only must we continue to operate as efficiently as possible but, like Caesar's wife, be perceived to be above reproach," King said. "Any sign of 'fat' in our organization or display of waste will contribute to resentment by the public."

In short, it was time for belt-tightening again. Utility companies tend to be fairly stable and not as tempest-tossed by economic ups and downs as other businesses, nevertheless they are affected and are particularly open to public scrutiny.

After successfully operating throughout 1979 without rate increases, all of the utilities were compelled to apply to the board for substantial rate relief in 1980. As an example of what was happening to costs, at the beginning of the seventies

Battle River Unit 3 cost the company twenty-eight million dollars, equivalent to one hundred and eighty-six dollars per kilowatt of installed capacity. But the fifth unit, completed in 1981, cost about two hundred and sixty million dollars, seven hundred and fifteen dollars per kilowatt.

Alberta 75 Years Old — 1980

The year 1980 marked the province's seventy-fifth anniversary. To help commemorate the anniversary, Canadian Utilities commissioned Canadian sculptor John Weaver to do a bronze rendering, scaled to one-quarter life size, of two men working on an early cable tool drilling rig.

In selecting the subject, Canadian Utilities recognized the role that the petroleum industry has played in the development of the province and the companies. One of five castings was presented to the province of Alberta and is on permanent display at the Provincial Museum of Alberta in Edmonton. Another was presented to the National Museum of Science and Technology in Ottawa. Others were retained by the company for display in company offices, and one was presented to the oil and gas industry for display in the Glenbow Museum in Calgary.

The eighties brought an increasing amount of re-examination of federal-provincial relationships. It had been a hundred years since Sir Adolphe-Basile Routhier, the great grandfather of Northwestern's general supervisor of plant records Guy Poirier, wrote the French words for O Canada. Alberta was no longer the colonial wilderness frontier it had been in 1880.

One of the very few men in Alberta whose lifetime spanned that hundred years was Richard Gavin Reid, who was Alberta's oldest surviving ex-premier when he died during the province's seventy-fifth year at the age of 101.

Dick Reid, as he was known to his many company friends, joined the staff of Canadian Utilities in 1949 as a research librarian and retired in 1974. After beginning his political career at Buffalo Coulee in his younger days, Reid became president of the United Farmers of Alberta in 1921. He led the UFA government as premier after J.E. Brownlee resigned in 1934, but thirteen months later his government was ousted by William Aberhart's Social Credit party. He left politics two years later.

Sadly the companies have occasionally lost men in leadership positions while they were in their prime. Such was the case with Wilson G. Sterling, senior vice-president and chief operating officer of Alberta Power, who died on July 8, 1980 at the age of forty-eight. He had served with the company since 1953 and made an outstanding contribution to the industry in Alberta. He was succeeded by Keith Provost, a vice-president of Alberta Power since 1971.

Hydroelectric Potential

In the early 1980s, Canadian Utilities joined with several other utility companies in studies of the hydroelectric potential of a number of sites in the north. A submission was filed with the provincial government calling for a hydroelectric development on the Peace River near Dunvegan, with hopes of completing it by the early 1990s.

While the studies of the Peace River hydro potential were going on, studies began on another site which it seemed had even greater potential, perhaps with less capital investment per megawatt of electricity produced. This was on the Slave River, near Fort Smith, Northwest Territories.

Development of the Slave River hydroelectric project would cost about six billion dollars and aroused great interest in the provincial government, which hoped the mega project would help the faltering Alberta economy. The economics of such an undertaking depended in part on whether export markets could be found for surplus power. After preliminary studies the Slave River project was shelved indefinitely as was Dunvegan.

Safety, and Conservation Emphasized

Safety, dependability and *efficiency* — these are important watchwords. As the seventies went out and the eighties were ushered in, the companies stressed safety more than ever before.

"Safety doesn't just happen . . . it takes a lot of committee work," commented Canadian Western's safety supervisor, Bob Dalton, as Canadian Western received the president's award for the best safety record in 1979, having cut its personal injury accident frequency rate almost in half during the last year of the seventies.

Planned inspections are an important part of safety programs. Through spot checks of crews, stations and vehicles, unsafe conditions are corrected and recommendations made for improvement.

While the companies were still in the business of selling electricity and natural gas, they were also promoting conservation.

Promoting the wise use of energy, without waste, was done in various ways. There was a promotional brochure, for example, explaining how to insulate a home, and the companies took part in a form of aerial heat photography known as thermography, which indicated where heat loss was taking place from buildings in urban areas.

The interest in energy conservation represented a major shift from the "energy to burn" days when oil and gas were first discovered. Those were the days when Alberta's wealth of energy resources seemed unlimited and gas wells were often left to burn uncontrolled.

The gas companies continued their exploration and development programs in 1980, acquiring additional petroleum and natural gas leases and participating in the drilling of sixty-one wells. Thirty were successful and eighteen others were to undergo further evaluation.

Activities in the oil sands areas continued to move forward. The company's new office building in the downtown business section of Fort McMurray was officially opened February 12, 1980. Known as the Borealis Building, it was one of Fort McMurray's largest office buildings with provision for construction of an additional three storeys in the future.

New Taxes — 1981

An excise tax payable on natural gas distributed by the companies, imposed by the federal government under the new national energy program, gave rise to a tax bill of more than one hundred and twenty million dollars in 1981.

The October federal budget had the direct effect of increasing Canadian Utilities' 1981 fuel cost by an estimated eight hundred thousand dollars and also reduced the revenue received from oil industry customers due to the reduction in oil production and exploration activity.

However, Canadian Utilities' customers once again benefited from a ninety-five percent refund of federal income taxes as well as a hundred percent of Alberta income taxes paid by the companies. Announcements confirmed a federal government decision not to pursue the change in legislation that would have reduced the federal portion of the refund to only fifty percent of taxes paid.

New Projects and New Records — 1981

The highlight of the year 1981 was the completion and commissioning of Battle River Unit Number 5, Alberta Power's first 375-megawatt unit, which doubled the previous capacity of the plant to 735 megawatts — enough to power a city the size of Edmonton.

The first earth movers had crawled on to the site in the summer of 1977 to begin the giant construction project. During the winter, foundations were poured under a huge plastic bubble building. By January 1979 girders and steel beams were swinging into place as the 73-metre by 83-metre frame of the powerhouse started growing.

By the following August the steel was up and work under way on the one hundred and seventy-five-metre stack. The construction work force reached its peak in 1979 as seven hundred and fifty people labored on the site. Late in the summer of 1979 the fourteen-storey boiler cavity was installed, and by the end of the year the water treatment plant was operational.

The turbine/generator, manufactured by the Hitachi company in Japan, was nearly a quarter of a million kilograms of almost solid copper. It arrived in Edmonton by rail and was then transported to Battle River by road — the heaviest load ever to leave Edmonton by truck.

The boiler was fired up for its initial steam stage during the early summer of 1981, the turbine churned out the unit's full capacity of 375 megawatts on June 24, and the official opening took place in mid-September.

Although Battle River Unit 5 stole the show in 1981, the year was not uneventful for the gas companies by any means. Northwestern mailed out a cheque for almost twenty-three million dollars in January 1981 — the largest gas supply cheque ever issued by the company — to TransCanada Pipelines. The cheque covered gas purchases from thirteen locations throughout the system during December and part of November. Because the accounting department's cheque issuing machine handles only up to nine digits, the cheque had to be manually typed. During 1980 Northwestern's natural gas costs totalled two hundred and fifty million dollars.

Northwestern and Canadian Western chalked up new records for capital works projects and increases in numbers of customers in 1981. Combined capital expenditures for the gas companies during the year totalled eighty-one million dollars, up from seventy-six million the year before. A combined total of nearly thirty thousand new customers was added to the gas systems, including more than eight hundred new customers acquired by Canadian Western through the purchase of the Valley Gas Company in the Turner Valley area. An agreement was also reached with the municipality of Bow Island for the purchase of its distribution system, serving nearly seven hundred customers.

Northwestern completed a 5,200-horsepower compressor station at the Viking field, improving the company's capacity to meet customer requirements and transportation exchange agreements.

At Canadian Utilities' head office in Edmonton, several departments moved to the new twenty-storey Standard Life Centre adjacent to the Milner Building. A pedway connected the second floors of the two buildings. Located in the new building were CU Engineering, management information services, Alberta Power's administration and general services department and the engineering and construction department.

Dennis Yorath Dies

D ennis Yorath, one of the company's outstanding pioneers, died on May 8, 1981. He had retired from the boards of the companies in the mid-seventies. At that time the energy group made him an honorary director for his many contributions to the companies over the years.

Not only within the companies, but from the outside as well, Yorath received many accolades during his years of service. The University of Alberta, for example, made him an honorary doctor of laws.

His death brought back many memories of the early days of the companies. An institution in the company for which he laid the foundation more than half a century ago is the staff magazine, *The Courier*. It has the distinction of being one of the oldest continuously published house organs in North America. Founded in 1927, it survived the rigors of the great depression and the war years. In good times and bad, it was always there to foster what Dennis Yorath's father, Chris, called *esprit de corps* in the first editorial ever published by *The Courier*.

The magazine celebrated its fiftieth anniversary in 1977. "I was proud to be the first editor," Yorath said on that occasion. "The purpose of creating such a publication was to keep all members of our staff informed regularly of the companies' progress as well as keeping them up to date on company activities, be it business, sports, social or just plain fun. The main objective was to bring all our staff into one cohesive organization, even though there were many differences in operations and actions. I think this has been achieved."

The Courier gave rise to other magazines and publications. At first it covered news of both electric and natural gas operations, and then during the forties employees in the electrical operations launched a small magazine of their own called *The Spotlite*. This in turn gave rise, in the late fifties, to the magazine which is today Alberta Power's employee publication, *The Transmitter*.

Employee Suggestion System

D ennis Yorath was also responsible for launching, back in the spring of 1951, the employee suggestion system that Canadian Western and Northwestern continue to operate successfully to this day. One of the main criteria for suggestions recognized by awards was that they must be designed to provide savings in time, labor and money. In other words, to improve operating efficiency.

In instances where actual savings can be calculated, the person who designed the improvement and presented it as a suggestion is given a specific percentage of the calculated savings over the first year of operation.

An added incentive in the eighties was the introduction of the Suggester of the Year award as part of the total suggestion program. At Canadian Western's annual banquet in March 1986 that award went to Alice Peterson, who was also the recipient of the largest single award which had ever been presented by the companies. While the Suggester of the Year award at the banquet was only one hundred dollars, it was totally overshadowed by a cash award of nearly seven thousand seven hundred dollars which Peterson received in December 1985 for the suggestion that return envelopes mailed to customers with bills should in future be mailed only to the approximately thirty percent of customers who actually use them for payment of their bills. "Alice's idea was a fairly simple one," said suggestion committee chairman Don Sharpe. "It turned out to be a real sleeper. It caught us off guard. We didn't realize how valuable the idea would be."

Suggestions presented for awards are judged by a committee of ten members, five appointed by management and five by the employees' association.

New Calgary Head Office Building — 1982

C anadian Western has been in its new head office building at Eighth Street and Eleventh Avenue S.W. in Calgary since the fall of 1982. The move to the sixteen-storey office tower allowed the company to consolidate a number of its scattered office operations in one building. It is within walking distance of the service centre.

The building was constructed by ATCO Housing and Development Corporation. One of its most striking aspects is the view it provides of the mountains, the downtown and the south part of the city.

The main lobby features a museum and archives preserving many artifacts which illustrate Canadian Western's colorful three-quarters of a century of history. This unique collection was put together under the direction of Canadian Western's public relations department. There are expanded library facilities in the new building and a Blue Flame Kitchen that can hold audiences of up to a hundred people.

A new Midnapore Operations Centre opened in December 1981, serving the south section of Calgary and the towns immediately south of the city. Next came the Whitehorn Operations Centre at 3055 – 37 Avenue N.E., serving towns to the east as well as the northeast section of Calgary, with half again as many customers as Lethbridge. It includes thirty-six towns in the districts of Trochu, Strathmore and Brooks. The Whitehorn Operations Centre opened in August 1982.

The old Service Centre on Eleventh Avenue S.W. was given responsibility for serving customers' needs in the central and northwestern sections of Calgary and the district towns west and north of the city. Future plans included another centre to cover the northwest area.

Construction activity at Northwestern in 1982 and 1983 centered on Edmonton's south side. On land located just south of the company's main control station at 82 Avenue and 56 Street, a heavy equipment and repair depot was completed. To this was added a fleet repair facility, completed in 1984. A mile southeast, construction of an operations centre began in the spring of 1983. Named the East Side Operations Base, it provided a consolidated regional operating centre for customer service, production, transmission and distribution staff.

ATCOR Resources Limited — 1982

I n the spring of 1982, Canadian Utilities' specialized subsidiaries in engineering, petrochemicals and oil and gas exploration were amalgamated into a new company called ATCOR Resources Limited. The amalgamation came about when Canadian Utilities acquired the oil and gas assets owned by various ATCO subsidiaries. These were combined with Canadian Utilities' own non-utility operations to form ATCOR. The name was chosen to reflect the tie to ATCO, while identifying the company with the resource industry.

Dr. John Wood, president of ATCO Industries (N.A.) Ltd., was appointed president and chief executive officer of the new company.

ATCOR was made up of CU Ethane, CU Engineering, CU Resources and ATCO Gas and Oil. The amalgamation improved efficiency, productivity and communication, creating an environment in which growth would exceed what the companies could achieve singly.

Petrochemicals have been one of ATCOR's major activities. The CU Ethane partnership with Dome Petroleum was only a beginning. ATCOR's objectives include not only the marketing of natural gas liquids, but possibly also byproducts from Alberta Power's thermal generating plants. Further primary thrusts of the company are in resource exploration and production.

ATCOR also has been involved in marketing natural gas to the industrial sector, using the transportation systems of the utility companies, making it the largest marketer in Alberta.

Canadian Utilities Centre — 1983

C anadian Utilities and its parent company, ATCO Ltd., built a new office tower on what was formerly the parking lot located on the west side of the Milner Building in Edmonton. This is the new corporate head office building, known as the Canadian Utilities Centre. Its doors opened to the public in November 1983.

The new twenty-storey office tower is an architectural landmark for downtown Edmonton. Its design features a seven-storey-high atrium lobby, expressed on the exterior of the building by a large cathedral-like archway. The CU Centre contains close to twenty-five thousand square metres of office space, plus four levels of underground parking.

As you walk into the lobby of this ultra-modern structure your attention is immediately captured by a sculpture by Edmonton artist Garry Jones. It consists of groupings of suspended acrylic prisms, eighteen in all, which reflect natural and artificial light to produce varied rainbow effects which are constantly changing throughout the day.

Salt Cavern Storage Facility — 1984

N orthwestern Utilities in 1980 identified the need for increased natural gas storage facilities for peak-day use. Salt cavern facilities were chosen over several alternatives (including new compressors, pipelines and various other storage methods). Project costs and details were presented to the board of directors in February 1982, and work on the first cavern started in April. Injection began in October 1984, and the facility was officially opened the following month. At a cost of thirty-five million dollars, the salt caverns would become the largest single capital project in Northwestern's history.

The caverns are located on a half-section of land northeast of Edmonton near Fort Saskatchewan. Five caverns lie eighteen hundred metres beneath the ground in a four hundred million year-old salt formation that covers a large area of northeastern Alberta and has been used to store other gases and liquids. The site can be expanded to include twenty-three caverns as they are needed to keep pace with growth.

The caverns were developed by water injection into the salt formation. The water dissolved the salt, forming an impervious cavern that allows no gas migration. Sonar surveys periodically monitor the caverns' shape and growth. The teardrop-shaped fully-developed caverns measure about seventy metres high and seventy metres in diameter and take up to two years to complete.

Maximum pressure of the caverns is twenty-eight thousand kPa or more than four thousand pounds per square inch. During winter, the facility is ready to deliver gas at flow rates designed to meet system requirements. Gas injection occurs for about two hundred days from April to October to refill the caverns.

Tumbler Ridge and Lloydminster Added — 1984

Northwestern now serves customers from Tumbler Ridge, B.C. to Lloydminster on the Alberta-Saskatchewan border.

Tumbler Ridge is a mining community about sixty-five kilometres southwest of Dawson Creek, and is part of a three-billion-dollar development to open up the area to coal mining. By way of Northland Utilities in Dawson Creek, Northwestern now provides natural gas service to Tumbler Ridge. The announcement that the franchise had been granted to Northwestern through its B.C. subsidiary, Northland, was made by the B.C. Utilities Commission in April 1982.

On the eastern side of Alberta, in the spring of 1984, Northwestern purchased the controlling interest in the Lloydminster Gas Company Limited, which had been held by Chieftain Developments Ltd. Northwestern subsequently bought up the additional shares held by other owners, to give the company complete ownership of Lloydminster Gas.

The new ownership became public at the beginning of 1985, when the Northwestern sign went on the building and Lloydminster became the base for Northwestern's East District operations. Northwestern's extensive natural gas grid now stretches from British Columbia into Saskatchewan.

Lloydminster Gas Company had more than half a century of distinguished and colorful history. The Lloydminster office is on the Saskatchewan side of Canada's only trans-border city, and the original gas company at Lloydminster has the distinction of having brought in Saskatchewan's first commercially viable natural gas well in 1934. The company was founded by the late O.C. Yates, the CPR station agent in Lloydminster at the height of the depression. The first well was drilled with an old coal-fired cable tool rig.

Natural gas operations were supplemented by a small oil refinery built in the nearby community of Dina in the late thirties. It was a "tea kettle" operation which extracted oil products from crude mainly by using heat generated by a coal-fired steam plant.

The primitive Dina refinery was followed by the more sophisticated plant of Excelsior Refineries Ltd. At the same time, Husky Oil and Refining Limited came into being and oil production was stepped up considerably in the area. Lloydminster Gas supplied natural gas to both of these companies.

The system was expanded from Lloydminster to the nearby communities of Blackfoot and Kitscoty. Then Chieftain Development of Edmonton came along. Chieftain had gas reserves in that area, and had plans to extend gas service farther into Saskatchewan. An amalgamation of the two companies was brought about when Chieftain bought Yates' controlling interest.

While Northwestern's acquisition of the Lloydminster Gas Company was a major expansion, Northwestern had been serving the Husky Refinery at Lloydminster since the mid-fifties. Then as the community grew in subsequent years, Northwestern began selling gas to the Lloydminster Gas Company as well.

Northwestern's Districts Defined

In 1985 Lloydminster became the hub of Northwestern's East District. The company now operates primarily in three districts, the other two being the Red Deer District and the Grande Prairie District. Although some of the management for the Red Deer and East Districts is still carried out from Edmonton, customer service in particular is now headquartered in the two centres.

The East District stretches from Fort McMurray in the north to Oyen in the south, and from the Saskatchewan side of Lloydminster in the east to Camrose in the west. The Red Deer District includes Swan Hills and Jasper.

Top Management Changes — 1984

Chief executive officer of CU, Edge King, retired at the beginning of June 1984. The *Edmonton Journal* paid him special tribute in a feature story in its business section, calling him "Alberta's Mr. Utilities" and noting that he helped Canadian Utilities weather double-digit inflation and the National Energy Program, "which hit the highly regulated company like a ton of bricks."

As King stood before shareholders at his last annual meeting of the company in the spring, he pointed out the coincidence that his dates in office as president coincided to the month with those of Pierre Elliott Trudeau as prime minister of Canada. "While it was no great trick to keep the company's balance sheet in better shape than Trudeau kept Canada's, I still find some satisfaction in drawing the comparison," King said in his address to shareholders.

King stepped down leaving Canadian Utilities worth $2.2 billion dollars, earning eighty-seven million dollars on $1.4 billion dollars in revenues, and able to boast of being one of only six Canadian companies with a Triple A credit rating.

His term of office included the two hundred and eighty-eight million dollar preferred share issue launched at the beginning of the eighties. It was one of the largest successful share issues in Canadian history, and signalled the end of the largest take-over bid in Alberta history — the bid by TransAlta Utilities to buy controlling interest in Canadian Utilities.

"The Alberta consumer is getting a good deal by having two major electric utilities in competition with each other," King stated on his retirement. "If you don't think so, just look elsewhere and compare power and natural gas rates." Government-owned utilities, he said, have grown so large they are no longer responsive to either the consumer or the government. Hydro Quebec's budget, for example, is bigger than that of the province.

The esteem in which Edge King was held by staff members in the Canadian Utilities group was obvious in the retirement parties held for him. Of special significance was a sculpture of The Lineman, by artist John Weaver, commissioned to honor the retiring president. One casting of the limited-edition bronze sculpture was presented to King, one is located on the twentieth floor of the Canadian Utilities Centre; and a third is on display in the Calgary office.

Upon King's retirement the board appointed Ron Southern as chief executive officer as well as board chairman. At the time Southern could foresee many changes, mainly related to the downturn of the economy in general, which he expected would put Canadian Utilities, along with everyone else, in a squeeze.

Southern described himself as an optimist, and boasted about the "immense capabilities of the people who make up the Canadian Utilities group of companies." At the same time he admitted that some of the things which are happening in society frighten him: developments like alarming unemployment rates, the danger of extraordinarily high interest rates, the problems of government deficits, and the continued hardships of simply being in business.

The challenges which lie ahead, he said, are of "large proportions and will require the very best efforts of each and every one of us to be successful."

John Wood New President — 1984

D r. John Wood was named the new president and chief operating officer of Canadian Utilities. The move was a natural one for him. He had served not only on the board of ATCO Ltd. but also on the boards of all its operating companies, and as president and chief executive officer of ATCOR Resources Limited.

An Albertan by birth (Calgary, 1931) Wood graduated from the University of British Columbia in 1953 with a degree in civil engineering, and from Stanford

University in 1956 with a PhD in civil engineering and engineering mechanics. He spent six years with Space Technology Laboratories Inc., and then founded his own company, Mechanics Research Inc., an engineering firm specializing in structural dynamics research in the missile, aerospace and oil industries.

In 1966 Mechanics Research Inc. became a subsidiary of ATCO and Dr. Wood became senior vice-president, engineering and research for ATCO. Two years later, in 1968, he was appointed senior vice-president, eastern region, responsible for monitoring and directing the management of ATCO subsidiaries and divisions within the eastern region.

As senior vice-president, planning, a position he attained in 1975, Wood was responsible for co-ordinating all aspects of planning within the ATCO group of companies.

His interest in space-age technology quickly carried over into the Canadian Utilities group, as he talked, for example, of adapting mini-computers to the task of automating meter reading for the electric and natural gas utilities. He saw the possibility, too, of non-utility operations getting involved in the manufacture of such sophisticated electronic gadgetry.

Another major change announced at the time of Edge King's retirement was the appointment of William R. Horton as executive vice-president of utilities for Canadian Utilities as well as president of each of the utility subsidiaries — Northwestern, Canadian Western and Alberta Power. Edge King commended this triumvirate of power to the staff in his last presidential bulletin, in which his final words were: "The company is in good hands."

The three, in fact, complemented each other in a unique way. Southern was the entrepreneur. He lived and breathed business, and he didn't mind admitting it. "I'm a child of business," he said, referring to the growth of ATCO from a small family trailer rental business to a worldwide enterprise employing thousands. And profitability, he said, is to a significant degree the yardstick by which you measure how well the company is achieving its other goals of providing good service to customers and motivation for its employees.

Wood, on the other hand, was the people person. "You can't run a company like this sitting in an office," he said. "You've got to get out and meet the people and see what they're doing so that you know what they're talking about because you've been there."

As for Horton, there's not much about utilities that escapes his eye. He is a past chairman of the Public Utilities Board. During his ten years on the PUB, seven as chairman, he had many opportunities to observe the companies in action. He established a reputation for his knowledge and integrity, and for maintaining the PUB as an independent body. Horton first became a member of the PUB in 1973. His appointment coincided with the beginning of a series of events — the OPEC oil embargo, the oil shortage and the rapid increase in oil and gas prices — that were to have an enormous impact on utilities in Alberta.

Management by Objectives

T he presidential style of Wood emphasized management by objectives. "We've laid out very tough objectives for the various companies — primarily improvements in their operation," he noted in an interview. "I'm a strong believer in setting those kinds of objectives and making sure people commit to the objectives and achieve them."

He talked about setting personal objectives, departmental objectives and company objectives that would be reviewed every month and modified to meet the rapidly changing business environment.

Wood practices what he preaches. He derives a lot of personal satisfaction from outlining goals and achieving them on a daily, monthly and yearly basis. "You commit to something and you achieve it," he comments. "That to me is a great thrill."

"We cannot lose sight of the fact that the utility business is competitive even here in Alberta," he says. "It has to be a highly productive company and it has to be an efficient company — not just to improve the earnings of the company, but the public impression."

He believes government regulatory bodies will begin to request management audits of utility companies to zero in on whether the companies are being run efficiently.

"I would rather take the positive approach that we initiate management reviews and not have the Public Utilities Board forcing them on us," he said. "I really am talking about this company becoming more competitive, more efficient and more productive."

Group Accident and Sickness Fund

C anadian Utilities' Group Accident and Sickness Fund celebrated its fiftieth anniversary in March of 1985. The fund has come a long way since its founding.

In the early thirties, during the great depression, the employees of Canadian Western, Canadian Utilities and Northwestern Utilities had a group accident and sickness policy of sorts with a company called the General Accident Assurance Company. In the fall of 1934 this company decided it did not wish to continue insuring the utilities group, and it cancelled its coverage effective March 31, 1935.

Meetings of the employees of the group of utilities were held to establish a self-insured plan to replace the cancelled coverage. A proposed memorandum of coverage was drawn up by Dennis Yorath. It was accepted by the group, and a board of administration, consisting of two representatives from each company, was elected.

Premiums were to be paid partly by the companies and partly by the employees. The primary aim of the fund thus established was to provide mutual assistance to its members, who through illness or injury might become overburdened financially through the cost of medical care and loss of earnings.

The first trustees of the fund were Yorath, Frank W. Paterson (CWNG) and Thomas A. Montgomery (CUL). Yorath was appointed secretary. It was decided not to incorporate under the Societies Act and today the fund is still an unincorporated trust.

During the depression and the Second World War the companies managed to keep their sickness and accident fund in healthy shape despite many hardships. It was not until the spring of 1948, long after the war was over, that a full-time secretary was appointed to take care of the day-to-day administration. The years that followed saw more improvements, including better coverage for employees, pensioners, spouses and dependants of employees. (For a more complete history of the Group Accident and Sickness Fund, see Appendix.)

Dafoe, Twa Head Utilities — 1986

There were no changes among the directors and officers of CU during 1986. However, the company's utility subsidiaries announced a number of appointments.

Bruce Dafoe was appointed president of the two gas companies and Craighton Twa became president of Alberta Power. Dafoe joined Northwestern in 1954, following graduation from the University of Alberta with a Bachelor of Science degree in chemical engineering. He advanced through a succession of management positions, and prior to his new appointment was senior vice-president of Canadian Western and Northwestern. Twa joined the company in 1959, following graduation from the University of Alberta with a Bachelor of Science degree in electrical engineering. He also advanced through a succession of positions and prior to his new appointment was senior vice-president and general manager of Alberta Power.

A number of other senior appointments were also made. For both gas companies, W. Laurence Graburn became vice-president and general manager, gas supply; Glyn W. Richards, vice-president, rate administration; and Gerald W. Welsh, vice-president, gas supply engineering.

For Canadian Western, John Fisher was appointed senior vice-president and general manager; John W. Fildes, vice-president, operations; J. Douglas Graham, vice-president, engineering and construction; Thomas J. Storey, vice-president and controller; and John M. Willsher, vice-president, administration and marketing.

For Northwestern, R. Graham Lock became senior vice-president and general manager; Robert Armstrong, vice-president, engineering and construction; Denis

M. Ellard, vice-president, administration and marketing; Ronald M. Masse, vice-president and controller; and Gordon K. Munk, vice-president, operations.

Expanding ATCOR Resources

A nother prominent member of the management team was William A. Elser, who was appointed president of ATCOR Resources in 1986. Elser occupied the position formerly held by Wood.

Prior to his appointment, Elser served as ATCOR's executive vice-president and chief operating officer. He joined the ATCO group in 1975 as president of ATCO Gas and Oil Ltd., having formerly been president of the exploration and development division of Ashland Canada Ltd. He is a graduate in petroleum engineering from the Colorado School of Mines.

Soon after ATCOR was formed through the amalgamation of ATCO Gas and Oil with the non-utility assets of the Canadian Utilities group, the engineering consulting division (formerly CU Engineering, then ATCOR Engineering) was discontinued because of severe slowdown of activities.

More than offsetting the two million dollar reduction in engineering operations during 1983 was a four million dollar increase in exploration and production activities and a six million dollar gain in natural gas marketing operations.

ATCOR became increasingly involved in frontier exploration. The company entered into a joint exploration venture with ATCO Ltd., Texaco Canada Resources Ltd. and Sun Life Assurance Company of Canada. The venture was called AT&S Exploration Ltd. Through this investment ATCOR came to own petroleum and natural gas rights and crude oil and natural gas reserves on Canada Lands developed through an exploration program totalling nearly two hundred and fifty million dollars.

ATCOR was engaged primarily in three areas of operation — oil and gas exploration and development, natural gas marketing and petrochemicals production. During 1983 the ethane extraction plant in South Edmonton, in which the company owned a fifty percent joint venture interest with Dome Petroleum, processed a daily average of almost six million cubic metres of natural gas, which resulted in a daily average recovery of more than seven hundred cubic metres of liquid petroleum gases. ATCOR had plans to develop the plant to a capacity of nearly nine million cubic metres of natural gas per day.

In June 1986, ATCOR Resources Limited was re-organized to become CU Enterprises Inc. ATCOR Ltd., which is the operating arm of CU Enterprises, specializes in oil and gas exploration and production activities, including the processing and marketing of natural gas.

Frontier exploration is still one of the interests of ATCOR Ltd., and in this respect it continues its association with AT&S, a joint exploration company in which ATCOR holds a thirty percent interest. In 1986 it completed its planned frontier exploration program. The highlight of the 1986 effort was at Amauligak in the Beaufort Sea where a three-well delineation program confirmed the presence of an estimated eight hundred million gross barrels of oil reserves.

The Amauligak discovery is particularly significant for it represents a world-class discovery. Its development could lead to the delineation of and the production from earlier discoveries in the Mackenzie Delta-Beaufort Sea area and the establishment of a whole new oil and gas exploration and producing region in Canada. Development of Amauligak and the construction of a pipeline from the Mackenzie Delta to Alberta would together represent a multi-billion dollar megaproject with many associated investment opportunities and economic benefits to Canada and the company.

An associate company, also a subsidiary of CU Enterprises Inc., is CU Energy Marketing Inc., a Delaware company which intends to import gas into the United States for resale.

Canadian Utilities Computer Facility — 1986

The continued demand for computing resources within the Canadian Utilities organization prompted the acquisition of an Amdahl 5870 computer in 1985.

This computer, the largest ever purchased by Canadian Utilities, can compute at a rate of twenty-one million instructions per second. This power is required to support corporate applications such as customer billing, accounting, purchasing and inventory, payroll, and gas management as well as the ad hoc processing required for such activities as financial planning and "what-if" analysis.

In order to store all the data required to run the corporation, in excess of seventy billion bytes of disk storage has been installed to provide instant access to data. Additionally, large batch data files and backup copies of the disk files are stored on new, innovative tape cartridges.

Corporate applications support employees in all locations. In order to allow these people to use the computer, a network with over one thousand terminals has been installed spanning Alberta and reaching into British Columbia and the Yukon.

Junior Citizen Awards Program

The year 1986 marked the twenty-fifth anniversary of Alberta's Junior Citizen of the Year Awards.

The awards program, sponsored by Alberta Power Limited and TransAlta Utilities in co-operation with the Alberta Weekly Newspapers Association, has been honoring individual young men and women since 1962. Group awards have been included in the program since 1964.

The program helps recognize young, concerned Albertans who are making significant contributions to the lives of their families, friends, neighbors, and their communities. Over the past twenty-five years more than three hundred exceptional young Albertans have been awarded the title. An annual awards ceremony, presided over by the Lieutenant-Governor of Alberta, provides the opportunity to present each winner with a citation, a cash award, and an Alberta Junior Citizen lapel pin.

Alberta Power also co-sponsors the Grant MacEwan Conservation Award. The award is given annually to the Alberta 4-H member who best promotes, practises and demonstrates conservation after attending the Alberta 4-H Conservation Camp, sponsored by Alberta Power Limited and TransAlta Utilities.

Sheerness Plant — 1986

T he first unit at Sheerness went into commercial operation in January 1986. Once the project had received government approval, Alberta Power signed an agreement with TransAlta Utilities to share equally the cost and output of Sheerness. Under the terms of the agreement, Alberta Power is the managing owner. This is the first joint ownership agreement ever negotiated for a power plant in Alberta and is one of the few instances of shared ownership in Canada.

Construction of Unit One was a five-year undertaking. The first earth movers went onto the site in the summer of 1981. The underground services, water, natural gas, sewer and fire protection, were installed first, as the first units of the construction camp were being built, followed by erection of the Anderson substation, two kilometres south of the plant site. An inflatable bubble larger than a football field, was placed over the area of the powerhouse foundations while the foundations were being poured during the winter of 1981–1982. The substation was energized initially at 25 kilovolts to provide construction power, and later commissioned at 240 kilovolts to allow electricity produced at the Sheerness plant to be fed into the provincial interconnected grid.

Sheerness Unit One burns about two hundred and sixty-five tons of coal an hour when generating power at peak capacity. The thirteen-hundred-acre artificial lake that serves as a cooling pond for the plant is filled with water piped from the Red Deer River, forty kilometres away. Water from the line not only cools the generating station, it also provides for the irrigation of a potential eleven thousand acres of land in the area, as well as providing the water supply for the town of Hanna. In the past Hanna has been plagued continually with low water supplies.

More than sixteen hundred people visited the plant on June 20, 1986 during the Open House celebrating the official opening of Unit One. Unit Two is currently scheduled for completion in 1990 although this timetable depends on the growth of electrical demand in the province..

Bigfoot, Brutus and Reclamation

L ook out Bigfoot, here comes Brutus!
Bigfoot and Brutus are the nicknames for huge "walking" draglines that remove overburden from coal seams at Battle River. Bigfoot received its name as a result of a name-the-dragline contest among Alberta Power employees.

Picture a double garage filled with earth and rock. That's how big a bucketful these draglines remove in one bite. Bigfoot and Brutus walk on "shoes," each of which measures about twelve feet by seventy feet (nearly four metres wide and over twenty-one metres long). The shoes pull the metal hulk of the machine along, as it slowly plods its way across the coalfields.

Brutus weighs nearly forty-two hundred tons, about the same as eleven fully-loaded Boeing 747 airplanes.

From the coalfield, sixty-six-ton haulers transport nature's gleaming black stored-up energy to the power plant, where it is dumped into an underground conveyor, pulverized and then blown into a furnace that stands as tall as a fourteen-storey building.

Alberta Power's coal-fired generating stations incorporate some of the newest power plant technology in North America. According to statistics of the Canadian Electrical Association for coal-fired units of more than sixty megawatts, Alberta Power's four units have consistently placed among the top ten units in Canada in terms of reliability.

What about land reclamation where the coal has been mined? Alberta Power, in co-operation with the mining companies which supply coal for the Battle River and Sheerness stations, pride themselves in the fact that they have returned the land to a level of productivity equal to or better than what it was before the coal was mined.

Reclamation of land follows a series of planned steps beginning with the removal of topsoil by scrapers. This soil is stockpiled for later use. Subsurface earth and rock, in turn, is stored in huge spoil piles. After the coal has been mined, the spoil piles are levelled by bulldozers, and again covered with the topsoil. Cereal or forage crops are planted the following spring.

Various crops, such as wheat and alfalfa, are growing well on hundreds of hectares of reclaimed land. In a joint program between the Alberta government and industry, researchers have studied different kinds of soil and rock and how best to reclaim them. For example, some experiments have mixed bottom ash from the generating station with the clay to see if the ash's calcium content will break up the clay, making it more hospitable to plant roots.

Computerized Meter Reading

R esearch in automated meter reading culminated in 1986 when Canadian Western introduced computerized meter reading equipment in Calgary's

Midnapore area and in High River on an experimental basis. The experiment worked so well that Canadian Western has implemented computerized meter reading throughout its service areas.

"The system has functioned almost flawlessly," says project co-ordinator Bob Kendrick. "If the figures from Midnapore are representative of the company, the savings could mean a payback of about three and a half years."

The most attractive feature of this system is that in the next few years it will bring the printing of bills on-site. A miniature printer carried by the meter reader will print bills identical to those now printed by the mainframe computer.

Northwestern Utilities and Alberta Power adopted the same meter reading system, starting in 1987.

Natural Gas for Vehicles

C anadian Western's Roy Nourse, always a leader in promoting natural gas as the best fuel for cars and trucks, continued to make this one of his leading activities until he retired in 1987. "Natural gas vehicles probably offer the biggest opportunity for sale of natural gas at the consumer level since the widespread acceptance of natural gas for heating," was his message in the mid-eighties in his capacity as the company's supervisor of special sales projects and corporate services.

While many businessmen were agitating for more gas and oil exports, Nourse was preaching that natural gas should be used wherever possible in the transportation industry "and leave the oil for export." Canadian Western and Northwestern each had their own natural gas pumping stations for company vehicles and also for outside customers. Other prominent leaders in the field who were doing the same included Husky Oil and its parent company, NOVA, an Alberta Corporation. They were reinforced by corporations like CNG Fuel Systems, founded by Canadian Hunter Exploration.

Roy Nourse was also quick in reminding vehicle manufacturers that the internal combustion engine, when it was invented more than a century ago, was designed to operate on methane gas, or coal gas, which was not nearly as complicated chemically as gasoline, and it is only today that engineers are rediscovering not only the simplicity of running cars and trucks on natural gas, but also the superior economics of it and its cleanliness environmentally.

The gas companies continued converting their vehicles, and in the mid-eighties had well over a hundred of them running on natural gas. The biggest drawback in marketing the concept for mass consumption in Alberta was that propane, which in this province was an abundant by-product of the natural gas industry, was cheap and easy to get, so many companies chose propane instead, even though natural gas had been proven to be superior to propane as a fuel.

New Corporate Ventures

A TCO and Canadian Utilities have identified the operation and maintenance needs of the new North Warning System to be built in Canada's North as an opportunity for growth in the non-utility area. An agreement was signed between Canada and the United States on March 18, 1985, calling for modernization of the North American Air Defence system in the far North. The needs of the new system provide an opportunity compatible with the skills already developed in the CU-ATCO group of companies.

To meet these challenges the group set up a new firm called the Frontec Logistics Corporation, better known as FRONTEC.

"FRONTEC will have the benefit not only of our long-standing corporate relationships in the North but also of our commitment to training and employing northerners," says CU board chairman Ron Southern.

The modern North Warning System will replace the Distant Early Warning Line (DEW Line). It is funded on a 60/40 basis by the United States and Canada, and will consist of about fifty short and long-range radar stations across Alaska, the Canadian Arctic and the Labrador coast.

Working in difficult terrain and in the far North comes naturally to Canadian Utilities personnel. An example of the kind of work they do is the construction of a major extension of the company's 240-kilovolt transmission system into northeastern Alberta, currently in progress. The one hundred and thirty million dollar project adds five hundred and fifty kilometres of line to the Alberta grid, much of it built across muskeg. The transmission project requires negotiations with four hundred landowners and a demanding approval process involving ten provincial government departments.

Canadian Utilities' experience in microwave communications is another technical capability which qualifies it uniquely for operations in the North. A digital microwave network of more than sixteen hundred kilometres, much of which is the equivalent of one hundred and ninety-two voice channels, forms the communications backbone of Canadian Utilities' utility operations. This system provides for protection, monitoring and control of generation and transmission equipment throughout both the electrical and gas pipeline grids.

The reliability and efficiency with which Canadian Utilities has carried out its operations in the far North resulted in an agreement between its Yukon subsidiary, Yukon Electrical, and the territorial government to assume the operation of the generating units and other facilities owned by the Northern Canada Power Commission when control of those facilities was transferred from the federal to the territorial government.

Another new project, a joint venture between Canadian Utilities and ATCO, is the CATS Defence Support System. The federal government and CATS are participating in the second phase of developing a moving tank target system.

The simulated tank is a remotely controlled target incorporating hit detection for military training purposes. The moving target can operate in a pre-programed mode or be controlled directly by a training officer who can manipulate several targets simultaneously.

CHAPTER 11

Seventy-Five Years of Service

Seventy-Fifth Anniversary

The year 1987 marked the seventy-fifth anniversary of the Canadian Utilities group. It was three-quarters of a century since it all began in the Bow Island field with the bringing in of Old Glory and the subsequent introduction of natural gas service to Calgary, Lethbridge and other southern Alberta communities.

Natural gas revenues were down significantly as a result of an unusually mild winter. The warmer than normal weather had one advantage however, it made construction work easier in Edmonton, where Northwestern was in the first stages of a ten-year pipeline replacement program — a one hundred million dollar undertaking.

The 1986 replacement represented three important firsts for Northwestern.

It was the first time Northwestern had used six-inch plastic pipe and the first time the company had inserted any significant length of polyethylene pipe into steel pipe. It was also the first time a contractor had been used on an urban distribution project.

The project involved the insertion of six-inch plastic pipe into existing 12-inch steel pipe, installed from 1923–1933. The existing intermediate-pressure line had developed a marked increase in the number of leaks, causing maintenance and repair costs to mushroom.

Approximately two hundred kilometres of pipe and thirty thousand services will be replaced in Edmonton, some by insertion and some by direct burial.

Most of the old pipeline which will be replaced is located in the downtown and older residential areas near the North Saskatchewan River.

At the close of 1986, Canadian Western completed the replacement of its main line between Taber and Burdett, which was the final section to be installed in an eight-year program that totally replaced the 1912 main line from the Bow Island field to Calgary. Canadian Western's largest capital project of 1987 was the replacement of the 1924 Foremost transmission line south of Bow Island.

For Canadian Western the seventy-fifth anniversary activities rolled into high gear early in 1987, kicking off with the anniversary theme highlighting the long-service awards banquet, which was appropriately held on Valentine's Day.

Anniversary receptions for community leaders and long-time customers were held in the five communities where service began in 1912: Lethbridge, Calgary, Brooks, Okotoks and Nanton. A special guest at many of the anniversary activities was Founding President Eugene Coste (portrayed by Calgary actor Brian Gromoff), who brought to life the excitement and challenges of the company's early years. Another major anniversary achievement was the publication of *75 Favorites*, the Blue Flame Kitchen's first hard-cover cookbook.

The year was also special for Canadian Western because of its high-profile preparations for the XV Olympic Winter Games. The company drew widespread praise for the giant flame installed and tested on top of the 190-metre-high Calgary Tower. By contributing the Calgary Tower flame — as well as the official Olympic flame at McMahon Stadium and smaller flames at the sport venues and the Olympic Plaza — Canadian Western qualified as an Official Supplier to the Games. This status, combined with ATCO's involvement as an Official Sponsor, enabled Canadian Western and associated companies to prepare an extensive Olympic hosting program for guests from across Canada and around the world.

Canadian Utilities extended special recognition to the southern Alberta natural gas operations, which were the founding members of the group of companies seventy-five years ago, by holding its annual meeting of shareholders in Calgary for the first time. The meeting was held on May 20, 1987, at the Calgary Convention Centre.

For Alberta Power, 1987 was a diamond anniversary year — the diamond is usually recognized as a symbol for sixtieth as well as seventy-fifth anniversaries. It was sixty years since the electric power side of Canadian Utilities experienced its modest beginnings in east-central Alberta and in Saskatchewan.

President's Awards

The idea of putting a natural gas flame on top of the Calgary Tower came from the imagination of public relations manager Gene Zadvorny. In recognition of Gene's role in guiding the project to completion, he was honored with the President's Award at the company's Awards Banquet in March 1988.

A Northwestern agency serviceman in Grande Prairie, Don Lowe, was similarly honored at Northwestern's Awards Banquet. Don was credited with saving the life of a drowning boy whom he pulled from a pool of water on a farm near TeePee Creek on February 20, 1987.

President's Summary

C anadian Utilities President John Wood presented an address to the Calgary Rotary Club on April 7, titled Alberta's Little Known Corporate Giant. The speech provides an appropriate summary of Canadian Utilities' seventy-five year record of service, and indicates the direction the group is headed as it looks to the future. It captured so well the spirit of the group of companies in its seventy-fifth year that we can think of no more appropriate way of summarizing the company's history than to quote that address in its entirety.

Speaking to the Calgary Rotary Club, April 7, Canadian Utilities' president, John Wood, said:

If I were to ask most Albertans to name an Alberta-based investor-owned company with over two and a half billion dollars in assets, employing more than four thousand employees, a company that has achieved impressive earnings right through the current recession; that consistently records over seventeen percent return on equity and has increased dividends every year for the past fifteen years; and a company that profoundly affects the lives of eighty percent of all Albertans, I would be surprised if I heard many right answers.

There are companies that meet one or two of these criteria but only one, I believe, that meets them all, that is the company that I am privileged to represent, Canadian Utilities Limited, the tenth largest Alberta-based, investor-owned company in terms of assets, and of these 10, number one in return on equity.

CU is a remarkable Alberta success story that is not as well known as it deserves to be. The reason for this is mainly that Canadian Utilities, as a holding company, has chosen to be known less for itself than for its operating companies: Alberta Power, Canadian Western Natural Gas, Northwestern Utilities and its non-utility subsidiary ATCOR Ltd. CU's primary reason for existence in the fifteen years since its formation as a holding company has been to raise the enormous sums of capital required by its utility subsidiaries, particularly during the booming seventies. Between 1972 and 1987 CU issued over two billion dollars in securities to finance the growth of its three major utilities. This money plus re-invested earnings has been plowed into power plants, pipelines, electrical transmission and distribution facilities, and other projects essential to our growing province. Through taxes, payroll and other operations and maintenance expenditures, the company has contributed another three billion dollars to the Alberta economy in the same 15-year period. This has meant thousands of jobs throughout the province, even during a time when many companies have been forced to lay off employees.

Canadian Utilities traces its beginnings to a flare lighting ceremony in Lethbridge seventy-five years ago on July 12, 1912. This occasion marked the beginning of natural gas service in Lethbridge and was followed a few days later by a similar event in Calgary. The company that had been incorporated to provide the service was Canadian Western Natural Gas Company Limited, the same company that serves Lethbridge and Calgary and much of the rest of southern Alberta today.

The Alberta Natural Gas story began three years earlier when Eugene Coste, formerly a consulting geological engineer for the CPR, brought in the "Old Glory" well on the South Saskatchewan River near Bow Island. Coste had acquired a lease on the Bow Island site from the CPR. He had persuaded Sir Clifford Sifton, former minister of the interior, and Sir William Mackenzie, president of the Canadian Northern Railway, that building a pipeline from the Bow Island field was a sound investment. He then incorporated the company that was first known as the Canadian Western Natural Gas, Light, Heat and Power Company Limited, and proceeded to raise money to finance his first venture.

The line from Bow Island to Calgary was sixteen inches in diameter and one hundred and seventy miles long. It was completed in just eighty-six days and was the longest sixteen-inch line in North America at that time.

Early pipelaying was done by pick and shovel, helped by a steam powered ditching machine. Pipe for the lines was hauled by a horse-drawn wagon. The old livery stable where the horses were kept was located across the street from City Hall in Calgary.

In 1913, after the end of Canadian Western's first full year of operation, the company was serving over 6,000 customers. By 1914, there were 20 wells producing in the Bow Island field.

Northwestern Utilities Limited, Canadian Western's sister company based in Edmonton, was established in 1923 to bring natural gas from the Viking field to the province's capital. Northwestern has had a similarly illustrious history serving the citizens of north-central Alberta.

The name Canadian Utilities Limited was originally given to an amalgamation of small electric power systems in east-central Alberta in 1928. This company expanded in the rural north-central and east-central regions of the province and ultimately into the Yukon and Northwest Territories. In 1972, the name Canadian Utilities Limited was assigned to the holding company and the electric utility became known as Alberta Power Limited.

During the early years, it was almost impossible to get people in Alberta to invest in a local utility company. There wasn't a great deal of money around to be invested, and much of what was around was still going into development of family farms or industries related to agriculture.

To raise large amounts of money, companies usually went to major world centers like London and New York. It was not surprising then, that the controlling interest in the CU group was held by an organization from outside Canada — IU International of Philadelphia.

That changed in 1980 when ATCO Ltd. of Calgary purchased the shares held by IU, giving ATCO the controlling interest in Canadian Utilities. Today CU is virtually one hundred percent Canadian-owned.

The company today serves over six hundred thousand natural gas utility customers and one hundred and fifty thousand electric utility customers. Most are in Alberta; however, through small subsidiaries we serve parts of the Yukon, the Northwest Territories, British Columbia and Saskatchewan.

As you are probably aware, Alberta is the last major stronghold of investor-owned electric utilities in Canada with CU and TransAlta Utilities providing eighty percent of the total Alberta load. Naturally, we are convinced that this has been of great benefit to the province. While there is an element of healthy competition between the two companies, where it has been advantageous to Albertans for us to co-operate we have done so. For example, the construction of the Sheerness generating station is a joint project of Alberta Power and Trans-Alta Utilities, with Alberta Power performing as the operator.

As mentioned earlier, CU has assets in excess of two and one half billion dollars and four thousand employees. We recently reported a fifteen percent increase in earnings from 1986 over 1985 and have managed to maintain healthy earnings throughout the recession. This has been accomplished, in part, through rigorous cost control programs that I believe have made us among the most efficient utility companies in North America.

Contrary to popular belief, Alberta's investor-owned utilities do not enjoy guaranteed profits. The utilities submit rate applications to the Public Utilities Board on a prospective or future test-year basis. Included among forecast costs to be recovered in the rates is an amount for return on investment. Even if this return is approved in total by the Public Utilities Board, which rarely happens, there is no guaranty that it will, in fact, be achieved. Variances between forecast and actual costs and revenues due to abnormally warm weather, forecasting errors or unpredictable events can slash profits. So management is faced with the same pressure to perform and the same daunting uncertainties as the managements of other private sector industries.

One phenomenon we share with practically all Alberta companies these days is a sharp decline in growth rate. This is reflected in declining figures for growth in assets, reduced need for new financing and slower growth in numbers of customers. Electric power consumption is an exception. Because of increased use of electric power for oilfield pumping and the start-up of a number of energy projects in northern Alberta, Alberta Power consumption figures actually increased fourteen percent last year.

Turning to our non-utility operations for a moment, ATCOR Ltd., CU's major non-utility subsidiary, headquartered here in Calgary, is Canada's largest marketer of natural gas direct to final users. It is also actively involved in natural gas processing and oil and gas exploration and development.

ATCOR has a significant interest in the Gulf-Amauligak discovery in the Beaufort Sea. This is a truly world-class find with an estimated eight hundred million barrels of oil. Its development could lead to the delineation of and production from earlier discoveries in the Beaufort-Mackenzie Delta area and the establishment of a whole new oil and gas exploration region in Canada. Development of Amauligak and the construction of a pipeline from the Mackenzie Delta to Alberta would represent a multi-billion dollar megaproject with many associated investment opportunities and economic benefits to the north, to Alberta, and to Canadian Utilities Limited.

CU is actively involved in a number of other promising non-utility enterprises. For example, another subsidiary, Frontec Logistics Corp., a joint venture company owned equally by Canadian Utilities and ATCO, is bidding on the management, operation and maintenance of the planned North Warning System, which is to replace the DEW Line by 1992.

Also relative to Canada's north, Alberta Power's Yukon subsidiary was selected by the territorial government to provide transition management services as electric power assets are transferred from the Northern Canada Power Commission to the Yukon government.

As you have probably guessed, one of my personal objectives this year is to make Alberta's "little-known corporate giant" a little better known. Alberta success stories are rare of late. I believe the CU story is one in which all Albertans can take pride.

The history of the company parallels that of the province and if the past is prologue, then we in CU and all of us as Albertans can look forward to a future full of achievement.

Index to Appendices

APPENDIX A

Current Senior Officers & Former Presidents

Current Senior Officers

R. D. SOUTHERN
Canadian Utilities Limited
Chairman of the Board
and Chief Executive Officer

J. D. WOOD
Canadian Utilities Limited
President
and Chief Operating Officer

C. S. RICHARDSON
Canadian Utilities Limited
Deputy Chairman of the Board
and Chief Financial Officer

W. R. HORTON
Canadian Utilities Limited
Executive Vice President
Utilities

B. M. DAFOE
Northwestern Utilities Limited
President
Canadian Western Natural Gas
Company Limited
President

W. A. ELSER
ATCOR Ltd.
President
and Chief Executive Officer

C. O. TWA
Alberta Power Limited
President

A. J. L. FISHER
Canadian Western Natural Gas
Company Limited
Senior Vice President and General Manager

R. G. LOCK
Northwestern Utilities Limited
Senior Vice President
and General Manager

286

Former Presidents
(In Alphabetical Order)

F. A. BROWNIE

E. COSTE

J. C. DALE

B. M. HILL

E. G. HILL

W. R. HORTON

E. W. KING

J. E. MAYBIN

H. R. MILNER

H. B. PEARSON

M. E. STEWART

B. F. WILSON

C. J. YORATH

D. K. YORATH

Chairmen, Presidents & Directors

Canadian Western Natural Gas Company Limited

HISTORY OF CHAIRMEN

Chairmen	Years Served	Chairmen	Years Served
Hon. C. Sifton	1911 – 1914	D.K. Yorath	1962 – 1970
E. Coste	1914 – 1922	J.E. Maybin	1970 – 1978
E.W. Bowness	1946 – 1949	R.D. Southern	1981 –
H.R. Milner	1949 – 1962		

HISTORY OF PRESIDENTS

Presidents	Years Served	Presidents	Years Served
E. Coste	1911 – 1922	B.F. Willson	1962 – 1965
H.B. Pearson	1922 – 1925	M.E. Stewart	1965 – 1968
C.J. Yorath	1925 – 1932	J.E. Maybin	1968 – 1969
H.R. Milner	1932 – 1949	E.W. King	1969 – 1984
F.A. Brownie	1949 – 1956	W.R. Horton	1984 – 1986
H.R. Milner	1956 – 1956	B.M. Dafoe	1986 –
D.K. Yorath	1956 – 1962		

HISTORY OF DIRECTORS

Directors	Years Served	Directors	Years Served
D.A. Coste	1911 – 1912	I.K. Kerr, Sr.	1914 – 1922
Hon. C. Sifton	1911 – 1925	T.A. McAuley	1914 – 1923
J. Bain	1911 – 1915	J.W. Sifton	1915 – 1925
P. Burns	1911 – 1913	J.R.L. Starr	1915 – 1925
N.S. Russell	1911 – 1923	J.H. Spence	1916 – 1920
E. Coste	1912 – 1922	D.L. Redman	1917 – 1918
J.A. Dennis	1912 – 1912	D. Coste	1919 – 1922
T.M. Fyshe	1912 – 1914	H.B. Pearson	1920 – 1925
C.A. Masten	1912 – 1916	P. Burns	1922 – 1923
W.H. McLaws	1912 – 1917	A.E. Cross	1922 – 1932
A. McLeod	1912 – 1914	H.S. Tims	1922 – 1934

Canadian Western Natural Gas — History of Directors (Continued)

Directors	Years Served	Directors	Years Served
J. Burns	1923 – 1925	G.T. Valentine	1958 – 1959
J.W. Davidson	1923 – 1930	K.L. MacFadyen	1959 – 1973
P.D. Mellon	1923 – 1969	R.S. Munn	1959 – 1970
F.W. Bacon	1925 – 1931	H.M. Hunter	1961 – 1967
P.R. Johnson	1925 – 1933	M.E. Hartnett	1961 – 1966
H.A. Sifton	1925 – 1925	J.E. O'Connor	1961 – 1980
C.J. Yorath	1925 – 1932	D.E. Batchelor	1964 – 1978
A.G. Baalim	1926 – 1965	A.C. Anderson	1965 – 1979
P.M. Chandler	1926 – 1931	J.E. Maybin	1965 – 1981
M.K. DuVal	1930 – 1931	M.E. Stewart	1965 – 1973
F.W. Seymour	1931 – 1942	J.M. Seabrook	1966 – 1972
A.F. Traver	1931 – 1933	G.L. Crawford	1967 –
A. Vermeer	1931 – 1932	D.B. Smith	1968 – 1973
H.S. Watts	1932 – 1947	R.N. Dalby	1969 – 1976
H.R. Milner	1932 – 1969	J.C. Dale	1969 – 1970
J. Garrett	1932 – 1946	E.W. King	1969 – 1986
E.W. Bowness	1933 – 1956	K.A. Biggs	1973 – 1981
S.E. Slipper	1933 – 1940	D.J.A. Cross	1977 –
P.M. Chandler	1934 – 1935	J.H. Pletcher	1977 – 1982
F.A. Smith	1937 – 1959	A.J.L. Fisher	1979 –
D.K. Yorath	1940 – 1949	D.L. Tait	1980 –
T.S. Watson	1942 – 1946	J.A. Campbell	1981 –
F.A. Brownie	1946 – 1956	G.N. Diamond	1981 – 1983
A.D. McNab	1946 – 1951	W.D. Grace	1981 – 1985
H.E. Timmins	1947 – 1957	R.D. Southern	1981 –
R.C. McPherson	1949 – 1966	J.D. Wood	1981 –
F. Stapells	1949 – 1962	B.M. Dafoe	1982 –
H. Butcher III	1951 – 1968	F.G. Swanson	1982 – 1987
D.K. Yorath	1956 – 1976	W.A. Elser	1984 –
H.W. Francis	1956 – 1958	W.R. Horton	1984 –
B.F. Willson	1956 – 1965	C.S. Richardson	1984 –
F.C. Manning	1957 – 1972		

Northwestern Utilities Limited

HISTORY OF CHAIRMEN

Chairmen	Years Served	Chairmen	Years Served
P.M. Chandler	1924 – 1931	D.K. Yorath	1962 – 1969
F.W. Seymour	1931 – 1934	J.E. Maybin	1969 – 1974
E.W. Bowness	1946 – 1949	R.D. Southern	1981 –
H.R. Milner	1949 – 1962		

Northwestern Utilities Limited (Continued)
HISTORY OF PRESIDENTS

Presidents	Years Served	Presidents	Years Served
E.G. Hill	1923 – 1924	B.F. Willson	1962 – 1965
C.J. Yorath	1924 – 1932	M.E. Stewart	1965 – 1968
H.R. Milner	1932 – 1949	J.E. Maybin	1968 – 1969
F.A. Brownie	1949 – 1956	E.W. King	1969 – 1984
H.R. Milner	1956 – 1956	W.R. Horton	1984 – 1986
D.K. Yorath	1956 – 1962	B.M. Dafoe	1986 –

HISTORY OF DIRECTORS

Directors	Years Served	Directors	Years Served
E.H. Wands	1923 – 1924	H.S. Watts	1932 – 1946
E.G. Hill	1923 – 1924	P.D. Mellon	1932 – 1946
J.H. Spence	1923 – 1925	E.W. Bowness	1932 – 1954
P.M. Chandler	1923 – 1931	H.S. Tims	1932 – 1934
F.W. Bacon	1923 – 1931	C.H. Spencer	1933 – 1937
D.C. Henny	1923 – 1926	A.F. Harvey	1933 – 1934
P.R. Johnson	1923 – 1932	W.F. Corl	1933 – 1935
G. de B. Keim	1923 – 1924	P.M. Chandler	1934 – 1936
S. Rogers	1923 – 1932	H.W. Braden	1934 – 1936
T.A. McAuley	1923 – 1928	R. Martland	1935 – 1958
J.L. Lilienthal	1923 – 1926	F.H. Russell	1936 – 1949
R.P. Buell	1924 – 1924	F.A. Smith	1937 – 1959
A.S. Kimberly	1924 – 1931	D.A. McIntosh	1939 – 1939
C.J. Yorath	1924 – 1932	T.S. Watson	1942 – 1946
G. de B. Keim	1924 – 1930	A.D. McNab	1946 – 1951
P.A. Thomson	1925 – 1927	J. Garrett	1946 – 1948
H.C. Flood	1925 – 1929	F.A. Brownie	1946 – 1956
R.P. Buell	1925 – 1928	H.W. Francis	1946 – 1958
J. Garrett	1926 – 1948	R.C. McPherson	1948 – 1949
H.R. Milner	1926 – 1969	D.K. Yorath	1949 – 1976
A.H. Gilmour	1927 – 1933	O.C. McIntyre	1949 – 1968
H.C. Phelan	1928 – 1931	A.M. MacDonald	1949 – 1963
M.K. DuVal	1929 – 1931	J.R. Munro	1949 – 1960
F.W. Seymour	1931 – 1941	H. Butcher III	1951 – 1968
P.A. Erlach	1931 – 1932	G. Gaetz	1954 – 1955
A. Vermeer	1931 – 1932	F.P. Layton	1956 – 1956
A.F. Traver	1931 – 1933	P.L.P. Macdonnell	1956 – 1956
J.P. Reilly	1931 – 1933	R.C. McPherson	1956 – 1968
D.K. Yorath	1932 – 1932	B.F. Willson	1956 – 1965

Northwestern Utilities Limited — History of Directors (Continued)

Directors	Years Served	Directors	Years Served
F.P. Layton	1958 – 1958	J.L. Schlosser	1972 –
P.L.P. Macdonnell	1958 – 1958	K.A. Biggs	1973 – 1981
J.C. Dale	1958 – 1970	H. Hole	1974 –
A.G. Stewart	1958 – 1969	J.E. Maybin	1974 – 1981
K.L. MacFadyen	1959 – 1973	A.H. Mitchell	1975 – 1986
F.T. Jenner	1960 – 1972	J.H. Pletcher	1977 – 1982
G. Gaetz	1960 – 1966	B.M. Dafoe	1979 –
J.L. McIntyre	1960 – 1971	J.E. Barrett	1981 –
M.E. Stewart	1960 – 1973	A. Schieman	1981 – 1984
Dr. R.M. Parsons	1962 – 1974	R.D. Southern	1981 –
P.L.P. Macdonnell	1963 – 1963	P.G. White	1981 – 1982
J.B. Whelihan	1963 – 1965	J.D. Wood	1981 –
J.M. Seabrook	1965 – 1972	W.D. Grace	1982 – 1985
J.E. Maybin	1965 – 1974	R.G. Lock	1982 –
A.R. McBain	1966 –	W.A. Elser	1984 –
D.B. Collier	1968 – 1975	W.R. Horton	1984 –
W.S. McGregor	1968 – 1972	C.S. Richardson	1984 –
E.W. King	1969 – 1986	J.E. Lougheed	1986 –
R.N. Dalby	1969 – 1976	S.D. McGregor	1986 –
D.B. Smith	1969 – 1973		

Canadian Utilities Limited

HISTORY OF CHAIRMEN

Chairmen	Years Served	Chairmen	Years Served
P.M. Chandler	1928 – 1931	J.C. Dale	1968 – 1969
F.W. Seymour	1931 – 1934	J.E. Maybin	1969 – 1981
E.W. Bowness	1946 – 1949	R.D. Southern	1981 –
H.R. Milner	1949 – 1968		

HISTORY OF PRESIDENTS

Presidents	Years Served	Presidents	Years Served
C.J. Yorath	1927 – 1932	H.R. Milner	1956 – 1956
H.R. Milner	1932 – 1949	J.C. Dale	1956 – 1968
B.M. Hill	1949 – 1954	E.W. King	1968 – 1984
F.A. Brownie	1954 – 1956	J.D. Wood	1984 –

Canadian Utilities Limited (Continued)

HISTORY OF DIRECTORS

Directors	Years Served	Directors	Years Served
J. Garrett	1927 – 1928	K.L. MacFadyen	1959 – 1973
C.J. Yorath	1927 – 1932	B.V. Massie	1960 – 1969
H.R. Milner	1927 – 1969	J.N. Ford	1963 – 1969
P.M. Chandler	1927 – 1931	E.W. King	1968 –
F.W. Bacon	1927 – 1931	J.M. Seabrook	1968 – 1980
H.S. Tims	1928 – 1934	D.R.B. McArthur	1969 –
H.S. Watts	1929 – 1946	F.C. Manning	1969 – 1972
F.W. Seymour	1931 – 1941	A.F. Shortell	1969 – 1972
A.F. Traver	1931 – 1933	J.E. Maybin	1969 – 1981
E.W. Bowness	1932 – 1952	M.E. Stewart	1969 – 1973
D.K. Yorath	1933 – 1949	G.L. Crawford	1972 –
B.M. Hill	1934 – 1963	F.T. Jenner	1972 – 1976
F.A. Smith	1937 – 1959	W.S. McGregor	1972 –
T.S. Watson	1942 – 1946	P.L.P. Macdonnell	1973 – 1983
A.D. McNab	1945 – 1951	W.D.H. Gardiner	1974 – 1980
F.A. Brownie	1946 – 1956	W.S. McLeese	1974 – 1980
J.G. MacGregor	1946 – 1950	R.F. Calman	1976 – 1980
H.E. Timmins	1946 – 1947	K.A. Biggs	1977 – 1981
G.E. Kelly	1947 – 1968	C.N.W. Woodward	1977 – 1979
G.L. Cooke	1949 – 1969	R.D. Southern	1977 – 1979
W. Poxon	1949 – 1957	R.D. Southern	1980 –
J.E. Thomson	1949 – 1959	W.L. Britton	1980 –
J.C. Dale	1951 – 1970	C.S. Richardson	1980 –
H. Butcher III	1951 – 1968	N.W. Robertson	1980 –
R. Belzil	1952 – 1954	V.L. Horte	1981 –
W.J. Lambert	1954 – 1960	B.K. French	1981 –
R. Martland	1956 – 1956	R.W.A. Laidlaw	1981 –
H.W. Francis	1956 – 1958	D.M. Ritchie	1981 –
R. Martland	1957 – 1958	J.D. Wood	1981 –
F.P. Layton	1958 – 1968	W.D. Grace	1981 – 1985
J.N. Ford	1958 – 1958	H.E. Joudrie	1982 –
D.K. Yorath	1958 – 1976	C.M. Leitch	1984 –
L.F. Snyder	1959 – 1972	W.R. Horton	1985 –

Alberta Power Limited

HISTORY OF CHAIRMEN

Chairmen	Years Served	Chairmen	Years Served
J.E. Maybin	1971 – 1973	R.D. Southern	1981 –

Alberta Power Limited (Continued)

HISTORY OF PRESIDENTS

Presidents	Years Served	Presidents	Years Served
E.W. King	1971 – 1984	C.O. Twa	1986 –
W.R. Horton	1984 – 1986		

HISTORY OF DIRECTORS

Directors	Years Served	Directors	Years Served
J.E. Maybin	1971 – 1973	K. Provost	1980 – 1985
E.W. King	1971 – 1986	W.L. Britton	1981 –
K.L. MacFadyen	1971 – 1973	W.A. Kmet	1981 –
D.K. Yorath	1971 – 1976	C.S. Richardson	1981 –
P.L.P. Macdonnell	1971 – 1972	C.N. Simpson	1981 – 1981
A.F. Shortell	1972 – 1976	J.D. Wood	1981 –
R.B. Hougen	1972 –	K.D. Zahnd	1981 –
K.A. Biggs	1973 – 1981	K.B. Purdie	1981 – 1981
G. Ford	1973 –	R.D. Southern	1981 –
R.N. Dalby	1973 – 1976	W.D. Grace	1981 – 1985
J.E. Maybin	1974 – 1981	C.N. Simpson	1982 – 1985
R.A. Snyder	1976 –	W.R. Horton	1984 –
R.J. Nelson	1977 – 1985	C.O. Twa	1985 –
W.G. Sterling	1977 – 1980		

CU Enterprises Inc.
(ATCOR Ltd.)

HISTORY OF CHAIRMEN

Chairmen	Years Served
R.D. Southern	1982 –

HISTORY OF PRESIDENTS

Presidents	Years Served	Presidents	Years Served
J.D. Wood	1982 – 1984	W.A. Elser	1984 –

HISTORY OF DIRECTORS

Directors	Years Served	Directors	Years Served
W.D. Grace	1982 – 1985	C.S. Richardson	1982 –
E.W. King	1982 – 1986	N.W. Robertson	1982 –

CU Enterprises Inc. (ATCOR Ltd.) — History of Directors (Continued)

Directors	Years Served	Directors	Years Served
R.D. Southern	1982 –	R.W.A. Laidlaw	1984 –
W.A. Elser	1984 –	J.D. Wood	1984 –
W.R. Horton	1984 –		

Honored Employees

Employee Association Presidents

CANADIAN WESTERN NATURAL GAS COMPANY LIMITED
NATURAL GAS EMPLOYEES' WELFARE ASSOCIATION

Presidents	Years Served	Presidents	Years Served
Bill Reid	1958	Chuck Restell	1972
Tom Grafton	1959	Dennis McIvor	1973
Lou Benini	1960	Bob Fisk	1974
Carl Windsor	1961	Chuck Restell	1975
Ray McDougall	1962	Jack MacDonald	1976
Earl Moore	1963	Gordon Lee	1977
Jim Henry	1964	George Sutton	1978
Bud Proctor	1965	Jim MacLean	1979 – 1980
Dick Farmer	1966	Stan Chapman	1981 – 1982
John Ellison	1967	Ken DeMille	1983
Jim Nichol	1968	Kristy Hutton	1984
Len Marshall	1969	Roger Miller	1985
Neil Shaben	1970	Wes Witherspoon	1986
Bill Kushnir	1971	Tom Funk	1987

NORTHWESTERN UTILITIES LIMITED
NATURAL GAS EMPLOYEE BENEFITS ASSOCIATION

Presidents	Years Served	Presidents	Years Served
Ken Wolsey	1958	Gerry White	1971 – 1972
Bob McClymont	1959	Ed Neumann	1973 – 1974
Peter Marples	1960	Trevor Smith/	1975
Duke Reynolds	1961	John MacDonald	
Dave Lawson	1962	John MacDonald	1976
John Peets	1963 – 1965	Dennis Berge	1977 – 1978
Bill Hite	1966	Graham Morris	1979
Ron Gibbons	1967	Cam Ross/	1980
Chuck Moore	1968 – 1969	Trevor Smith	
Bud Townsend	1970	Wayne Ogden	1981

Employee Association Presidents — Northwestern Utilities (Continued)

Presidents	Years Served	Presidents	Years Served
George Ambler	1982 – 1984	Jim Orchin	1986
Bill Lingley	1985	Bruce Ratcliff	1987

ALBERTA POWER LIMITED EMPLOYEE ASSOCIATION

Presidents	Years Served	Presidents	Years Served
Tom Wharton	1969	Mike Cooper	1980
Pat McGuire	1970	Ken Fate	1981
Ken Anderson	1971 – 1972	Bryan Johnson	1982
Dave Ziegler	1973 – 1974	Earl Stewart	1983
Jim Haiste	1975 – 1976	Brian Taylor	1984
Bill Porter	1977	Larry Tutt	1985
Peter Walmsley	1978	Bryan Rosenberger	1986
Jim Douglas	1979	Dave Sexsmith	1987

Suggester-of-the-Year Award Winners

CANADIAN WESTERN NATURAL GAS COMPANY LIMITED

Award Winners	Year	Award Winners	Year
Jim Howie	1957	Allan Gall	1973
Earl Moore/	1958	Layne Ment	1974
Bill Reid		Roger Miller	1975
Earl Purdy	1959	Ken Morgan	1976 & 1977
Irvin Johnson	1962 & 1965	Bob Townsend/	1978
Ray Bodman	1963	Glen Graham	
Art Atkinson	1964	Abe Rafih	1979
Earl Moore	1966	Ross Briosi/	1980
Bert Volgelenzang	1967	Dale Filkowski	
De Jong		Frank Gee	1981
Richard Powys-	1968	Brenda Roeke	1982 & 1984
Lybbe		Reah Tharby	1983
Ray McDougall	1969	Laurie Brazeau	1985
Tommy McLean	1970	Alice Peterson	1986
Dave Durnie	1971	Grant Gale/	1987
John Chase	1972	Troy Jamieson	

Suggester-of-the-Year Award Winners (Continued)

NORTHWESTERN UTILITIES LIMITED

Award Winners	Year	Award Winners	Year
Adam Knoll	1960	Dennis Hutton	1975
George Gregoreschuk	1961	Napoleon Legroulx	1976
Lloyd Delisle	1962	Jim Sharrow	1977
Nick Esak	1963	William Wiens	1978
Charles Desilets	1964	Harold Christiansen	1979
John Maybin	1965	Linda Fuller	1980
Eric Beniston	1966	George Ostashek	1981
Karl Ploc	1967	Julie Huot	1982
Robin Estlin	1968	Herbert Lauman	1983
Oliver Robin	1969	Garry Gould	1984
Nicholas Borynec	1970	Murray Hafso/	1985
William Tennant	1971	Arnold Sagmoen	
Tom Wilkerson	1972	Jim Bacon	1986
Gary Gray	1973	Bill Fownes	1987
Arthur Goutbeck	1974		

President's Award Winners

Award Winners	Year	Award Winners	Year
Norman Bowser/	1968*	Bill Dyck/	1984
Mills Parker/		Bill Dobson	
Roger Wagar		Tim McEvoy	1986
Ronald Krisa	1968	Ed Ladret	1987
Pal Ferguson	1976	Don Lowe/	1988
Bill McNeill	1980	Gene Zadvorny	

*The President's Award was established in 1968 by Murray E. Stewart, then President of Canadian Western Natural Gas Company Limited and Northwestern Utilities Limited.

APPENDIX D

Utility Systems Maps

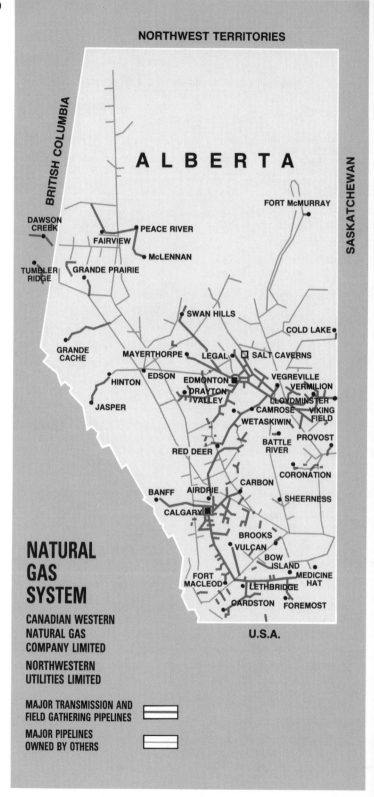

NORTHWEST TERRITORIES

BRITISH COLUMBIA

SASKATCHEWAN

ALBERTA

FORT McMURRAY

DAWSON CREEK

PEACE RIVER

FAIRVIEW

McLENNAN

TUMBLER RIDGE

GRANDE PRAIRIE

SWAN HILLS

COLD LAKE

GRANDE CACHE

MAYERTHORPE

LEGAL

SALT CAVERNS

HINTON

EDSON

EDMONTON

VEGREVILLE

VERMILION

DRAYTON VALLEY

LLOYDMINSTER

JASPER

CAMROSE

VIKING FIELD

WETASKIWIN

BATTLE RIVER

PROVOST

RED DEER

CORONATION

CARBON

BANFF

AIRDRIE

SHEERNESS

CALGARY

BROOKS

VULCAN

BOW ISLAND

FORT MACLEOD

MEDICINE HAT

LETHBRIDGE

CARDSTON

FOREMOST

U.S.A.

NATURAL GAS SYSTEM

CANADIAN WESTERN
NATURAL GAS
COMPANY LIMITED

NORTHWESTERN
UTILITIES LIMITED

MAJOR TRANSMISSION AND
FIELD GATHERING PIPELINES

MAJOR PIPELINES
OWNED BY OTHERS

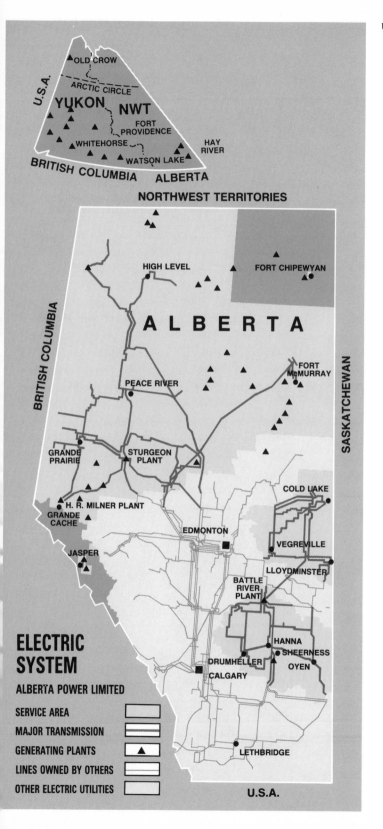

OLD CROW

ARCTIC CIRCLE

U.S.A.

YUKON   NWT

FORT
PROVIDENCE

WHITEHORSE

HAY
RIVER

WATSON LAKE

BRITISH COLUMBIA   ALBERTA

NORTHWEST TERRITORIES

HIGH LEVEL

FORT CHIPEWYAN

ALBERTA

BRITISH COLUMBIA

SASKATCHEWAN

PEACE RIVER

FORT
McMURRAY

GRANDE
PRAIRIE

STURGEON
PLANT

COLD LAKE

H. R. MILNER PLANT

GRANDE
CACHE

EDMONTON

VEGREVILLE

JASPER

LLOYDMINSTER

BATTLE
RIVER
PLANT

HANNA
SHEERNESS

**ELECTRIC
SYSTEM**

DRUMHELLER

OYEN

CALGARY

ALBERTA POWER LIMITED

SERVICE AREA

MAJOR TRANSMISSION

GENERATING PLANTS ▲

LINES OWNED BY OTHERS

OTHER ELECTRIC UTILITIES

LETHBRIDGE

U.S.A.

Communities Served
& Start-of-Service by the Companies

Canadian Western Natural Gas Company Limited

Community	Served Since	Community	Served Since
Acme	1959	Claresholm	1913
Airdrie	1956	Cluny	1976
Aldersyde	1970	Coaldale	1947
Banff	1951	Coalhurst	1955
Barnwell	1947	Cochrane	1952
Barons	1959	Conrich	1960
Bassano	1960	Cowley	1971
Beaver Mines	1981	Cranford	1956
Beiseker	1959	Cremona	1962
Bellevue	1962	Crossfield	1956
Big Valley	1965	Dalemead	1976
Black Diamond	1930	Delburne	1956
Blairmore	1962	DeWinton	1955
Bow Island	1982	Diamond City	1956
Bowden	1956	Didsbury	1956
Bragg Creek	1969	Duchess	1960
Brocket	1974	Elnora	1960
Brooks	1912	Enchant	1956
Burdett	1930	Exshaw	1951
Calgary	1912	Foremost	1930
Canmore	1960	Fort Macleod	1913
Carbon	1959	Frank	1962
Cardston	1955	Gem	1960
Carmangay	1959	Gleichen	1976
Carseland	1977	Glenwood	1969
Cayley	1930	Granum	1913
Cessford	1964	Grassy Lake	1954
Champion	1959	Harvie Heights	1965
Cheadle	1977	High River	1927
Chestermere Lake	1970	Hillcrest	1962
Chin	1977	Hillspring	1969

Canadian Western Natural Gas — Communities Served (Continued)

Community	Served Since	Community	Served Since
Hussar	1960	Picture Butte	1956
Huxley	1960	Purple Springs	1966
Indus	1976	Raymond	1955
Innisfail	1955	Redwood Meadows	1978
Iron Springs	1967	Rockyford	1960
Irricana	1959	Rosebud	1960
Kathyrn	1960	Rosemary	1960
Keoma	1960	Seebe	1951
Kirkcaldy	1959	Shaughnessy	1956
Lac Des Arcs	1971	Shepard	1971
Langdon	1977	Spring Coulee	1955
Lethbridge	1912	Standard	1960
Linden	1960	Standoff	1970
Lomond	1973	Stavely	1927
Longview	1981	Stirling	1955
Magrath	1955	Strathmore	1959
Milk River	1971	Swalwell	1960
Monarch	1949	Taber	1929
Morley	1952	Torrington	1960
Mountain View	1966	Turin	1967
Namaka	1974	Trochu	1960
Nanton	1912	Turner Valley	1981
Nobleford	1956	Vauxhall	1957
Okotoks	1912	Vulcan	1959
Olds	1956	Wardlow	1981
Parkland	1927	Welling	1955
Penhold	1956	Wimborne	1960

Northwestern Utilities Limited

Community	Served Since	Community	Served Since
Alberta Beach	1968	Beaverlodge	1964
Alix	1959	Bentley	1960
Amisk	1969	Berwyn	1972
Argentia Beach	1982	Bittern Lake	1949
Bashaw	1959	Blackfalds	1949

Northwestern Utilities Limited — Communities Served (Continued)

Community	Served Since	Community	Served Since
Bon Accord	1954	Irma	1951
Breton	1959	Itaska Beach	1982
Bruderheim	1956	Jasper	1972
Camrose	1946	Lacombe	1946
Caroline	1962	Lamont	1956
Chipman	1956	Lavoy	1957
Clive	1961	Legal	1953
Clyde	1967	Lloydminster	1984
Cold Lake	1979	Lougheed	1970
Consort	1958	Mannville	1954
Coronation	1979	Mayerthorpe	1966
Czar	1969	McLennan	1972
Donnelly	1972	Millet	1956
Drayton Valley	1957	Minburn	1957
Eaglesham	1972	Mirror	1959
Eckville	1961	Mundare	1956
Edgerton	1972	Nampa	1972
Edmonton	1923	Onoway	1956
Edson	1956	Oyen	1958
Entwistle	1957	Peace River	1972
Evansburg	1957	Point Alison	1974
Falher	1972	Ponoka	1946
Fairview	1972	Provost	1959
Fort McMurray	1972	Red Deer	1947
Fox Creek	1972	Rimbey	1960
Gibbons	1953	Rocky Mountain House	1961
Girouxville	1972	Rycroft	1972
Golden Days	1982	Ryley	1923
Grand Centre	1979	Sangudo	1966
Grande Prairie	1972	Seba Beach	1957
Grimshaw	1972	Sexsmith	1972
Hardisty	1967	Sherwood Park	1955
Hines Creek	1972	Silver Beach	1957
Hinton	1956	Spirit River	1972
Holden	1923	Spruce Grove	1955
Hughenden	1969	St. Albert	1951
Hythe	1964	Stony Plain	1955
Innisfree	1957	Swan Hills	1965

Northwestern Utilities Limited — Communities Served (Continued)

Community	Served Since	Community	Served Since
Sylvan Lake	1956	Viking	1923
Thorsby	1959	Warburg	1959
Tofield	1923	Wetaskiwin	1946
Vegreville	1940	Whitecourt	1963
Vermilion	1941	Wildwood	1957
Veteran	1968		

Northland Utilities (B.C.) Limited

Community	Served Since	Community	Served Since
Dawson Creek	1951	Rolla	1963
Pouce Coupe	1954	Tumbler Ridge	1983

Northland Utilities (NWT) Limited

Community	Served Since	Community	Served Since
Fort Providence	1964	Hay River	1951

Alberta Power Limited

Community	Served Since	Community	Served Since
Alliance	1928	Forestburg	1928
Andrew	1931	Fort Chipewyan	1959
Beaverlodge	1930	Fort MacKay	1969
Bonnyville	1947	Fort McMurray	1953
Castor	1927	Fort Providence	1964
Cold Lake	1956	Fort Vermilion	1957
Consort	1954	Grand Centre	1957
Coronation	1928	Grande Cache	1970
Drumheller	1927	Grande Prairie	1928
Fairview	1937	Grimshaw	1940
Falher	1943	Hanna	1927

Alberta Power Limited — Communities Served (Continued)

Community	Served Since	Community	Served Since
Hay River	1951	Spirit River	1952
High Level	1970	Stettler	1928
High Prairie	1945	St. Paul	1938
Jasper	1942	Swan Hills	1960
Lloydminster	1927	Three Hills	1928
Manning	1957	Two Hills	1936
Peace River	1934	Valleyview	1958
Rainbow Lake	1968	Vegreville	1927
Slave Lake	1957	Vermilion	1947
Smoky Lake	1946		

The Yukon Electrical Company Limited

Community	Served Since	Community	Served Since
Dawson*	1987	Old Crow	1964
Faro*	1987	Watson Lake	1959
Haines Junction	1958	Whitehorse	1958

*Served on behalf of Yukon Energy Corporation

Brief Histories

History of the Group Accident and Sickness Fund

Health care for employees was a rarity in the 1930s when the three Alberta utility companies pioneered a program they would administer themselves for the benefit of their staffs. It continues today as a unique company service for both employees and pensioners.

Called the Group Accident and Sickness Fund it has come a long way since it was founded on March 31, 1935.

During its first year the fund provided coverage for fewer than five hundred employees. Premiums collected from the staff amounted to seventeen thousand dollars. Just over five thousand dollars was paid out in claims.

In contrast, in a recent year the fund received $1.3 million in premiums and paid out more than $1.2 million in claims. It had assets well over half a million dollars.

Approximately four thousand employees are participating in the fund today — staff members of Alberta Power, Canadian Western Natural Gas, Northwestern Utilities, Canadian Utilities and ATCOR Ltd., along with associate and subsidiary companies. Taking into account the dependents of these employees, along with pensioners who have retired and their dependents, the fund is covering more than ten thousand persons.

From its modest beginnings the fund has become increasingly sophisticated. It now provides salary indemnity benefits for a period of two years, relative to non-occupational sickness or injury. In addition a schedule of coverages is provided for prescription drugs, ambulance services, glasses, hearing aids, limited hospital and home nursing services, semi-private hospital ward fees (Alberta rates) and limited travelling and accommodation expenses associated with covered benefits not available in outlying rural communities.

Within the parameters laid down by the trustees, the fund also makes loans to employees from its reserves.

FOUNDERS OF THE FUND

In the early thirties, during the great depression, the employees of Canadian Western Natural Gas, Light, Heat and Power Company Limited, Canadian Utilities Limited and Northwestern Utilities Limited had a group accident and sickness policy of sorts with a company called the General Accident Assurance Company. In the fall of 1934 this company decided it did not wish to continue insuring the utilities group and it cancelled its coverage effective midnight, March 31, 1935.

Meetings of the employees of the group of utilities were held to establish a self-insured plan to replace the cancelled coverage. A proposed memorandum of coverage was drawn up by Dennis Yorath. It was accepted by the group, and a board of administration, consisting of two representatives from each company, was elected.

The source of income was established in a premium schedule, to be paid partly by the companies and partly by employees. The primary aim of the fund was to provide mutual assistance to its members, who through illness or injury might become overburdened financially through the cost of medical care and loss of earnings.

The first trustees of the fund were Dennis Yorath and Frank Paterson of Canadian Western and Thomas Montgomery of Canadian Utilities. Yorath was appointed secretary. Additional members of the board of administrators were Lee Drumheller, Canadian Utilities; C. W. Brown, Canadian Western; Ted Megas and W.N. Watkins both from Northwestern. The trustees and administrators managed the fund and paid claims based on schedules of coverage provided for in the agreement.

Accident indemnity provided coverage from the fourteenth day if the disability exceeded thirty days, with a maximum of one year's coverage. The insured was covered for sickness from the fourteenth day for a maximum of a year. Employees over sixty years of age could not claim for more than thirteen weeks of benefit for the same or related illnesses within the same twelve consecutive months. Coverage for medical fees was subject to a maximum of $60, with $10 deductible. If the illness was not a disabling illness, the maximum medical fee was $25.

It was decided not to incorporate under the Societies Act. Today the fund is still an unincorporated trust.

During the depression and the Second World War the companies managed to keep their Accident and Sickness Fund in healthy shape despite many hardships. It was not until the spring of 1948, long after the war was over, that a full-time secretary was appointed to take care of the day-to-day administration.

That was a good year. Not only did the board appoint a full-time secretary in the person of Gordon Tranter, they also increased the coverage substantially. A family coverage plan was developed and limited coverage was extended to pensioners.

The years that followed saw more improvements, including better coverage for spouses and full health coverage for dependents of employees.

Gordon Tranter retired from the companies on November 30, 1957, and was replaced by Bob Nobes as secretary of the fund. Hal Robbins was chairman at

306

the time. Looking back today and recalling the early years of the fund, he reminisces: "It was touch and go for a small group which was not backed by any assets to speak of. We probably never operated at a profit if you included the cost of the secretary and the people who handled the fund. This was all paid for by the company. It was only in this way that in my time we gradually built up a nest egg of around two hundred thousand dollars."

The year 1959 brought another milestone. A committee was established to make a study of the salary indemnity provisions and premium structure. An actuarial consultant was retained to make a complete survey and report on the overall operation of the fund. The result was that a new schedule of premiums was established, salary indemnity provisions were upgraded and permanent disability benefits were increased.

MEDICARE BRINGS CHANGES

In the early sixties the fund was paying out so much in claims and benefits that it was operating at a deficit, so the premiums had to be increased. Additional revenues came in at a rate of about nine thousand dollars per year, and the fund was again on sound footing.

The year 1967 brought medicare, both federal and provincial. The fund was obliged to make adjustments to its provisions of coverage. The deductible on physicians' services was discontinued and various other changes were made. In the months that followed a complete restructuring of the fund was required and on July 1, 1969, when medicare became operative in Alberta, this was put into effect.

In the early seventies the long-term disability benefit policy held by Dominion Life Assurance Company came up for renewal. Bids were requested from the insurance market. Sun Life Assurance came in with the best package and received the contract.

The late seventies saw still more improvements in coverage provided by the fund, including better payments for such expenses as dentistry, glasses and hearing aids. Coverage was introduced, too, to help pay for the services of clinical psychologists.

As the fund has grown over half a century, the trustees, made up of company and employee representatives, have kept it responsive to the changing needs of employees, amending the agreement as needed to provide new or higher benefits to keep up with inflation, and deleting from the fund coverages assumed by various government programs.

Today the management of the Group Accident and Sickness Fund is a full-time responsibility of a secretary, an administrator and several claims adjudicators. These staff officers assess and pay claims, maintain up-to-date records on members and their families and generally manage and administer the trust fund in accordance with the policies and guidelines established by the board of trustees.

History of the Pensioners Associations

The Courier of January 1945 reported that Northwestern Utilities pensioner A.W. (Art) Holmes had suggested the formation of a pensioners association. It was to be purely experimental, to see what interest there was in providing retired employees with the opportunity to keep in touch with fellow pensioners and the company in which they had been employed.

The first meeting attracted seven pensioners, and the interest shown continued through subsequent meetings until January 1947, when the association was formally established, an executive elected and a constitution and program of activities developed. The association became known as Northwestern Utilities Old Timers Association (NUOTA).

Art Holmes and Bill Watkins were elected the first president and secretary-treasurer respectively, and plans were laid to hold periodic social and dinner meetings.

Not much changed in the association for more than a decade. Art Holmes remained as president for sixteen continuous years. During those years the principal activities of the association consisted of quarterly meetings and the annual company-sponsored Christmas dinner.

The ongoing interest of the original members, augmented by the enthusiasm of new members, confirmed the value of the association. Following the resignation of Art Holmes as president in 1961, Jim Robinson was elected to fill that office. He continued in the chair until 1965 when he was succeeded by Doug Watson, who in turn was followed in 1967 by Jack Thorogood.

When Jack Thorogood took over as president with A.E. (Eddie) Shiels as secretary, thirteen members attended his first meeting. Thorogood and his executive continued in office until November 1973 when Glen Millard became president. Eddie Shiels continued as secretary until the fall of 1975. Attendance at meetings averaged from ten to twelve members during the sixties, increasing to twenty-five in the seventies and forty-five in the eighties.

Membership, as first recorded in 1967, stood at ninety with fifty-five of these residing in the Edmonton area. Following the restructuring of the companies in 1972, the name of the association was tentatively referred to as the Canadian Utilities Old Timers Association and included members from both the old and new Canadian Utilities as well as Northwestern Utilities.

ALBERTA POWER JOINS THE RANKS

The electric utilities had never formed a pensioners association of their own as their pensioners were too widely scattered throughout their service area. However, in May 1974 when the Canadian Utilities Pensioners Association

(Northern) was formed, the new association included in its ranks pensioners from Alberta Power and Canadian Utilities.

In 1978 Ernie Harrison became the first Alberta Power pensioner to hold an executive position in the association. Anna Murphy, also of Alberta Power, became the first female pensioner to hold office and was secretary for four years.

The membership of over one hundred and forty, which was achieved by the late seventies, included seventy-two Edmonton area residents and twenty newly added retirees mainly in and around the Drumheller area.

The fourteen presidents of the northern chapter of the pensioners association, which served the group from 1967 to 1987, were as follows:

1967-73	Jack Thorogood	1980-81	Steve Hawrelak
1973-75	Glen Millard	1981-82	Ben Banks
1975-76	John Peets	1982-83	Austin Nicoll
1976-77	Roy Mabey	1983-84	Jack Livingstone
1977-78	Graham Dale	1984-85	Ted Tutt
1978-79	Ernie Harrison	1985-86	John Gray
1979-80	Walter Prausa	1986-87	Walter Mitchell

CANADIAN WESTERN PENSIONERS ORGANIZE

The Canadian Western Pensioners' Association began in the early fifties and, like its northern counterpart, was at first known as the Old Timers Association. Its inaugural meeting was held Friday evening, April 24, 1953 at the company's main office in Calgary.

Officers elected for the first year were: president, George Wrathall; vice-president, Frank Platt and secretary-treasurer, Joe Chase. The meetings of old timers in those early days were all-male events, except for a female touch with the preparation of food and refreshments by the home service department.

Joe Chase served as the first secretary of the southern association, and was one of its leading lights during its formative years. The inter-company personnel departments took an active part in helping to organize events.

The team of Phil Clarke, Boyd Willett and Hal Robbins shepherded many of the early activities of the Canadian Western association and arranged the necessary co-ordination with company management.

The Canadian Western group's first president, George Wrathall, was followed by nineteen presidents over the years. Here is the complete list:

1955	George Wrathall	1963	Joe Chase
1956-57	Wilf Gray	1964	Doc Alexander
1958-59	Fred Humphries	1965	Porter Mellon
1960	Tommy Dodds	1966	Oscar Doten
1961-62	Harry Patten	1967	George Craig

1968	Dave Dunn	1978-79	Joe Clitheroe
1969	Lloyd McPhee	1980-81	Art Smith
1970-73	Harry Hunter	1981-82	Tom Fowler
1974-75	Boyd Willett	1982-84	Harold McFadyen
1976-78	Hal Robbins	1984-87	Tom Grafton

It was during Lloyd McPhee's term of office in 1969 that the group decided it would rather be known as the "pensioners" than the "Old Timers". From that point on the name of the association became officially the Canadian Western Pensioners Association.

In the late sixties the women began joining the ranks of the association. Among the first names were Ida Nelson, Nell Macartney and Marie McCaffary.

The highlights of association activities have included some outstanding bus trips. In the fall of 1978, for example, an overnight trip took the group to Adams River in B.C. to see the peak of the salmon run which occurs every four years. Bus trips were made to Watson Lodge in the Kananaskis Valley, featuring the cooking of steak dinners on gas barbecues.

In 1986 a trip was made to Drumheller to tour the new provincial museum, and 1987 saw two buses, carrying a total of 82 pensioners, visiting all the venues of the 1988 Olympic Winter Games.

"It is obvious a strong *esprit de corps* exists among the members of CWPA," said Hal Robbins in a report on the group's activities. "Now over two hundred employees from the company, representing many different positions and occupations, meld together in one common bond of fellowship."

On May 2, 1985 the total number of pensioners in the CU group of companies hit the five-hundred mark. Since reaching that milestone, the numbers are growing at a rate of more than sixteen a year.

History of ATCO Ltd.

A TCO Ltd. is the Alberta based holding company for a worldwide organization of companies engaged principally in the areas of energy and resources. Formerly best known for its innovative work in the supply of transportable industrial structures, ATCO Group has expanded its operations in recent years to embrace other areas of energy development and servicing.

Like many family businesses, ATCO started almost from scratch, with four thousand dollars saved up by a Calgary fireman and his teenage son to launch a utility trailer rental business in 1946, with the goal of earning money to send the son to medical school. Many large corporations, of course, have had a similarly humble start, but ATCO is different. Different because most of the original players still manage it, continuing to shape an industrial giant that is a model of creative entrepreneurship.

The Calgary fireman, whose desire for something better for his son led to ATCO's beginning, was S. Donald Southern, who in 1987, at the age of seventy-eight, held the title of board chairman. The son, Ronald D. Southern, now deputy chairman and chief executive officer, is noted for his foresight as corporate planner and motivator. "He has the ability to look ahead and judge what a turn in the economy is going to mean for the company," one of his executives said.

From the beginning, Ron Southern worked in the business alongside his father, greasing wheels and running errands, while the elder Southern continued for a time with the fire department.

As the first halting steps were taken in building the business, major changes in the North American way of life were brewing. A burgeoning standard of living strained existing sources of energy and other resources, sending men into the frontier areas in search of oil and gas, or to develop hydro, mining, pipeline and forestry projects. This rising living standard also meant construction workers and oilfield crews were no longer content to put up with the kind of accommodation that until then had been standard: work camps of hastily assembled sheds or tents. And the harshness of the weather in these new development areas meant that such accommodation was impractical, if not downright dangerous.

At first the demand developed for family housing on wheels. The Southerns began retailing trailers supplied by a California manufacturer, and within five years the Alberta Trailer Company (from which the current name was derived) was Western Canada's most successful dealership for what we now term mobile homes.

As the frontiers were pushed back further, an oilfield driller who had bought mobile homes from the Southerns came to their first employee, ace salesman E.N. (Slim) Farch (who later headed their Australian and Saudi Arabian operations) with another need — bunkhouses for single persons. The remoteness of the location in which these were required precluded building them on site, and no shelter strong enough to withstand being dragged across miles of roadless terrain was available from manufacturers. A new product had to be devised.

With great difficulty, this first order — for seven bunkhouses — was filled. And thus began the manufacturing operations that spurred ATCO's growth in a multinational corporation that in peak years created housing for as many as fifty thousand workers.

Not long after the first order was handled, Ron Southern left the University of Alberta with an undergraduate degree, abandoning his initial plan of being a doctor for the vast challenge of helping to run a growing business.

One early employee working with him was C.S. (Cam) Richardson, now senior vice-president, finance. A former schoolmate of Ron's, he had been an income tax assessor for six years before being enticed into the fledgling firm.

Another of the first employees was G.P. (Gerry) Kiefer, a post-war immigrant from Germany who put his carpentry skills to work on the early orders, originating production methods. Kiefer today holds the position of senior vice-president, special projects.

COMPANY ISSUES PUBLIC SHARES

As word spread of ATCO's capabilities, larger and more sophisticated projects came their way. One large-scale contract, obtained in 1959, was for the supply of housing for the Minuteman missile sites project in the southwestern United States.

By 1968 the company's sales exceeded forty two million dollars, putting it on a scale that could no longer be financed privately, so public share offerings were made. This new financing and strong markets permitted rapid expansion throughout the 1970's with plants established in Eastern Canada, British Columbia, the United States and Saudi Arabia, in addition to Australian operations which were established in 1961. The company's Calgary factory was rebuilt as the largest and most modern of its type in the world.

Another landmark project was housing for the Trans-Alaska Pipeline. The first orders began arriving early in 1974. By the time the last order was filled, sixteen months later, camps for fifteen thousand men had been created — ninety percent of the housing required for the project.

The executive directly involved in obtaining the Alaska contracts was N.W. (Norm) Robertson, who started with ATCO in 1961, after an early career with Canadian Western Natural Gas Company Limited. Recognized early for his executive talent, he was promoted through a succession of positions to become ATCO's president and chief operating officer in 1984.

In 1978, another major diversification for the company was the purchase of Thomson Industries Limited, one of the leading oilfield contract drillers and well services in Canada and the U.S. Expanded and renamed ATCO Drilling, the Energy Services Group is headed by John Hlavka, the former Thomson Industries general manager.

ATCO ACQUIRES CONTROLLING INTEREST IN CU

A year after the Thomson purchase, ATCO bought controlling interest in Canadian Utilities Limited. The three hundred twenty-five million dollar CU purchase confirmed ATCO's stated intention to pursue opportunities in the energy resources field. More than that, it provided a stable base which has allowed ATCO to expand its initiations in the company's various areas of expertise. Canadian Utilities' president, Dr. John D. Wood, is an ATCO executive with twenty-one years of service, having joined the organization in 1966 when it acquired the engineering and research company he headed.

ATCO had entered the oil and gas business on a modest scale in 1975. Later, the assets that had been built up were rolled together with the non-utility assets of Canadian Utilities into a new subsidiary now called ATCOR Ltd. ATCOR is involved in oil and gas exploration and production, natural gas processing and natural gas marketing. On a larger scale, a partnership that includes ATCOR, Texaco Canada Resources Ltd. and Sun Life Assurance — AT&S Exploration Ltd. — owns a share in 5.6 million hectares on the Tuktoyaktuk peninsula in the Beaufort Sea, including the massive discoveries made in the Amauligak formation of up to eight hundred million gross barrels of oil. ATCO Ltd. also has invested directly into this project, giving the ATCO Group, in total, a very significant interest. A priority for the company and its partners is getting this oil to market, at first by tanker, and in the future by a new Mackenzie Valley pipeline.

ATCO tackled one of its most technically advanced projects to date, when it engineered a six hundred fifty-man construction camp and a one hundred fifty-man base operations centre for the world's first offshore oil production facility on Alaska's North Slope.

Manufacturing is no longer the major area of operations for ATCO. Although the company maintains the world's largest stock of transportable buildings for sale or lease, changes in direction have been occurring over several years, and in effect, have transformed the corporate profile dramatically.

ATCO Development Corporation was formed to develop and build major commercial projects. Numerous office structures have been created by this division since its formation in 1975, including the Canadian Utilities head office building in Edmonton and the Canadian Western Natural Gas headquarters in Calgary (also the location of ATCO's worldwide head office). Additionally, the division has built major shopping centres and other commercial projects, and manages buildings both in its own portfolio and for other clients.

Always looking for business opportunities, the company undertook a number of interesting projects related to the 1988 Winter Olympic Games in Calgary.

Housing for more than three thousand Olympic family members was created in two locations — Calgary and Canmore — to provide a high standard of accommodation while avoiding the problem of oversupply of housing after the Games.

Another major facility related to the 1988 Winter Olympic Games, a temporary fifty thousand square foot broadcast centre for ABC Sports, was installed by ATCO in the Roundup Centre at Calgary's Stampede Park. ATCO also provided temporary buildings at nine Olympic venues, for ABC Sports to shelter their equipment.

The forty-year journey that has transformed a four thousand dollar father-and-son enterprise into a multi-national corporation with over $3.3 billion in assets and annual revenues of over $1.5 billion, has been an adventurous one for the Southerns, the early employees who have travelled with them and the more than five thousand five hundred people who work for ATCO's worldwide operations today. Their adaptability, their determination and their drive to achieve, have created a remarkable example of excellence on the Canadian business scene.

Chronology

1883 Natural gas discovered at Langevin, near Medicine Hat.

1889 Eugene Coste brought in first commercial natural gas well in Ontario on January 23.

1897 Geological survey of Canada drilled natural gas well near Pelican Rapids in Northern Alberta.

1901 The Yukon Electrical Company Limited incorporated.

1905 Alberta became a province on September 2.

1909 In February Eugene Coste and Frosty Martin brought in Old Glory, discovery well in the Bow Island field.

1911 The Canadian Western Natural Gas, Light, Heat and Power Company Limited was incorporated on July 19.

1912 On April 22 construction started on the twelve-inch, 170-mile pipeline from Bow Island to Calgary. It was completed in eighty-six days.

Flare-lighting ceremonies in Lethbridge on July 12, and Calgary on July 17 signalled arrival of natural gas in southern Alberta.

In October, the first homes in Lethbridge were served with natural gas.

Nanton, Okotoks and Brooks were also served by Canadian Western.

1913 Fort Macleod, Granum and Claresholm served with natural gas.

Construction started on new office building in Calgary at 215 Sixth Avenue West.

The Edmonton Industrial Association Drilling Company began drilling in the Viking field.

1914 Natural gas struck near Viking on November 4, with an open flow of nine million cubic feet.

1915 City of Calgary challenged Canadian Western's franchise rights to serve the entire city. The matter was finally settled by the Supreme Court of Canada in 1917 in favor of Canadian Western.

1915 Alberta established the Board of Public Utility Commissioners on November 4.

1917 A line blowout occurred at Chin Coulee leaving Lethbridge without gas for seventy-two hours.

1918 Chin Coulee gas well No. 1 was brought in on November 11.

1919 The Drumheller Power Company was formed from the re-organization of the North-west Engineering and Supply Company of Calgary.

1920 Gas pressure in the Bow Island field began diminishing rapidly, signalling the need to find additional sources of gas.

1921 Board of Public Utility Commissioners approved rate increase for Canadian Western from thirty-five to forty-eight cents per thousand cubic feet, provided the company built a pipeline to obtain additional gas from Turner Valley by December 31, and pursued the search for additional reserves.

Christopher J. Yorath became commissioner for the City of Edmonton.

1922 Calgary received its first gas from Turner Valley on January 1.

H.B. Pearson, who had been with Canadian Western since 1912, became president of the company, succeeding Eugene Coste, who resigned and moved to Toronto.

1923 Northwestern Utilities Limited was incorporated on May 26, and opened its first office in the Agency Building on Jasper Avenue in Edmonton.

Northwestern Utilities contracted with the engineering firm of Ford, Bacon and Davis to build a pipeline from the Viking field.

First trainload of pipe for the Viking line arrived July 6.

Northwestern Utilities moved its Edmonton office to a building at the corner of 103 Street and Jasper Avenue on August 1.

Natural gas from the Viking field reached Edmonton on October 27. Service to the city was inaugurated with a flare-lighting ceremony on November 9.

Union Power Company Limited bought Drumheller Power Company. Union Power later merged with Canadian Utilities Limited.

1924 Contract with Ford, Bacon and Davis expired September 30 and Edgar G. Hill, engineering firm's manager, resigned as first president of Northwestern Utilities.

Christopher J. Yorath became president of Northwestern Utilities in October. At that time controlling interest in both Northwestern and Ford, Bacon and Davis was held by International Utilities Corporation.

1924 Canadian Western Natural Gas Company conducted its first customer stock ownership campaign with marked success.

1925 Christopher J. Yorath became president and managing director of Canadian Western on June 15.

In December Canadian Western appointed International Utilities Corporation as its agent in the United States.

1926 Canadian Western employees sold more than two thousand preference shares in the company to more than seven hundred subscribers. Some three and a half million dollars worth of these shares eventually were sold.

1927 The first issue of *The Courier* was published in April 1927. It is still being published today as a magazine for the employees of Canadian Western and Northwestern Utilities.

Walter Schlosser established Northern Light and Power Ltd. at Indian Head, Saskatchewan.

Mid-West Utilities, Limited, a subsidiary of International Utilities Corporation, was incorporated May 18. First purchase, Vegreville Utilities Limited; subsequent ones included plants in Hanna and Raymond. Christopher J. Yorath was named president. (The company was to change its name to Canadian Utilities, Limited a year later — see 1928.)

Union Power Company Limited at Drumheller became an associate company of Mid-West Utilities.

Canadian Western installed its first mechanical billing machines, replacing hand billing in ledgers.

1928 A break in the Viking line on January 1 caused a major gas outage in Edmonton.

Mid-West Utilities acquired the power plant and distribution system in Grande Prairie on March 1 and had a new plant in operation by September.

Mid-West Utilities' name was changed to Canadian Utilities, Limited on June 12.

Canadian Utilities' office moved to Calgary from Edmonton.

The power plant at Stettler was purchased by Canadian Utilities.

Canadian Utilities extended operations in the Watrous district of Saskatchewan and acquired the diesel power plant at Yorkton.

1929 Drumheller power plant was rebuilt and generating capacity increased.

Canadian Utilities bought Northern Light and Power in Saskatchewan on March 1.

1929 Home service department formed by Canadian Western in October, under the direction of Hesperia Lee Aylsworth.

Power line built by Union Power to tie the Castor-Coronation area with the high voltage line serving Stettler from the Drumheller plant.

Canada's first mobile rail car generating plant built by Canadian Utilities.

1930 Northwestern Utilities launched home service department in March under the direction of Kathleen Esch.

Canadian Utilities entered into agreement with Calgary Power for purchase of electricity in bulk in the Vegreville district.

Northwestern moved into its consolidated offices at 10124 – 104 Street, Edmonton.

Underground storage of compressed natural gas started at Bow Island, the second field in the world to be used for storage.

Control of the utilities group was acquired by Dominion Gas and Electric Company, a subsidiary of the American Commonwealths Power Corporation. On July 1, 1944 control was again acquired by International Utilities. This occurred after Dominion Gas and Electric Ltd. merged with International Utilities.

1931 Ratepayers of Prince Albert, Saskatchewan, voted January 14 to sell their power plant to Canadian Utilities. Plant was taken over in April.

A major break in Northwestern Utilities' main line caused a city-wide outage of gas in Edmonton.

1932 Fire destroyed the Corona Hotel on Jasper Avenue, Edmonton, on February 21. Lawsuits totalling three hundred and sixty thousand dollars were filed against Northwestern Utilities. The case went eventually to the Privy Council which, in 1934, ruled in favor of the claimants.

Christopher J. Yorath, president and managing director of the utility group, died on April 2 at the age of fifty-two.

Horatio Ray Milner, K.C. was elected president and managing director of the utilities on May 6.

Northwestern Utilities became the first gas company in Canada to start odorizing natural gas as a safety procedure.

The Turner Valley Gas Conservation Board was formed to regulate production from the field.

Canadian Western, taking advantage of a heavy discount on sterling, redeemed much of its debenture stock at a considerable saving.

1933 Union Power installed a travelling electrical appliance display on a two-ton truck chassis to promote load growth.

1934 The gas companies staged Western Canada's first displays of gas appliances and heating equipment at the Calgary Stampede and the Edmonton Exhibition.

Canadian Western designed and installed North America's first natural gas-fired hog-singeing apparatus in the Burns packing plant in Calgary. Burns installed similar equipment in Edmonton.

Northwestern Utilities extended its distribution system to the town of Jasper Place on Edmonton's western outskirts.

Lloydminster Gas Company brought in Saskatchewan's first commercial natural gas well.

B.C. Power Commission bought electric systems at Nanaimo and Duncan from Dominion Gas and Electric.

1935 Canadian Utilities acquired the assets of Drumheller-based Union Power on August 1.

Canadian Western's new office building was completed in Calgary.

The first Social Credit government was elected in Alberta.

Canadian Utilities initiated first "Better Light . . . Better Sight" campaign in Canada.

1936 Canadian Utilities acquired Calgary Power's franchise and facilities in St. Paul in exchange for Canadian Utilities' property at Raymond.

The companies acquired their first aircraft, a four-seater Stinson Reliant monoplane.

1937 Deepest well to date in the British Empire sunk to depth of 8,990 feet near High River was unsuccessful.

Northwestern Utilities purchased property north of 105 Avenue for a pipe yard in Edmonton.

Canadian Utilities installed new generating equipment in Prince Albert plant, making it largest plant in company's system.

1938 Petroleum and Natural Gas Conservation Board established on July 1 by Alberta government.

Canadian Utilities renewed franchises with twenty-three towns and villages.

1939 In Calgary an appliance approval committee was formed by Canadian Western and the City of Calgary. Henceforth gas appliances could not be installed unless they were tested and approved in the company's laboratory.

Canadian Western opened its new office in Lethbridge on November 3.

1939 Canadian Utilities conducted first rural electrification experimental program at Swalwell.

1940 Eugene Coste, father of the natural gas industry in Canada, died in Toronto at the age of eighty-one.

Vegreville supplied with natural gas by Northwestern Utilities.

1941 Canadian Utilities' first mobile radio system began operating at Drumheller in July. First installation consisted of a 200-watt transmitter and two mobile sets.

Canadian Utilities renewed franchise with Prince Albert, Saskatchewan for ten years.

1942 Electric service by Canadian Utilities was turned on in Fort St. John, B.C. on the Alaska Highway, on November 10.

Canadian Utilities became the first electric utility in Western Canada to adopt Reddy Kilowatt as its symbol.

1943 Transmission line break occurred in Edmonton on January 20 when the temperature was fifty-two degrees below zero (Fahrenheit).

Study launched into farm electrification in Alberta by a committee from Canadian Utilities, Calgary Power and the University of Alberta.

1944 Canadian Utilities began service to its first major rural electrification project on October 19, connecting seventy-eight farms in the Drumheller District.

First electrified oil well in Alberta connected by Canadian Utilities.

1945 Walter Schlosser and Warren DuBois founded Northland Utilities Limited, serving gas and electric customers in the Peace River area of Alberta.

1946 Fire in Northwestern Utilities' head office building in Edmonton caused thirty thousand dollars worth of damage in February.

Northwestern Utilities connected a number of communities to the natural gas system on its southern extension to Red Deer. Flare-lighting ceremonies marked the start of service: Camrose, August 15; Wetaskiwin, August 16; Ponoka, October 18; and Lacombe, December 2.

Canadian Utilities' fourth farm experimental area (north of Vegreville) was energized.

1947 On January 1 Canadian Utilities operations in Saskatchewan were taken over by the Saskatchewan Power Commission.

Leduc oil strike on February 13 ushered in the new era of Alberta oilfield development.

1947 The power plant and distribution system at Vermilion were purchased by Canadian Utilities on August 1.

Red Deer supplied with gas service August 22 from a 100-mile line connecting to the main Viking line at Poe.

The Canadian Western Natural Gas, Light, Heat and Power Company changed its name to Canadian Western Natural Gas Company Limited.

On Christmas Eve power was turned on for fifty rural families in the Grande Prairie District.

1948 In a province-wide plebiscite August 17 majority of Albertans voted against government take-over of the power companies.

Canadian Utilities moved its office from Calgary back to Edmonton in June.

New power plant at Drumheller went into operation in October.

Canadian Utilities constructs first steel transmission towers (between Vermilion and St. Paul).

1949 On January 26 the new Canadian Utilities plant at Vermilion was officially opened.

Horatio R. Milner became chairman of the energy group on April 28, after seventeen years as president.

Canadian Utilities connected its first rural electrification association east of Drumheller.

First permit to transport natural gas outside Alberta granted by province to Northland Utilities, which began gas service to Dawson Creek, B.C.

In the Drumheller district a 66-kilovolt tie line between Canadian Utilities and Calgary Power was energized on September 30.

Northwestern Utilities Employees Association organized in September. Ben Banks was elected chairman.

Northwestern Utilities opened its Edmonton North Yard on November 9.

Canadian Western's first mobile radio system installed in Calgary.

1950 The first load of pipe for the line to the Jumping Pound field arrived in Calgary in October.

Northwestern Utilities built twenty-inch line to connect its system to Leduc field. It was largest diameter gas line in Canada at that time.

On October 23, Canadian Western turned the sod for its new office building at Sixth Avenue and First Street Southwest in Calgary.

Flare-lighting ceremony marked the start of service to Fort Saskatchewan on October 27.

1950 Canadian Utilities employees formed an employee association. T.K. Cornborough elected first president.

1951 A mountain in Jasper National Park was named in honor of J.G. Pattison, an employee of Canadian Western who was awarded the Victoria Cross posthumously in the First World War.

Natural gas officially turned on in Banff with a flare-lighting ceremony on October 27.

The gas companies started the employee suggestion system.

Canadian Utilities contracted to supply power to the armed forces base at Cold Lake.

Canadian Western Employees Association held its first meeting, electing Walt Hopson chairman.

Canadian Utilities and Ducks Unlimited built the Morecambe Dam, to conserve water in the Vermilion Lakes.

1952 Canadian Western officially opened its new office building at 140 Sixth Avenue Southwest in Calgary, on July 5.

Canadian Western and Northwestern each installed their fifty thousandth gas meter.

Brigadier J.C. Jefferson of Northwestern went to Ottawa on loan to the national civil defence program.

1953 Dust in Jumping Pound line to Calgary caused interruption of gas service to several thousand Calgary customers.

1954 On November 26 Canadian Utilities commissioned Canada's first natural gas turbine generator at Vermilion. A new plant at Fairview was also put into service.

Canadian Utilities announced plans to build new generating station on the Battle River near Forestburg.

Canadian Utilities entered a joint agreement with Northland Utilities to operate a gas-fired plant in Fairview.

1955 New generator at Grande Prairie plant was commissioned in December by Alberta Industries and Labour Minister Ray Reierson.

A motion picture, Meet Your Gas Company, was produced by Canadian Western and Northwestern.

On September 6 the energy group began converting to IBM punch card billing.

Northwestern Utilities opened its new meter repair shop and office buildings on 112 Street, Edmonton.

1956 F. Austin Brownie, president of the three energy companies, died on January 23 at the age of forty-seven.

Horatio R. Milner succeeded Brownie as president of the companies on January 27.

Canadian Utilities completed the first 30-megawatt unit at the Battle River plant.

On April 21, the spillway at Canadian Utilities' Battle River dam site broke away and was swept downstream by the swollen river.

Canadian Western began construction on May 1 of its northern extension to the vicinity of Red Deer. Premier Ernest Manning "turned on" the extension on September 28.

On July 1, the B.C. Power Commission took over the Canadian Utilities operations at Fort St. John, B.C.

Canadian Utilities began acquiring distribution rights in the Slave Lake area.

First 138-kilovolt line in Canadian Utilities system built from Battle River plant to Vermilion using H-frame construction.

1957 On January 2, Canadian Utilities took over the operations of McMurray Light and Power Company then serving two hundred and thirty customers at McMurray and Waterways.

At a sod turning ceremony on April 30, Horatio R. Milner signalled start of construction of the Milner Building in Edmonton.

Alberta natural gas started flowing east via Alberta Gas Trunk Line and TransCanada Pipelines on July 23.

First issue of *The Transmitter,* Canadian Utilities' staff magazine, was published in November.

During the year a six-floor addition to Canadian Western's head office in Calgary was completed.

1958 Gas companies' submission to Royal Commission on Energy urged that Alberta should have rolling thirty-year supply before gas is exported.

On April 1 Canadian Utilities purchased The Yukon Electrical Company Limited and Yukon Hydro Company Limited.

Sturgeon gas turbine, south of Valleyview, began production of electricity for Grande Prairie and Peace River areas.

City of Edmonton power plant installed its first natural gas turbine.

1959 In April the Milner Building in Edmonton was completed and on April 17 Canadian Utilities staff moved from its office above the Seven Seas Restaurant on Jasper Avenue, and Northwestern Utilities moved from its building on 104 Street.

1959 Northwestern Utilities switched to therm billing.

Canadian Utilities was asked by Cities Service Research and Development Company (now Suncor) to supply power to its Mildred Lake operation in the Athabasca oil sands.

Canadian Utilities installed a power plant at Fort Chipewyan.

Canadian Utilities awarded contract for first all-Canadian gas turbine for its Vermilion plant.

Canadian Utilities bought two hundred and fifty thousand shares in Peace River Power Development Company in B.C. Horatio R. Milner was appointed a director.

1960 Name of Alberta's Board of Public Utility Commissioners was changed to Public Utilities Board.

A motion picture, The Turn of a Valve, was produced by the gas companies.

Stettler was the first community to switch streetlights to mercury vapor lamps.

1961 In February Canadian Utilities hauled a seven-ton diesel generator to McMurray, the first such freight shipment to go in by road.

Controlling interest in Northland Utilities Limited was purchased by International Utilities and on June 19 Northland became a member of the energy group.

On August 1 the province of British Columbia took over B.C. Electric Co. Ltd.

On August 3 International Utilities announced the appointment of Horatio R. Milner as chairman of the board, with International's principal office in Toronto.

Northland staff moved into the Milner Building in October.

1962 In February Dennis Yorath was elected chairman of the board of the gas companies. Bruce Wilson became president.

Canadian Western's fiftieth anniversary was marked in July by the unveiling of plaques in the Calgary office by Mayor Harry Hays, and in the Lethbridge office by Mayor E.C. Lonsdale.

New corporate symbol adopted by the gas companies.

Canadian Utilities' last property in B.C., a small diesel plant and distribution system at Hudson Hope, taken over by B.C. Hydro and Power Authority.

1963 The Peace River country was connected to the province-wide power grid by a 72,000-volt tie line.

1963 Hillcrest Junior High School in Edmonton became Canada's first "total energy" school, using natural gas for every energy requirement.

1964 Canadian Utilities commissioned the second generating unit at the Battle River station.

Yukon Electrical built a plant to serve Old Crow, a community eighty miles inside the Arctic Circle.

Severe gas emergency on an extremely cold day averted by dedicated staff of gas companies after failure of an automatic valve at Nevis.

Gas companies became leaders in the use of plastic pipe for rural service. Canadian Western installed more than a million feet.

1965 First generation computer installed in Milner Building.

Northwestern's new service centre opened in Red Deer.

Canadian Utilities introduced the first truck-trailer mobile generating stations in Alberta, built to supply power to oilfields.

International Utilities' directors met in Edmonton for first time.

International Utilities acquired Canadian Coachways Limited.

1966 Canadian Western built and installed world's largest gas burner, with flare twenty feet high, atop a derrick at petroleum exposition in Calgary.

Canadian Western's new Lethbridge service centre, 410 Stafford Drive, opened for business on October 24.

The Simonette power plant in the Peace River country went on line in December.

On New Year's Eve Alberta's Lieutenant-Governor J.W. (Grant) MacEwan lit a natural gas torch on the legislature grounds to usher in Canada's centennial year, 1967.

1967 Companies' centennial project, publication of *Alberta . . . A Natural History,* became a best seller.

Northwestern added one hundredth community to its system.

Canadian Western installed Alberta's tallest gas service in the 613-foot Calgary Tower.

Canadian Western installed first remote meter reading device.

1968 Northland Utilities received the franchise to provide natural gas service to Fort McMurray in March. A flare-lighting ceremony on August 28 marked start of service.

Dunston Apartment Block explosion in Edmonton destroyed the building with loss of two lives.

1969 Canadian Western became one of Canada's first utilities to switch to natural gas fuel for service vehicles.

On March 29, Northwestern Utilities' high pressure station in north Red Deer was destroyed by fire of unknown origin.

On April 18, Horatio R. Milner retired at the age of seventy and was appointed honorary chairman of the board for the energy group.

Dennis Yorath became chairman of the executive committee of International Utilities. John Maybin became chairman and Edge King president of the Alberta energy companies.

First twenty-four-inch gas line laid in Calgary.

On July 30, Northwestern Utilities installed its one hundred thousandth natural gas service line in Edmonton.

Canadian Utilities 150-megawatt Battle River Unit No. 3 generator went into production in the fall.

Work began on a power plant for Grande Cache.

1970 The Blue Flame rocket car, fueled by liquefied natural gas, streaked to a land speed record of 622.5 miles per hour on the salt flats of Utah.

1971 Northwestern Utilities brought in a well in the Fort Saskatchewan field with the highest deliverability in the company's dry gas fields.

International Utilities reverted to U.S. residency at the year end.

At year end Canadian Utilities became the holding company and parent of Canadian Western, Northwestern Utilities and Alberta Power Limited which had been incorporated October 26 to take-over the electrical operations.

1972 New H.R. Milner Generating Station at Grande Cache went into production on July 20.

The new Natural Gas Control Centre and No. 1 Gate Station of Northwestern Utilities was officially opened in Edmonton on October 21.

A November storm built up ice three to four inches thick on power lines, causing havoc in the Drumheller District.

Alberta's electric utilities formed the Electric Utility Planning Council.

Construction started on Northwestern's new gate station and heavy equipment repair depot in Edmonton.

Canada's first experimental fuel cell powered by natural gas was unveiled by Canadian Western and Engineered Homes in Calgary.

1973 Northwestern Utilities' fiftieth anniversary was celebrated in Edmonton with a flare-lighting ceremony at the civic centre on November 9.

1973 Gas companies sponsored award-winning film: Ernest Brown, Pioneer Photographer.

Gas companies joined twenty-seven-company consortium planning a pipeline from the Arctic.

CU Engineering Limited formed.

1974 Fire in the power plant at Jasper destroyed five generators and almost the entire plant in February.

Alberta Government instituted natural gas rebate program to help shield customers in province from impact of international price increases.

CU board chairman established an office in Toronto.

Dennis Yorath and the pilot of the company aircraft, Molly Reilly, and her husband Jack were inducted into Canada's Aviation Hall of Fame.

Northwestern completed first section of twenty-four-inch line from Alberta Gas Trunk line at Homeglen-Rimbey.

1975 Horatio R. Milner died on May 24 at the age of eighty-six in his summer home on Vancouver Island.

Alberta Power completed Battle River generating Unit No. 4.

On December 15, Northwestern's Jasper district agent, Palmer Ferguson, saved the lives of two Jasper residents when a gas explosion demolished the building they were in.

Gas companies installed IBM 3741 data system.

Fort McMurray went on the interconnected Alberta grid of 240-kilovolt electric transmission lines following completion of a power line from Slave Lake.

1976 Canadian Utilities' largest debenture issue in its history was successful in raising fifty million dollars in new capital.

Canadian Fertilizer Limited, Canadian Western's largest customer, went into production.

Canadian Western completed its Temple regulating station.

1977 CU Resources Limited formed.

Ron Southern, president of ATCO Ltd., was appointed a director of Canadian Utilities.

Alberta Power marked its fiftieth anniversary with banquets in each of its six original communities.

1978 CU Ethane Limited went into production at its plant on southern outskirts of Edmonton.

1978 Northwestern's maximum daily demand for natural gas exceeded one billion cubic feet.

1979 D.R.B. McArthur, a director of Canadian Utilities, was appointed chairman of Canada's Metric Commission.

New computer facility, the IBM 3032, installed in Milner Building, Edmonton — the first of its kind in Western Canada.

Total assets of Canadian Utilities passed the billion dollar mark.

1980 ATCO Ltd. purchased IU International's fifty-eight percent interest in Canadian Utilities.

Ron Southern, president of ATCO Ltd., was elected chairman of the board of Canadian Utilities.

Wilson Sterling, senior vice-president and chief operating officer of Alberta Power, died on July 8.

Richard G. Reid, former premier of Alberta and a former employee of Canadian Utilities, died at the age of one hundred and one.

Energy Resources Conservation Board turned down Alberta Power's application to build a transmission line to interconnect with Saskatchewan Power.

Canadian Utilities presented Alberta with cable tool drilling rig sculpture by John Weaver in commemoration of Alberta's 75th anniversary.

Alberta Power becomes the first electric utility in Canada to put a fibre-optic system into permanent use, controlling and protecting generating equipment.

1981 Jack Dale, former president of Canadian Utilities, died on March 3.

Dennis Yorath, former chief executive officer of the energy group, died on May 8.

Canadian Western opened its Midnapore operations centre in south Calgary.

Generator No. 5 (the companies' first 375-megawatt unit) was commissioned on September 16, at Alberta Power's Battle River Station.

Northwestern sent a cheque for $22.7 million to TransCanada Pipelines, the largest gas supply cheque ever issued by the company.

Calgary Power Limited changed its name to TransAlta Utilities Corporation in May.

1982 Construction began on the Sheerness Generating Station.

CU Ethane, CU Engineering, CU Resources and ATCO Gas and Oil amalgamated into the new ATCOR Resources Limited.

1982 Canadian Western sold its head office building at 140 Sixth Avenue South-west in Calgary and moved in the fall to the new Canadian Western Centre at 909 Eleventh Avenue Southwest.

Canadian Western opened its Whitehorn operations centre in northeast Calgary.

Northwestern began construction of salt caverns in Fort Saskatchewan area for storage of natural gas.

Alberta government established Electric Energy Marketing Agency.

Northland Utilities revived as name of electric subsidiary established for Northwest Territories.

1983 The Canadian Utilities group moved in November from the Milner Build-ing to the new Canadian Utilities Centre in Edmonton.

1984 Egerton W. King retired as president of Canadian Utilities on June 1 and was succeeded by Dr. John D. Wood.

Public Utilities Board assigned remaining unallocated service areas in prov-ince to Alberta Power and TransAlta Utilities.

1985 Northwestern Utilities took over the operations of the Lloydminster Gas Company Limited on January 1. Lloydminster became the base for North-western Utilities' East District operations.

IBM 3081 replaced by Amdahl 5870 as heart of CU's main computer system.

1986 First unit of Alberta Power's Sheerness Generating Station went into com-mercial operation in January. An official opening of the plant was held on June 20.

Frontec Resources Corp. incorporated.

Bruce M. Dafoe appointed president of Northwestern Utilities Limited and Canadian Western Natural Gas Company Limited.

Craighton O. Twa appointed president of Alberta Power Limited.

William A. Elser appointed president of ATCOR Resources Limited.

ATCOR Resources Limited became CU Enterprises Inc. and ATCOR Ltd. became its operating arm.

Completion of program to replace Canadian Western's 1912 main line.

1987 Canadian Western marked its 75th anniversary and prepared for its role as official supplier of the flames for the XV Olympic Winter Games.

Alberta Power marked its sixtieth anniversary.

Canadian Utilities held its annual meeting of shareholders in Calgary for the first time in honor of Canadian Western's seventy-fifth anniversary.

Index